Democracy or Authoritarianism

The first Islamist parties to come to power through democratic means in the Muslim world were those in Turkey, Tunisia, and Egypt. The Justice and Development Party (AKP) won the 2002 election in Turkey, and Ennahda (Renaissance Party) in Tunisia and the Muslim Brotherhood in Egypt were both elected in the wake of the Arab uprisings of 2010–11. Yet only Ennahda could be said to have fulfilled its democratic promise, with both the Turkish and Egyptian governments reverting to authoritarianism. Drawing upon extensive fieldwork in three countries, Sebnem Gumuscu explains why some Islamist governments adhered to democratic principles and others took an authoritarian turn following electoral success. Using accessible language, Gumuscu clearly introduces key theories and considers how intraparty affairs impacted each party's commitment to democracy. Through a comparative lens, Gumuscu identifies broader trends in Islamist governments and explains the complex web of internal dynamics that led political parties to either advance or subvert democracy.

Sebnem Gumuscu is Associate Professor of political science at Middlebury College. She has done extensive fieldwork in the Middle East and published widely on Islamist parties, democracy, and authoritarianism in prestigious journals. She has previously published *Democracy, Identity, and Foreign Policy in Turkey: Hegemony through Transformation* (coauthor, 2014).

Democracy or Authoritarianism
Islamist Governments in Turkey, Egypt, and Tunisia

Sebnem Gumuscu
Middlebury College, Vermont

Shaftesbury Road, Cambridge CB2 8EA, United Kingdom

One Liberty Plaza, 20th Floor, New York, NY 10006, USA

477 Williamstown Road, Port Melbourne, VIC 3207, Australia

314–321, 3rd Floor, Plot 3, Splendor Forum, Jasola District Centre, New Delhi – 110025, India

103 Penang Road, #05–06/07, Visioncrest Commercial, Singapore 238467

Cambridge University Press is part of Cambridge University Press & Assessment, a department of the University of Cambridge.

We share the University's mission to contribute to society through the pursuit of education, learning and research at the highest international levels of excellence.

www.cambridge.org
Information on this title: www.cambridge.org/9781009178235
DOI: 10.1017/9781009178259

© Sebnem Gumuscu 2023

This publication is in copyright. Subject to statutory exception and to the provisions of relevant collective licensing agreements, no reproduction of any part may take place without the written permission of Cambridge University Press & Assessment.

First published 2023

A catalogue record for this publication is available from the British Library.

Library of Congress Cataloging-in-Publication Data
Names: Gumuscu, Sebnem, 1979– author.
Title: Democracy or authoritarianism : Islamist governments in Turkey, Egypt, and Tunisia / Sebnem Gumuscu.
Description: Cambridge, United Kingdom ; New York, NY : Cambridge University Press, 2023. | Includes bibliographical references and index.
Identifiers: LCCN 2022036228 | ISBN 9781009178235 (hardback) | ISBN 9781009178259 (ebook)
Subjects: LCSH: Political parties – Turkey. | Political parties – Egypt. | Political parties – Tunisia. | Democracy – Turkey. | Democracy – Egypt. | Democracy – Tunisia. | Islam and politics – Turkey. | Islam and politics – Egypt. | Islam and politics – Tunisia.
Classification: LCC JQ1809.A795 G86 2023 | DDC 320.55/7–dc23/eng/20221021
LC record available at https://lccn.loc.gov/2022036228

ISBN 978-1-009-17823-5 Hardback

Cambridge University Press & Assessment has no responsibility for the persistence or accuracy of URLs for external or third-party internet websites referred to in this publication and does not guarantee that any content on such websites is, or will remain, accurate or appropriate.

Contents

List of Figures	*page* vi
Acknowledgments	vii
List of Abbreviations	ix
Introduction	1
1 Modernization, Inclusion, and Power: Explaining Islamist Parties' Democratic Commitments	23
2 A Theory of Intraparty Politics: Resources and Coalitions	61
3 The AKP's Pivot from Liberal Democracy to Electoral Islamism	82
4 Electoral Islamism and Killing the Dream of a Democratic Muslim Brotherhood	143
5 Ennahda's Path toward Liberal Islamism	202
Conclusion	255
Interviews	267
Bibliography	269
Index	293

Figures

1. Intraparty dynamics and Islamist party attitudes in Turkey, Egypt, and Tunisia *page* 14
2. Urban population in Turkey, Egypt, and Tunisia (percentage) 36
3. Economic development in Turkey, Egypt, and Tunisia (GNI/capita in current US$) 37
4. A theory of party behavior 65
5. Building and sustaining dominant coalitions 70
6. Liberal democracy in Turkey, 2002–2021 132

Acknowledgments

It took me a long time to write this book. I spent months in three countries doing fieldwork extended over several years and then spent many more months making sense of the stories of three parties that came to power in these countries. Countless people helped me along the way. First and foremost, I am grateful to all those who shared their time, experiences, and insights with me in the field. Without their input, this book would be at best incomplete and at worst inaccurate. I was also lucky to have friends that made these field trips enjoyable. I am particularly grateful to my sister, Ebru Mert, who traveled with me to different cities in Turkey. My friend Nora Fisher Onar joined me on another trip to Egypt. My classmates and interlocutors in Tunisia made field interviews so much easier.

Then my gratitude goes to all my writing buddies who made writing less solitary and more "fun." Didem Candeğer deserves special thanks for listening to my endless laments for months as I wrote the first draft of this book. Also thanks to the employees at Caribou who for months served us the most critical input, coffee, and tea, as we embarked on our intellectual journeys. I should also thank Mustafa Nuri Mert for being my personal barista at other times. I collected more writing buddies as I continued writing and rewriting. Sayaka Abe, Ilkim Buke-Okyar, Deniz Karakaş, Feyda Sayan-Cengiz, and Şebnem Yardımcı-Geyikçi helped me with the final push.

I am also grateful to all those who heard different versions of this project and shared their thoughts: Erik Bleich, Nadia Horning, Jillian Schwedler, Chris Klyza, Mine Eder, Murat Akan, Yeşim Arat, Zeynep Gambetti, Sultan Tepe, Ilke Civelekoğlu, Ersin Kalaycıoğlu, Zeki Sarıgil, Ilker Aytürk, Zana Çıtak Aytürk, Meral Uğur Çınar, and participants at panels at APSA 2018, ESPA 2019, MPSA 2019, Colloquia at Boğaziçi, Bilkent, and Özyeğin Universities, and the City University of New York Graduate Workshop.

Danielle Lussier, Berk Esen, and Dean Schafer served as discussants in these presentations. John Tallmadge, Mert Arslanalp, Orion Lewis,

Till Weber, Febe Armanios, and Georges Fahmi read individual chapters and made excellent suggestions that enriched the manuscript. Jessica Teets and Dean Schafer read multiple versions of multiple chapters and offered comments on substance and organization that helped me to make the manuscript tighter. They deserve special thanks. Nora Fisher Onar, Ekrem Karakoç, and Garda Ramadhito read the entire manuscript and provided thorough and insightful comments. The students in my senior seminar also read several different versions and helped me refine my arguments. To all of them, I am truly grateful.

Special thanks to my colleagues at the Political Science Department at Boğaziçi University for giving me an academic home during my academic leave. My trips to the field were made possible by a Project on Middle East Political Science Travel–Research–Engagement grant and the generous support of Middlebury College, which did not only fund this project in its different stages but also gave me time to write this book. So many of my students took part in different stages of this project, from research to writing and formatting. Razan Jabari, David Rubenstein, Isabella Mauceri, Ege Yüzbaş, Lily Jones, and Vera Roussef have my gratitude for their meticulous work.

Finally, I thank the three anonymous reviewers for their helpful comments and my editors at Cambridge University Press – Maria Marsh, Atifa Jiwa, and Daniel Brown – for keeping the publication process smooth and stress-free. Thanks to Kenan Sharpe for final proofreading and preparing the index.

Without friends, family, and my therapist, I could not have completed this undertaking. My friends, parents, and beloved Tarçın gave me the emotional support I needed throughout this journey. My sister, Ebru Mert, always joked that I would never finish this book. It is to her I dedicate it.

Abbreviations

AKP	Adalet ve Kalkınma Partisi (Justice and Development Party)
AQIM	Al-Qaeda in the Islamic Maghreb
BJP	Bharatiya Janata Party
CA	Constituent Assembly (in Egypt and Tunisia)
CC	Constitutional Court (in Turkey)
CEDAW	Convention on the Elimination of All Forms of Discrimination against Women
CHP	Cumhuriyet Halk Partisi (Republican People's Party)
CPJ	Committee to Protect Journalists
CPR	Congrès pour la République (Congress for the Republic)
CSO	Civil Society Organization
DEVA	Demokrasi ve Atılım Partisi (Democracy and Progress Party)
DYP	Doğru Yol Partisi (True Path Party)
ECHR	European Court of Human Rights
EMT	Exclusion–Moderation Thesis
EU	European Union
FIS	Front Islamique du Salut (Islamic Salvation Front)
FJP	Hizbal Hurriya wal-Adala (Freedom and Justice Party)
FP	Fazilet Partisi (Virtue Party)
GP	Gelecek Partisi (Future Party)
HDP	Halkların Demokrasi Partisi (Peoples' Democratic Party)
HSYK	Hakimler Savcılar Yüksek Kurulu (Sumpreme Council of Judges and Prosecutors)
IAF	Islamic Action Front
IMT	Inclusion–Moderation Thesis
ISIS	Islamic State of Iraq and Syria
MNP	Milli Nizam Partisi (National Order Party)
MSP	Milli Selamet Partisi (National Salvation Party)
MTI	Mouvement de la Tendance Islamique (Harakat al-Ittijah al-Islami or Islamic Tendency Movement)

NSC	National Security Council
NSF	National Salvation Front
NT	Nidaa Tounes
RCD	Rassemblement Constitutionnel Démocratique (Democratic Constitutional Rally)
RP	Refah Partisi (Welfare Party)
RSF	Reporters sans Frontières (Reporters without Borders)
RTUK	Radyo Televizyon Üst Kurulu (Higher Council of Radio and Television)
SCAF	Supreme Council of Armed Forces
SP	Saadet Partisi (Felicity Party)
UGTE	Union Générale Tunisian des Etudiants (General Union of Tunisian Students)
UGTT	Union Générale Tunisienne du Travail (Tunisian General Trade Union)
UTICA	Union Tunisienne de l'industrie, du Commerce et de l'artisanat (Tunisian Union of Industry, Trade and Handicrafts)

Introduction

On a December day in 2010, twenty-eight-year-old street vendor Mohamed Bouazizi set himself ablaze in a small Tunisian town. Earlier that day, local authorities had confiscated his fruit cart and publicly humiliated him. Soon, Bouazizi's act of desperation and search for dignity ignited protests in his hometown. The proverbial fire quickly spread to neighboring mining towns and shortly reached the coastal cities. Bouazizi's self-sacrifice ignited a revolution that toppled the autocratic regime in Tunisia in twenty-four days. This was just the beginning. The Tunisian uprising inspired millions in the region as they poured onto the streets of Cairo, Amman, Rabat, Sena, and Tripoli to demand jobs, freedom, and dignity. The people had revolted before with similar demands, but this time was different. This time they succeeded in overthrowing their long-time dictators in Tunisia, Egypt, Yemen, and Libya and gained concessions in Morocco and Jordan. Observers, hopeful, dubbed the revolutionary wave the "Arab Spring."

As the revolutionary dust settled, the reality of regime change hit many. Transitions required organized actors with resources and mobilizational capacity. Political parties sprouted up with the hope of translating the revolutionary momentum into democratic regimes. It soon became clear that the youthful revolutionaries were unorganized, divided, and without resources. The most organized actors with mobilizational capacity turned out to be Islamist movements.[1] They already had formed a formidable opposition under the former autocratic regimes. As these regimes fell one after another, Islamists made critical advances. With the fall of dictators, Islamists in exile returned, those in prison regained their freedom, and together they

---

[1] I adopt Hegghammer's definition of Islamism, which is "activism justified by primary reference to Islam" (see Hegghammer, "Should I Stay or Should I Go?"). Scholars often adopt "a call for application of Sharia rule" as the definitive criterion for Islamism (see Mandaville, *Islam and Politics*). I agree with Masoud (*Counting Islam*, 1) that this criterion is problematic since non-Islamist parties may call for sharia rule as well. It is also common that other Islamist parties do not explicitly call for sharia rule and yet still justify their activism by primary reference to Islam, as we observe in the case of Turkey.

established legally recognized political parties. Their strong grassroots and wide membership delivered them victories in transitional elections.

Witnessing Islamists' ascent, analysts revisited the old debate on Islamism and democracy. For skeptics, Islamists posed a threat to democratic transitions; the Arab Spring, for them, was now an "Islamist Winter." They recycled the arguments of Bernard Lewis or Samuel Huntington, who expected Islamists to build autocratic regimes based on Islamic principles. In Lewis' words, "[f]or Islamists, democracy ... [was] a one-way road on which there [was] no return, no rejection of the sovereignty of God, as exercised through His chosen representatives. Their electoral policy has been classically summarized as 'One man (men only), one vote, once.'"[2] This skepticism stemmed from essentialism that treated Islam as an antidemocratic force.[3] Islamists who promised to apply Islamic principles to politics were inadvertently a threat to democracy.

Others contested the essentialist take and entertained the transformative impact of sociopolitical contexts on Islamist movements. For them, Islam lacked an unchanging political essence but offered a multiplicity of interpretations.[4] What Muslims make of Islam mattered more in discerning the relationship between Islamism and democracy. And these formulations were open to continuous change; Muslims articulated and rearticulated their political visions with rising opportunities and in interaction with their political rivals as well as their environments. Political institutions and opportunities, previous learning experiences, and the behavior of other political actors, all mattered.

In reality, Islamist movements have a track record of change under different contexts. The Adalet ve Kalkınma Partisi (Justice and Development Party, hereafter AKP) in Turkey was an excellent case in point. Having roots in Islamism dating back to the 1970s, the party came to power in 2002 with a promise of "moderation" and commitment to liberal democracy. Operating within a secular political framework, the

---

[2] Lewis, *The Crisis of Islam*, 111–12.

[3] Essentialists suggest that there is no separation of religion and politics in Islam, which also rejects any separation between private and public spheres, whereby the sole authority is vested in God. See Lewis, *The Shaping of the Modern Middle East*, 54–56; Kedourie, *Democracy and Arab Political Culture*, 5–6; Huntington, "Will More Countries Become Democratic?" 208. Huntington also suggested in his famous "clash of civilizations" thesis that Islamists would be the gravest threat not only to democracy in their own societies but also to Western civilization at the global level. See Huntington, *The Clash of Civilizations and the Remaking of World Order*.

[4] Anti-essentialists argued that understanding the relation between Islam, Islamists, and democracy requires a closer analysis of each and every society under scrutiny, for there is no one Islam but many tendencies and interpretations which may or may not be compatible with democratic values. See, for instance, Esposito and Voll, *Islam and Democracy*; Bayat, *Making Islam Democratic*.

Introduction

party leaders took several democratizing steps to improve political rights and civil liberties in the country. For many, the AKP proved Islamists' democratic habituation. That is why many treated Turkey as a "model" for the transitioning countries in the Arab world.

Islamists in the region also picked up the reference and tried to calm skeptics' fears by highlighting their resemblance to the AKP. Such assurances and their unmatched mobilizational capacity delivered electoral victories. Harakat al-Nahda (Renaissance Movement, hereafter Ennahda) in Tunisia and the Muslim Brotherhood's (Ikhwan al-Muslimeen) Hizb al-Hurriya wal-Adala (Freedom and Justice Party, hereafter FJP) in Egypt joined the AKP in Turkey as freely elected Islamist parties in power. Upon their wins, the party leaders promised to bring democracy to their countries.

A decade later, only Ennahda has fulfilled its promise. The party worked with other stakeholders to build the only democratic regime in the Arab world.[5] Surprisingly, the AKP, the "model" for the Arab world, took an authoritarian turn after 2011. In a few years, Turkey was no longer a democracy.[6] Egypt also reverted to authoritarian rule, albeit under different circumstances. The Brotherhood dominated the transition at the cost of alienating most Egyptians. Its exclusionary practices and ambiguous democratic platform created a perfect pretext for the military intervention of 2013. The movement has since fallen into disarray as Abdel Fattah el-Sisi, Egypt's new president, cut the democratic experience short.

What caused the different trajectories of these three Islamist parties in power? Why has Ennahda adhered to democratic principles while the AKP and the Muslim Brotherhood adopted hegemonic, majoritarian, and exclusionary politics? Is Islamism (and Islam) at odds with democracy as skeptics claim?

Islamists' track record in power seems to vindicate essentialists' claim about the anti-democratic tendencies of Islamism. I argue, however, that these assertions are not only misleading but also inaccurate. The Islamist experience in Turkey, Tunisia, and Egypt clearly shows that Islam's political manifestation is varied. The three countries prove that the relationship between Islamism and democracy is complex. Essentialists' reductionism fails to capture this complexity. How Islamists relate to democratic practices has changed over time as well as across and within different countries. Some Islamists have undermined democracy once in power, whereas others strengthened and nourished it.

---

[5] In the summer of 2021, President Kais Saied, elected as a political outsider in 2019, issued emergency measures and suspended parliament for an indefinite period. His power grab put the nascent Tunisian democracy to a test, which is still ongoing at the time of writing.
[6] Esen and Gumuscu, "Rising Competitive Authoritarianism in Turkey."

A key finding of this book is that all three of these Islamist parties indeed internalized democratic procedures to a great extent, contrary to essentialists' claims. Both the AKP after 2011 and the Brotherhood in Egypt until 2013 showed clear commitment to electoral politics. Elections for Islamists were not a "one time, one man, one vote" affair as Lewis suggested. It was a clear political choice.

Equally crucial, some Islamists went beyond electoralism to commit to liberal democratic principles. These "liberal Islamists," as I call them, even after coming to power, have adhered to pluralism, institutional forbearance, and mutual tolerance in addition to electoral politics.

Islamism is therefore never monolithic. Instead, a central claim of this book is that mainstream Islamist parties include various groups that self-position along a spectrum of "electoralism" and "liberalism." This plurality of positions eschew essentialism and invites further analysis.

This book, relying on original research in three countries, explains why some Islamist parties commit to democracy while others undermine it. I trace these parties' democratic experience by unpacking intra-party dynamics, particularly the diverging perceptions of political power, democracy, and civil liberties. I find that Islamist parties are comprised of groups with different understandings of democracy. While most Islamists converge on the centrality of elections, they disagree on the norms underpinning electoral politics. *Electoralists* carry majoritarian and exclusionary tendencies, while *liberals* commit to pluralist and inclusionary politics.

Yet it is not the absence of liberals among Islamists that explains why some Islamist parties remain committed to democracy while others do not. Rather, the balance of power among factions determines the party's trajectory. Most mainstream Islamist parties, the focus of this book, host both groups and many fence-sitters within their organization. While liberals' dominance produces democratic commitments at the party level, their weakness can also determine the hegemonic posture of Islamist parties. To put it differently, wherever liberal Islamists dominate, they keep their parties committed to liberal democracy. Otherwise, electoralists inject majoritarian and exclusionary tendencies into their parties.

Liberal Islamists within each movement have gained prominence in all three countries, yet only in Tunisia – and briefly in Turkey – could they successfully transform the Islamist movement into a democratic force. In Egypt, liberal Islamists tried and failed to induce a similar transformation in the Brotherhood and remained marginal within mainstream Islamism. What are the reasons behind this disparity? Why have liberal Islamists in Tunisia succeeded in carrying out a large-scale democratization which led to the marginalization of electoralists while their Egyptian counterparts failed and became marginalized themselves? Why did liberal Islamists in Turkey succeed initially only to lose their position to electoralists later? These questions are the focus of this book.

I argue that power distribution among different factions determines the course of an Islamist party. The key to power balances, in turn, lies in organizational resources. When a faction commands key resources, it can build a tight incentive structure, which is required to form a dominant alliance within the party. Selective and collective incentives offered to members cultivate loyalties and convert fence-sitters and even some rivals into allies. Extra-party resources often fortify organizational resources and build a virtuous cycle of dominance for the ruling alliance. I trace the internal struggle over organizational resources in all three parties and explain why and how liberals prevailed in Ennahda but not in the AKP or the Muslim Brotherhood.

This approach advances our understanding of Islamist party behavior in key respects. Existing accounts focus on the transformative impact of external factors on either individual Islamists or the entire party organization as a group. Scholars have done brilliant work in unpacking the origins of democratic commitments, both electoral and liberal, among Islamists, as I discuss in Chapter 1. They have studied the impact of external factors such as inclusion and exclusion on Islamists' democratic attitudes. In certain cases, these studies documented how "inclusion" in formal politics allowed Islamists to spread their message to wider audiences, win the hearts and minds of Muslims, and obtain power. Thus, electoral politics became a protective shield against state repression, a means to capture power, establish a more Islamic society, *and* maintain legitimacy. Such internalization, scholars posit, stems from strategic calculations.

Sustained political participation, some scholars have also argued, taught Islamists, at least some of them, the value of democratic politics beyond its immediate benefits. Sometimes it was the transformative impact of political learning and political socialization with ideological rivals, while at other times it was Islamists' common experience with the political other under repression or living in exile in democratic countries that altered their political preferences. Regardless of the trigger, they came to internalize democratic norms and principles at a deeper ideological level and appreciate the democratic system and its inherent qualities. Hence, my terminology: "liberal Islamists."

These accounts offer compelling explanations of individuals' ideological transformation induced by inclusion and/or exclusion. However, they fail to explain why some Islamists commit to democratic norms as a result of such experiences, while others do not. They also suffer from the problem of indeterminacy. As a result, ideological change remains a puzzle, often overdetermined and hard to theorize. In addition, with their focus on individuals' experiences, these accounts also fail to overcome the aggregation problem: how members' personal experiences translate to the party level. The question of why some Islamist parties adhere to democratic principles while others adopt hegemonic, majoritarian, and exclusionary politics once in power remains unanswered.

More recently, scholarly attention has focused on the impact of external factors on party behavior. Accordingly, the military, secular civil society, popular protests, regional developments, or international pressures have explained the actions of Islamist parties. The stronger the pressure from outsiders, the greater the incentives for Islamists to commit to democracy.

Often absent in these accounts is the divergence of responses to such external stimulus among Islamists. After their rise to power, different Islamists approached crises and constraints in distinct ways. When faced with similar challenges, some Islamists recognized incentives for collaboration and engagement, while others within the same party perceived threats. They disagreed, for instance, on what political protests signified; or they estimated their party's social support and political power differently; or they read regional developments in a very different light. Interestingly, all factions operated within the same context and faced similar constraints and incentives. Yet their perceptions of their political rivals and what the best course of action was in a specific context diverged markedly.

Such accounts oftentimes retrospectively rationalize party behavior instead of explaining how parties formulate their strategies. This hindsight bias obscures internal struggles over party behavior and strategy and explains away the entire causal mechanism behind party behavior. These explanations assume that parties are monolithic and unitary, and that they formulate the most rational strategy under given circumstances. Such assumptions are faulty. All political parties, including Islamists, host a diversity of opinions and preferences.

I argue that party behavior in a particular instance is not the *only* rational choice the actors could make under given circumstances but a product of internal coalition-building efforts of different factions. This implies that a party's response to the exact same stimulus can be completely different according to different factions.

A more rigorous analysis, thus, requires a closer look at intraparty politics. We need to move beyond the individual level to unpack power dynamics within political parties, often treated as unitary actors. Political factions offer an analytically useful level of analysis that both supersedes the individual level and addresses the issue of aggregation. Indeed, factions form major sources of party change,[7] taking primacy over external factors such as electoral defeats, social dynamics, or economic crises. In other words, the impact of such external factors should be placed within the broader framework of intraparty politics.

In this book, I analyze intraparty politics to identify Islamist groups with diverging democratic attitudes. By focusing on factions, I explain how individual preferences (and political attitudes) aggregate within party organizations while discerning how intraparty dynamics mediate the impact of external factors on party behavior. This approach allows us to overcome the weaknesses of existing accounts, as I discuss in the next chapter. Building on the studies of Islamist change at the individual level, in Chapter 2 I offer a theory of aggregation using factions as the major unit of analysis.

My aim is not to offer a theory of ideological moderation for individual Islamists. Instead, I study the aggregation of preferences with changing incentive structures within a party, as factions try to build larger coalitions. This book thus explains why *some* parties adhere to democratic norms, while others choose not to. In contrast to answers that foreground the transformative effect of external factors on Islamists, I argue that intraparty struggles take primacy in shaping Islamist party trajectories.

Islamism and Democracy

The question of democracy gained urgency among Islamists with the emergence of political opportunities often through regime-induced political openings: in the 1950s in Turkey and in the 1970s and 1980s for most of the Arab world. Mainstream Islamist movements, the focus of this book, responded by forming parties seeking the integration of Islam, politics, and society.[8]

These Islamist parties are ideological parties[9] that seek to reform the political system in line with their political vision.[10] As such, they belong to the family of political parties motivated by a distinct worldview, that is, Catholics, socialists, communists and so on. Like any other ideological party, they come in different shades as their political programs, objectives, and methods diverge significantly. This is particularly the case when it comes to their relationship with democracy. They often partake in electoral politics to fulfill different aims. For some the aim

---

[7] DiSalvo, *Engines of Change*.
[8] In some cases, Islamists were not allowed to form parties, so they ran as independents or formed alliances with existing parties.
[9] Sartori, *Parties and Party Systems*.
[10] Note that these parties do not include mainstream parties that instrumentalize Islam to gain votes or stay in power such as United Malays National Organisation in Malaysia, center-right parties in Turkey, and the National Democratic Party in Egypt, among others.

is to capture the state; for others democracy is an end in itself. These political attitudes do not originate from what essentialists imagine as a singular Islam but arise from different interpretations of Islam that inform actors' preferences along with broader political, social, and economic contexts. That is why no two "Islamisms" are alike.[11]

When given the option to participate in elections, at first many Islamists were ambivalent, but later they embraced electoral politics following sustained political activism in the 1970s and 1980s. Many Islamists treated elections as another way of winning the hearts and minds of Muslims. The National Salvation and Welfare Parties in Turkey, the Islamic Action Front in Jordan, the Islamic Salvation Front in Algeria, the Islah Party in Yemen, Hamas in Palestine, Hadas in Kuwait, Hezbollah in Lebanon, and the Muslim Brotherhood in Egypt, among others, participated in elections and won seats in parliament or municipal governments.[12]

Once several Islamist parties embraced political participation in different countries, they also emerged as the strongest opposition to the authoritarian practices of existing regimes. In the face of repression, they took up the mantle of democratic reforms and human rights against authoritarian infringements. They thus started to speak the language of civil liberties and political rights. Skeptics believed that this was dissimulation, a claim hard to test until Islamists gained political power.

Momentous events like the Arab uprisings created the conditions for Islamists' recent surge, allowing analysts to assess the extent of Islamist change and incumbency's effects on their democratic attitudes. Islamists' rise to power, however, occurred amid revolutionary upheaval, which generated institutional flux, whereby institutional incentives were uncertain or nonexistent. More importantly, Islamist parties are hardly fringe parties that need to move to the center to win elections. In point of fact, these parties had built strong social movements and enjoyed certain advantages over their weak secular rivals. As a result, Islamist parties often – and certainly in the three cases studied in this book – emerged as a dominant political force in their societies.

Despite such uncertainty and their capacity to redesign institutions, I find that Islamist parties in all three cases showed high level of commitment to electoral politics even when institutional incentives to do so

---

[11] Tezcür, *Muslim Reformers in Iran and Turkey*. Also see Yadav, "Understanding 'What Islamists Want'"; Schwedler, "Can Islamists Become Moderates?" Ashour, *The Deradicalization of Jihadists*; Ayoob and Lussier, *The Many Faces of Political Islam*.

[12] Turkish Islamism enjoyed greater rights and freedoms due to country's democratic institutions, although they could never explicitly call for an Islamic system due to restrictions imposed on political parties by the secular constitution.

remained weak. Skeptics' fear of "one man, one vote, one time" turned out to be misplaced. Both strategic and ideological factors, I argue, effected this outcome.

For some Islamists, elections were a strategic means to come into and remain in power with a strong popular mandate. Such mandate allowed these parties to capture the state and Islamize their societies. Elections also offered an ideological and institutional solution to a puzzle Islamists grappled with for a long time. Islamist movements, often seeking the Islamization of social and political life, rarely offered an alternative to the institutions of the modern nation-state. Islamist ideologues and activists such as Sayyid Abul A'la Maududi or Hassan al-Banna kept postponing questions of an Islamic model of governance to an indeterminate future. The only specifics they offered pertained to the ideal ruler: a virtuous, pious man who would govern the society in an Islamic fashion with the help of virtuous civil servants.[13] This ambiguity was partly due to the silence of the Qur'an and the Sunna (Prophet Muhammad's example) on governance/political systems and was partly a result of Islamists' dialectical relationship with their political contexts.[14]

This institutional and theoretical underdevelopment was key in Islamists' adaptation to their local circumstances, as it allowed for their internalization of democratic procedures, as they had been fixated on individual virtue rather than institutional development as a crucial pillar of an Islamic polity and had no answer to the question of selection of the "rightful rulers." Democracy, at least its procedural aspects, offered the best available solution to one of the critical issues for mainstream Islamist parties. So in contrast to scholars who argue that Islamism is inherently authoritarian, I assert that these Islamist parties are committed to elections as an indispensable mechanism for selecting decision-makers. As such, democracy filled a major vacuum in the Islamist political imaginary. Yet what they gathered from "democracy" differed markedly.

The experience of Islamist parties in power soon proved the limits of their democratic habituation. Indeed, several Islamists reversed their

---

[13] Roy, *The Failure of Political Islam*; for examples see Maududi, *The Political Theory of Islam*; Kısakürek, *Ideolocya Örgüsü*.

[14] For instance, for Hassan al-Banna, the founder of the Muslim Brotherhood in Egypt, the emphasis was on "social Islam" and not the establishment of an Islamic state. Islamization of the state would come through "greater attention to religion and spirituality across all sectors of all public life, [hiring] more graduates of religious schools, and encouraging greater religiosity in the part of the populace." In the late 1930s, Banna issued open calls to the palace to initiate Islamizing reforms. His successors translated this vision into full implementation of the sharia only after Anwar Sadat changed the Egyptian constitution in 1974, stating that the source of legislation in Egypt is the sharia (Mandaville, *Islam and Politics*, 77–79).

earlier commitment to civil liberties and democratic norms such as pluralism and mutual tolerance after coming to power yet without foregoing their commitment to *electoralism* (echoing right-wing populists elsewhere). Other Islamists, in contrast, experienced substantial ideological change through inclusion in or exclusion from the political system. After coming to power, they remained unwaveringly committed to democratic norms such as pluralism, mutual tolerance, and institutional forbearance.

The Outcome of Interest: Islamist Parties' Democratic Commitments

This book focuses on Islamists' democratic commitments. The outcome of interest is therefore democratization, and not "moderation." The latter is often used by scholars but also widely criticized for its ambiguity.[15] Democratization is a much clearer and more analytically useful alternative, since it can be tracked in a more systematic fashion.

There is no singular definition or understanding of democracy. Since democracy can be perceived in different ways, democratization may also occur in different degrees. In its minimalist conceptualization, offered by Schumpeter, democracy is "the institutional arrangements for arriving at political decisions in which individuals acquire the power to decide by means of a competitive struggle for the people's vote."[16] Schumpeterian democracy rings a majoritarian tune, and those who subscribe to it may focus more on its procedural aspects than its normative requirements. As such, democracy may quickly devolve into an instrument of amassing power, rather than being an end in itself, as recently seen in many democracies and hybrid regimes.

In contrast, a thicker understanding of democracy would recognize the centrality of certain principles, including pluralism, regular give-and-take, and mutual compromise. As Levitsky and Ziblatt specify, there are two crucial norms that form the basis of democracy: institutional forbearance

---

[15] Scholar often use the concept of "moderation" to define Islamists' ideological change. The theories of moderation of Islamists do not necessarily define moderation as democratization (except Wickham, who sets a higher bar for moderation – i.e., liberal and democratic commitments). Some define it as a change in worldview which falls short of democratic politics. Regardless, the concept of "moderation" is quite problematic, as several scholars have already pointed out. Parties hold different positions on a variety of issues; Islamists are no exception. The concept appears more confusing than clarifying. For a thorough critique of the concept, see Schwedler, "Can Islamists Become Moderates?" Brown, *When Victory Is Not an Option*; Wickham, *The Muslim Brotherhood*; Künkler and Brocker, "Religious Parties"; Netterstrøm, "The Islamists' Compromise in Tunisia."

[16] Schumpeter, *Capitalism, Socialism and Democracy*, 269.

and mutual toleration.[17] This means whoever wins the electoral game in round one should not abuse their access to state power (institutional forbearance) to pack the courts and politicize key institutions or to undermine civil liberties and rights of their opponents (mutual tolerance). That way, if they lose in round two, they have other chances to compete, making elections not a zero-sum but an iterated game. These norms are closer to Robert Dahl's thicker, yet still procedural, conceptualization of democracy. In a widely accepted formulation, Dahl lists free, fair, and regular elections, universal suffrage, right to office, absence of veto powers over elected officials, and freedom of expression, information, and assembly as key components of democratic rule. Building on Dahl's definition, I add the rule of law, pluralism, and protection of minorities[18] as indispensable features of democratic rule to ensure that democracy does not translate into the tyranny of a majority.

Islamists do not always agree on the underlying principles or implications of democratic politics. Some Islamists, who I call *electoralists*, internalize democracy as the best available procedure to select the rightful leaders in a community, as I stated above. Their perception of democracy remains procedural, majoritarian, and populist. They adopt a hegemonic position with respect to other political groups in violation of political pluralism and infringe on the rule of law and civil liberties in line with the spirit of majoritarianism. It is their self-fashioned ideological and moral superiority that informs their right to rule in a hegemonic manner. So they refuse to commit to democratic norms such as pluralism, deliberation, mutual tolerance, and forbearance. When they treat democracy as only elections, they act with a sense of moral superiority that rejects limits on majority rule and opens the gates to democratic backsliding and even breakdown.

Not all Islamists are electoralists, though. In fact, some, who I call *liberals*, commit to norms of deliberation, engagement, pluralism, and power-sharing. They prioritize democratic principles and politics over their partisan interests, which is a key pillar of democracy, as Levitsky and Ziblatt suggest. These Islamists, in contrast, view their movement on par with their rivals and shun any sense of moral superiority; for them, democracy, with its liberal norms and values, is the closest one can get to the ideal Islamic society premised on justice and freedom. This understanding supports pluralism and minority rights.

---

[17] For a discussion of these democratic norms, see Levitsky and Ziblatt, *How Democracies Die*.
[18] Scheppele makes a compelling case for the indispensable need for liberal checks and balances and protection of individual liberties for a sustainable democracy. I follow her definition of liberalism in this book. See Scheppele, "Autocratic Legalism," for further details.

An Islamist party's political trajectory ultimately rests on the balance of power between liberals and electoralists. When liberals dominate, the party adheres to democratic principles and advocates pluralism and power-sharing. Even after attaining political power, they resist "righteous majoritarianism" and advocate a pluralist democratic system with safeguards for civil liberties for all groups and individuals. In contrast, when electoralists dominate, they become a force for polarization, zero-sum politics, and top-down Islamization, reflecting a majoritarian view of democracy and a tendency to monopolize power by excluding and delegitimizing the opposition.

Despite amassing substantial power, electoralists do not forego electoral politics for the reasons I listed above. Meanwhile, their hegemonic understanding of Islamism informs their understanding of democracy. Their belief in "righteous majoritarianism," as Pahwa calls it,[19] primes their style of governance and justifies the systematic violation of the civil liberties of those who contest their vision.

The Cases of Turkey and Egypt vs Tunisia: When and Why Electoralists Prevail

Why study Islamist parties? Islamist parties are assumed to be monolithic entities with high internal coherence and an ideology that is inherently antidemocratic or fixed, as I pointed out earlier. As such, they are often treated as something distinct to which theories of party politics may not apply. Studying Islamist parties in light of these theories allows us to explore how widely the mechanisms we identified in our study of parties in advanced democracies travel. This endeavor hence minimizes the distance between Islamist and non-Islamist parties while challenging common assumptions about Islamism to show that Islamist parties are like any other political party. That said, the study of ideological pluralism in parties based on a religious tradition and unpacking the conditions under which liberal or authoritarian tendencies prevail is instructive for all political parties that harbor both authoritarian and liberal wings. This study, then, offers key insights into party capture by populist factions in recent years and why and how nonpopulist factions are losing their grip on their parties.

Why study these three parties? Since Islamist parties in these three countries came to power in free and fair elections and formed governments with substantial influence over the design of political institutions,

---

[19] Pahwa, "Pathways of Islamist Adaptation."

they constitute excellent cases to trace Islamists' democratic commitments in power.[20] The Islamist movements in Turkey, Egypt, and Tunisia also deserve an in-depth analysis for other reasons. Unpacking the AKP experience since 2002 is important due to its widespread regional appeal. In the wake of Arab uprisings, the AKP government in Turkey was treated as a model for the coexistence of democracy and Islam by leaders of both the Brotherhood and Ennahda. After coming to power in 2002, the AKP registered political success by winning consecutive elections, generating extensive economic growth, and beginning accession talks with the European Union. However, the AKP reversed its course midstream, a move that ultimately undermined Turkish democracy. This within-case variation in the outcome of interest – namely, the adoption by Islamists of liberal norms after coming to power only to abandon them later – significantly enriches the comparative analysis and makes for an interesting empirical puzzle.

The Brotherhood in Egypt, on the other hand, is the most established and influential Islamist movement with several chapters in the Middle East and North Africa. Its influence on other Islamist movements, in both Turkey and Tunisia, cannot be disputed. Finally, Ennahda is also of critical importance because its leader, Rached Ghannouchi, is not just a political leader but also a philosopher and ideologue who has written extensively on Islam and democracy and inspired generations of Islamists in multiple countries, including Turkey and Egypt. More importantly, Ennahda has steered Tunisia toward democracy along with other stakeholders and has registered Tunisia as the only democracy in the Arab world for several election cycles until recently. This party with a clearly democratic platform has sustained a pluralist agenda while compromising with other political actors to democratize Tunisia.

---

[20] Elsewhere in the Muslim world, Islamists made meaningful electoral advances, but they either failed to establish governments or were denied power. For instance, the Justice and Development Party in Morocco governs under the shadow of the king, consociationalism in Lebanon and its restricted appeal hand Hezbollah limited power, the power of Islamist parties in Indonesia is circumscribed to regional governments, while many other Islamist parties are denied freedom of organization or the opportunity to run in competitive elections, as is the case in Jordan, Kuwait, Algeria, Yemen, Libya, and Syria. The FIS in Algeria, Hamas in Palestine, and the Shi'a parties in Iraq are exceptions, since they also had electoral victories in relatively free and fair elections. However, the military intervened in Algeria before the FIS could register an electoral victory in the second round of elections in 1991, while Hamas was denied the opportunity to govern Palestine by external actors in 2006, and the post-invasion circumstances complicated Iraqi politics and led to state failure instead of opening the way for the establishment of a government under Islamist parties. For more on Islamist parties' political opportunities in Iraq, Lebanon, and Palestine, see Hamzawy and Brown, "Islamist Parties and Democracy."

Islamist Party Commitment to Democracy

Dominant faction	Liberal democracy	Electoral democracy
Liberals	AKP 2001–2007 Ennahda 2011–	
Electoralists	AKP 2001–2002	Ennahda 1989–1990 AKP 2008– Muslim Brotherhood 2011–2013

Figure 1 Intraparty dynamics and Islamist party attitudes in Turkey, Egypt, and Tunisia
Source: the author

In this book, I explain why the AKP slid into authoritarianism and back to ideological rigidity, although it was established as a moderate splinter party; why the Brotherhood failed to commit to democratic norms after coming to power; and why Ennahda followed a different path and displayed sustained commitment to democracy, mutual tolerance, and compromise in its encounters with other political actors. As Figure 1 summarizes, liberal Islamists had the upper hand in the AKP until 2007 and in Ennahda since the 1990s, while electoralist Islamists had dominated the Brotherhood before and after they rose to power in Egypt. Chapter 2 offers a theoretical explanation for these shifts, and the empirical chapters illustrate how the theory plays out in individual cases.

Methodology

I adopt a comparative approach to reveal similarities and differences across cases and test for the impact of such differences on the outcome of interest. A comparative approach combined with process tracing in all three cases allows for causal inference and testing for competing explanations. This combination of methods allow me to explain why Ennahda remained committed to liberal democratic norms, whereas the Muslim Brotherhood did not, and why the AKP initially committed to such norms only to abandon them later. Variation across cases and changes within each case over time provide a fertile ground for comparative analysis.

Methodology 15

All three cases, for instance, belong to the same branch of Islamism: They are mainstream political movements that prioritize gradual political and social change (reformism) through formal institutions rather than revolutionary or violent upheaval. All three are also based on strong social movements, which makes them "movement parties" even when they are not legalized by the ruling regimes, as was the case before the revolution in Egypt and Tunisia.[21] Even then both Ennahda and the Brotherhood acted as institutionalized and bureaucratized movement parties with bylaws, internal elections, and executive and legislative branches. Perhaps more importantly, they showed a clear desire to participate in formal politics and ran in elections when permitted on electoral platforms defined by the organization. The Turkish Milli Görüş (National Outlook) movement, which gave birth to the AKP in 2001, enjoyed greater political freedoms, while its parties were also embedded in a social movement.[22] Of course, the three parties had differences when it came to the primacy of politics within the broader social movement. This was a point of contention within each movement, and factions, in Ennahda and the Brotherhood in particular, rallied around a particular position, that is, primacy of the *da'wa* (preaching) vs politics. This issue was largely resolved in the Milli Görüş movement by the early 1980s in favor of political activism, while it preoccupied factions in the other two movements, as I discuss later. Such internal debates are part of the outcome I intend to explain.

In addition, before coming to power, all three parties endorsed competitive politics, political pluralism, and civil liberties. The three parties also proved to be dominant actors in their respective contexts. Their competition remained weak and fragmented, while they maintained strong grassroots networks and a tight organizational structure. This comparative strength secured their political dominance even when their electoral fortunes remained relatively modest. Such crucial similarities among parties notwithstanding, the three countries also diverge in several respects. I return to these differences and their implications for democratic commitments in Chapter 1. Despite their differences, simultaneous revolutionary moments in Tunisia and Egypt allow for a fruitful paired comparison. When combined with case variation in Turkey, all three cases permit

[21] For the concept of "movement party," see Kitschelt, "Movement Parties"; for a discussion on the Muslim Brotherhood and Ennahda's transition from movements to parties, see Zollner, "The Metamorphosis of Social Movements into Political Parties."
[22] The Milli Görüş movement had organic ties to associations that were established to raise funds for religious schools and to mobilize youth (Milli Gençlik Vakfı) and immigrant workers in Europe (Avrupa Milli Görüş Teşkilatı). The movement also ran social welfare programs for lower-income families through the party branches and later through local municipalities. The AKP later replicated this frame at a larger scale.

controlling for different factors. Several such factors that seemed important in a single case – structural, institutional, and contextual – lost their analytical value when all three cases were studied together, as I show in the next chapter and discuss in greater detail in the empirical chapters. Examining all three cases allowed me to surpass the pitfalls of single case studies which miss the chance of finding common patterns.

Through process tracing in all three cases, I also identify causal mechanisms. Specifically, I trace the internal workings of each party within their broader political context to specify causal chains and their observable implications.[23] I also test alternative causal explanations based on external pressures. Process tracing reveals the multiplicity of paths that an Islamist party could take at different junctures. Using this method, in conjunction with comparative analysis, I trace why and how a party ends up adopting a strategy, and not others, as its "dominant strategy."

Process tracing in a comparative study requires rich fieldwork in all three countries. A topic such as intraparty politics, which is hard to observe as party members are not willing to reveal their differences, requires the collection of data from various sources. The book relies primarily on semi-structured interviews with prominent members of Islamist parties in all three countries as well as party platforms, official statements, media interviews, and memoirs of Islamic activists collected during field trips and online. Collecting information on a phenomenon from multiple sources helped me minimize missing data as I traced the process in its observable implications.[24]

A second layer of primary data comes from several interviews conducted with non-Islamic activists, analysts, and journalists. Such conversations complemented interviews I conducted with Islamists and enriched my understanding of the context within which Islamists operated. I used purposive and snowball sampling technique to select respondents among the leading Muslim Brothers, Ennahda, and AKP officials, as well as non-Islamist party representatives, columnists, civil society activists, businessmen, union leaders, and intellectuals. At times I met with interlocutors to build connections with party members, and at others, I reached out directly to party leaders whom I identified through official documents of the party and news archives. When I started this research, I had a good sense of intraparty conflicts in the Muslim Brotherhood and Milli Görüş but had limited knowledge of such splits in the AKP and Ennahda. My understanding of internal disagreements in these parties crystallized during fieldwork.

---

[23] Gonzalez Ocantos and Laporte, "Process Tracing and the Problem of Missing Data."
[24] Ibid.

Methodology

In the field, I relied on the networks I had built in Turkey and Egypt for my dissertation.[25] I also built new connections in Tunisia through my connections in Turkey and Egypt. My first field trip was to Turkey in 2011 to gain a deeper understanding of the AKP's growing dominance in the country. As part of this new field study, I observed the party campaign for the 2011 national election in one of its strongholds, Istanbul, Turkey's largest city. I did house visits with an AKP nominee and witnessed the party's interactions with its supporters. I also observed the workings of local branches and interviewed party activists at the district and neighborhood levels to get a sense of the party structure.

With the onset of the Arab uprisings, I went back to the field to do research on Islamists' role in democratic transitions. I went to Tunisia in 2012 to observe the postrevolutionary developments and meet with representatives of Islamist and non-Islamist political organizations. My goal was to grasp Ennahda's role and political attitudes throughout the transition. I joined an exchange program organized in Tunis and traveled around the country to meet with activists and civil society representatives in Kasserine, Sfax, Sidi Bouzid, and Gafsa. The group interviews during the program often revolved around the causes of the revolution, Islamists' perception of democracy, and the heightened polarization in the society.

I went back to Egypt in January 2013 during the second anniversary of the revolution to conduct another set of interviews in Cairo. I intended to observe Egypt under Morsi's rule and inquire about the impact of his (and the Brotherhood's) decisions on the transition process. I ended up meeting with several former members of the Brotherhood, activists from different parts of the political spectrum, and civil society representatives.

With the AKP's increasing authoritarianism, I returned to Turkey to observe the party's transformation more closely. In January 2014, I took two trips to Istanbul and Ankara to interview liberals purged from the AKP. By then, the party was already on an authoritarian path, and Erdoğan successfully quelled intraparty struggles by purging his rivals within the party organization. I went back to Turkey in 2017 for additional interviews in Istanbul, Ankara, and Bursa, where I met with several founding members of the party who had previously served in AKP governments and played a critical role in Turkey's democratic reforms in the

---

[25] In the summer of 2006 and 2007, I traveled to Egypt to interview prominent names among both electoralists and liberals within the Brotherhood. I also interviewed former members of the Muslim Brotherhood who left the movement to establish the Wasat Party in 1996. In this project, I studied ideological moderation of Islamists in Turkey and Egypt through internal splits in the Milli Görüş movement and the Muslim Brotherhood. I also rely on my observations from these trips in this book.

party's first term in power. I supplemented these interviews with further conversations with experts of political Islam in Turkey. In the meantime, I monitored five local and general elections from March 2014 to June 2019. I also conducted participant observation in several AKP events, including the party's major rally in Istanbul that concluded its electoral campaign of June 2015 elections and democracy rallies organized after the 2016 failed coup attempt. Such opportunities for participant observation were critical to deciphering the party's pivot to hegemonic Islamism.

In 2016, I started another cycle of interviews with Brotherhood members, this time in Istanbul. Thousands of Brothers went into exile in the wake of the coup in 2013. Hundreds relocated to Istanbul, several of whom I met to discuss what went wrong in Egypt's transition. The Brothers I spoke with included a diverse group including liberal and electoralist, old and young, and former and current members of the organization.

In the summer of 2017, I returned to Tunisia to meet with high-ranking figures in Ennahda. I frequented the Tunisian parliament to interview deputies from the party and observe their legislative activities. I ended up meeting the majority of the party's executive bureau as well as the party chairman and his deputies. I also had the opportunity to converse with non-Islamist members of the parliament who had been working with Ennahda deputies since the transition. The trip also allowed me to speak with analysts who closely observe Tunisian politics.

After I completed the field trips, I conducted several more online interviews with prominent names in Ennahda and the Brotherhood to enrich the material and clarify a few questions.

In the end, I met with more than 120 Islamists and analysts, some of them multiple times, for more than 130 interviews. Most interviews lasted about an hour, and a few took several hours. All the interviews were in Turkish, Arabic, or English. For the interviews carried out in Arabic, I had an interpreter to make sure that my comprehension was accurate. Because all three countries now have more autocratic regimes than they had when I began this research, I have anonymized my contacts unless they are among the top leadership or their views are already public.

Outline

Chapter 1 starts with a discussion of the role of external factors on Islamist party behavior informed by three major perspectives: structural factors such as modernization and economic development, institutional factors including inclusion and exclusion, and balance of power considerations informed by rational choice. I argue that external factors often play a secondary role in shaping party behavior; instead, intraparty dynamics determine the impact of external pressures on the organization as different factions frame external impetus in divergent ways in line with their own ideological and strategic positions. For instance, both *liberals* and *electoralists* in the AKP, the Muslim Brotherhood, and Ennahda developed different strategies under similar circumstances and attributed conflicting meanings to the actions of their rivals. In each case, factions disagreed on the best course of action for the party.

In Chapter 2, I offer a theory of interfactional politics to unpack party trajectory. Organizational resources, I argue, determine internal balances of power and the formation of internal coalitions. A faction that controls specific resources in the party organization builds an incentive structure indispensable for erecting intraparty alliances. The larger the resource pool, the greater the odds of building a dominant coalition. Extended incumbency reinforces this dominance by way of expanding a party's resource pool and allowing the ruling faction greater access to such resources to build broader internal coalitions with selective rewards and sanctions.

As Chapters 3 through 5 uncover, in all three cases a dominant coalition sidelined its rivals to set the course of the party by capturing organizational resources and building solid incentive structures. The rise of a dominant coalition was predicated on two factors, one internal and the other external to the party. Internally, a party's foundational moments provided the opening factions needed to vie for resources and build new incentive structures. These foundational moments included the AKP's formation in 2001, the Muslim Brotherhood's second founding in the 1980s, and Ennahda's second founding in 2012. In the case of the AKP and Ennahda, the foundational moments coincided with an external shock that brought the two parties to power. In these two cases, unlike the case of the Brotherhood, factions also utilized expanding public and private resources to build dominant coalitions in their organizations (the AKP for a longer period than Ennahda).

As Chapter 3 demonstrates, liberals in the AKP left their imprint on the first two AKP governments (2002–07), known for their ambitious reformist agenda that carried Turkey to European Union candidacy. In this chapter, I analyze the internal struggles within the party, often neglected by scholars, based on interviews I conducted with its founding members. Particularly important is the marginalization of the liberals starting in 2007, the resultant monopolization of power in the hands of Recep Tayyip Erdoğan (the leader of the electoralists), and the growing authoritarianism in the country. I discuss in detail key organizational resources and their changing distribution across factions in favor of electoralists. Capitalizing on the institutional flux at the time of party formation, electoralists changed the party rules, written by liberals, and allowed the party leader to command all recruitment and promotion within the organization. Combined with their access to party finances, electoralists built an extensive incentive structure that they used to reward their supporters and punish dissenters through the allocation of positions within the government, parliament, and party organization. Their growing control over the party's internal communication as well as the national media further consolidated their position in the party. While a few liberals and many fence-sitters joined this alliance, others first strived to keep the party on a liberal democratic path. When they realized they no longer had any power in the organization, they left.

Electoralists in the Brotherhood, in a similar fashion, successfully thwarted threats liberals posed to their leadership in the movement. Chapter 4 explores the Muslim Brotherhood's internal politics since its second founding in the 1980s to document the increasing prominence of electoralists, also known as the old guard, in the movement at the expense of liberal reformist voices. Relying on extensive fieldwork and interviews, I identify three critical waves of purges within the movement: the establishment of the Wasat Party by reformists leaving the Brotherhood after a long internal strife in 1996, the internal elections of 2010 that marginalized liberal voices remaining inside the organization, and the 2011 revolution and expulsion of remaining liberals from the movement. Electoralists' growing control over the executive offices of the Brotherhood after the death of General Guide Omar al-Tilmisani along with the intentional recruitment among rural Egyptians underpinned their dominance. Their command over the movements' internal communication, indoctrination, and financial resources further entrenched their control. The old guard's manipulation of party rules and rigging of the 2009 internal elections secured their hold on to power at the time of the revolution in 2011. When Mohamed Morsi, as the nominee of the old guard, was elected as president in 2012, he carried the righteous majoritarianism of his faction to power. Liberals, now purged from the movement, heavily criticized Morsi's actions in office, but to no avail. The chapter concludes with an assessment of the key decisions made by the leadership over the course of Morsi's presidency and their impact on the political crisis of 2013, which ended Egypt's democratic transition.

Chapter 5 studies the contrasting case of Ennahda and its history with a focus on the party's trajectory since its first founding in the 1980s. At the time, the party hosted both radicals and democrats, and thanks to the strong collective incentives they could offer, radicals had the upper hand in the movement. Democrats, led by Ghannouchi, tried but failed to keep Ennahda on a democratic path. After 20 years of exile, the party's second founding in 2012 reshuffled the cards. Ghannouchi, who regained party leadership in exile, capitalized on the foundational moment and the democratic transition to build a liberal alliance within Ennahda. After coming to power, liberal democrats under Ghannouchi's leadership sought consensus and compromise with their political rivals. They encountered criticism from within but managed to reinforce their command over the party organization by recruiting liberal-minded members, allocating public positions to their supporters, and expanding their control over intraparty debates. This heightened control over the party allowed liberals to sideline electoralists within the party who had been pushing for a more assertive and hegemonic posture for Ennahda.

Although the empirical chapters trace the changing balances of power among factions in all three cases, each of these chapters is organized differently to follow key moments in each country. Real life is messy, and it is not always easy to fit political events into neat boxes, as much as we would like to. Those readers who would prefer the same structure repeat in all three chapters will be disappointed. Yet a different organization, I believe, would be more frustrating since it would be confusing and harder to follow. Instead, the chapters trace the evolution of all three parties over time with a particular focus on intraparty struggles.

The final chapter concludes with a discussion of how this framework travels to other cases, Islamist and non-Islamist parties alike, and the implications of this study for party capture and democracy.

The framework I offer in this book is dynamic and flexible enough to explain change within a party across time. It both sheds light on the past course of a party *and* offers a causal explanation for potential changes that may take place in the future. The theory, therefore, applies to other parties, such as right-wing parties, which often include majoritarian and antipluralist tendencies within. As such, this book provides keys to understanding party capture and how autocratic factions prevail.

The book hence adds to the broader conversation on democratization and democratic backsliding and the study of hybrid regimes, whereby electoral politics still carry great significance, yet the ruling elite systematically violates pluralism and civil liberties essential for a well-functioning democracy. The role of political parties in democratization and democratic backsliding is undeniable. If we are to understand parties and their role in democratic advancement and backsliding, we need to pay greater attention to intraparty politics. This book explains why.

Finally, this study informs policymakers and the broader international community on the diversity of Islamist actors by shattering the myth of monolithic Islamism. That is, there is a third option besides jihadi violence/"war on terror" and anti-Islamist authoritarian rule in the Muslim world. This third option requires better coordination among democrats, Islamist and non-Islamist alike. By displaying the complexity of Islamist politics, this study offers paths of dialogue among political actors in Muslim societies by questioning the false binaries that undermine trust between Islamists and non-Islamists.

1 Modernization, Inclusion, and Power
Explaining Islamist Parties' Democratic Commitments

Why do some parties commit to democratic principles while others do not? Can democracy socialize political actors? Or is it essentially vulnerable to the attacks of such actors who can come to power through free and fair elections only to destroy democracy? With the recent surge of right-wing populism from the United States and India to Brazil and Hungary, these questions have once again gained urgency. Illustrative of a fundamental paradox, democracies have faced similar threats from political parties before. In fact, socialists, Catholics, and fascists in the nineteenth and early twentieth centuries instrumentalized democratic routes to power to alter the system in line with their worldview. After these parties joined the democratic game, some accepted it as the "only game in town," while others undermined it.

In their efforts to discover the conditions under which ideological parties commit to democracy, some scholars highlight structural factors and broader socioeconomic trends such as modernization and economic development. Meanwhile, others underscore institutional constraints on actors' behavior, attributing democratic commitments to the taming effects of institutions. Inclusion in the system, they suggest, transform actors with authoritarian tendencies, as in the case of socialist or Catholic parties. Yet not all actors embrace democracy despite their political inclusion in the system, as in the case of fascist parties.

Do structural changes, such as modernization, transform authoritarian actors into committed democrats? Or do institutions rein in the authoritarian tendencies of political actors through political socialization and democratic habituation? This chapter critically reviews the scholarly debate surrounding these questions with a particular focus on Islamist parties.

Islamism indeed offers a fertile ground to study the relationship between political parties and democracy. Some observers have singled out Islamism as particularly antidemocratic, a claim that is, as I have already detailed, empirically unsupported.[1] Other scholars, in contrast, reject this essentialist

---
[1] See Mozaffari, "What Is Islamism" and Hamid, *Temptations of Power*.

approach to argue that Islamists do not carry an unchanging and antidemocratic essence.[2] Instead, they suggest, like the socialist and Catholic parties of Europe, the sociopolitical contexts within which such parties operate shape their political preferences. This line of scholarship is theoretically and empirically more rigorous than essentialist accounts, although they also suffer from some key shortcomings. Here, I discuss three main approaches to Islamist change motivated by structural, institutional, and rational choice theories and their strengths and weaknesses before advancing a complementary framework to unpack the democratic trajectories of Islamist parties.

This chapter surveys existing accounts of Islamists' democratic commitments starting with macrolevel changes pertaining to modernization and continuing with meso- (institutional) and microlevel analyses (rational choice) of political parties and individuals. Macrolevel theories along with the inclusion–moderation thesis offer key insights as to how and why Islamist parties in all three countries might have accepted democracy as their preferred system. Yet these theories fail to explain the differences within each party and why some Islamist parties adhered to liberal norms while others committed to majoritarianism after coming to power. The studies that unpack ideational change at the individual level induced by inclusion or exclusion shed greater light on the origins of internal splits within Islamist parties. But they fail to address the issue of aggregation – or, to put it differently, why liberal Islamists prevail in some parties but not in others. Different individuals develop different reactions to the same external impetus. Some Islamists learn and internalize democratic norms when faced with exclusion and repression, while others pursue confrontation and radicalism. Still others, upon their inclusion to the system, instrumentalize electoral politics to pursue Islamist majoritarianism, whereas many adhere to liberal norms and strive to build democratic institutions. When faced with certain constraints and incentives, they develop competing rationalities. Existing studies largely fail to account for this diversity and very few explain how and why a certain strategy gains currency within a party. This, I posit, is a question of power and resources. I theorize this causal relationship in the next chapter.

Here, I start with a critical survey of structural factors that may account for divergent outcomes in the three countries of interest in this book. Specifically, I trace the history of modernization in Turkey, Egypt, and Tunisia and discuss the role of socioeconomic factors on the democratization of Islamist parties. This section also aims to give a historical context to the three cases studied in this book.

[2] See, for instance, Ayoob and Lussier, *The Many Faces of Political Islam;* Esposito, *The Islamic Threat: Myth or Reality?*

Next, I explore the impact of institutions on party behavior and ideology. Specifically, I discuss the inclusion-moderation thesis to test its claims against the evidence we now have with the rise of Islamist parties to power. Although this thesis suggests that institutions, via electoral considerations and governmental concerns, often tame ideological parties, these constraints do not always yield sustained commitment to democratic principles. This survey reveals the limits of the institutional effects of inclusion. The ideational effects of inclusion offer invaluable insights for ideological change of some, if not all, Islamists. The second part of this section discusses these contributions and their limits in detail.

Finally, I turn to the strategic calculations of Islamist actors as determinants of Islamist party behavior. Specifically, I discuss the role played by external factors, including regional and international developments, in each case. As this critical survey reveals, such accounts offer important yet partial insights into Islamist party behavior.

Modernization and Democratization

Seminal theories of comparative politics that underscore structural factors may shed some light on the trajectories of the three parties in question. Modernization theory, for instance, predicts greater commitment to democracy as societies undergo modernization. With the rise of modernity, the significance of tradition, religion, and personal and communal ties associated with rural lifestyles decline, and in their stead come secularization, scientific education, professional specialization, impersonal ties, and an (often) individualistic and urban lifestyle.[3] For some, the decline of tradition and the rise of a modern society inevitably lead to democratization.[4] Several scholars, in agreement with the basic premises of modernization theory, add economic development as a key causal mechanism that ties modernization to democratization.[5] Many argue that democracy finds a stronger foothold in wealthier societies where urbanization, education, and professional specialization define the social structure and the middle classes expand and become a dominant force.[6] Such theories, extended to the case of Islamist parties by scholars

---

[3] See, for instance, Parsons, *Talcott Parsons on Institutions and Social Evolution*.
[4] Rostow, *Politics and the Stages of Growth*.
[5] For a recent study that revives the theory, see Boix and Stokes, "Endogenous Democratization."
[6] See the seminal work of Lipset, "Some Social Requisites of Democracy." There is a long-lasting debate on the mechanisms that tie economic development to democracy. Some highlight growing resources and the power of educated, urbanized, wealthier citizens vis-à-vis their ruler, while others underline the increasing costs of authoritarian practices in wealthier societies. See Inglehart and Welzel, *Modernization, Cultural Change, and*

like Nasr, imply that Islamists commit to democracy in countries with higher levels of modernization, economic development, and a sizable middle class.[7]

All three cases in this study share similarities with respect to their modernization processes. They all have a long history of state-building, secularization, and economic development dating back to the nineteenth century. In an attempt at defensive modernization,[8] the ruling elite in the Ottoman Empire and its nominal provinces of Egypt and Tunisia emulated European institutions to preclude further decline. Such reforms were oriented toward centralization and expansion of state capacity through top-down reform.

State-Building in Turkey, Egypt, and Tunisia

Facing European imperialism, the Ottoman elite pursued centralizing reforms over the course of the nineteenth century to build a strong state with loyal subjects and a vibrant economy. Collectively labeled the *tanzimat* (regulations), these successive measures aimed to build a modern tax administration, formidable army, an education system to train civilian and military bureaucrats, and a centralized and largely secular legal system. Economic measures accompanied such reforms to modernize the imperial economy according to capitalist production and commerce. For that purpose, the state established factories and encouraged private investment in manufacturing while investing in infrastructure by building ports, railroads, and telegraph lines.

Most of these reforms were met with mixed success and resistance from different quarters of society.[9] Partial centralization failed to deliver expected tax revenues, while ambitious infrastructural projects cost the imperial coffers a heavy debt burden. Turkey, the heartland of the Ottoman Empire, avoided colonial rule yet still bore the brunt of European economic and military domination through the nineteenth and early twentieth centuries, losing its territories, markets, and financial independence. Still, modernizing reforms changed the Ottoman state in a drastic fashion and cultivated the seeds of further modernization through its nascent administrative, education, and legal systems under the republican elite, as I will discuss shortly.

Democracy; Rueschemeyer et al., *Capitalist Development and Democracy*; Stokes et al., *Brokers, Voters, and Clientelism*.
[7] Nasr, "The Rise of Muslim Democracy."
[8] For a rich and detailed discussion of defensive developmentalism, see Gelvin, *Modern Middle East*.
[9] Ibid.

Egypt's modernization also dated back to the early nineteenth century. In the wake of Napoleon's invasion, Muhammad Ali Pasha, an Ottoman officer of Albanian origin, arrived in Egypt to thwart French forces. He chose to stay instead of leaving for another position in the imperial bureaucracy with the intention of building his own dynasty on those fertile soils. Under his rule, Egypt remained a nominal Ottoman province with de facto independence. Muhammad Ali Pasha began extensive modernization not only in the state apparatus but also in agriculture and manufacturing. He built a formidable army, a modern taxation system, new administrative units, irrigation systems, textile factories, as well as railways and military and civilian academies. Quite successful in these reforms, this Ottoman province outperformed the imperial heartland militarily and economically. Yet Muhammad Ali's plans were deeply frustrated by his own ambitions and ensuing British interference. After threatening the Sublime Porte through territorial expansionism, he was forced to reduce the size of his army and ban monopolies over cotton production and manufacturing. Thus, the Egyptian economy was reduced to a supplier of cheap raw materials for global markets. His successors only deepened such frustrations when they undertook major projects for the sake of late development. Chief among them was the Suez Canal, which not only amplified the strategic significance of the country but also created a huge debt burden with its mounting costs. The international context was not helpful either, with cotton prices taking a hit with the end of the American Civil War. The British, taking advantage of the fiscal crisis in Egypt, occupied the country in 1881. British troops would remain in the country until 1954. Despite such setbacks, the ruling elite managed to kick-start modernization of both the state and the economy, which would continue for almost another century.[10]

Tunisia, like Egypt, remained under Ottoman rule until the late nineteenth century, albeit with a significant degree of autonomy. Under Ahmad Bey's (1837–55) leadership, Tunisia also underwent defensive modernization, as did Egypt and the Ottoman heartland, in response to European ascendance (as well as in response to Ottoman centralizing efforts). These reforms concerned the emulation of Western institutions in public administration, justice, military, and education. Like their modernist counterparts, the Tunisian rulers built a modern standing army, overhauled the taxation system, and established higher education institutions to train military officers. Ahmad Bey also started conscription, monopolized the export of agricultural products, created a nascent industry, and invested in infrastructure, which proved to be, along with

[10] Ibid.

other reforms, quite costly.[11] Tunisians borrowed from Europeans to cover these costs, went bankrupt, and eventually fell under French rule in 1881. The country remained a French protectorate until it gained its independence in 1956 under Habib Bourguiba's leadership. As Gelvin aptly puts it, despite growing European influence, along with Turkey and Egypt, Tunisia proved to be unique among other states of the region with its long history of state-building and professionalized civil and military bureaucracies.[12]

Religion and Secularism

Turkey was the first to gain independence (1923); Egypt (1954) and Tunisia (1956) followed suit. The modernization process continued after independence in a more ambitious fashion, touching all aspects of life from religious affairs to economic development. Even though their societies were predominantly Muslim, the ruling elite in Turkey, Egypt, and Tunisia pushed for greater secularization of both state and society. The Turkish and Tunisian regimes sustained an assertive secular order, whereas in Egypt, Nasser's assertive secularism was somewhat diluted by his successors after his death in 1970. All three countries also experimented with developmentalism to fortify newly gained political independence with sustained economic development.

In the wake of World War I, the Ottoman Empire was completely dismantled. The British and the French divided up its Arab-populated territories and invaded the Turkish mainland with the help of Greeks. The Turkish nationalist movement, formed by Mustafa Kemal (later Atatürk), had to fight a war of independence to oust these occupying forces. Soon after the nationalists' surprising victory in 1922, they replaced the monarchy with a secular republic in 1923. A series of Westernizing reforms followed. The elite of the new regime, in a top-down fashion, abolished the Caliphate – the only institution, albeit in a symbolic sense, that represented the unity of the Muslim world – and overhauled the Islamic education and legal systems as well as religious networks in the society. Through sweeping changes, from daily attire and education to the penal and personal status code, the republican elite made sure the new society conformed to "Western" standards. A crucial part of this reform program entailed accelerating late Ottoman secularization of the legal and education systems, the subordination of religion to the state, and breaking the backbone of socioreligious networks represented by traditional Sufi

---

[11] For more, see Perkins, *A History of Modern Tunisia*.
[12] Gelvin, *The Modern Middle East*.

brotherhoods. Specifically, the ruling elite abolished the Islamic foundations (waqfs), thereby ending the financial independence of religious networks in Turkish society. The regime also abolished the Islamic law (sharia) as well as Islamic courts and replaced them with secular legal codes largely borrowed from Europe. The most critical change concerned the regulation of family matters, which had been governed by Islamic law for centuries. The republican elite replaced Islamic family law with the Swiss secular personal status code. In this new legal framework, women were given equal rights in marriage, inheritance, and divorce while polygamy was banned. A few years later, women were also given suffrage rights as well as the right to education and work. These secular principles were institutionalized in a constitutional amendment in 1934, declaring the Turkish Republic a secular state. The republican elite also desired to control Islam, making sure that its predominant interpretation not only conformed to the secular republican regime but also supported the creation of the ideal citizen loyal to the Turkish state. The Directorate of Religious Affairs (Diyanet) was established in 1924 to meet the religious needs of Muslims, enlighten society in religious matters, and manage places of worship. The directorate sought to monopolize the country's religious terrain, as every preacher and religious official became a state employee, and it oversaw every mosque in the country. In short, the republican elite aimed to diminish the role of Islam in public life by controlling and confining it largely to the private life of individuals.

The nationalist elite in Egypt largely echoed these sentiments. After coming to power in 1952 through the Free Officers coup, Gamal Abdel Nasser, the leader of the republican–nationalist cadres, also pursued a strictly secular agenda, though perhaps less assertive than Turkey's. He undermined the financial and judicial–institutional power of the Islamic establishment and curtailed the power of social (and political) Islam organized under the banner of the Muslim Brotherhood. Nasser distanced himself from the Brotherhood soon after his ascent to power and clamped down on the movement, executing several of its leaders and imprisoning thousands of members. Like Atatürk, Nasser also undermined Islam's institutional power by confiscating waqf property and abolishing sharia courts. Perhaps like Atatürk did in Turkey, Nasser sought to subordinate the largest Islamic institution, Al-Azhar Mosque University, for political expediency. He undermined Al-Azhar's autonomy as the government took control of the institution through the appointment of its administrators and teachers and a redesign of its schools and curriculum. Thus, Islam, as interpreted by the most profound Islamic institution in the country, could justify Nasser's developmentalist and Arab socialist programs.

While he waged a political war against Islamic organizations, Nasser did not go for full secularization of the legal system. Perhaps, the most important difference between Atatürk and Nasser concerned the changes to family affairs. On the one hand, Nasser refused to heed the Muslim Brothers' calls for veiling and recognized suffrage and social rights for women, that is, the rights to work and to maternity leave and childcare. On the other hand, he kept the Islamic family law largely intact, allowing for polygamy and discriminatory practices in divorce, inheritance, and child custody. Nasser also did not go as far as Atatürk in institutionalizing his secularizing measures; instead, he kept Islam as the religion of the state in the 1954 constitution while separating state affairs from religious doctrines.

The Tunisian republican elite was no different in its secular orientation. Habib Bourguiba, the founding father of the modern Tunisian state, established a secular republic based on Tunisian national identity. Taking his inspiration from Atatürk, Bourguiba pursued a very similar reform agenda in his country's formative years. Soon after independence in 1956, Bourguiba took several steps to exert the state's control over Islam by ending the autonomy of an array of religious institutions and curtailing their power in public life. More specifically, the government confiscated the property financing mosques and Qur'an schools through land management, placed Islamic courts within the national judicial system allowing for the appointment of more progressive judges who would support his reforms, and placed the Al-Zaytuna Mosque University, the institutional counterpart of Al-Azhar in Tunisia, under the Ministry of Education and turned it into the Faculty of Theology at the University of Tunis, practically ending the institutional autonomy of one of the oldest Islamic institutions in the region.

Bourguiba proved to be more ambitious than Nasser in arranging family affairs. The government passed the most progressive personal status code in the Arab world that handed women equal rights in marriage and divorce and improved their status in matters of inheritance and child custody. The code also banned polygamy while setting a minimum age for marriage.[13] Instead of following Atatürk's example in pushing Islam to private life though, Bourguiba, much like Nasser, made sure to provide Islamic justifications for his actions posing as a Muslim reformer, despite his lack of religious training. For Bourguiba, his reforms were perfectly compatible with Islam and in line with *ijtihad* (independent reasoning). Although the 1959 constitution kept Islam as the religion of the country, there was no role recognized for Islamic principles and injunctions in state affairs.

---

[13] See Perkins, *A History of Modern Tunisia*.

Economic Development

In short, all three countries went through similar processes of state-building and secularization with limited differences. Modernization is, of course, more than nation-state-building and secularization. It also involves, to a great extent, economic change and development. Much like their state- and nation-building experience, the three countries also share several similarities in their economic development trajectories. The most important commonality among the three concerns the overall economic structure. Unlike their oil-rich neighbors in the region, all three countries lack rich natural resources that could create rentier effects and inhibit the modernization process.[14] With limited natural resources and motivated by the goal of economic independence, the ruling elite in these three cases pursued developmentalism under the guidance of the state. The state, in all three cases, undertook a major role in capital accumulation and industrialization, and invested heavily in human development through extensive undertakings in education and healthcare. Developmentalist policies and economic growth boosted urbanization and occupational specialization, while the state's extensive role in social policies increased literacy rates and raised overall education levels for large segments of the population. Women, in particular, benefited from such programs.

Once these programs proved unsustainable due to high costs, the three countries switched to neoliberalization starting in the 1970s and 1980s, allowing for greater space for private initiative and enterprise. Still, the middle classes expanded and society has become more diverse in all three cases first under state-led developmentalism and later under the neoliberal economic model. Islamists also received their fair share of this expansion, as I will discuss shortly.

Most of these reforms were carried out in an autocratic fashion, as the nationalist elite in all three countries toppled monarchies to build secular developmentalist republics upon independence. Single-party rule marked the political system in all three countries in their early years. Their regime trajectories, however, later diverged. Turkey remained under single-party rule between 1923 and 1950, when it transitioned to multiparty politics with the first free and fair elections of the republican era. The Turkish state largely maintained its assertive secular outlook even after the transition to multiparty politics. Yet after 1950, religious networks in society recovered, thanks to the support of right-wing governments. The Turkish

---

[14] Egypt and Tunisia have more revenues accruing from oil and mineral extraction than Turkey. For more on the rentier effects of oil on modernization, see Ross, "Does Oil Hinder Democracy?"

state, presumably the most secular of the three, also reconciled with Islam without changing the constitutional framework after 1980, when the military intervened and changed the official ideology of the state to the Turkish–Islamic synthesis.[15] The goal was to counter the growing appeal of leftist movements among the youth by raising conservative generations. As part of this new ideological frame, the military elite injected Islam into the education system and introduced mandatory religion courses for all students. The state also opened greater space for religious orders and organizations in different venues of life.[16]

Egypt's secular framework was also diluted following Nasser's death in 1970. Anwar Sadat portrayed himself as the "believer president" to prop up his popularity among conservatives in a desire to counterbalance left-leaning Nasserists. Turning this discursive shift into institutional change, two constitutional amendments in 1971 and 1980 recognized Islamic law (sharia) as the principal source of legislation. The goal was to buttress regime legitimacy as its popularity started to decline with the demise of pan-Arabism. Such changes notwithstanding, the legislative and executive functions remained largely secular in practice as the Egyptian parliament followed secular norms in legislation.

Similarly, in Tunisia, Habib Bourguiba, who led the independence movement and the secularization of society, relaxed his assertive secularism in the 1970s and 1980s to counterbalance the power of the leftist opposition. The constitution remained intact, yet the regime allowed for greater visibility of Islam on college campuses and among the youth. Ben Ali, however, reversed this trend and brought Bourguiba's early secularism back and largely limited the visibility of Islam in public space, privatizing religious sensibilities for all Tunisians in the 1990s and 2000s, a topic I will turn to in Chapter 5.

The Islamist movements studied in this book emerged in these national contexts. They not only reacted to top-down secularization but also benefited handsomely from economic modernization, as I will discuss shortly. The roots of these movements go back to the nineteenth-century trauma Muslim societies experienced in their visible decline vis-à-vis Europe. And Islamism largely revolved around the questions and existential crises raised by the processes of modernization and state/nation-building under an increasingly secular frame in the nineteenth and twentieth centuries. The division of the Muslim world into separate political units with clear borders and the end of the caliphate pushed those who wanted to maintain

---

[15] See Toprak, "Religion as State Ideology"; Lord, *Religious Politics in Turkey*.
[16] One key group in this effort is the Gülen movement, which would follow a quietist path until the 2000s and ally with the AKP after 2007. For further details, see Chapter 3.

a greater role for Islam in public life to innovate and think about what role Islam could play in a modern nation-state.[17] The question of how to maintain an Islamic order in the age of modernity and secularization proved to be a crucial piece of the puzzle. In the end, all Islamists reacted to the top-down secularization of public life. For them, the emerging national identities had to be centered around religion. They thus advocated a return to the authentic identity of their societies whose essence was inextricable from Islam.[18] These movements also agreed that Islam was not only a religion but also a holistic system offering a panacea to societal ills.

The rise of an almighty institution – the modern state – with extensive control over society pushed several (but not all) Islamist groups to seek the capture of the state, through revolution, social reform, or elections. Some groups took an explicitly political direction as they sought to establish an Islamic polity. Others have taken a discursive and reformist turn to advance Islamic values at the societal level to form an Islamic society without initially altering the institutional structure. They sought the re-Islamization of their societies through grassroots activism and proselytization. Such social transformation would lead to the Islamization of decision-makers and the state cadres that would later transform the society in a more Islamic direction. These twin routes, political and social, later merged and became increasingly intertwined.

The three Islamist movements studied here grappled with the issue of political activism in a nation-state built around secular principles. The new sociopolitical context, which was the product of century-long modernization, imposed new realities on these movements. All three adapted to the modern state system and welcomed and benefited from the ruling elite's greater accommodation of Islamic practices and identities in the public space after the 1970s. They discovered opportunities of expansion in social, political, and economic life, and published periodicals, cultivated intellectual circles, established strongholds on college campuses, and founded civil society organizations (CSOs) and charities, all while constructing Islamic parallel sectors in education, healthcare, social services, and business.

---

[17] Despite similarities, these structural/institutional realities/factors have not led to a singular form of Islamism (much like communism has not led to a singular ideology but a family of ideologies). Some accepted and internalized the newly defined borders that separated the Muslim *ummah* and agreed to operate within these states with the aim of increasing the power and presence of Islam in these newly established entities, while others adopted a more internationalist outlook seeking to overthrow what they deem arbitrary and artificial lines of demarcation (Hizbut Tahrir, ISIS). This book focuses on the first group.

[18] For a thorough discussion of Islamism and identity politics, see Yavuz, *Islamic Political Identity in Turkey*.

In all three cases, Islamist activists mostly come from middle-class backgrounds,[19] and they have received their fair share of benefits from economic growth and upward social mobility. Islamist movements, in Turkey and Egypt in particular, benefited from economic liberalization as they found opportunities to expand their economic activities through more inclusive institutions and reforms after the early 1980s. As I have explained elsewhere, these reforms facilitated the growth of an Islamic middle class in both Turkey and Egypt.[20] This enrichment further empowered Islamic activism in these countries. Yet these movements also found the state's growing accommodation of Islam insufficient. For them, Islam promised solutions to the social, economic, and political problems these countries faced, and to instate these solutions, they decided to take up and expand political activism.[21]

Turkish Islamists mobilized largely under the banner of the Milli Görüş movement and established successive political parties, while the Muslim Brotherhood in Egypt recovered from Nasser's repression in the 1970s and merged their social and political activism on college campuses, through professional associations, as well in parliament. In Tunisia, Islamic activism on college campuses in the 1970s gave birth to the Islamic Tendency Movement (later rebranded Ennahda) that monopolized the terrain of political Islam in the 1980s.

Although the ruling elite in these countries sought Islam's help to counterbalance the left and accrue legitimacy after the 1970s, they remained vigilant about Islamism. In that vein, all three states prohibited the establishment of religious parties while opening some space for Islamic activism punctuated by occasional repression.[22] The elites' oscillation between accommodation and repression created a troubled relationship between Islamists and the state (i.e., the military, judiciary, and the ruling elite), as I will discuss later. Regardless, to varying degrees, Islamist movements have had opportunities for political participation in all three countries.[23] Whenever given the chance, these Islamist movements adapted to electoral politics (and democracy) as the main frame within which they operated. They established political parties when they were allowed to or ran in elections as independents when they were not. Their goal was to bring

---

[19] Ibid.; Clark, *Islam, Charity, Activism*; Gumuscu, "Class, Status, and Party."
[20] Gumuscu, "Class, Status, and Party."
[21] For a detailed discussion of this framework, see Wiktorowicz, *Islamic Activism*; Eligur, *The Mobilization of Political Islam in Turkey*.
[22] Ben Ali's Tunisia was the most repressive of the three, as Islamic activism was largely eradicated in the country in the 1990s, as I will discuss in greater detail in Chapter 5.
[23] Again, Ennahda in Tunisia may be a partial case here, as it was forced into exile in 1991. Islamist movements remained quite active in the 1980s in the country.

Islam back into the political sphere, often through the existing institutional framework drawn by the secular modernist elite.

Indeed, scholars, myself included, argue that the growing middle-class base for Islamist movements has driven their growing commitments to democratic politics in the 1990s and 2000s.[24] As argued by scholars such as Lipset and Friedman, economic development and modernization are closely associated with democracy; social changes brought by economic growth give birth to higher levels of education, urbanization, secularization, and specialization, often accepted as prerequisites of democracy. The expansion of the middle classes is also part and parcel of the presumed connection between economic development and democracy. In line with these explanations, the AKP started off with a strong prodemocratic agenda departing from the authoritarian tendencies of its predecessors. Similarly, both the Brotherhood and Ennahda embraced electoral mechanisms and civil liberties and called for free and fair elections in their countries. Echoing Nasr, it is safe to suggest that Islamists' middle-class orientation, coupled with overall modernization in these countries, has contributed to their growing commitments to electoral politics.[25]

In short, modernization in all three states unfolded somewhat similarly as they shared the desire to build secular nations and modern economies, mostly in a top-down fashion, and molded Islamist movements into modern movements. In the end, in line with increasing modernization, Islamist movements socialized not only into the modern state system and economy but also modern electoral politics. Such similarities in their broader modernization experience notwithstanding, the three countries still exhibited some differences at the time of Islamists' ascent to power. Twentieth-century reforms yielded somewhat differing levels of education, urbanization, income level, and religiosity in each country. Can these differences then shed light on the diverging trajectories of the three parties in power – AKP's pivot from liberalism to electoralism, Brotherhood's persistent electoralism, and Ennahda's liberalism?

In terms of income levels, all three were lower-middle-income countries at the time Islamists came to power. When the AKP won the 2002 elections, Turkey was at the higher tail of lower-middle-income category with very high levels of urbanization and adult literacy (87 percent in 2004 as reported by the World Bank). In 2011, Tunisia had about the same and Egypt had slightly lower per capita income (still lower-middle-income), with Tunisia enjoying higher levels of urbanization and adult literacy

---

[24] Nasr, "The Rise of Muslim Democracy"; Yavuz, *Secularism and Muslim Democracy in Turkey*; Gumuscu, "Class, Status, Party"; Demiralp, "The Rise of Islamic Capital."
[25] Nasr, "The Rise of Muslim Democracy."

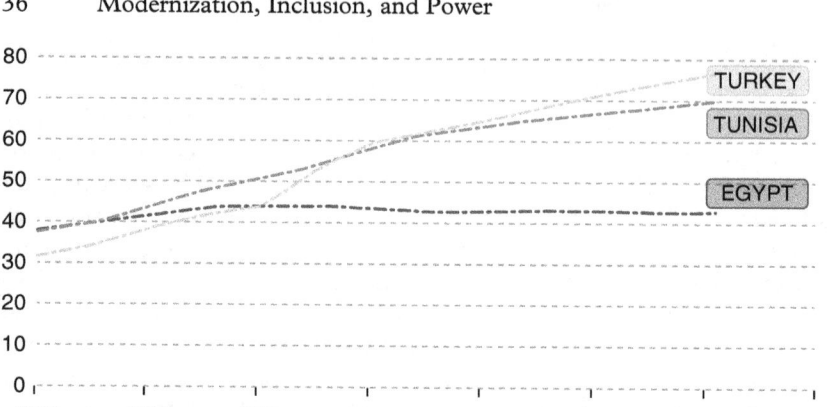

Figure 2 Urban population in Turkey, Egypt, and Tunisia (percentage)
Source: World Bank

(79 percent) compared to Egypt (43 percent; see Figure 2 for levels of urbanization and Figure 3 for economic development).

While the Turkish economy had significant troubles in the 1990s, both Egypt and Tunisia registered substantial (albeit uneven) economic growth driven by neoliberal reform programs over the decade preceding the revolution. All three parties, however, faced economic challenges when they took over the government. After coming to power, the AKP rapidly stabilized the Turkish economy, registered sustained economic growth (as shown in Figures 2 and 3), as well as expansion in urbanization and adult literacy, reaching 96 percent in 2017.[26] The country also enjoyed relative economic stability and lower levels of inflation until 2018, largely avoiding the ripple effects of the 2008 global financial crisis.[27] Hence, the Turkish society got richer as well as more urbanized and educated under AKP rule (at least until 2018). The Brotherhood's Morsi did not serve his full term, and the Egyptian economy remained in a crisis mode throughout his year in power. Ennahda had more time and opportunities to fix the Tunisian economy than the Brotherhood, but still, along with other actors, they failed to fix high unemployment and sluggish growth rates in Tunisia, increasing the vulnerability of the political system.

---

[26] Turkish economic growth tapered off after 2014 and entered a recession in 2018, but this decline succeeded AKP's authoritarian turn after 2011, rather than preceding it.
[27] Przeworski and Limongi, among others, argue that economic stability consolidates democracy. See, Przeworski and Limongi, "Modernization: Theories and Facts." Turkish economic stability in this period thus refutes their hypothesis; for further details, see Esen and Gumuscu, "Why Did Turkish Democracy Collapse?"

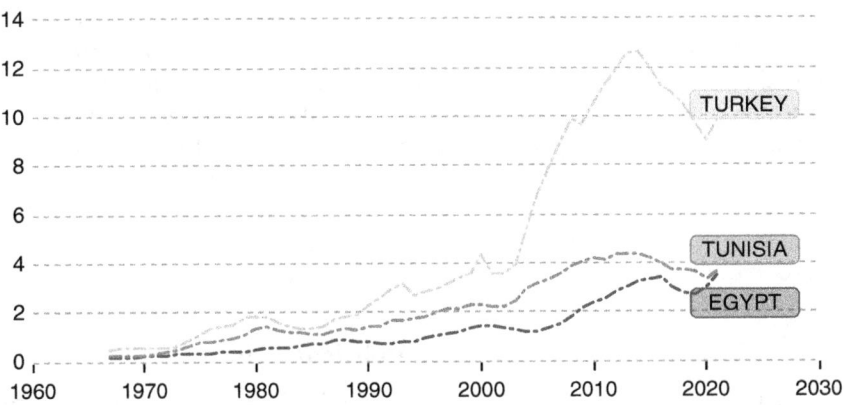

Figure 3 Economic development in Turkey, Egypt, and Tunisia (GNI/capita in current US$)
Source: World Bank

If modernization and a high level of economic development culminated in democratic preferences, then we would expect the AKP to exhibit the highest level of democratic commitment among the three, thanks to Turkey's overall development and middle-class orientation of Islamists. Indeed, the AKP committed to liberal democracy in its first term in power, yet later pivoted to an increasingly majoritarian understanding of democracy amid increasing growth, economic development, and expanding education and urbanization. Such an unexpected turn culminating in democratic underperformance defied explanations connecting modernization and democratization, hence upending the basic premises of modernization theory.[28] It is hard to decipher this dramatic pivot by macrostructural changes; what we need is a closer look at political actors, their political calculus, and intra-party dynamics, a topic I will turn to later in this chapter and in Chapter 3.

By a similar logic, Islamists in Egypt and Tunisia would then exhibit commitment to electoral democracy, again thanks to their middle-class status, but perhaps relatively weaker commitments to liberal norms due to the lower levels of economic development of these countries. Yet Tunisia and Egypt diverged significantly in their democratic transitions as Ennahda committed to liberal democracy and the Brotherhood

---

[28] I discuss the AKP's authoritarian turn and its theory-upending qualities elsewhere. See, Esen and Gumuscu, "Why Did Turkish Democracy Collapse?" Also see Brownlee, "Why Turkey's Authoritarian Descent Shakes Up Democratic Theory"; Sarfati, "How Turkey's Slide to Authoritarianism Defies Modernization Theory."

pursued electoral democracy, despite coming from similar backgrounds. Tunisia overperformed given its relatively modest levels of urbanization, education, and economic development, largely, I argue, thanks to the dominance of liberal Islamists within the ranks of Ennahda. By way of contrast, one could suggest that Islamists in Egypt conformed to expectations with its lower levels of development and urbanization.[29] These factors seem compelling when each country is studied individually. By comparative logic, however, structural conditions in these three cases fail to explain the differences in Islamists' democratic commitments.

Sociopolitical Trends and Political Cleavages

A possible explanation for differences among the democratic commitments of Islamists in Turkey, Tunisia, and Egypt is that the extent of modernization had divergent impacts on sociopolitical trends in these three countries and shaped the political calculus of these actors. Often, analysts point to high levels of conservatism in Egypt to explain the Brotherhood's actions in government. Similarly, they point to the secular and moderate nature of Tunisian society to elucidate Ennahda's liberal commitments.[30]

Masoud, for instance, offers a compelling argument that connects antecedent socioeconomic conditions such as modernization to the balance of power among different actors and their ensuing strategies. He argues that Islamists were dominant in Egypt but not in Tunisia, thanks to the divergent levels of modernization of the two countries. In Egypt, religious associations dominated the relatively weak civil society, offering a great advantage to Islamists. The Tunisian society, Masoud contends, has been more modernized and had greater associational pluralism, thereby leveling the playing field between Islamists and non-Islamists. Because, Masoud suggests, dominant political actors have no reason to commit to democracy, the Brotherhood had weaker commitments to democracy than Ennahda in Tunisia.[31]

The argument is quite compelling but only sheds partial light on the differences observed in Tunisia and Egypt and also fails to answer

---

[29] Masoud, *Counting Islam*.
[30] See, for instance, Hamid, *Temptations of Power*.
[31] Masoud follows a line of scholarship advanced by Rustow, O'Donnell and Schmitter, Przeworski, and Huntington, among others, that the dominance of a single political party does not bode well with democracy. According to Masoud, when non-Islamists in Egypt realized that they could not defeat Islamists at the ballot box – because of their inherent disadvantage in mobilizing the society vis-à-vis Islamists – they called for a military intervention. Although this may be a compelling argument that explains the weak democratic commitments of secular or non-Islamist actors, it does not tell us why an Islamist party committed to democracy in Tunisia but not in Egypt or Turkey.

several questions posed in this book. Let us start with Tunisia. In contrast to observers' depiction of the Tunisian society as relatively moderate and even secular, there existed strong societal support for a greater role for Islam in public affairs. A poll conducted in January 2014 (at the time when the draft constitution was ratified in the Constituent Assembly [CA]) reveals noteworthy trends: 50 percent of respondents believed that Islamic principles should be considered when making policy or law, and another 20 percent claimed that Islamic texts should form the foundations of making all policies and laws.[32] Another poll in 2011 showed that the support for secularism stood at 27 percent, while 65 percent of respondents envisioned a political system that was somewhat secular/religious or strongly religious.[33] Although support for Islam in public life does not necessarily signify support for Islamists, as Masoud reminds us,[34] the survey trends clearly showed that Tunisians also sought a greater Islamist presence in politics. In several polls conducted in 2011 and 2012, the average support for Islamist parties in politics hovered around 67 percent.[35] In short, the majority of the Tunisian people desired a greater role for Islam in politics, and Islamism proved to be a dominant force in Tunisian politics in the wake of the revolution.

Despite such strong support for Islamic politics, liberal leaders of Ennahda refused to maximize political gains and dominate the transition. For instance, in the first elections after the revolution, Ennahda strongly supported a representative electoral system to ensure that the party did not dominate the new assembly (still, it won 42 percent of the seats thanks to its extensive popular support). Moreover, the party sustained its liberal, pluralist, and conciliatory political style even when they were confronted by different actors, despite strong objections from electoralists within the party, as I will discuss at length in Chapter 5. Indeed, several leaders in the party recognized the popular demand for a more assertive Islamist politics. Still, they stayed on a liberal democratic course and resisted polarizing the Tunisian society for partisan gains.[36]

What about Egypt? It is safe to claim that the Egyptian society was the most religiously conservative of the three. Yet this high level of religiosity did not directly translate into support for Islamism. In an Arab Barometer survey in 2011, although an overwhelming majority of respondents identified as religious or somewhat religious, 80 percent of them agreed

---

[32] *IRI*, "Survey of Tunisian Public Opinion June–July 2014."
[33] *IRI*, "Survey of Tunisian Public Opinion March 2011."
[34] Masoud, *Counting Islam*.
[35] *IRI*, "Survey of Tunisian Public Opinion April 2012."
[36] Interviews with Ennahda officials in July 2017.

that religion is a private matter that should be separated from political and social affairs. In the same survey, only 20 percent of respondents desired a system based on Islamic law without parties and elections; likewise, only 20 percent of respondents supported a system in which only Islamist parties could compete. A staggering 83 percent rejected the statement that Islam and democracy are incompatible. Along these lines, 73 percent stated that laws should follow the wishes of the people, and 80 percent said that laws should be in accordance with sharia.[37]

Similarly, in a Pew survey conducted in 2013, 74 percent of respondents in Egypt supported instating Islamic law as the law of the country (as opposed to 12 percent of respondents in Turkey and 56 percent of respondents in Tunisia).[38] Yet such support did not mean wide-scale support for Islamism. In fact, despite high levels of support for sharia rule in Egypt, this support did not translate into electoral support for Mohammed Morsi in the 2012 presidential elections. He only received 25 percent of the votes in the first round (with a voter turnout of 46 percent), even though the Brotherhood had the strongest party machine in the country. A total of 75 percent of the electorate who turned out to vote cast their ballots for non-Islamist or liberal Islamist candidates. In the second round, Morsi secured a narrow victory which he owed to the fact that his rival was Hosni Mubarak's last prime minister, Ahmed Shafik. The narrow majority Morsi attained did not stem from Egyptians' overwhelming Islamist tendencies, as some claim, but from the institutional and political context. Still, unlike Ennahda's leaders, electoralists in the Brotherhood took this victory to mean widespread support for their ideological agenda, as I will show in Chapter 4. Owing more than half of his electoral support to the opposition, Morsi refused to compromise and intended to monopolize power at the expense of revolutionary forces. Liberal Brothers, in contrast, recognized the modest support for the Brotherhood and rejected the majoritarian tendencies of the electoralists.

In contrast, a greater role for Islam in politics has found scant support among the Turkish people. In a poll conducted in 2002, the year the AKP came to power, only 9.5 percent of respondents expressed support for the instatement of Islamic law. In 2006, four years into AKP's first term in office, the support slightly increased to 15 percent, while the party's vote share increased from 34 percent in 2002 to 47 percent in 2007.[39] Still, support for turning Islamic law into the law of the land stood at a

---

[37] Arab Barometer Survey, June 2011.
[38] Pew Research Center, *The World's Muslims*.
[39] Carkoglu and Toprak, *Religion, Society, and Politics*.

mere 12 percent in a Pew survey conducted in 2013.[40] Yet such limited support for Islamic law did not deter the AKP under Erdoğan's leadership from polarizing society along secular–Islamic fault lines. Starting in its third term in power, the AKP pursued a gradual program of hegemonic Islamization, as I show in Chapter 3, despite the opposition of liberal voices within the party and from the strong secular civil society. The AKP, under electoralists' leadership, translated its electoral dominance into a mandate for Islamization.

In short, the Tunisian society was not as "moderate" or secular as many argued, and the Turkish society was not as supportive of an Islamist agenda as Erdoğan portrayed it to be. Still, echoing Berman, both the AKP and Ennahda took initiative and attempted to mold the political scene to their liking, in favor of majoritarianism and polarization in the former, and for inclusion and liberalism in the latter.

Perhaps more importantly, these parties were not monoliths. Different factions within each party perceived their political reality differently. Despite its clear dominance in Tunisian politics, the leading faction in Ennahda, unlike the leading factions in the Brotherhood and the AKP, did not assume their electoral success to be a mandate for majority rule. They remained on a course of conciliation and compromise. The factions at the helm of the other two parties, in contrast, interpreted their electoral success (and weakness of the opposition) as no need for compromise.

The paths of the three parties diverged after the first elections that brought them to power. The AKP moved on to consolidate its dominance[41]; the military intervention ended the democratic transition in Egypt before a second election, while Ennahda suffered some electoral losses in 2014 and again in 2019. For many, Ennahda's electoral decline stemmed from its conciliatory attitude throughout the transition and its growing distance from hegemonic Islamism, not the other way around.[42] Despite such losses, the party stayed on course, as I will show in Chapter 5. This is an outcome neither long-term modernization nor sociocultural trends can explain. This gap invites analyses beyond macrostructural narratives. A more accurate understanding requires, therefore, a closer look at actors, their individual experiences, the constraints and incentives they face, and how these affect Islamists' behavior and ideology.

---

[40] Pew Research Center, *The World's Muslims*.
[41] For a detailed discussion of AKP's dominance, see Gumuscu, "The Emerging Predominant Party System" and Gumuscu, "Dominance and Democratic Backsliding."
[42] Many party officials agreed with this assessment during my interviews in 2017.

Explaining Islamist Change: Actors and Institutional Constraints

So far, I have outlined the long-term political and economic trends and how they informed Islamist politics. Now I turn to the impact of institutions that are presumed to induce action from political actors – in this case, Islamists – through a set of incentives and constraints. Can institutional constraints, for instance, explain why some Islamist parties commit to democracy while others do not? Can incentives and constraints provided by democratic inclusion and exclusion shape their democratic commitments?

In the extensive scholarly literature on the relationship between democratic inclusion and political moderation, scholars have spent considerable time unpacking what they call the "paradox of democracy," that nondemocratic actors can come to power through free and fair elections and go on to subvert democracy. Many posited that the socializing effects of democracy, namely inclusion-moderation thesis and its variants, would appear in the transformative effects of the democratic game on political actors. One can identify two main branches of this thesis: institutional and ideational.[43] First, I summarize the institutional variant of the thesis and discuss its application to Islamist movements. Then, I turn to the ideational variants of the thesis and its premises vis-à-vis Islamists' democratic commitments for a critical assessment.

Inclusion and the Transformative Impact of Institutions

According to the institutional (and predominant) variant of the inclusion-moderation thesis, two specific mechanisms come into play for ideological parties: electoral concerns and governance concerns. The first suggests that parties move toward the political center to win more votes.[44] Scholars have long argued that parties are primarily concerned with winning elections and will change their positions with changing external impetus, such as inclusion in the electoral system and electoral pressures.[45]

---

[43] I would like to thank one of the anonymous referees for this distinction.
[44] The most well-known formulation of this theory is Downs, "An Economic Theory of Political Action in a Democracy."
[45] Duverger, *Political Parties*; Downs, "An Economic Theory of Political Action in a Democracy." Some add nuance to this argument by positing that different parties give different responses to particular stimuli. Accordingly, changes in a competitive situation would generate the most decisive and immediate effect on parties with a primary goal of vote maximization or office maximization but not on those that advocate an ideology. Harmel and Janda, "An Integrated Theory of Party Goals and Party Change."

The second mechanism implies that once they come to power, parties embrace governance concerns, that is, attending to the daily needs of the people rather than running subversive or revolutionary schemes.[46] Those who argue that inclusion induces behavioral moderation also expect this process to induce ideological change as a result of participation in legal politics.[47]

Socialist parties in Europe, for instance, preferred strategies designed to maximize electoral support and thereby replaced their ideal of socialist victory with more centrist policies and programs.[48] Similarly, radical political parties in "third-wave" democracies and communist parties in postcommunist democracies, when faced with a trade-off between radicalism and inclusion, often opted for the latter.[49] Religious parties are no exceptions. A religious party, such as Catholic parties of nineteenth-century Europe, rests its program on a religious tradition and seeks to establish a polity inspired by these principles. It, therefore, lacks complete control over its platform, unlike other mass-based parties.[50] Despite this key difference, Kalyvas and Kersbergen argue, incentives and sanctions embedded in electoral politics moderate religious parties as political interests take precedence over dogmatic rigidity.[51]

The inclusion-moderation thesis has also been widely scrutinized by scholars.[52] First, the thesis overestimates parties' willingness to change with the intention of maximizing their votes. Political parties are conservative organizations and are resistant to change. For instance, bad electoral performances failed to induce change in Christian democratic parties in the 1990s.[53] Ideological parties are particularly resistant to change, as they may incur higher costs than mainstream parties when they shift position. That is why many maintain ideological rigidity even under electoral pressures.[54]

More importantly, parties are not, as these theses suggest, passive recipients of socioeconomic, cultural, or electoral pressures.[55] In Berman's

---

[46] Berman, "Taming Extremist Parties."
[47] For instance, see Przeworski and Sprague, *Paper Stones*; Kalyvas, *The Rise of Christian Democracy in Europe*.
[48] For more, see Przeworski and Sprague, *Paper Stones*.
[49] Huntington, "Democracy's Third Wave"; for a similar argument on postcommunist parties, see Grzymala-Busse, *Redeeming the Communist Past*.
[50] Gunther and Diamond, "Species of Political Parties."
[51] Kalyvas and van Kersbergen, "Christian Democracy."
[52] For an exemplary review, see, for instance, Tepe, "The Inclusion–Moderation Thesis."
[53] Duncan, "Lately, Things Just Don't Seem the Same"; Harmel et al., "Performance, Leadership, Factions and Party Change."
[54] Adams et al., "Are Niche Parties Fundamentally Different from Mainstream Parties?" Sanchez-Cuenca, "Party Moderation and Politicians' Ideological Rigidity."
[55] Wilson, "The Sources of Party Change: The Social Democratic Parties of Britain, France, Germany, and Spain."

words, "while exogenous social, economic, and cultural changes may shape the environment political parties face, they do not determine how parties will actually respond to these challenges."[56] In fact, parties shape their environments through their ideological, organizational, and mobilizational capacity. After all, this is their raison d'être. In short, parties are impactful actors, not victims of their environments.[57] They can rearticulate the political identities and preferences of their supporters, polarize the political spectrum, and accrue electoral benefits without feeling the need to compromise their ideological positions.

Right-wing populist parties in recent years illustrate this point. Such parties, whereby populism and the extremism/far-right merge, have proven to be immune to pressures of electoral competition and governance.[58] They successfully build electoral coalitions without foregoing their authoritarian tendencies, as we see in the case of Fidesz in Hungary and the Bharatiya Janata Party (BJP) in India. In fact, these parties turn extremist positions into mainstream ones by capitalizing on their ideological flexibility and popularity.[59] Besides, right-wing populist parties do not moderate their words or actions once in office either. The BJP's example in India along with several other populist parties is quite informative in this regard, as the leaders of the party continue to embrace polarization, demonization, violence, and repression even after coming to power. In other words, rather than merely being the victims of their environments, parties define, articulate, and aggregate interests, signal what is important to their constituency, and shape their worldviews.[60]

If electoral pressures, governance concerns, and socioeconomic changes hold limited impact on party behavior in other contexts, their impact on Islamist parties is even less. Islamist parties, like other religious or right-wing populist parties, often emerge from strong social movements that equip them with exceptional mobilizational capacity and organizational strength.[61] Relatedly, despite their strong ideological positions, Islamist parties violate the dominant assumption that ideological parties receive limited support from the electorate. Because they often rest on strong social movements and grassroots, they can count on extensive popular support in competitive elections. Such popular support for Islamist parties,

---

[56] Berman, "The Life of the Party," 105.
[57] Ibid., 102.
[58] Heinisch, "Success in Opposition–Failure in Government."
[59] Ibid.; Albertazzi and McDonnell, *Populists in Power*; McDonnell and Cabrera, "The Right-Wing Populism of India's BJP."
[60] Iversen, "The Logics of Electoral Politics."
[61] One of the first treatments of Islamist activism as a social movement is Wiktorowicz, *Islamic Activism*. For Islamists' mobilizational capacity, see Wickham, *Mobilizing Islam*.

as also seen in the cases studied in this book, thereby challenges the most critical expectation of the inclusion-moderation thesis that remaining in perennial opposition tames such movements over time.

In contrast, secular political parties are quite weak in many Muslim countries.[62] In most cases, such parties are either associated with an authoritarian past and failed ideologies or co-opted if not already crushed by repressive regimes. Secular parties also lack the networks, organizational infrastructure, and ideological affinity that Islamist movements often enjoy. As Tessler suggests, left-wing parties and organizations are exposed to state repression since they cannot hide behind the protective cloak of Islam. Islamist parties, in contrast, can rely on local mosques and religious foundations to recruit and mobilize supporters and raise funds even under the watchful eye of authoritarian rulers.[63]

Associational advantages hence matter. Masoud underscores the prevalence of patronage ties to explain Islamists' electoral advantages and political dominance in Egypt. Islamists, he argues, build strong patronage ties with their middle-class constituencies through predominantly religious associations, while their leftist counterparts lack a similar associational connection to their constituencies.[64]

Such factors create an imbalance between Islamists and their more secular counterparts and allow them to win popular mandates when given the opportunity to run in free and fair elections. In fact, their organizational and mobilizational capacity, combined with their ideological appeal, may lead to quick success under competitive regimes and culminate in political dominance soon after their incorporation into the system.[65] Once the party is in government, it may use its power to shape society and the new political system after its own vision, altering both to its advantage. In other words, electoral pressures for Islamist parties may not be as strong as scholars assume, thanks to their heightened mobilizational capacity.

Governance concerns may not be enough to transform Islamist parties either. The argument suggests that once in government, antisystem parties cannot afford to engage in ideological battles, since they would be busy solving the problems of their electorate.[66] The main

---

[62] For a thorough analysis of the imbalance between secular and Islamist parties, see Tessler, *The Origins of Popular Support for Islamist Movements*.
[63] Tessler, *The Origins of Popular Support for Islamist Movements*.
[64] Masoud, *Counting Islam*.
[65] See Masoud, *Counting Islam*, for an excellent discussion on how Islamists dominate the electoral scene.
[66] Berman, "Taming Extremist Parties."

assumption is that ideological parties may not meet the demands of the people and endorse their ideological agenda at the same time. But Islamists are well-known for effectively serving their constituencies – even when they are in opposition – while simultaneously pursuing an ideological agenda. From Hezbollah in Lebanon to Muslim Brotherhood in Egypt, activists provide their constituencies with goods such as education, childcare, vocational training and employment opportunities, as well as basic needs such as food, cheap housing, clothes, and healthcare.[67] And wherever they control local governments, their municipal services often supersede their political rivals. Such a wide range of social services and, in some cases, high-quality municipal governance offered by Islamist parties further strengthen their ideological appeal. Such attributes render Islamists powerful actors in a competitive political environment. Hence, as the broader literature on political parties suggests, electoral constraints are hardly a source of change for Islamist parties.[68]

Besides, the institutional constraints underlined by the inclusion-moderation thesis lose their utility in times of political transitions such as the Arab uprisings, when institutions are collapsing and the rules of the political game are in the making. In such moments, as Schwedler rightfully observes, ideological commitments and attitudes gain greater force than the prestige of collapsing institutions.[69] One does not need a revolution to overhaul a system either. When political actors establish their dominance with sustained electoral support, they may very well carry the strong popular mandate to redesign institutions.[70] When a political actor establishes its dominance, whether through a revolution or successive electoral victories, institutional constraints remain at the mercy of the government, bringing forth actors' ideological commitments.[71]

Going beyond Institutionalism: Ideological Effects of Inclusion

What about the ideological impact of inclusion, then? Can participation in democratic politics socialize nondemocratic actors into genuine democrats? The institutional variant of the inclusion-moderation thesis does not elaborate on the ideological effects of inclusion but rather

---

[67] An excellent study on Islamist social services is Clark, *Islam, Charity, and Activism*.
[68] In fact, an Islamist incumbent party may invest in ideological polarization when faced with a crisis to consolidate its support base. This is what the AKP and the Brotherhood did in power as I show in Chapters 3 and 4.
[69] Schwedler, "Islamists in Power?"
[70] Panebianco, *Political Parties*; Pempel, *Uncommon Democracies*.
[71] See, for instance, Panebianco, *Political Parties*; Schedler, "The Logic of Electoral Authoritarianism."

assumes a linear (and inevitable) progression toward greater commitment to democracy upon inclusion, an empirically suspect claim.[72] The ideational variant of the thesis, in contrast, unpacks these mechanisms by explaining how inclusion leads to ideological moderation by distinguishing behavioral/strategic change from ideological transformation. The difference between the two is simple; the latter requires a substantive transformation in the goals and political principles of the party (in addition to its political strategies). Scholars of Islamism identify several mechanisms of ideological change among Islamists, such as political learning through cooperation across ideological lines,[73] internal party debate,[74] charismatic leadership,[75] internal splits, and generational change.[76]

Indeed, as I noted earlier, when given the opportunity, many Islamist movements joined electoral politics. They hoped, in a strategic fashion, to extend their message to broader segments of society through political participation while seeking legitimacy and thereby protection from state repression. In certain cases, scholars have suggested, such strategic changes led to ideological transformation among Islamists.

Wickham, for instance, posits that through inclusion, both the means and ends of Islamist movements change over time.[77] For her, new experiences and/or exposure to new ideas through various forms of political engagement can trigger self-conscious shifts in actors' commitments.[78] For instance, inclusion in formal politics allows Islamists to engage with their ideological rivals through a process of political learning. As Islamists work with state officials and other parties on issues of common concern, they modify their political beliefs and find democracy more appealing.[79] In the 1980s and 1990s, the younger members of the Brotherhood, for instance, had the opportunity to socialize and collaborate with secular

---

[72] Schwedler, *Faith in Moderation*, 149. Democratic habituation may not take place despite sustained inclusion. A recent case in point is the BJP, a right-wing populist party capitalizing on Hindu nationalism in India, that pursued polarization and violence instead of revising its political goals upon inclusion. One could also consider increasing authoritarianism among established parties, such as the Republican Party in the United States.
[73] Wickham, "The Path to Moderation"; Ashour, *The De-radicalization of Jihadists*; Browers, *Political Ideology in the Arab World*; El-Ghobashy, "The Metamorphosis of the Egyptian Muslim Brothers"; McCarthy, *Inside Tunisia's al-Nahda*.
[74] Schwedler, *Faith in Moderation*.
[75] Ashour, *The De-radicalization of Jihadists*; Yadav, "Understanding What Islamists Want."
[76] El-Ghobashy, "The Metamorphosis of the Egyptian Muslim Brothers."
[77] Wickham, *The Muslim Brotherhood*, 14.
[78] Ibid., 8–10.
[79] Wickham, "The Path to Moderation." Also see El-Ghobashy, "The Metamorphosis."

colleagues in professional associations in Egypt. This experience taught them the value of democratic practices and initiated what El-Ghobashy calls "the metamorphosis" of the Brotherhood.[80] Similarly, inclusion led to moderation in the IAF in Jordan as Islamists worked jointly with their ideological rivals in the Higher Committee for the Coordination of National Opposition Parties to call for democracy in Jordan.[81]

Political learning has indeed served as a major mechanism of ideological transformation of several Islamists. However, the experience is not uniform across individuals or parties. First, the same political experience may induce diverse learning outcomes in different actors. As Wickham concedes, individuals' idiosyncrasies preclude us from expecting the same set of reactions from Islamists sharing the same political experience.[82] In fact, the same experiences and processes produce very different attitudes among Islamists within the same movement or party. Schwedler's work on the IAF in Jordan and the Islah Party in Yemen reveals such differences. While inclusion led to ideological change in the IAF, it has not triggered a similar transformation in the case of Islah Party.[83] Moreover, ideological moderation remained limited and selective in the case of the IAF since the party refused to discuss those issues pertaining to sharia and kept cooperation with its ideological rivals limited to the issues of procedural democracy.[84]

Existing theories of political learning fail to explain why political actors with similar experiences usually have divergent learning experiences or why political learning has its limits. Levy offers an explanation that "people interpret historical experience through the lens of their own analytical assumptions and worldviews […] in a way that *reinforces their views*, so as to rally support for their preferred policies, whether they be driven by views of the national interest or partisan political interests."[85] Insofar as the political learning thesis fails to theorize when individuals (do not) learn, as Schwedler points out, political learning offers an insightful "description" of moderation and not an explanation.[86]

---

[80] El-Ghobashy, "The metamorphosis".
[81] Schwedler, *Faith in Moderation*; Clark, "The Conditions of Islamist Moderation."
[82] Wickham, *The Muslim Brotherhood*, 8–10.
[83] Schwedler, *Faith in Moderation*.
[84] Clark, "The Conditions of Islamist Moderation." Although Islamist parties in Egypt, Kuwait, and Palestine embraced peaceful and legal political activity, ideological transformation among them often remained limited since political openings prior to the Arab uprisings of 2011 were quite constrained and elections were neither free nor fair. For a thorough discussion of such constraints and their effects, see Brown, *When Victory Is Not an Option*.
[85] Quoted in Çavdar, "Islamist 'New Thinking' in Turkey," 480.
[86] Schwedler, *Faith in Moderation*.

Explaining Islamist Change

A second, and more serious, pitfall of the political learning thesis concerns the question of aggregation. Because political learning occurs at the individual level, the thesis cannot explain how individual experiences diffuse and shape group decisions and translate into broader changes at the party level.[87] "The learning of a collective," as Revanal claims, "is different from the learning of an individual." For collective learning to take place "[l]essons must be internalized in some enduring, objective, consistent, and therefore predictable way."[88] The political learning thesis, with its focus on individual experiences, fails to provide us with keys to such processes, and this gap requires a closer look at the internal dynamics of Islamist movements.

Schwedler, in her comparative study of the IAF and Islah parties, offers a way to resolve the issue of aggregation. She identifies internal party debates in interaction with the political opportunity structures as the main mechanism of ideological moderation.[89] These debates, echoing Renaval, determine the boundaries of imaginable (justifiable and unjustifiable) practices, a process that shifts the worldview of the entire movement toward greater openness. She observes that internal debates within Jordan's IAF shifted the red lines of the movement from justification of political participation to internalization of several democratic practices. In the case of the Islah Party, the factionalized nature of the party with deep ideological divisions precluded similar internal debates and thus moderation. Power dynamics, specifically the weakness of moderate voices of the Muslim Brothers vis-à-vis radical figures such as Abdul Majeed al-Zindani, play a critical role in this outcome.

I argue, instead, that internal debates are products of the power dynamics within the Islamist movement and serve as a mechanism of collective learning only when factions who are willing to carry out such debates are at the helm. The driving factor behind IAF's moderation then, I assert, concerns the balance of power among different factions instead of internal debates. Obviously, moderates in the IAF dominated the party and established internal debate as the primary mechanism to resolve ideological differences, as opposed to radicals in the Islah Party who dismissed such debates.[90]

Ashour resolves some of these issues pertaining to the ideational impact of inclusion in his study of deradicalization of violent Islamist movements.[91] He

---

[87] Wickham, *The Muslim Brotherhood*; Gumuscu, "Class, Status, and Party."
[88] Quoted in Çavdar, "Islamist 'New Thinking' in Turkey," 484.
[89] Schwedler, *Faith in Moderation*.
[90] The fact that moderates within the Islah Party sustained such debates among themselves without carrying them to the party level supports this claim.
[91] Ashour, *The De-radicalization of Jihadists*.

identifies interactions within the movement, akin to Schwedler, and political learning, echoing Wickham, as mechanisms of ideological transformation. By adding the leadership factor embodied in a credible, pious, theologically knowledgeable figure as a key catalyst in providing legitimacy to deradicalization, Ashour adds nuance to existing studies and implicitly introduces power dynamics to the process of ideational change.[92] Like many other political parties, Islamist parties and movements change when the dominant faction pursues change. Yet Ashour stops short of offering a systematic analysis of intra-party struggles, which I will offer in the next chapter.

Inclusion–Moderation in Turkey, Egypt, and Tunisia

How do these theories apply to Islamist parties in Turkey, Egypt, and Tunisia? Can institutional constraints and incentives help us understand why Ennahda remained committed to democratic norms while the AKP and the Brotherhood did not? I now turn to this question to survey plausible explanations (and their shortcomings) for the divergent paths of the three Islamist parties (see Table 1 for a summary).

As I noted earlier, in all three countries, secular regimes set incentives for Islamist parties to play the electoral game while placing constraints on their Islamic agenda. That is, the regimes combined inclusion and threat of exclusion to socialize these parties. Before the onset of the uprisings in 2011, only Turkey among the three cases had established democratic institutions. That is how, despite its undemocratic secular practices and occasional military interventions, Turkey offered the greatest space for Islamist political participation upon the condition that they accepted the secular nature of the state. Turkish Islamists have actively participated in politics under the banner of legal parties since 1970, checked by the Constitutional Court for their secular credentials and shut down whenever they engaged in antisecular activities. The same provision indeed existed in Tunisia and Egypt, whereby Islamist movements enjoyed different levels of accommodation by these secular regimes. Tunisian Islamists had the opportunity to run in elections in the 1980s when the ruling elite experimented with top-down liberalization, only to face heavy repression under Ben Ali, who forced Ennahda into exile in the early 1990s. In Egypt, in contrast, Nasser heavily repressed and criminalized the Brotherhood in the 1960s, as I discussed earlier, while his successors Anwar Sadat and Hosni Mubarak allowed the movement to participate in politics through controlled elections and civil associational life

---

[92] Ibid.; Yadav also draws attention to charismatic leadership.

Table 1 *Factors that shape Islamist party behavior*

	Turkey	Egypt	Tunisia
Structure			
State-building	Nineteenth century led by modernist elite	Nineteenth century led by modernist elite	Nineteenth century led by modernist elite
Political economy	Non-rentier, lower-middle-income (2002)	Non-rentier, lower-middle-income (2011)	Non-rentier, lower-middle-income (2011)
Education (literacy)	high	medium	high
Urbanization	high	medium	high
Support for Islam in politics	low	high	high
Institutions			
Regime type	Single-party authoritarian → multiparty democracy (1950)	Single-party authoritarian	Single-party authoritarian
Inclusion/exclusion	Inclusion as a legal party with periodic sanctions	Inclusion as an illegal movement with periodic sanctions	Brief inclusion followed by sustained exclusion and repression
Democratic commitment of the party	**Liberal to electoral**	**Electoral**	**Liberal**

Source: Compiled by the author based on the World Bank Data, Gelvin 2016, various public opinion surveys.

as independents while denying legal status to the movement. Waves of repression punctuated such accommodation, as thousands of Muslim Brothers were tried in military courts and imprisoned on a regular basis.

Several studies suggested that the threat of exclusion and incentives for inclusion pressured Islamists to moderate in Turkey in the late 1990s. The primary mechanism in the process entailed both strategic calculation and political learning.[93] Once Islamists realized that challenging the secular nature of the state was not feasible (discussed in greater detail in Chapter 3), they capitalized on the incentive to remain in the system.[94] Turkish

---

[93] Cizre and Çınar, "Turkey 2002"; Çavdar, "Islamists' New Thinking in Turkey." Çavdar notes that not all Islamists learn the same way.
[94] Insel, "The AKP and Normalizing Democracy in Turkey"; Atacan, "Explaining Religious Politics"; Özbudun, "From Political Islam to Conservative Democracy."

Islamism had experienced ideological change within the context of electoral incentives coupled with judicial sanctions in the late 1990s.[95] The future leaders of the AKP learned the value of democracy in this process, the argument goes, as selective incentives for inclusion, combined with such sanctions, induced ideological transformation in Turkish Islamism.[96]

The Brothers in Egypt also enjoyed growing opportunities for inclusion in the system after Mubarak took over in 1981. The movement, denied legal party status because of its explicit Islamic character, still ran in elections with independent candidates and won seats in parliament. Such participation in formal politics allowed the movement to reach out to different parts of the society with limited political risks. However, as I noted before, the regime still occasionally cracked down on the Brotherhood. The combination of inclusion and the threat of exclusion, many suggested, pushed the movement toward a more democratic position and the Brotherhood raised the banner of political liberalization, free and fair elections, and respect for political freedoms in the 1990s and 2000s.[97]

The case of Ennahda differed somewhat from its counterparts in Turkey and Egypt. Islamists were very briefly included in the political system in the 1980s, and this inclusion was followed by a period of intense repression starting in the 1990s. Scholars attribute Ennahda's ideological moderation to this intense exclusion. Cavatorta and Merone, for instance, highlight exclusion in the form of political and social marginalization under the Ben Ali regime as a driving factor of Nahdawis' (as Ennahda members are called) ideological moderation.[98] Likewise, for McCarthy, Ennahda's democratization was a product of Nahdawis' long-term political exclusion and their prison experience, which exposed them to long debates with leftists in prisons.[99] Nugent agrees with McCarthy on the impact of repression. She finds that Ben Ali's blanket repression of leftists and Islamists reduced the political distance between the two and facilitated their collaboration after the revolution.[100]

Certainly, these experiences shaped the democratic attitudes of individual Islamists to a large degree. Many experimented with electoral practices, worked with their ideological rivals, and learned the value of democratic rights and norms. However, these lessons were not uniform

---

[95] For a thorough analysis of this transformation, see Mecham, "From the Ashes of Virtue."
[96] Mecham, "From the Ashes of Virtue"; Somer, "Moderate Islam and Secularist Opposition"; Yavuz, *Secularism and Muslim Democracy*.
[97] Wickham, *The Muslim Brotherhood*.
[98] Cavatorta and Merone, "Moderation through Exclusion?"
[99] McCarthy, *Inside Tunisia's al-Nahda*.
[100] Nugent, "The Psychology of Repression and Polarization."

across the movement, and significant differences have arisen within the ranks of Islamists. Some pursued democracy for strategic reasons and for its instrumental value, while others experienced ideological change and bridged Islamic norms with democratic ones. To what extent these norms were internalized within the movement was not clear until after the rise of the three parties to power, first in Turkey and then in Tunisia and Egypt. For instance, there was simply no way to know to what extent the democratic commitments were strategic and instrumental as opposed to ideological; to what extent these democratic commitments were internalized and the lessons were learned collectively; and to what extent individual experiences translated into group behavior. Many of these assertions were tested rigorously after these parties won elections.

If inclusion primed Islamist parties' subsequent behavior toward greater commitment to democracy, then we would expect the AKP to be the most and Ennahda to be the least democratic of the three. After all, Turkish Islamists had the longest experience with multiparty politics and their Tunisian counterparts had the shortest. The experience of Egyptian Islamists under Mubarak's electoral authoritarian regime fell somewhere in between. Sustained political participation in Turkey, however, has not secured Islamists' long-term commitment to democracy. The earlier commitment to democratic norms was traded for majoritarian Islamism after 2011. This reversal raised several questions about the effect of democratic incentives and the learning curve of Islamists, as I will discuss in Chapter 3. Equally surprising, severe repression and exclusion of Islamists in Tunisia did not lead to a similar shift for Ennahda after their ascent to power. The party remained committed to liberal democracy throughout its term and refrained from instrumentalizing electoral politics in a majoritarian fashion. Despite operating in a lesser repressive environment than Ennahda, the Brotherhood opted for majoritarian Islamism after Morsi's election as president. Clearly, inclusion had mixed results for long-lasting democratization in these cases, although it might have played a critical role in the internalization of electoral politics.

What about electoral and governance pressures? Could different levels of electoral strength, then, explain AKP's and Brotherhood's hegemonic turn and Ennahda's democratic commitments? Has Ennahda stayed on the path of democracy because it was electorally weak? Masoud, for instance, argues that Islamists in Tunisia were forced to compromise and work with non-Islamists because they could not dominate the founding elections and the playing field was even. In contrast, he asserts, Islamists in Egypt dominated the founding elections, so they had no reason to commit to democracy.[101]

---

[101] Masoud, "Not Ready for Democracy."

In fact, all three parties were clear victors of the first elections that brought them to power. The AKP came to power with 34 percent of the votes, Ennahda received 37 percent, and Brotherhood's FJP received 37 percent. (Morsi received 25 percent of the votes in the first round of presidential elections, as I discussed above.) All three proved to be the best organized political party in their countries with strong ties to the electorate through their local organizations, dominating their closest rivals in these elections. In fact, Ennahda's success over its rivals was much more impressive compared to both the AKP and the Brotherhood, given the fact that the Tunisian electoral system favored smaller parties.

The translation of vote shares to seats in parliament has shown significant differences though. These vote shares yielded disproportionate power to the AKP in its first term with 66 percent of the seats, while Ennahda had 41 percent, and the FJP had 47 percent. The "relative weakness" of Ennahda in terms of seats, however, was its own doing. The party endorsed a perfectly representative electoral system in the founding elections, handing over seats to smaller parties so as not to dominate the CA. Both the AKP and the Brotherhood, in contrast, benefited from majoritarian institutions and electoral rules that inflated their electoral power and showed no intention to change these rules that favored them over their rivals. For Turkey, this was the 10 percent electoral threshold, which basically erased smaller parties from the political scene in favor of bigger parties; for Egypt, it was the presidential system, which culminated in a winner-takes-all logic instead of proportional representation and power-sharing.

Although Islamists under different party banners had a stronger showing in Egypt than the other two cases, such support was restricted to the parliamentary elections. The Brotherhood's FJP and Salafi Nour Party together captured around 70 percent of the seats in the founding elections. Yet Egypt's parliament, unlike in Turkey and Tunisia, was not the executive branch during the transition; it was the presidency. The Brotherhood's candidate Mohammed Morsi only received 25 percent of the votes in the first round and had a narrow victory in the second round, as I noted above. Indeed, veteran Brotherhood member Abdel Moneim Aboul Fotouh told me in an interview that an accurate estimate of the Brotherhood's electoral support would hover around 25 percent in free and fair elections. The first round of the presidential race affirmed his assessment. Indeed, people who voted for the Brotherhood in the parliamentary elections supported other candidates in the presidential race.

In short, early electoral differences among the three parties were not as pronounced and were partly the function of institutional differences and the parties' deliberate choices. What about long-term electoral pressures and governance concerns? Here, the Turkish and Tunisian cases help us decipher the answer. For both cases, electoral and governance pressures fail to explain parties' behavior. Of the three, only the AKP managed to win successive elections and establish political dominance.[102] In its first two terms, the party received these votes as a centrist party – and there were no incentives for it to pivot far-right. There were no powerful right-wing contenders on the Turkish political scene, nor was there any demand for an Islamic hegemonic agenda from society, as I discussed earlier. By way of contrast, Ennahda had incentives to shift to the right, as the party base demanded explicitly Islamic politics from the party leadership, which resisted this pressure. In the end, the party ended up losing votes in subsequent elections and some members left to join political coalitions with a hegemonic Islamic agenda.[103] In short, accounts that underline electoral pressures as determinant of party behavior cannot explain the AKP's pivot to hegemonic Islamism or Ennahda's sustained commitments to liberal democracy. As we see in both cases, party leadership has determined the reaction of the party to electoral pressures.

Balance of Power Considerations and Political Strategies

The AKP's recent turn to hegemonic Islamism and the Brotherhood's clear majoritarian tendencies seem to challenge the inclusion-moderation and political learning theses, at least at the group level, and vindicate the thesis that the moderation was primarily strategic, as advanced by Hamid and others. These scholars argued that when there are no forces that keep Islamists in line, there is no reason for Islamists to follow democratic norms. Islamists' sustained commitment to democracy, they implied, required external pressure on such parties because they are ultimately motivated by survival.[104] The argument implies that when such veto powers are weakened, that is, under competitive regimes, Islamists will monopolize power with the intention of Islamizing society. In short, exclusion can induce behavioral change, yet, for Hamid, this change is short-term, tactical, and cosmetic.[105]

That is partly why recent analyses concur on the impact of external f/actors on Islamist party trajectories, suggesting that interaction

---

[102] I have unpacked AKP's dominance elsewhere with a coauthor. See Keyman and Gumuscu, *Democracy, Identity, Foreign Policy*. Also see Gumuscu, "The Emerging Predominant Party System."
[103] Lorch and Chakroun, "Salafism Meets Populism."
[104] Hamid, *Temptations of Power*.
[105] Ibid.

among different actors and their balance of power considerations dictate Islamists' democratic commitments. One can identify several sources of external pressure from within and outside of a society, including the military establishment, the judiciary, civil society, popular protests, and regional and international politics, among others.

For instance, scholars have attributed the AKP's transformation from a centrist party into a hegemonic Islamic party to the waning influence of the Turkish military and judiciary after 2010 and shallow ideological change among the ranks of the AKP.[106] These veto powers put pressure on the party in its first term to make sure the party complied with the secular republican principles entrenched in the constitution. Following the controversial presidential elections in 2007, the party chose to confront the veto powers and weaken them through legalistic measures. With the declining power of the secular establishment, the AKP could have very well stayed on a democratic course, yet it chose not to, hinting at leaders' weak democratic commitments.

This account sheds some light on the political calculus of AKP leadership, but it remains incomplete and reductionist. For instance, it overlooks significant disagreements among the party ranks that arise in the wake of the party's dominance. The argument attributes a singular strategy and homogenous ideology to the party, an empirically questionable assertion. As I show in Chapter 3, a split indeed occurred within the AKP in the wake of the decline of the secular establishment. While one faction took the new power matrix as a pass for hegemonic rule, others remained committed to pluralism. By unpacking the balance of power among different groups inside the party, Chapter 3 offers a more accurate account of AKP's trajectory than existing accounts.

Similarly, the veto powers received their due credit in such analyses of Egypt for keeping the Muslim Brotherhood in check. Both the military and the judiciary, and later popular protests, put pressure on Brothers, who, however, chose to accommodate the military while confronting the judiciary and the protesters. None of the veto powers showed any sign of decline, and the judiciary signaled its willingness to balance the Brotherhood government. Morsi, however, defied the courts and undermined horizontal checks in the system in favor of the presidency. When protesters took to the streets to contest the legitimacy of his actions, Morsi chose to delegitimize and demonize them while polarizing Egyptian politics. For him, he had greater legitimacy than other actors in the system.

---

[106] See, for instance, Yeşilada and Rubin, *Islamization of Turkey under the AKP Rule*; Çavdar, "Islamists' New Thinking in Turkey"; Baran, "Turkey Divided"; Kubicek, "Majoritarian Democracy in Turkey."

Neither societal pressure nor the military's or judiciary's vetoes could deter Morsi from his strong attachment to electoralism.

By way of contrast, in Tunisia, there were no veto powers in the military or the judiciary. Instead, it was civil society along with protests that put pressure on Ennahda. Wolf, for instance, suggests that Ennahda's leader, Rached Ghannouchi, strategically embraced nonviolence and developed the doctrine of Islamic democracy because of the pressure of the Tunisian civil society and the international community over the party.[107]

Indeed, the wave of protests in July 2013 and pressure from the organized civil society challenged Ennahda. In response to this popular mobilization, unlike their counterparts in Turkey and Egypt, the leaders of Ennahda engaged with opposition leaders and CSOs for a peaceful resolution to the crisis instead of opting for polarization and demonization of their rivals. Unlike the Brotherhood in Egypt, Ennahda had no reason to fear a military takeover. The secular parties were far from posing a serious threat to the party. Besides, there was strong internal push within the party to dismiss protesters' demands. Still, Ennahda leaders responded to external pressures with compromise, while the other two parties embraced confrontation and hegemonic politics.

This fact also raises doubts about the role of regional developments in shaping party trajectories. Some claim that the military intervention in Egypt against the Brotherhood left an imprint on Turkey and Tunisia, altering their threat perception and hence their behavior. However, as discussed above, neither party had a reason to fear a military intervention by the summer of 2013. The AKP had already sidelined the Turkish armed forces through political and judicial measures, thanks to its partner, the Gülen movement, which had been infiltrating the military and the judiciary since the 1980s. Besides, the AKP had already risen to hegemony in Turkey and had no reason to fear any backlash from the secular establishment. Similarly, the Tunisian military was weak and politically inactive, unlike the Egyptian armed forces. It posed no threat to Ennahda, and there was no viable autocratic alternative to Ben Ali's regime.

One could extend the list of external f/actors to explain the divergent trajectory of Islamist parties in these three countries. Clearly, these factors have an impact on party behavior. Based on a retrospective reading of events, such arguments sound quite plausible. Yet these accounts are incomplete and often gravitate toward reductionism. First, they assume that Islamist parties are unitary and dismiss ideological and behavioral

---

[107] Wolf, *Political Islam in Tunisia*, 96–97.

pluralism within these organizations. So they study group-level change at the surface level without accounting for internal processes and disagreements.

These accounts either assume that there is a singular homogenous ideology that defines party goals or that survival and maximization of partisan gains drive the behavior of Islamist parties. I assert, in light of the empirical evidence I will discuss in greater detail later, that there are a plethora of political objectives within Islamist parties. Partly due to their experiences and learning curves, some adhere to democratic norms and prioritize them over partisan goals. In contrast, other Islamists within the same party pursue the maximization of power by any means possible, often by instrumentalizing electoral politics. In short, the existing accounts preclude such ideological pluralism and identify any democratization as strategically motivated.

These accounts also present the strategy that a party adopts as the *only* rational strategy available to it. Given the plurality of the positions within each party, such explanations are not empirically accurate, since there might be multiple rational strategies.[108]

Indeed, when faced with external pressures, significant internal disagreements have arisen within all three parties. Under the same set of constraints, different factions disagreed on what constituted the best strategy for their party. Each faction read the external pressures exerted by veto powers, popular protests, international actors, and regional developments in a different light. Liberal Islamists prioritized democracy-building over partisan gains, anchored their actions in international organizations and alliances, perceived the opposition as legitimate partners, and took protests and civil society seriously. Electoralists, in contrast, capitalized on their electoral mandates, dismissed external/international pressures as Islamophobic, delegitimized the opposition, and viewed popular protests and civil society activism as signs of the opposition's electoral weakness. Each faction acted *rationally* to find the best strategy to fulfill their goals, given external constraints and their perception of the power balances. Depending on their preferences, ideas, and interests, they arrived at different conclusions. These different visions clashed within the party to produce a dominant strategy and charter the course of the organization. What scholars have depicted thus far as party strategy has been, in fact, the strategy of the dominant faction that happened to prevail in internal power struggles.

Such accounts based on external pressures hence suffer from hindsight bias. This leads to the rationalization of all choices made by actors after

---

[108] I thank Dean Schafer for making this point more explicit.

the fact, rendering these explanations unfalsifiable.[109] For instance, the AKP's repressive measures against protests in the absence of the threat of a military takeover, the Brotherhood's choice to confront the protesters despite the real threat of a counterrevolution, and Ennahda's strategy to compromise with a much lower threat of a counterrevolution are all rationalized in hindsight by strategic calculations. These accounts obscure and dismiss competing strategies discussed within parties while presenting the strategy of the dominant alliance as the *only rational strategy*. As such, these accounts are partial at best, since they do not explore the full range of actions and strategies available to a party and why in the end one strategy prevails over the others. Without unpacking internal power dynamics, I argue, we cannot solve the puzzle of party behavior.

Conclusion

Islamist movements were born into modernity and have come to grips with the rise of nation-states, economic development, urbanization, secularization, and modern education. They have also socialized into electoral politics as structural changes created a sizable middle class among the ranks of Islamist movements, and the opportunity space created by ruling regimes expanded and offered incentives for inclusion while keeping the threat of exclusion real. These long-term structural factors and medium-term institutional factors transformed Islamists into actors willing to play the game of democracy. However, this long-term transformation has not generated a uniform perception of democratic politics among Islamists. Some internalized democratic norms and committed to pluralism, deliberation, and conciliation, while others perceived democracy to be a numbers' game, where the winner took all and had a right to impose its ideological agenda in a hegemonic fashion. More recent accounts often fail to capture this diversity and assume that all Islamist parties are majoritarian in their orientation. They can commit to democracy only when counterbalanced by non-Islamist forces, be it secular parties and civil society, veto powers in the state, or regional and international actors. The reality is more complex and nuanced.

These accounts share a common shortcoming. They prioritize factors external to political parties – be it modernization, inclusion, and balance of power considerations – over internal factors. Such external

---

[109] Waldner and Lust, "Unwelcome Change."

forces certainly bear an impact on the behavior of Islamist parties. However, they do not dictate a particular behavior for these organizations. Individual Islamists react differently to the same external stimuli, draw different lessons from similar experiences, and develop different strategies under the same circumstances. Existing accounts overlook such differences and fail to explain how such individual experiences translate into party behavior. This chapter explains why without unpacking party organizations, we cannot shed light on how certain strategies, ideological positions, or political narratives win over others within the party apparatus. It is the internal struggle for power that shapes a party's trajectory in office. The next chapter explains how.

2 A Theory of Intraparty Politics
Resources and Coalitions

All political parties represent a variety of interests and policy preferences. Islamist parties are no exception. What determines (Islamist) party behavior is the aggregation of such preferences and the balance of power among different groups with divergent political attitudes. Islamist parties do not fail to commit to democracy because they are filled with antidemocratic actors. In fact, they host both liberal and illiberal voices within, much like contemporary right-wing parties or past socialist or Catholic parties.[1] Given the multiplicity of voices within Islamist parties, a theory that explains their behavior requires a systematic study of intraparty dynamics.

This chapter builds on the existing studies of behavioral and ideological change induced by inclusion and exclusion. The main goal is to advance these studies and address the issue of aggregation while filling in the gap left by the group-level explanations. To this end, I turn to intraparty dynamics. The aim herein is twofold. First, I trace how individual preferences aggregate into group preferences in the form of factional politics. Second, I explore the conditions under which one faction prevails over others. At the core of both processes lie access to organizational resources and control over the incentive structure. Intraparty struggles are about building and sustaining coalitions within the organization. The goal is to capture and control the party. Once a dominant coalition emerges, it aligns the party's trajectory with its own worldview and strategy.

Studying factions offers an intermediate level of analysis that allows us to go beyond the individual level and resolve the issue of aggregation – how individual preferences translate to the party level – while also avoiding the faulty assumption of parties as monolithic entities. Specifically, factional analysis overcomes the hindsight bias many studies carry, as they seek an explanation for Islamist party behavior. What many deem the "obvious strategy" available to an Islamist party under a given set

---

[1] See Brown, *When Victory Is Not an Option*; Kalyvas, "Commitment Problems"; Sokhey and Yildirim, "Economic Liberalization and Political Moderation."

of circumstances is indeed one strategy among many the party could adopt. In fact, multiple possible strategies emerge and compete inside the party when prompted by an external event, as I discussed in the previous chapter.

The impact of external factors on political party behavior, I argue, works through factional politics. A growing body of literature on party politics already contends that external factors and internal factors – such as intraparty dynamics, leadership, and dominant factions – act together to bring about change in political parties.[2] Going a step further, I argue that internal factors have primacy over external factors in charting a party's course. Specifically, whichever faction commands greater resources within the party builds the dominant alliance. This coalition then dominates the party's trajectory. The dominant alliance's perceptions, interests, and ideological positioning in turn shape the party's strategy in response to a wide range of external factors from popular protests to regional developments. Thus, external events do not dictate Islamist party behavior; rather, the dominant alliances within the party do.

Factional analysis also offers a dynamic analytical framework. Attending to factions explains changes and reversals in party positions with changing internal balances of power instead of insisting on a teleological and linear path toward democracy, as the inclusion-moderation thesis does. In short, studying internal power struggles allows us to trace party change and build empirically accurate and theoretically rigorous arguments. Building on this discussion on intraparty dynamics, this chapter accounts for why some Islamist parties commit to democratic norms (i.e., pluralism) in power, while others adhere to a minimalist and electoral democracy (i.e., majoritarianism).

Parties' Interactions with the External: What Explains Party Behavior?

Parties operate in a sociopolitical environment. They pursue their goals in interaction with their rivals and supporters. They formulate policies, define and aggregate interests, establish and represent political identities, and thereby shape politics. They constitute politics and are constituted by it in turn. Yet parties, as Berman brilliantly puts it, are not victims of their environments.[3]

---

[2] Panebianco, *Political Parties: Organization and Power*; Ignazi, "The Silent Counter-Revolution."
[3] Berman, "The Life of the Party," 102.

Exogenous factors that do not account for internal party dynamics can explain neither party behavior nor the timing, direction, or limits of party change. As Berman argues, "exogenous social, economic, and cultural changes [...] do not determine how parties will actually respond to these challenges."[4] When faced with an external event, parties may welcome it as an opportunity for transforming their agenda, organization, and ideology. At other times, they may strongly resist change brought by a momentous event. And sometimes they may spearhead change without an external impetus; they become the bearer of a momentous event.[5]

The perceptions, interests, and ideology of a dominant alliance, I argue, determine a party's behavior. Factions carry certain policy preferences, which stem from their interests and ideological convictions. They, instead of parties as a whole, coordinate activists, officials, interest groups, and intellectuals to develop and rationalize their public agenda and policy process.[6] They are powerful "engines of change" and forces of the status quo.[7]

Recent studies indeed show that parties do not change, even in the face of substantial environmental changes, unless party leadership or a dominant faction perceives the necessity to change and convinces the rest of the party of such a necessity.[8] Wilson, in his study of social democratic parties in Western Europe in the post-Cold War era, concludes that party leadership plays a key role in party transformation: "Party change is really an internal matter, with the key to change found in the attitudes and behavior of party leaders and reformers."[9]

Going a step further, in her study of the European left, Sanchez-Cuenca finds that external factors do not play a role unless the balance of power between different groups permits change.[10] Specifically, Budge et al. posit that "party change is an internal factional process rather than strategic decisions taken by unitary actors"; internal ideological conflicts among factions drive policy shifts, while the magnitude of such shifts correlates with the relative strength of the dominant faction.[11]

---

[4] Ibid., 105
[5] Deschouwer quoted in Harmel and Janda, "An Integrated Theory of Party Goal and Party Change," 263–64.
[6] DiSalvo, *Engines of Change*, xii–iii.
[7] Ibid.
[8] Bille, "Leadership Change and Party Change"; Harmel et al., "Performance, Leadership, Factions, and Party Change"; Wilson, "The Sources of Party Change." Also see, Tepe, "Moderation of Religious Parties".
[9] Wilson, "The Sources of Party Change," 265.
[10] Sanchez-Cuenca, "Party Moderation and Politicians' Ideological Rigidity."
[11] Budge, Ezrow, and McDonald, "Ideology, Party Factionalism and Policy Change."

The behavior of political parties in postwar democracies confirms these findings. For instance, political parties in the United Kingdom and Germany after 1950 displayed a change in policy and organization even in the absence of an "external shock" when a new dominant faction succeeded in building a coherent coalition in the party.[12] Similarly, left-wing parties in Europe, for instance, have not altered their goals or revised their programs before the balance of power between the more dogmatic and pragmatic members in the party changed in favor of the latter.[13]

Similarly, the Catholic Party in Belgium, an ideological party based on a religious worldview, adopted a prodemocracy attitude because the moderate Catholics overcame the resistance of the radicals, who rejected democratic institutions altogether. Although Kalyvas points out the role of the Catholic Church and its strategic calculation as the cause of such democratic habituation, a crucial component of the moderation process involved the organizational control of the moderates over the party organization and their dominance over the radicals.[14]

External factors, I argue, affect party behavior only through intraparty dynamics. That is, a party does not respond to an external stimulus as a whole; instead, the dominant coalition articulates the party's response. Then, a party may respond to the exact same event in different ways depending on who controls the organization.[15]

Needless to say, exogenous factors may give rise to diverging reactions within a party, generating fissures. Such disagreements may generate rivalry and produce new factions, change the type of factionalism (personalist vs ideological), and/or intensify existing divisions.[16] Figure 4 summarizes these processes. The impact of exogenous factors on party behavior, however, still depends on internal balances of power. Depending on the power structure, an external event may not affect a party at all; it may trigger a substantial transformation of the party or lead to party split.[17] What determines internal power balances then? I now turn to this question.

---

[12] Harmel and Tan, "Party Actors and Party Change."
[13] Sanchez-Cuenca, "Party Moderation and Politicians' Ideological Rigidity."
[14] Kalyvas, "Democracy and Religious Politics."
[15] This variation also explains why some parties fail and collapse, while others survive and succeed. Although actors are rational, they make strategic mistakes and carry misperceptions or miscalculations. Many of their actions may seem unnecessarily confrontational, misguided, or well-planned after the fact.
[16] Ayan Musil and Dikici Bilgin, "Types of Outcomes in Factional Rivalries."
[17] For more on under what conditions factional rivalry lead to leadership removal or party split, see ibid.

Parties as Coalitions

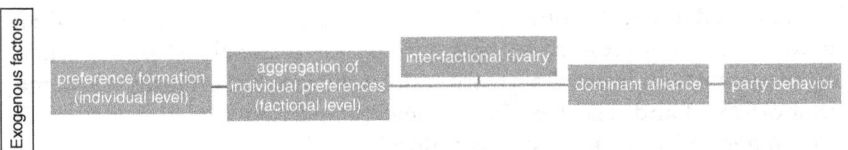

Figure 4 A theory of party behavior
Source: the author

Parties as Coalitions

A political party is where individuals meet to aggregate their interests. Because parties are large organizations, the aggregation process often produces disagreements and conflicts.[18] A party is itself, Katz and Mair assert, a political system with different coalitions of forces striving for dominance.[19] Members with different political views, preferences, interests, and visions come together to form subgroups within the party organization. They compete or collaborate with each other to capture the control of the party and its resources to direct the organization in line with their preferences, interests, and/or values.[20] As a result, individuals form constellations of rival groups and a party turns into what Sartori calls "a loose confederation of sub-parties."[21]

Yet these subgroups, Sartori posits, are largely invisible. Because factionalism is seen as a source of weakness by political elites, they conceal their factionalism to present coherence and unity to the electorate.[22] Observers often mistake factions' invisibility as their absence, especially when subunits are not as organized. Their invisibility does not signify factions' absence, however. In fact, the study of a political party is, in Sartori's words, incomplete and inaccurate "unless it probes how subunits enter and alter [it]."[23]

I use the word "faction" in the broader sense of the term to signify subunits that act together within political parties. Factions are distinct in their political preferences and what they envision for the party. They may

---

[18] Sartori, *Parties and Party Systems*, 71.
[19] Katz and Mair, *Party Organizations*. Boucek also writes, "Parties are not unitary actors but collections of individuals and coalitions of sub-party groups with common but also divergent preferences and interests with competing claims on party resources." Boucek, "The Structure and Dynamics of Intra-party Politics in Europe," 454.
[20] For a discussion on types of party factions, see Zariski, "Party Factions and Comparative Politics."
[21] Sartori, *Parties and Party Systems*, 72.
[22] For other concerns, see Boucek, "The Structure and Dynamics of Intra-party Politics in Europe," 459.
[23] Sartori, *Parties and Party Systems*, 71.

be organized and autonomous (operating their own network of loyalties, holding their congresses, seeking money for themselves) or minimally autonomous with limited networks and resources.[24] Similarly, some may be short-lived and dissolve after achieving a particular goal, while others last longer and become institutionalized – such as in Japan and Italy.[25]

Factions may be motivated by different goals. They may rally behind a leader and constitute a personalist faction. Or they may come together to support a particular policy agenda. Sometimes the two goals coalesce. Members may also form factions "to change (or prevent the change of) the values, norms, ideas, expectations, and rules of the political game."[26] Needless to say, not everyone in a party has a faction or a wing. Many do, however, while some remain independent or sit on the fence. Similarly, factions are not fixed but fluid. As members change their political preferences, they may also change their factions and personal allegiances. Idiosyncratic factors, individual experiences (discussed in Chapter 1), and incentive structures within a party (discussed below), all affect members' decisions to break away from one faction and join another.

A single faction is often too weak to control the entire organization, so they form alliances. Independents, careerists, or fence-sitters as well as other factions represent potential allies. From their strife emerges a dominant coalition. And this coalition is always an alliance of alliances.[27]

But how are dominant coalitions formed? Panebianco's seminal work on political parties, which centers on sources of organizational power, offers crucial insights. Building on his study, I unpack intraparty coalition-building in three stages: vertical power games, horizontal power games, and maintaining coalitions.[28] In all three stages, actors spend "trump cards" such as recruitment, rules, finances, internal communication, expertise/competency, and environmental relations to prevail in internal power games.[29] I argue that each trump card serves a different function, and their roles differ across different stages of the game.

Selective and Collective Incentives in Vertical Power Games

To build a dominant coalition, factions first need to strengthen their vertical ties to party activists and outside supporters. The ability to

---

[24] Ibid., 76.
[25] Boucek, "The Structure and Dynamics of Intra-party Politics in Europe," 458.
[26] DiSalvo, *Engines of Change*, 6.
[27] Panebianco, *Political Parties*, 39.
[28] Panebianco discusses vertical power games in detail while leaving aside horizontal power games – the center of my theory.
[29] Panebianco, *Political Parties*, 33.

offer incentives is indispensable for building and sustaining alliances at this stage. Faction leaders, as they try to expand their coalition, deploy such incentives to build a follower base while co-opting and recruiting fence-sitters, independents, and even their rivals. Such incentives may re/define the interests and preferences of party members and encourage them to switch sides.

Leaders may offer selective and collective incentives to their potential and actual supporters within and outside the party.[30] Selective incentives include status within (and outside) the party organization as well as particularistic and material benefits given to individuals such as positions, welfare benefits, services, and networks; meanwhile, collective incentives promise solidarity, salvation, meaning, and a sense of ideological and moral power. All activists and supporters receive a myriad of selective and collective incentives and respond to them in different ways depending on their ideas and interests.

Key organizational resources – recruitment, finances, and internal communication – are critical to building strong incentive structures. Control over organizational recruitment and party finances is crucial to pooling selective incentives (material and status), whereas internal communication and environmental relations (and media power) facilitate collective incentives in vertical power games. It is a combination of such resources that gives a particular group the ability to build coalitions, which form "the distribution center of organizational incentives within the party."[31]

The first organizational resource is *recruitment*. Recruitment is primarily related to organizational borders, determining who can and cannot join the organization.[32] As such, it offers both an identity and status to potential activists and defines the identity and character of the party. Yet recruitment also concerns internal promotions, appointments, nominations, and career advancement opportunities. As such, leaders who oversee recruitment can leverage it to reward their supporters and sanction opponents.[33]

Equally important in building a formidable incentive structure is *party finance*. Often, a party has a multitude of monetary resources: members' dues, state funds, and individual or organizational financiers. While the first two directly flow to party headquarters, the third can be predicated upon personal and privileged contacts independent of party executive

---

[30] This section draws on Panebianco's discussion of selective and collective incentives.
[31] Panebianco, *Political Parties*, 37.
[32] Ibid., 33.
[33] Sartori, *Parties and Party Systems*, 97.

organs. Such financial power is critical for the survival of the party organization and the continuity of collective and selective incentives. First, funds are essential to spread the message of the party, which is crucial to the construction of a collective identity. Campaign finance is particularly important. Second, those who hold financial power also provide material incentives as they build clientelistic relations with party members and ensure their daily survival with the financial benefits they offer.[34] Financial resources accruing to the dominant alliance through organizational or individual connections reinforce its organizational control, as Panebianco suggests.[35]

It is possible that organizational resources are distributed across different factions, which capitalize on their resources to build and expand their faction. Horizontal power games among factions with different resources determine the dominant alliance. This is the second stage of building intraparty dominance.[36]

From Vertical to Horizontal Power Games: Co-opting or Purging Rivals

The vertical ties, built around incentives, play a crucial role in interfactional horizontal power games by putting a certain group at a more favorable position vis-à-vis others. Those with a stronger following among party activists and supporters carry certain advantages in horizontal games. Selective and collective incentives also matter in interelite rivalry. These trump cards such as recruitment and promotion and party finance can also be leveraged in coalition-building among factions. It is not unusual, for instance, for a leading faction to co-opt other factions as well as independents and fence-sitters among the party elite. A faction that controls recruitment and promotion can build alliances with other factions or co-opt their members through the promise of office (or nominations) and advancement. The same goes for party finances; factions that control funds can use discretion over their use to reward allies with campaign finance and other material perks while sanctioning their rivals. This creates incentives for others to join a coalition with them.

Other trump cards may also increase the leverage of certain groups in internal negotiations, which are crucial in horizontal power games. Chief

---

[34] Boucek rightfully acknowledges the significance of patronage distribution. See Boucek, "The Structure and Dynamics of Intra-party Politics in Europe," 475.
[35] Panebianco, *Political Parties*, 35.
[36] It is important to note that vertical and horizontal power games do not always follow a consecutive order; they may also unfold simultaneously.

Parties as Coalitions

among these are party rules, internal communication, competency, and environmental relations. The first two resources are particularly crucial for intrafactional rivalry, and when used in a strategic fashion, such resources may tilt the playing field in favor of a certain alliance and assure its sustained dominance.

Rules are central to horizontal power games. Because parties are formal organizations, they operate on *formal (and informal) rules*, even in cases they do not hold legal status. Party bylaws act like constitutions and regulate a wide range of issues from internal elections and decision-making to electoral nominations. As Panebianco aptly notes, they are decisive in power relations within parties.[37] A faction with greater control over organizational rules (possibly thanks to stronger vertical ties to party activists) can formulate, revise, or manipulate party rules in a self-serving fashion. At the same time, formal rules "tend to reflect the existing balance of power within the party as a political system, and hence any shifts in that balance are likely to be reflected, at least eventually, in discernible modifications in the rules."[38]

Internal means of communication matter as well. This trump card assures circulation of the message of a faction/alliance within the party organization. Whoever controls it can gain an advantage over others in building collective incentives for party activists and supporters. Those who control recruitment often control *internal communication*. Through internal communication, factions spread their ideological and political messages and exert ideational power. To the extent a faction distributes, manipulates, delays, or suppresses information within the party organization, they create an uneven playing field.[39] For instance, a leading faction may make it increasingly difficult for its rivals to reach out to the rank and file and spread their ideological message, thereby monopolizing internal debates at the expense of their rivals. In other words, rivals to the dominant alliance and their ideas become largely invisible. In such cases, a faction may leverage internal communication to construct collective incentives for party activists and convey an ideological agenda. Thus, combined with other resources, internal communication may help build and entrench dominant alliances.

A final trump card that actors hold in intraparty horizontal games is *competency*. This resource refers to individual expertise and empowers those who hold them in internal negotiations. Competency may be the most widespread and individualized power in political parties, yet it is

---

[37] Panebianco, *Political Parties*, 35.
[38] Katz and Mair, *Party Organizations*, 6.
[39] Panebianco, *Political Parties*, 36.

70 A Theory of Intraparty Politics

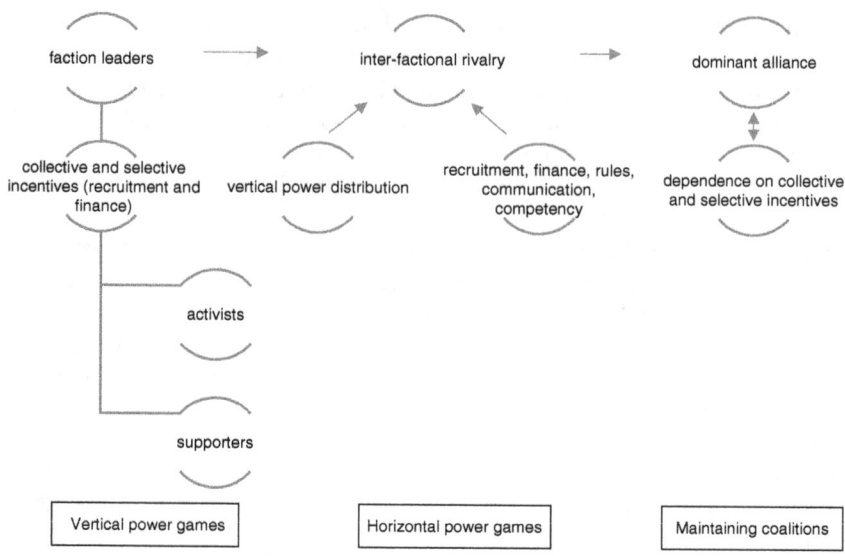

Figure 5 Building and sustaining dominant coalitions
Source: the author

also the most easily replaceable. Individual members can leverage their expertise to negotiate with faction leaders and receive incentives, but expertise without the support of other resources is unlikely to produce advantages at the collective/group level. Figure 5 summarizes the internal processes of alliance formation.

Often, those who capture recruitment and finance dominate the incentive structure and gain leverage over other factions. With strong vertical ties, they may capture party leadership, change party rules, and dominate internal communication to create an uneven playing field within the party organization. The sequence may also be reversed. A factional alliance may capture party leadership at a juncture and then control other resources to entrench their control over the organization.

Either way, capturing party leadership carries central importance. Leaders are crucial for several reasons. A major reason, as explained by Michels in his seminal work, is the oligarchic tendencies of political parties, which are divided between a few leaders and their mass followers.[40] In other words, leaders embody the party, speaking in the name of their mass followers.[41] They set the goals of the party – often contested by

---

[40] Michels, *Political Parties*, 70.
[41] Ibid., 98–99.

other factions – while dominating internal communication and providing collective incentives and identity to their followers. A charismatic leader or a powerful orator, Pridham asserts, can dominate party affairs.[42] Although such skills help a leader sustain his coalition, it is neither necessary nor sufficient for dominance. Leaders without such skills may still control the party machine if they secure the distribution of organizational, both collective and selective, incentives.[43]

Irrespective of their skills, party leaders have to play both vertical and horizontal games to build dominant alliances. These games require significant resources since both selective and collective incentives are crucial. When a leader rises to the helm of a party, different organizational resources may be distributed across different groups and individuals. Such distribution of power may put the leader in a precarious position and force them to negotiate with different actors within the party to form an alliance. Alternatively, as fence-sitters and rival factions witness the rise of a strong faction/alliance, they may choose to jump on the bandwagon to receive remunerations from the rising leadership. In short, if the leader and their faction can build strong incentive structures, they can build a dominant alliance within the party. This alliance then charts the direction of the party.

At certain critical junctures in a party's history, such resources are distributed and redistributed. Early phases of party formation, the period before the party is institutionalized, are particularly critical. Members of different factions seek to maximize political power and influence in the early years in a party's life. Party change in such moments is also likelier.[44] Another critical moment may be the death or retirement of a party leader that opens up the leadership position and allows for realignment within the party. With potential splits and the rise of new factions, resources are also redistributed as alliances are formed.

External events also matter as they may affect the allocation of resources among factions. An electoral victory, for instance, may expand a party's resources considerably, while a defeat shrinks its pool of resources, as I discuss in the next section.

Sustaining/Securing Dominant Alliances

A dominant coalition is always a precarious construction. As Massicard warns, factionalism should not be seen as a static phenomenon but as an

---

[42] Pridham, "Party Systems, Factionalism, and Patterns of Democratization," 17; also see Michels, *Political Parties*, 98–99.
[43] Panebianco, *Political Parties*, 40.
[44] Künkler and Brocker, "Religious Parties."

ongoing process of human management, balance keeping, retribution, reconciliation, and bargaining. The management of both party resources and rewards is oriented toward the reproduction of factions and their continued or expanded control over resources.[45] Thus, negotiations continue to take place between the dominant coalition and its following, and within the dominant coalition itself.

A dominant coalition is likely to reproduce itself relatively easily if its vertical ties are strong. Popular support matters. If party leadership is popular and electorally successful, its alliances within the party organization will be sturdier. Strong popular support may also translate into government offices, whether local or national. Being in government strengthens dominant alliances in the party since *access to public resources* in the form of public office, bureaucratic appointments, policymaking, and implementation can expand the pool of incentives, both collective and selective, that leaders tap into for their existing and potential supporters.[46] A leader with such resources can easily build and sustain larger coalitions. Their rivals, in contrast, may find it hard to challenge an incumbent leader and their alliance that has electoral popularity and access to public resources.

This does not mean that party leaders are doomed if they lose an election. Although internal rivals may gain ground when their party loses an election, electoral defeat does not always induce leadership change. Depending on a leader's access to organizational sources, they may successfully thwart such threats. Party rules, for instance, are critical. By manipulating the rules of the game in the party, leaders may hang onto power, often forcing party splits.

Benefits also matter. To the extent that both activists and supporters are dependent on the dominant alliance for renumeration/benefits, even when the party is not in government, there is a greater likelihood of sustained dominance, though this requires extensive resources. As Panebianco adds, alliances are more tenuous when party activists or supporters can find alternative sources of benefits/privileges.[47] For instance, lower-income groups are unlikely to find an alternate source of empowerment than party activism, while the middle classes may find such renumeration elsewhere. Irrespective of one's socioeconomic standing, a party member

---

[45] Massicard and Watts, *Negotiating Political Power in Turkey*, 69.
[46] Massicard underlines the significance of social support in internal party dynamics; she argues that factions utilize such support at the local level to gain dominance within the party through their alliances with groups in society (kinship, ideological, associational), neighborhood communities, chambers – at the local level though. Massicard, "The Uses of Team Rivalry," 69–71.
[47] Panebianco, *Political Parties*, 40.

may depend on the strong collective incentives that a party has to offer, unmatched by any other organization. Leaders of ideological and religious parties often provide such incentives. Under such conditions of material and ideational dependency, activists and supporters alike may remain loyal to party leadership and help reproduce their dominance in the organization.

Explaining Islamist Party Behavior

How does this theory help us decipher Islamist party behavior? As in the case of any other party, external events do not dictate an Islamist party's behavior in power, let alone its democratic commitments. When faced with repression, for instance, some Islamists embrace democracy, whereas others turn to violence or do not alter their behavior or attitudes at all. The same is true for electoral outcomes, pressures coming from domestic or international actors, popular mobilization, or any key development in their country or region. When faced with these circumstances, individual Islamists and, later, factions, perceive their rivals' intentions differently or assess their party's power and capacity in different ways. Some underestimate this power, while others overestimate it.

Wickham rightfully notes the subjective nature of political preference formation under institutional, as well as other, constraints. Islamists' reaction to external impetus varies depending on their past experiences, values, beliefs, and ideational processes. As Blyth affirms, "structures are not irrelevant, but they do not come with instruction sheets [and] different agents hold different mental models regardless of their similarities in structural positions."[48] There may be an infinite number of factors that shape an Islamist's preference, as is the case for any political actor. So it is almost impossible to "determine a priori how Islamists will respond to a given set of institutional cues" because actors may interpret "the costs and benefits associated with any given course of action" in diverse ways.[49]

What then explains Islamist parties' varied commitment to democratic principles after coming to power? External factors such as modernization, repression, inclusion, electoral pressures, and so on may all induce changes in Islamists' political preferences at the individual level. These individual-level changes are already established in the literature, which I discussed in Chapter 1. Scholars are correct to highlight these processes. What they miss is preference aggregation and how individual-level

---

[48] Blyth, "Structures Do Not Come with an Instruction Sheet," 697.
[49] Wickham, *The Muslim Brotherhood*, 9–11.

changes effect group-level change. One cannot answer this question by treating Islamist parties as unitary actors because, as Wickham posits, there is no "matrix of ideological and behavioral shifts that applies to the cadres of the Islamist movement as a whole."[50] What we need is a systematic analysis of their intraparty struggles.

To explain variation in the behavior of Islamist parties in power, we should unpack party organizations to study disagreement and conflicts within. These parties are indeed composed of different tendencies with diverging political preferences, including their perceptions of democracy.

Islamist activists, like their counterparts in other movements, see factionalism as a source of weakness. They often go to extreme measures to conceal their internal disagreements and project an image of strength and unity. Revealing these differences, for them, undermines the party's mission. Regardless, scholars have identified and studied disagreements within Islamist parties. For instance, Kalyvas explores splits within the FIS in Algeria; Ehteshami and Tezcür separately study factional conflict in Iran; Schwedler focuses on internal divisions in the IAF in Jordan and Islah Party in Yemen; Yadav examines differences within Hezbollah in Lebanon; and Hwang unpacks intraparty splits in the Malaysian Islamic Party and the Prosperous Justice Party in Indonesia.[51]

Political Islam in Turkey or Egypt is no exception. El-Ghobashy, for instance, analyzes generational change within the Muslim Brotherhood as a source of its internal disagreements and the rise of a new wing with a different worldview among the Brothers.[52] Wickham successfully traces such internal disagreements in the Brotherhood through the revolution and its aftermath. She insists that the Brotherhood is not a unitary actor, highlighting disagreements within the organization over ideology and strategy.[53] Students of Turkish politics have also detected internal splits within Islamist parties. Several scholars, including myself, have studied the struggle between reformists and hardliners in the Milli Görüş movement in the 1990s.[54]

---

[50] Ibid., 4.
[51] Kalyvas, "Commitment Problems in Emerging Democracies"; Ehteshami, *After Khomeini*; Tezcür, *Muslim Reformers in Iran and Turkey*; Schwedler, *Faith in Moderation*; Yadav, "Understanding 'What Islamists Want'"; Hwang "When Parties Swing."
[52] El-Ghobashy, "The Metamorphosis"; See also Trager, *Arab Fall*; Shehata and Stacher, "The Brotherhood Goes to Parliament"; Wickham, "The Path to Moderation."
[53] Wickham, *The Muslim Brotherhood*, 3.
[54] Tezcür, *Muslim Reformers in Iran and Turkey*; Mecham, "From the Ashes of Virtue, a Promise of Light"; Atacan, "Explaining Religious Politics at the Crossroad"; Gumuscu, "Class, Status, and Party."

Internal splits often became the "engine of change" in Islamist parties. The rise of a prodemocratic and pluralist middle generation (the university youth of the 1970s) within the Brotherhood caused a metamorphosis, according to El-Ghobashy. The leaders of the middle generation had been transformed by their political experiences and pushed for change from within.[55] Yet their power and influence remained limited, as Kandil and Trager separately show.[56] The transformation of Turkish Islamism also stemmed from internal splits within the Welfare Party.[57] Younger generations of Islamists in the 1980s and 1990s experimented with new political activism and challenged the party's old guard for a renewed outlook.

Such disputes often stemmed from necessities brought on by increased political participation. Islamist activists debated their movements' aims, character, identity, political vision, and appropriate tools. They had to resolve several issues. For movements that emerged from religious activism, the central issue concerned the balance between religious and political activism; they had to specify both their political *and* religious goals, and how they should interact. Such movements, along with parties without a religious network, have also faced immediate questions pertaining to the relationship between Islam and democracy. They needed to clarify their position regarding equal citizenship, pluralism, civil liberties, women's and minority rights, and the meaning of Islamic politics in a nation-state. The urgency of such matters forced Islamists to think about democratic politics and develop certain positions.

While mainstream Islamist movements almost universally embraced democratic procedures (elections, party politics, legislation), Islamists also disagreed on the meaning of democracy, the centrality of sharia, limits on civil liberties, or the extent of women's and minority rights. These tensions led to ambiguities and contradictions in electoral platforms and official statements.[58] Skeptics took such contradictions as signs of dissimulation (*takiyye* or *taqiyyah*), implying that Islamists were not genuine democrats. In fact, these contradictory statements manifested pluralism within Islamism. Different groups advanced diverging political positions and often their visions clashed, producing incoherent party visions.

As these Islamist parties came to power, two democratic positions crystallized within: At one end emerged a liberal and pluralist understanding; on the other emerged the procedural and majoritarian understanding. I call

---

[55] Wickham, *The Muslim Brotherhood*, 13.
[56] Trager, *Arab Fall*; Kandil, *Inside the Brotherhood*.
[57] Mecham, "From the Ashes of Virtue, a Promise of Light"; Atacan, "Explaining Religious Politics at the Crossroad"; Gumuscu, "Class, Status, and Party."
[58] Hamzawy, Ottoway, and Brown, "What Islamists Need to Be Clear About."

the first group *liberals*[59] and the second group *electoralists*.[60] This conceptualization diverges from those scholars who categorize Islamists according to their willingness to accept electoral politics, which obscures splits and disagreements within mainstream parties. The aim of this book is to reveal such schisms, particularly among those who had already embraced electoral politics. As discussed above, acceptance of formal political channels and participation in electoral politics do not necessarily imply commitment to democratic principles. Electoralists might in fact, accept the instrumental value of democracy to attain power in a strategic fashion while rejecting democratic norms and values for ideological reasons.

Three interrelated axes separate liberals and electoralists in power: (1) *perception of democracy*, which may be pluralistic or majoritarian; (2) *attitudes toward other political actors*, which may entail deliberative engagement or polarizing and delegitimizing strategies; and (3) *practice of power*, which may be inclusionary or exclusionary. Such electoral or liberal commitments among Islamists have translated into specific choices with respect to (1) institutional reform including constitutional changes; (2) the approach to state institutions such as the judicial branch, electoral councils, police forces, and education bureaucracy; (3) the treatment of political rivals in the opposition; and (4) the response to popular opposition and mobilization.

Some aspects of the two positions of liberals and electoralists were clear even before the Islamist parties studied here came to power. Others crystallized over time. As Islamist parties won elections and took over governance, they faced opportunities and constraints. The way individual Islamists have perceived, assessed, and interpreted these environmental conditions informed their democratic commitments. For some activists, this was a formative process; for others, it was a major shift from one end of the spectrum to the other. For still others, it entailed a reinforcement of prior attitudes. Not all Islamists neatly fit into these two boxes either. An Islamist can self-position anywhere along the "liberal–electoralist" spectrum at any point in time. Nor are these positions fixed. Electoralists can become liberals, or vice versa. An activist can change their position along this spectrum for several reasons. Although such changes, in Wickham's words, have been multifaceted, nonlinear, and ridden with contradictions and reversals,[61] incentive structures within the party have largely determined individual Islamists' choices and which faction they joined.

---

[59] "Liberalism," in the political sense of the term (not social or economic), signifies a commitment to civil liberties and the protection of minorities.

[60] Ashour also adopts a similar conceptual differentiation in *The De-radicalization of Jihadists*.

[61] Wickham, *The Muslim Brotherhood*, 2.

Individual experiences and ideational processes, well-documented by the scholars I have mentioned, play a critical role in this process. Yet organizational dynamics are as important in shaping an Islamist's political preference. Coalition-building within Islamist parties can exert an immediate impact on members' choices. First, different groups and their leaders often voice competing interpretations of a situation and what they deemed an appropriate strategy. Leaders articulate and represent such positions, and they also actively modify their followers' beliefs about what their interests are.[62] Second, as different groups vie for dominance within a party, they capture and mobilize organizational resources essential for building and sustaining a dominant alliance. The intraorganizational rivalry of different visions and the incentives they provide affect members' attitudes.

So what determines the distribution of organization resources across factions? One critical juncture where dominant coalitions were still in the making and resources were somewhat up for grabs was the moment of party formation. The death of a leader also played an important role in some cases, particularly when it coincided with foundational moments. At these moments for the three parties studied here, all three were still uninstitutionalized, and the likelihood of changing rules, capturing other organizational resources by manipulating internal mechanisms, and building clientelistic connections within the party was high.

External events, too, helped some of these factions when they coincided with the party's founding moment. The political opening in the Egyptian political system during the Brotherhood's second founding, the AKP's coming to power a year after its establishment, Ennahda's rise to power and its second founding in 2012 – all provided opportunities for factions to take. Those who could build strong vertical ties and capture organizational resources ended up forming dominant coalitions.

I now turn to the individual paths in each country. In Turkey, a group of Islamists left their mother movement to establish the AKP in 2001. This was a foundational moment for the party, and when it came to power in 2002, organizational resources were evenly distributed among liberals and electoralists. Although the latter held the party leadership after Erdoğan was elected as the party chairman, there were strong mechanisms in place to prevent him from monopolizing power. Besides, liberals held control over party rules and expertise, and partial control over recruitment and internal communication. Electoralists, meanwhile, wielded control over party finances and shared recruitment and internal communication with liberals. Coupling Erdoğan's position as the party

---

[62] Blyth, "Structures Do Not Come with an Instruction Sheet," 698.

chairman and popularity in the party with selective incentives to liberals, electoralists soon changed party rules and subverted intraparty democracy. Shortly after, the party leader monopolized recruitment and promotion as well as internal communication in addition to party finances. Empowered with public and private resources, thanks to its incumbency, electoralists were able to build strong clientelist ties with party members and supporters.

In contrast to Ennahda and the Muslim Brotherhood, the AKP sustained successive electoral victories after 2002. Good economic performance, expanding clientelist ties centered around party leadership, and growing control over the media handed electoralists strong vertical support. With such an advantage in vertical power games, they could easily sideline their rivals in horizontal power games. In fact, the electoralist faction dealt a major blow to the liberals when their leader Abdullah Gül was elected as president in 2007, the latter being a non-partisan position according to the constitution, which meant he had to resign from the party he established. The liberals had no matching vertical support or access to public or private resources that would allow them to build a new incentive structure. The fact that the party leadership continued to remain electorally successful – thus providing both collective and selective incentives to their supporters – also weakened whatever internal opposition was left. Some liberals joined the electoralist coalition, while others unsuccessfully attempted to capture the party and eventually left.

In line with these internal changes, the AKP's trajectory in power shifted over time. Until 2007, the AKP advanced political rights and civil liberties through inclusive reforms. In its deliberations, the AKP government included an array of actors from different political views in its decision-making processes and welcomed input from civil society in its constitutional reform processes. Other political actors at this time were equal partners with which the party could engage. As such, the AKP remained committed to mutual tolerance and institutional forbearance. After 2007, however, the party shifted toward righteous majoritarianism. Its commitment to mutual tolerance and institutional forbearance withered away. In 2010 and 2017, the AKP unilaterally introduced vast changes to the judicial and political systems through constitutional referenda. Unlike previous reforms, these referenda capitalized on exclusion, partisanship, and polarization to institutionalize a majoritarian political system. As such, the party instrumentalized elections as a tool to maximize its partisan gains at the expense of the opposition, which they depicted as enemies rather than equal partners. The AKP also securitized dissent and cracked down on protesters and civil society, violating the rights and liberties of citizens. Finally, thanks to its increasing power, the AKP government embarked on a process of Islamizing Turkish society. Liberals contested most of these measures taken by electoralists through party channels as well as public channels, but they were too weak to make an impact. In short, the AKP remained committed to liberal democracy as long as liberals had greater power within the party; once electoralists established their dominance, the party pivoted toward righteous majoritarianism.

For the Brotherhood, a critical juncture that realigned resources among factions was the movement's second founding in the 1980s, particularly after the passing of then General Guide Omar al-Tilmisani. The old guard took this opportunity to build an intricate incentive structure. While liberal reformists were concerned with political activism beyond the organization permitted by the recent liberalization of the regime, the old guard prioritized vertical ties through recruitment, promotion, and internal indoctrination. Manipulating internal rules using Mubarak's authoritarian rule as a pretext also helped them. Hence, they gained the upper hand in vertical power games and created an uneven playing field within the movement. Liberals, as they themselves admitted, overlooked vertical ties in the movement and instead focused on external relations. By the mid-1990s, the old guard had already built its dominance and established strong clientelistic networks; when liberal reformists waged an internal campaign for greater democracy and transparency in the movement in the 1990s, they lost. Several liberals left the movement (and others remained when they were threatened with expulsion). Whoever stayed sustained their critique throughout the 2000s; they were eventually either sidelined in a manipulated internal election in 2009 or co-opted. In the wake of the revolution in 2011, which could have been a critical juncture for the Brotherhood, liberals pushed for greater freedom and democracy within the movement and challenged the leadership. After all, the revolution empowered their message and ideas of mutual tolerance, pluralism, equal citizenship, and civil liberties. Yet they failed. The old guard mobilized its organizational resources to thwart this call and expelled hundreds of thousands from the movement. Those who were not expelled either stayed due to selective and collective incentives or left the movement to establish their own political parties.

During its brief term in government, the Brotherhood was committed to righteous majoritarianism and exclusionary politics. It resorted to polarization, instead of practicing mutual tolerance and forbearance, and refused to deem its political rivals as legitimate actors who deserved engagement and deliberation. Instead, for the electoralist old guard, the opposition, because they had lost the election, remained illegitimate and unfit to represent the will of the people. Besides, they were also enemies of the Brotherhood (and Islam). The Brothers, in the end, dominated the drafting of the constitution, while President Morsi preferred to rule by decree. They did not seek consensus, solicit input from different stakeholders (except from Salafis), or consider objections to the drafting process as legitimate. Morsi rushed the Brotherhood's draft constitution informed by hegemonic Islamism through a popular referendum. When the opposition mobilized against such majoritarian measures, the Brotherhood perceived them to be enemies and resorted to countermobilization rather than engagement and deliberation. The Brotherhood's righteous majoritarianism ignited a deep political conflict that ended with the coup in July 2013.

In contrast to the Brotherhood, Ennahda's second founding in 2012 coincided with the revolution. The rise of a dominant coalition in the party also unfolded over the course of the transition. The party returned from exile in 2011 to unite with its members in Tunisia and rebuild the organization. The new political context empowered the party's leader Rached Ghannouchi and other liberal Islamists with their discourse on democracy, political rights, and civil liberties over other groups that prioritized survival over democratization. Although leadership mattered to some degree in the process, it had to be conjoined with other factors to make a difference. Ghannouchi served as a popular leader with a significant following and commanded great respect as the founder and spiritual guide of the movement. He tilted the balance of power in favor of liberals throughout the transition whenever electoralist groups weighed in. For instance, his key interventions during the drafting of the constitution as well as popular mobilization in the summer of 2013 empowered liberals over electoralists. With this added advantage, liberals dominated recruitment and promotion, occupied important positions in the party and seats in the cabinet, changed party rules, and increasingly controlled internal communication. Liberals sidelined several Islamists who subscribed to righteous majoritarianism in election lists in 2014. By 2016, they were already entrenched in the party and introduced fundamental changes to the party's mission and identity. Public and private resources, although much less than what the AKP and Brotherhood possessed, also helped them in building selective incentives that they offered to form a dominant coalition.[63]

Thanks to liberals' dominance in Ennahda, the party's understanding of democracy remained liberal throughout the transition and beyond, as I detail in Chapter 5. Democracy was not just elections, they argued;

---

[63] Most recently, the question of electing a new party leader led to splits among liberals. I return to this topic in Chapter 5.

it comprised freedoms and rights for all. Instead of instrumentalizing democratic procedures to maximize partisan gains, the party supported more inclusionary and representative arrangements during the transition, often at its own expense.[64] Once successful, liberals then kept their party committed to pluralism, mutual tolerance, and institutional forbearance, following an inclusionary style of governance. As the assembly drafted the constitution, for instance, Ennahda deputies engaged with their political rivals and deliberated on numerous issues to seek consensus. The party also took its time to solicit input from different social groups in the draft constitution. Rather than polarizing the society along the secular–Islamist divide, liberals defeated any internal calls to invoke Islamic law in the new draft and supported freedom of conscience, to the dismay of several of its members. In the end, it took more than two years to draft the constitution, which was ratified by an overwhelming majority of deputies in the CA. Soon after, Ennahda willingly stepped down and let a technocratic government take the country to the 2014 elections. The party lost power in these elections and readily conceded, certifying the success of democratic transition in the country. Ennahda has lost electoral support since then and failed, alongside other parties, to secure the recovery of the Tunisian economy. Although recent democratic decline in Tunisia put the party to a test and generated new fissures within the liberal coalition itself, Ennahda's experience has overall shown that Islamist parties remain committed to liberal democracy when controlled by liberal factions.

In the next three chapters, I offer a detailed account of each party's trajectory.

---

[64] For instance, the party demanded proportional representation in the first elections after the revolution and established a coalition government with the two largest secular parties in the assembly.

3 The AKP's Pivot from Liberal Democracy to Electoral Islamism

The year 2005 was an extraordinary year for Turkey. In December 2004, the European Council ruled that Turkey had met the European Union political criteria for accession. A few months later, negotiations formally began and marked a moment the country had been waiting for since 1987. The same year, Turkey received its highest democracy scores to date from international organizations. The Washington DC-based Freedom House, for instance, commended Turkey's progress in enacting political reforms and advancing human rights protections. Again in 2005, the Turkish economy grew by 9.6 percent, a success unmatched by any government since 1976. The force behind such economic, political, and diplomatic achievements was the AKP, which came to power in 2002.

Only eight years later, in 2013, the same government was cracking down on peaceful protests in downtown Istanbul and the rest of the country. When protesters attempted to stop the destruction of Gezi Park, the government attempted to stop them by killing five and injuring thousands. The government repression that started in the Gezi protests quickly spiraled into a rapid authoritarian descent in the ensuing months. In the process, the AKP deeply politicized the judiciary, disciplined the media, purged dissidents, violated civil liberties, and undermined political rights in a systematic fashion. The party also ascribed ideological content to its authoritarian turn and accrued legitimacy by returning to Islamist frames of reference.

Starting off as a "conservative democratic" party with liberal tendencies, the AKP pivoted back to hegemonic Islamism with populist overtones over the years it ruled Turkey. In the process, it took the country on a roller coaster of political transformation from democratic reforms to authoritarian retreat. How can we make sense of this drastic shift? This chapter offers an answer.

Those who subscribe to the inclusion-moderation thesis were caught off guard since they foresaw a progressive democratic habituation once the party had taken the path of moderation in 2001.[1] For them, the AKP was the product of Islamists' democratic learning over decades of political participation under a secular system.[2] Without a doubt, the thesis has shed light on the origins of the AKP as a conservative democratic party. Yet its linear logic also obscured the reversible nature of democratic habituation and failed to make sense of this reversal. The Turkish case clearly demonstrated that moderation was reversible as an Islamist party came to power with a strong democratic mandate yet switched to a hegemonic and majoritarian posture in government.

How can we explain the AKP's pivot from liberal democracy to electoralism? Why did the party choose to conquer the state, in Somer's words, instead of democratizing it?[3] Why has the party reverted to an instrumentalist view of democracy informed by Islamism and away from the goal of democratic consolidation? Neither inclusion, with its ideational or institutional effects, nor strategic determinism can provide a satisfactory answer to the questions posed here, as discussed in Chapter 1.

The answer to such questions, I argue, lies in intraparty dynamics. The AKP that came to power in 2002 no longer exists. In fact, the party has never been a unitary actor with a singular political agenda. Rather, it has been a coalition of different groups with diverging political goals, attitudes, and views on democracy. Such differences became more evident over time as external events prompted responses from party members. Individual democratic commitments crystallized in the process; electoral and liberal understandings of democracy started to diverge. Disagreements and power struggles ensued within the party.[4]

The party's behavior was one possible option among many, and the dominant coalition within the party dictated its course. That is, the AKP did not revert to majoritarianism because it had no other option or because it lacked pluralism. The political crises discussed in this chapter

---

[1] To assess this transformation, students of Turkish politics resorted to the IMT: Tezcür, *Muslim Reformers in Iran and Turkey*; Gürses, "Islamists, Democracy and Turkey"; Atacan, "Explaining Religious Politics at the Crossroad"; Tanıyıcı, "Transformation of Political Islam in Turkey."
[2] Çavdar, "Islamist 'New Thinking' in Turkey."
[3] Somer, "Conquering versus Democratizing the State."
[4] Recently, scholars have focused on internal party dynamics to explain the moderation and "immoderation" of the AKP. Kirdiş, for instance, underlines the lack of internal pluralism and a strict hierarchy to explain why the AKP has immoderated. Wuthrich and Çiftçi, in partial agreement, suggest that a centralized party organization facilitates strategic action (in the form of moderation or radicalism) in response to external factors. While both studies highlight strategic thinking, hierarchical organization, and external factors as determinants of party behavior, they also overlook pluralism within the party and miss the opportunity to explore the origins of party hierarchy, intraparty conflicts, and their impact on party behavior. See Wuthrich and Çiftçi, "Islamist Parties" and Kirdiş, "Wolves in Sheep Clothing or Victims of Times?"

produced a multiplicity of reactions inside the party. There were several liberal voices within the AKP with diverging interpretations and strategic choices. But their voices have become much weaker over time. An electoralist alliance came to dominate the party organization and steered the party in a majoritarian direction.

The liberal wing of the AKP was not always weak though. At the outset, they left their imprint on the party platform, shaped organizational rules, and exercised partial control over recruitment. They enacted many of the reforms that the party was known for in its first term in power. Yet they started to lose such footholds to the electoralists led by Recep Tayyip Erdoğan. As an electoral wing emerged and captured organizational resources, it also changed the party's behavior. In the end, the electoralists' understanding of democracy defined the AKP's trajectory and took the country into a competitive authoritarian direction.[5]

Turkish electoralists' understanding of democracy stems from the traditional Milli Görüş movement, discussed in detail below, and relies on "righteous majoritarianism." They claim moral superiority over other political parties and delegitimize them as strangers to the religiocultural values of the Turkish society. For electoralists, the AKP embodies and protects the Muslim identity of the Turkish people and advances the cause of Islam in Turkey and abroad. Their rivals inside the party, until their recent departure, in contrast, rejected "righteous majoritarianism," advocated a pluralist democratic system with safeguards for civil liberties for all groups and individuals, and treated Islam as a private source of inspiration rather than a public mission.

This chapter offers an account of the AKP's swing from liberalism to electoralism. It discusses the AKP's origins, its trajectory in government, and how it has taken a hegemonic direction despite its branding in its inception as a conservative party with an explicitly democratic agenda. To explain this transformation, I identify major forces inside the AKP, their diverging understandings of democracy, and describe how one wing prevailed over the other to take the party into an electoralist Islamist direction. A key part of this process involves the rise of a dominant coalition under Erdoğan's leadership. His growing command over organizational resources weakened his rivals with more liberal democratic orientations. This chapter traces these processes and their political consequences.

---

[5] For more on this topic, see Esen and Gumuscu, "Rising Competitive Authoritarianism in Turkey."

The Origins of the AKP: The Milli Görüş Movement

Turkish Islamism springs from the collective trauma that the Muslim world suffered in the nineteenth century with the rise of European imperialism. Located at the heart of the Islamic world at the time, the elite of the Ottoman Empire sought to remedy the state's demise vis-à-vis its longstanding rivals in Europe. Some advocated emulation of the West, whose political, economic, and military institutions had proved superior. Those who wanted to salvage both the empire and Islam in the face of disintegration and increasing Western secularism suggested reviving Islam and its forgotten principles to address the problems Muslims faced with the rise of modernity. Representatives of both trends took turns carrying out a series of reforms over the course of the century to save the empire from collapse.

Thus, Islamism emerged as a potential survival strategy, along with Westernism and nationalism, from European domination in the nineteenth century, and its heyday was the reign of Abdülhamid II (1876–1909), who carried Islamic modernism to power and embraced pan-Islamism to unite the empire's Muslim subjects against European colonization.[6] The nationalist forces organized around the İttihat ve Terakki Cemiyeti (Committee of Union and Progress) ended the sultan's long reign in 1908 and brought Turkish nationalism to power. By the end of World War I, both Islamism and the empire had been defeated.

Although such reforms ultimately failed to prevent the disintegration of the Ottoman state, nationalist leaders managed to establish an independent nation-state on the imperial ruins. The allied powers invaded the Turkish mainland after the war, triggering a war of independence led by nationalist officers in the Ottoman Army. By 1922, they were victorious. In 1923, they established the Republic of Turkey, and in 1924 they abolished the caliphate. Successive secularizing reforms followed, as I discussed earlier.

Until 1950, single-party rule under the Republican People's Party (Cumhuriyet Halk Partisi, henceforth CHP) redesigned Turkey's political and social life. Under the CHP, Islamist movements remained under state repression and were mostly defeated and largely quiet. The transition to multiparty politics with free and fair elections in 1950 provided Islamist movements with breathing room. Thanks to the inclusive nature of the new regime, Islamic tendencies initially found a home in center-right parties. They lobbied the political elite to reverse some of the secular policies of the republic and revive Islam in public life.[7] Over time, those who sought a higher level of Islamization deemed such center–right

---

[6] For more, see Keddie, "Pan-Islamic Appeal."
[7] For a comprehensive study of Islamism in Turkey, see Bora, *Cereyanlar*.

parties too secular for their ideological tastes. The existing parties, many believed, also failed to represent the interests of conservative Muslims.[8] In 1970, a group of Islamists under the leadership of Necmettin Erbakan established the Milli Görüş movement and its first formal political party. The secular–religious cleavage in Turkish politics was thus formalized.[9]

The Turkish constitution and the Law of Political Parties, however, proscribe the establishment of religious parties. That is why the Milli Görüş movement threaded a cautious line. On the one hand, it aimed to appeal to the Islamic sentiments of the Turkish people and represent Islam in the political arena. On the other, it wanted to avoid triggering a reaction from the secular establishment. That is partly why the leaders of the movement used Islamic symbolism without calling for the establishment of an Islamic state. The constitutional Court still shut down the Milli Görüş parties when it deemed the use of such symbols as excessive and in violation of the secular principles of the republic. The movement persevered under pressure and formed five successive parties largely thanks to emerging opportunities they enjoyed during critical junctures.[10]

The leading cadres of the AKP come from the Milli Görüş movement. Many of them joined the movement in their youth and matured in its affiliated parties. Although they left the movement to establish the AKP as a centrist party in 2001, electoralists within the AKP soon returned to the traditional Islamist line, which I unpack in this section.

The ideology of the Milli Görüş movement remained incoherent and eclectic, like many of its counterparts in the Muslim world.[11] Several aspects of its political program remained ambiguous not only because the

---

[8] Some conservatives remained in the fold of center–right parties and flirted with Turkish nationalism. Their ultimate concern was to countermobilize against communism during the peak of the Cold War. Islamists and conservatives often converged on this goal. Turkish nationalist, conservative, and Islamist youth mobilized through anticommunist associations. This anticommunist tendency also put them on the state elite's good side during the 1970s and 1980s.

[9] A number of Islamic parties were established during the early republican era and soon after the transition to multiparty politics, but they only lasted a few months before being closed down for violating the secular principles of the republic.

[10] These five parties associated with the Milli Görüş movement are the MNP (1970–71); the MSP, (1972–80); the RP (1983–98); the FP (1997–2001); and the SP (2001–present). The SP has changed its political outlook in recent years partly in reaction to the AKP's growing authoritarianism. The party advocates a return to a democratic system with greater safeguards for civil liberties and pluralism. This shift gave birth to a split within the party when Erbakan's son established the RP in 2018 with Erdoğan's support with the claim that the SP no longer followed Erbakan's Milli Görüş vision. For more on opportunity structures in Turkish politics for Islamic activism, see Yavuz, *Islamic Political Identity in Turkey* and Eligür, *The Mobilization of Political Islam in Turkey*.

[11] Çakır, "Milli Görüş Hareketi"; Sarıbay, "Milli Nizam Hareketi'nin Kuruluşu ve Programının İçeriği." See also Yavuz, *Islamic Political Identity in Turkey*.

The Origins of the AKP: The Milli Görüş Movement

Turkish constitution proscribed clear references to Islam[12] (or any other religion for that matter) but also because Turkish political Islam, like its counterparts, lacked a coherent political vision. As such, the movement was shaped to a great extent by its sociopolitical context.

The major motive behind Islamist activism in Turkey was to revive Islam's "lost" glory and strength. Islamists remained discontent with the secular–republican project. This rejection of republican Westernization defined the Milli Görüş's goals, vision, and symbolism. The leaders of the movement argued that Westernization failed to accomplish political and economic independence; instead, it forced Turkey to imitate the West and reject its "true" identity, which was formed and informed by Islam.[13]

According to this view, the privatization of religion under the Westernized elite precluded a much-needed moral development. Moral decay and dependency resulted from this failed project. Both the republican elite, who had started top-down Westernization in the country, and their predecessors among the political elite were to blame. The Milli Görüş leaders claimed that Turkey could regain its independence only if it returned to its roots and eradicated the corrupting "Western" influence in cultural, economic, and social life. As such, the movement forcefully rejected elite-driven Turkish Westernization and embraced centralizing Islam in social and political life.[14]

Islamists described spiritual and material development as an exit from Turkey's century-long predicament: Spiritual development required Islamization, while material development entailed heavy industrialization. Islamization was a prerequisite for both material development and democratization because without an authentic identity, these modern processes would corrupt the society and as Süleyman Arif Emre, a prominent leader of the movement, posited in 1973, the rule of law and democratic order required moral development.[15]

The movement's rejection of the limited role the republican elite ascribed to Islam separates Islamists from their political rivals. Indeed, the Turkish political elite occasionally evoked Islam to confer legitimacy in different ways. While the secular republican elite invested in the Directorate of Religious Affairs (Diyanet) to control religion's popular and political manifestations (to make it apolitical in the early republican era or counter leftist movements from the 1980s onwards), center–right

---

[12] Sarıbay, *Türkiye'de Modernleşme, Din, ve Parti Politikası*, 117–28.
[13] Yavuz, *Islamic Political Identity in Turkey*.
[14] See, for instance, Erbakan's speeches in the 1970s to 1990s; also see the platforms of the MNP, MSP, and RP.
[15] Süleyman Arif Emre quoted in Sarıbay, *Türkiye'de Modernleşme, Din, ve Parti Politikası*, 111.

parties sought support from conservative parts of the society through a liberalization of the religious marketplace, expanding religious freedoms, and public displays of religiosity.[16] Even if they receive guidance and inspiration from their faith, non-Islamists neither turn Islam into a political program nor impose their faith onto their fellow citizens. They follow secular republican principles and keep their faith mostly private (even if they publicly perform some of their religious duties).

The Milli Görüş Movement and Democracy

To implement its twin projects of spiritual and material development, the Milli Görüş movement had to come to power. Socialized into the modern economy and politics and given incentives to participate in multiparty politics, the movement accepted elections, instead of revolutionary or violent alternatives, as the chief political means.[17] All five parties the movement established sought nonviolent activism, operated within the legal framework, and used democratic means to advance their agenda[18] even when faced with repression by the secular establishment.[19]

Commitment to electoral politics, however, did not signify commitment to democratic norms. The Milli Görüş's perception of democracy contained an instrumentalist, majoritarian, and antipluralist core that remained at clear odds with mutual tolerance and institutional forbearance, two essential norms for democratic survival. This core would later be revived and deployed by electoralists in the AKP, as I discuss later.

Instrumentalism

The path to power for the movement passed through elections, which would hand a popular mandate for Islamization. Electoral victories would also deliver control of the state, which the leaders believed could

---

[16] In her recent book, Lord argues that there is greater continuity between Turkey's Ottoman past, its republican secularism, and the most recent AKP experience. I argue otherwise and suggest that the way Islam entered politics in the republican era under the rule of the secular elite fundamentally differs from the Islamist imagination. The goal of the secular elite is to control Islam's dominant interpretations in the country and ensure that it serves the goals of the republic; in contrast, majoritarian Islamists seek state capture to Islamize society while at the same time instrumentalizing Islam to maintain their regime.

[17] Çalmuk, "Necmettin Erbakan."

[18] This commitment to multiparty politics existed in clear contrast to radical Islamism, which was on the rise in Turkey following the Islamic revolution in Iran in 1979. The Milli Görüş's commitment to democratic procedures and formal politics infuriated radicals, who blamed the movement's leaders for subduing the Islamist momentum in the country. Ibid.

[19] Even when Turkey's Constitutional Court shut down the RP and banned Erbakan from politics, he clearly eschewed violence and sustained his commitment to democratic procedures.

sanction a set of (Islamic) values by controlling and shaping individual behavior and prescribing religion as a practical guide in social and political life.[20] The charismatic leader of the movement, Erbakan, frequently confirmed this instrumentalism: "One should not forget that democracy is not an end in itself," he uttered, "instead it is a means to a greater end. That end is the establishment of the Order of Happiness,"[21] a reference to an Islamic ideal.

Çalmuk describes this as a tendency for unitary thinking and discourse. A former Islamist, Mehmet Bekaroğlu, in agreement with Çalmuk, claims that the Milli Görüş desired a strong state that could control every aspect of life. Islamists had no problem with a strong state or creating a new and more "ideal individual" using its power. Their aim was not to democratize the state, Bekaroğlu suggested; instead, Islamists wanted to control the state to Islamize the society.[22]

State personnel were central to the Islamization project, for they would serve as the agents of Islamization within the state apparatus. Such an attitude aligned well with the movement's state-centric view and revealed its desire to conquer the state for Islamist purposes. The movement hence prioritized establishing pious cadres in the state bureaucracy, besides just Diyanet, as a path toward an Islamic society.[23] Pious cadres with merit, a sense of justice, and virtue would resolve the issues within existing institutions, which mostly stemmed from officials' corruption. The Milli Nizam Partisi (National Order Party, henceforth MNP) platform from 1970, for instance, aimed to regulate bureaucratic recruitment on the basis of political affiliation and ban leftists from civil service, while hiring "virtuous" (read "pious" Muslim) civil servants.[24] State capture through partisan bureaucratic appointments would too become a major goal for electoralists in the AKP, as I will discuss later.

In practice, Islamization also required the complete overhaul of the education system, a central focus of Milli Görüş party platforms. Educational policy, Islamists maintained, formed a key part of organizing individuals' inner affairs.[25] To raise pious individuals and generations, the movement envisioned an education system founded entirely upon morality and spirituality to cultivate values such as piety, work ethic, and devotion

---

[20] Sarıbay, *Türkiye'de Modernleşme, Din, ve Parti Politikası*, 120–28.
[21] Erbakan, *Türkiye'nin Meseleleri ve Çözümleri*, 46.
[22] Quoted in Çalmuk, "Necmettin Erbakan," 553.
[23] The MNP platform is quite explicit about this goal. We see a similar emphasis on pious bureaucratic cadres in the Brotherhood. Its leader, Hassan al-Banna, was also quite explicit regarding the necessity of maintaining pious civil servants.
[24] Milli Nizam Partisi, "Program ve Tüzük," 9.
[25] Ibid.

to morality and family. Thus, both the Ministry of Education and the Directorate of Religious Affairs (Diyanet), in charge of religious instruction and practice in the county, were of central importance. Their extensive and expansive use would deliver the desired Islamization in the society.

A key aspect of Turkish political Islam hence involved the instrumentalization of democracy for Islamist purposes. The parties of the movement ran in elections and gained seats in the parliament to push for their Islamist agenda. When they got the chance to join coalition governments, these parties mobilized public resources for their Islamization project. For instance, for most of the 1970s, the Milli Selamet Partisi (National Salvation Party, MSP) was a junior partner in coalition governments established by parties from the center-left and center-right. The party used the few seats it acquired in the cabinet to advance the role of religion particularly in education. First, the party introduced mandatory religion courses to the curricula of elementary and secondary schools.[26] Then it reallocated public funds to build a thousand new mosques, recruit hundreds of new imams and Qur'an teachers, and expand the number of the Imam Hatip schools.[27] For Erbakan, the Imam Hatips were the movement's backyard, areas of recruitment and indoctrination for Islamists. Increasing their number became a priority for the movement. Of the 505 Imam Hatip schools built from 1951 to 1995, the MSP movement opened 233 in only the 4 years it was the junior partner in coalition governments (1974–78).[28] The AKP's electoralists would also put Islamic education and specifically Imam Hatips at the center of their government agenda.

Populist Majoritarianism

One should note the willingness of Milli Görüş to follow the path of the republican elite in carrying top-down reforms. Of course, although their methods showed great resemblance, as Bekaroğlu has suggested, the ideological content starkly differed from that of the republican project.[29] Also, the movement claimed to have a democratic mandate, which, they argued, republican secularism lacked. The movement claimed to be the true representative of the people whose authentic identity rested on Islamic values and teachings.

---

[26] Sarıbay, "Milli Nizam Hareketi'nin Kuruluşu ve Programının İçeriği," 584.
[27] These schools were originally established to train prayer leaders and preachers, yet the number of graduates from these schools far exceeded the need for religious personnel.
[28] Yeşilada, "The Refah Party Phenomenon in Turkey," 134.
[29] Interview with Mehmet Bekaroğlu, June 12, 2014.

The Milli Görüş Movement and Democracy

Milli Görüş's political view, much like the electoralist outlook in the AKP, had a loud populist ring to it.[30] The people, according to the movement, were virtuous Muslims who had been subject to the repression of the Westernized and immoral elite. Since the movement voiced the yearning of the "true people" for a return to their authentic identity and claim for power, this populist core carried a democratizing essence, for its primary concern was the empowerment of social groups who had felt excluded by the secular republican elite.[31]

Yet the movement's democratic mission is largely limited by its heavy majoritarianism. Once the movement acquired a popular mandate, the leaders presumed they could carry on with their project of moral development. Whatever the people wished – as long as it was in line with Islamic teachings – was acceptable and legitimate. Erbakan voiced this majoritarianism in different venues. In an interview conducted in Germany, he was asked if he could ever envision sharia rule in Turkey. This was a contentious issue in a secular country and one that Milli Görüş consistently avoided mostly for fear of a backlash. Still, Erbakan responded in the affirmative with a democratic twist: Sharia rule was theoretically possible, he claimed; countries governed by Islamic law were content with their legal structures. And when it came to Turkey, the parliament would decide whether or not Turkey should adopt sharia rule.[32] Again, in another interview in 1969, Erbakan suggested, "There are significant benefits in reviving the caliphate" and continued, "I'm not saying it should be revived. But if the people want it, anything is possible. Anything is possible."[33] In other words, if the people want sharia or the reinstatement of the caliphate, then there would be no reason not to do it. In fact, Erbakan implied that it would be antidemocratic not to instate the caliphate or sharia.

Thanks to its majoritarian core, the movement remained highly selective and instrumentalist in its conception of individual rights and liberties. The Milli Görüş parties almost exclusively focused on the freedom of belief and conscience and freedom of expression – central liberties for the advancement of the movement's agenda. This agenda clearly revolved around advancing communal rights (for Sunni Muslims), rather than protecting individual liberties. This emphasis made sense, since for them community came before the individual. Republican

---

[30] See Tuğal, "Islamism in Turkey," for a detailed discussion of Milli Görüş's Islamic populism.
[31] Yavuz, *Islamic Political Identity in Turkey*.
[32] Quoted in Sarıbay, *Türkiye'de Modernleşme, Din, ve Parti Politikası*, 119.
[33] Interview with Yılmaz Çetin, quoted in Çalmuk, "Necmettin Erbakan," 554.

secularism threatened Muslim's communal rights, and the movement sought to redress this issue through democratic activism. However, this defense for communal rights advanced democracy in so far as the movement fought for inclusion and justice. It was devoid of liberal norms. The same majoritarian perception of democracy could be quite toxic for individual rights and liberties when in power. The AKP experience after 2007 attests to this fact, as I discuss below.

The human rights and democratization section of one Milli Görüş party manifesto, for instance, discussed only the problems faced by devout Muslims in their encounters with the secular establishment.[34] The party did not mention any other violations of human rights targeting different social groups like ethnic and religious minorities (Kurds or Alevis). The movement's instrumentalism and majoritarianism also proved evident, for instance, in its perception of the press. The press was an educational institution and a key component of the movement's mission to achieve its cultural and moral objectives. So the party called for legal provisions proscribing immoral media coverage while reducing the media to an ideological instrument for the government in its fight against "destructive" political movements (i.e., socialism and communism).[35]

The Political Other and Antipluralism: Presenting the Movement as Islam

Thus far, I have shown the instrumentalist and majoritarian nature of the Milli Görüş vision. This ideological frame also rested on a binary and antipluralist worldview that pits the Islamic against the un-Islamic, thereby informing the movement's self-righteousness. The leaders articulated these two poles around two contrasting Islamic notions: *hakk* and *batıl*. *Hakk* is one of God's ninety-nine names in Islam and translates as "truth" and signifies godliness and the righteous path. *Batıl*, in contrast, means ungodly, alien, and inauthentic. The two notions, *hakk* and *batıl*, informed both the movement's self-perception and its perception of the political other. While Milli Görüş embodied Islam (and *hakk*),[36] others were associated with *batıl*, invalid and filled with falsehoods.

This polarized worldview that equated the movement with Islam also meant that other political parties were opponents of Islam. Such a dichotomy inadvertently undermined democratic essence and norms such as mutual tolerance since democracy rests upon a competition among equals. In Milli Görüş's conception, there were no equals. On the one hand, there

---

[34] Refah Partisi, "1995 Seçim Beyannamesi," 20–22.
[35] Milli Nizam Partisi, "Program ve Tüzük," 34.
[36] Bora, *Cereyanlar*, 475.

was the "ultimate truth" and its agents who claimed moral superiority, and, on the other hand, there was everyone else who diverged from the "truth."

Erbakan, on several occasions, underscored this moral superiority and the idea that Milli Görüş represented the one truth and divine justice.[37] By implication, all Muslims were expected to support the movement, since it was the sole representative of Islam in politics.[38] In a speech he delivered at a Refah Partisi (Welfare Party, RP) convention in 1993, Erbakan aptly summarized this view:

> There are no twelve parties in Turkey. There are only two. One is *the party of truth*, the "national outlook," and Mehmed the Conqueror's faith. The second includes every other party, because they are all the same. [...] They imitate the west, advocate European Union membership, and *act as enemies of Islam* under the banner of secularism. The Welfare Party [the RP] is the party of *hakk*, and the others are the party of *batıl*.[39] [emphasis added]

Thus, Islam and the movement became one and the same thing. Like the Muslim Brotherhood, which I will discuss in the next chapter, the movement claimed *da'wa* (simply, the call to Islam or preaching). And Islamic political activism under the banner of Milli Görüş turned into a religious duty.[40] That is why Erbakan would end his rallies with Prophet Muhammad's words, "Bear witness, I came and delivered the message,"[41] declaring that he had called his people to Islam.

For Erbakan, the salvation of the Turkish people depended on leaving (political) falsehood and returning to "truth." In a speech he delivered in 1991, he addressed his supporters:

> If you do not serve the RP, your prayers will not be accepted because there is no other way to be a Muslim. The Welfare Party is an army and you have to fight to make this army larger and stronger. This party is an army of Jihad. Are you a Muslim? Then you should be a soldier in this army... Those who work for the party go to heaven because to work for the party means to fight for the establishment of the Qur'anic order.[42]

Although "Jihad" in Islam has multiple meanings, it is widely understood as a sacred struggle. The struggle, for Erbakan, entailed a revival of Islam and constructing a virtuous society through peaceful Islamic activism.

---

[37] See, for instance, a televised interview with Erbakan: https://youtu.be/s_PttkC1akQ
[38] Çınar, "AKP ve İslami Hareketler: Defansif ve Dağıtıcı İktidar Kardeşliği," 310.
[39] Erbakan's speech at the AMGT Convention in 1991: https://youtu.be/5CnduUfr3E0. All translations are mine unless otherwise stated.
[40] Islamic references in his campaign rally from 1994 are illustrative. See, for example, the collective oath-taking at a party rally: https://youtu.be/ovv3UErVhSQ
[41] Çalmuk, "Necmettin Erbakan," 566.
[42] Quoted in *Anayasa Mahkemesi*, "Anayasa Mahkemesi Kararı Yargıtay Cumhuriyet Başsavcılığı – Refah Partisi Davasi."

In this "holy" endeavor, Erbakan and other party leaders referred to their activists as *"mücahid,"* those who wage jihad or work tirelessly to instate God's order. Later in the 1990s, party officials suggested that voting for the RP meant voting for Islam and obeying God's rules.

These features – instrumentalism, majoritarianism, antipluralism – characterized the movement and its parties well into the late 1980s. A series of developments in the 1980s onwards expanded its scope and produced disagreements within. As early as the 1980s, what Yavuz calls "a liberal wing" started to talk about pluralism and individual rights.[43] They aimed to distinguish the movement from Islam and open greater space for pluralism. The more conservative leadership, helmed by Erbakan, also received pressures from the far right, as radical Islamism made advances in the aftermath of the Iranian revolution in 1979. Erbakan desired to channel radical activism into his movement[44] without compromising his commitment to democratic politics. So he kept liberals at bay and instead raised the banner of an Islamic order more forcefully. The leaders' righteous majoritarianism played a critical role in this choice.

The tension between liberals and conservative leadership – which aimed to co-opt radicalism into democratic politics – was reflected in Erbakan's speeches. In 1993, for instance, in a speech written by liberal voices such as Bahri Zengin, Erbakan "differentiated majority democracy from pluralistic democracy and said that pluralism and diversity are a necessary framework for prosperity and a working democracy."[45] A year later, Erbakan painted a very different picture: "The RP will establish the Just Order [*Adil Düzen*]. This is a must," he said, and asked: "Will this transition be smooth or rough? Bloody or peaceful?" He ended on a majoritarian note : "60 million will decide."[46]

Amid growing internal disagreements, the movement went from the fringes of Turkish politics to its center, as its popularity rapidly increased in the 1980s and 1990s.[47] The movement, then organized under the

---

[43] Yavuz, *Islamic Political Identity in Turkey*, 225–26. In a speech written by liberals, Erbakan alluded to such liberal values only to counter them in his other speeches. Such contradictions raised doubts among skeptics about the democratic credentials of the movement.
[44] Bora, *Cereyanlar*.
[45] Yavuz, *Islamic Political Identity in Turkey*, 227.
[46] Erbakan, "1994 Speech in Welfare Party Parliamentary Group Meeting."
[47] The rising popularity of the Islamist Welfare Party in the 1990s was due partially to the destruction of the left in the wake of the 1980 coup, the new official ideology resting on Turkish–Islamic synthesis engraved in the 1982 constitution, and the failure of the existing parties to deal with the needs of the immigrant populations in the metropolitan areas. See Eligür, *The Mobilization of Political Islam in Turkey* and Gülalp, "Globalization and Political Islam."

banner of the RP, managed to win the municipalities of metropolitan areas such as Istanbul and Ankara in the 1994 local elections. A year later, it won the plurality of seats in the parliament. As the largest party in the legislative assembly, the RP formed a coalition government with the center–right True Path Party (Doğru Yol Partisi, DYP).

Closely intertwined with the rising popularity of the party was the rise of a new style of political activism within. A new generation of activists pursued a more vigorous political line and introduced new outreach strategies. A group led by Erdoğan in the party's Istanbul branch, for instance, pursued more "modern" *daʿwa* activism than the conservative leadership by reaching out to all sectors of the society, including pubs and brothels.[48] Yet this shift, for Çakır, was exclusively strategic: They aimed to popularize the movement, not liberalize it. In fact, Çakır suggested the younger generations shared the same worldview of the conservative leadership and even proved to be more skeptical of democracy and secularism.[49]

After successive victories in local and national government, prominent figures in the party opted for majoritarianism instead of liberalism. Several elected mayors and deputies from the ranks of the RP resorted to Islamic symbolism, equated their party with Islam, and displayed their instrumentalist and majoritarian tendencies. For instance, Erdoğan, elected the mayor of Istanbul in 1994, stated on different occasions that all power belonged to God, and the people could abolish secularism if they desired so. And, for him, democracy was not an end in itself; it was a means toward a greater end. So it resembled a train that one gets off when the time comes.[50] In another fiery and militant speech, he embraced Islamic symbolism and depicted his party as the embodiment of Islam quoting verses from Turkish poet Ziya Gökalp: "Minarets are our bayonets [*süngü*]/domes are our helmets/mosques are our barracks [*kışla*]/Muslims are our soldiers."[51] Many within the ranks of the party joined him in this excitement.

Islamists' political rise and their fiery statements triggered a strong reaction from the secular establishment. At a National Security Council (NSC) meeting on February 28, 1997, the generals presented a document to then Prime Minister Erbakan, detailing several steps to be taken

---

[48] Çakır, "Milli Görüş Hareketi," 549, 574.
[49] Ibid., 549.
[50] Erdoğan's interview with *Milliyet* in July 1996, quoted in Çakır and Çalmuk, *Recep Tayyip Erdoğan*, 212–13.
[51] These statements would incriminate Erdoğan for inciting hatred and enmity amongst the people in a court case concluded in 1998. He would receive a brief prison sentence and be banned from politics.

against the rising threat of political Islam in the country. The intervention, known as the "February 28 process,"[52] amounted to a major crackdown on Islamist movements. During this process, Erbakan was forced to resign and banned from politics along with other prominent leaders for several years, while his party was shut down by the Constitutional Court. Succeeding governments dominated by secular center–right and center–left parties reinstated the headscarf ban in universities, practically denying the right to higher education for veiled women and increased the duration of compulsory education to reduce the popular demand for Imam Hatip schools.

The Milli Görüş movement responded to this cycle of repression by establishing the Virtue Party (Fazilet Partisi, FP) and deviating from the traditional Islamist line toward a stronger emphasis on democracy, pluralism, human rights, and civil liberties.[53] The voice of liberals who had been previously silenced became louder. The conservative leadership was also onboard now, as they blamed their demise on the democratic deficit in the country.[54]

Many observers remained skeptical of this pivot toward liberalism and perceived it as purely strategic. Others suggested that repression and exclusion combined with incentives for moderation triggered ideological change among Islamists. Regardless, the February 28 process revealed a growing schism within the movement. Liberal reformers, previously sidelined, frequently criticized the Milli Görüş line and challenged the old guard on the basis of democracy, respect for human rights, and pluralism. This was not the only challenge that the leadership faced. The Istanbul branch of the movement, under Erdoğan's leadership, had been questioning the leaders' electoral and political strategies. Ultimately, at the FP party convention in 2000, liberal reformers led by Abdullah Gül and Bülent Arınç joined forces with Erdoğan's Istanbul branch to challenge the old guard for party leadership. This was a first in the history of the movement, which had a centralized and hierarchical structure with a strong cult of leadership.

Gül's group took the global post-Cold War democratic wave and universal human rights and liberties as their reference point. They specifically demanded intraparty democracy, primaries before elections, the transfer of funds to local branches, and the strengthening of the rank and file at the expense of the politburo in the making of party policies. For

---

[52] For a detailed analysis of this process, see Cizre and Çınar, "Turkey 2002."
[53] Mecham, "From the Ashes of Virtue, a Promise of Light."
[54] For details on the rise and demise of the FP, see ibid.

Gül, Milli Görüş could not successfully safeguard democratic rights in the country without first establishing democracy within the party.[55]

Erdoğan, in contrast, as I discussed above, focused on the proper outreach methods to expand the party base toward non-Islamic constituencies. He was eager to reform the party's electoral strategies to reach out to the widest electoral constituency possible through public service. For him, going beyond the mosque congregation was key to this effort and required door-to-door canvassing of all voters regardless of their ideologies.[56] The involvement of women in face-to-face interaction with voters was a key part of his strategy.[57] Yet the old guard was not particularly enthusiastic about his approach due to their more conservative outlook. Despite their apparent displeasure, Erdoğan's team applied this strategy in Istanbul, where he headed the RP branch and triumphed in the local mayoral elections in 1994. Aside from this strategic challenge, Erdoğan did not offer an ideological criticism of the movement. Instead, he remained a loyal follower of the Milli Görüş 's instrumentalism and spiritual developmentalism. In short, Erdoğan's group challenged the party leadership in its methods, a challenge practical in nature, while Gül's faction demanded stronger commitment to democratic principles within and outside of the party apparatus, a difference that was essentially ideological.

In the end, Gül's alliance lost the race for party leadership to Recai Kutan, Erbakan's close friend, by a very narrow margin. The slim margin of victory for the old guard signaled reformists' increasing popularity among the party base. However, soon after the congress, the Constitutional Court closed the FP in 2001 for its antisecularism. The rift between the reformists and the old guard was beyond repair. The old cadre went on to establish the Felicity Party (Saadet Partisi, SP), the final link in the Milli Görüş chain. Reformists, convinced that they could not reform the movement from within, decided to establish a new political party, namely the AKP, in August 2001.

The Birth of the AKP and Its Internal Dynamics

At the time of its establishment, the AKP was a coalition of two reformist wings among the Islamist cadres, what I call Ankara and Istanbul groups, who unsuccessfully joined forces to replace the old guard, as

---

[55] Abdullah Gül's speech in the FP Party Congress, May 14, 2001, www.youtube.com/watch?v=ZAvC5GLwoW0
[56] Çakır and Çalmuk, *Recep Tayyip Erdoğan*.
[57] Baykan, *The Justice and Development Party in Turkey*; Çakır and Çalmuk, *Recep Tayyip Erdoğan*.

already discussed. The differences between the two groups have only grown larger and more visible over the years in a way that characterized the internal conflicts of the new party.

The Ankara group emerged from within the parliamentary group of the FP, with more experience in parliament. They have had a more collaborative leadership with Abdullah Gül and Bülent Arınç heading their group and sharing their power with figures such as Abdüllatif Şener and Ertuğrul Yalçınbayır. These prominent figures sustained their adherence to democratic principles such as pluralism, freedom of expression and information, the rule of law, a pro-European Union stance, and intraparty democracy before and after coming to power. The Istanbul group, in contrast, had more experience in local governance than parliamentary politics. Led by Erdoğan, they wavered between liberalism and electoralism.

It was Gül's team, with a liberal democratic orientation, who penned both the party platform and bylaws. Both documents reflect their democratic attitudes and demands in the 2000 party convention. The group included several former deputies, mostly based in Turkey's capital Ankara. Gül and Arınç led this wing along with mid-level leaders such as Abdüllatif Şener, Ertuğrul Yalçınbayır, and Ersönmez Yarbay. They collectively penned the AKP platform that expressed their perception of democracy which included pluralism, guarantees for political rights and civil liberties, protection of minority rights, and engagement with political rivals in a civil and democratic manner. In other words, the platform articulated a liberal understanding of democracy instead of a majoritarian one.

Thanks to the liberal wing's overall influence, the AKP emerged as an economically liberal, politically pluralist, and socially conservative party. Its central political project was based on two main goals: (1) economic development and growth and (2) expansion of human rights and freedoms and consolidation of liberal democracy.

The party assigned no role to Islam in its pursuit of these aims and, different than Milli Görüş, rejected Islamism as a social, economic, and political project.[58] The AKP instead redefined Islam as a religion, and not an ideology, that comprises the norms and values which render life meaningful for devout Muslims. Islam was no longer *din wa dawla* (religion and state) or a sociopolitical program. The party did not claim to embody Islam either; instead, it rejected the use and abuse of religious values for political purposes, recognizing liberal conceptualization of

---

[58] Tekin, *AK Parti'nin Muhafazakâr Demokrat Kimliği*, 111.

secularism as a central component of democracy[59] that allowed believers to live in accord with their beliefs.[60]

The liberals in the AKP also replaced Milli Görüş's instrumentalist view of human rights as they committed to protecting the freedoms and rights of all citizens. To safeguard freedoms of thought, speech, conscience, and information – as well as the rights of women, and children – the party program urged the adoption of internationally accepted standards stated in the Universal Declaration of Human Rights, the European Convention on Human Rights, and the Helsinki Final Act.[61] Going well and above, the AKP also claimed that torture and death during interrogation, disappearing persons, and unsolved murders (mostly targeting leftists and Kurdish activists) were unacceptable in a democratic country and vowed the party would take all the necessary steps to eradicate such practices.[62] Such a wholesome take on rights and liberties marked a clear departure from other Milli Görüş parties, which had hardly mentioned freedoms unrelated to Islamic practices.

The new party's perception of democracy also diverged from the righteous majoritarianism and antipluralism of its predecessors. Political parties, the platform claimed, are essential to well-functioning democracies but are no agents of *truth*; instead, as civil organizations, they compete for power to address citizens' demands.[63] Also, the platform insisted, electoral success does not deliver absolute power to winners. Ruling parties have to respect minority rights, placed under constitutional guarantees.[64] Ertuğrul Yalçınbayır, a prominent figure within the liberal group and one of the authors of the platform, elaborated this point when I asked about their perception of democracy:

---

[59] "Adalet ve Kalkınma Partisi Programı," 15.
[60] Ibid., 7–8. An ongoing debate about secularism and its application in Turkey has occupied the political agenda since the establishment of the AKP. Kemalists insist on a Jacobin secularism (or, more appropriately, laïcité) that seeks to control Islam and ban all of its visible manifestations in public life. How one interprets the public sphere is another significant dimension of the issue, as the Kemalists reject a distinction between those who perform and those who receive service in public institutions. As such, a ban on headscarves applies to university students as well as professors. The AKP, on the other hand, demanded a reinterpretation of secularism in the language of the Anglo-Saxon tradition of freedom of conscience and religious practice and protecting religion from state intervention.
[61] Ibid., 14.
[62] Ibid., 15–16. It is often leftists who are victims of such violations. The Milli Görüş parties have never mentioned violations of human rights along these lines in their party manifestos.
[63] Ibid., 17.
[64] Ibid., 25–26

Democracy is a totality of values: participation, pluralism (not majoritarianism), accountability, transparency, and quality in governance. In our program, we claimed that our first priority is to fight corruption, nepotism, inequality, racism, partisanship, despotism. Democracy is not about elections; it is about justice, fundamental rights, and freedoms. These are ingrained in the AKP program.[65]

Liberals in the AKP also made sure that the new party would be democratic in its internal affairs. They were particularly wary of Erbakan's centralized and nondemocratic rule in Milli Görüş parties. In numerous interviews, Arınç, Yarbay, Şener, and Yalçınbayır repeatedly stated that their mission was to establish a party with strong internal democracy. Yarbay, for instance, the head of AKP's Ankara branch in 2001, had been quite critical of the hierarchical and authoritarian structure of the Milli Görüş tradition. He concurred that they established the AKP as a party of collective wisdom.[66] This was a key lesson they learned from their prior experience. Similarly, for Arınç, one of the authors of the bylaws, his aim was to replace leadership oligarchy and one-man rule with intraparty democracy and collective leadership.[67]

The founding leaders thus set the rules of the organization such that their party would not become a leader's party. Carrying the imprint of liberals like Yalçınbayır, the party bylaws reflected a deep appreciation of intraparty competition and democracy. To that end, liberals placed a three-term limit on party leaders, deputies, and mayors, and established intra-party election mechanisms for greater accountability. Accordingly, the party would select candidates through primaries, avoid making group decisions in parliament to increase deputies' independence, and determine party whips and members of central committees through elections.[68]

The party platform and bylaws thus displayed a substantial ideological transformation and a clear departure from the Milli Görüş line. Still, skeptics questioned the nature of this transformation. Was this a strategic move, an act of dissimulation, or a genuine ideological change indicating democratic habituation? The leaders of the new party faced a demanding public. The way different figures carried out such discussions also revealed early differences in their democratic attitudes.

Gül and Arınç, for instance, discussed their political transformations candidly and proved to be less combative when engaging with skeptics and more self-reflective of their transformation than Erdoğan ever was.

---

[65] Interview with Ertuğrul Yalçınbayır, January 13, 2017.
[66] Interview with Ersönmez Yarbay, June 24, 2014.
[67] Indeed, when his three terms ended, Arınç decided not to run, even though the three-term limit was already moot by then, as we will discuss later. See *HaberTürk*, "Gül parti kurmaz ama bizi imtihan etmeye kalkmasınlar."
[68] "Adalet ve Kalkınma Partisi Programı," 18–20.

Both leaders confirmed that they advocated Islamism in the past, yet they had changed their views in a fundamental way. Gül explained his new position in an interview:

> We have realized that religious politics do not benefit pious people or the country. A political party is not a *da'wa* organization. It is an instrument of public service. I may aspire to be a pious person, but those who support me should not vote for me because of my piety; they should support me because they trust that I can govern this country better than others.[69]

Erdoğan, in contrast, often refused to reflect on the nature of his political transformation and preferred to deny his earlier attachment to Islamist ideals. An early press conference he held with the intention to dispel suspicions about the political goals of the AKP was illustrative of his political line. In this press conference, he took only a few questions, refused to elaborate on the main points he made in his statement, and mocked journalists. He displayed a combative and polarizing attitude throughout the event. Party supporters who were present at the press conference cheered Erdoğan's dismissive attitude. The Turkish Journalists' Association released a statement afterward, inviting the party leaders to a more respectful exchange with the press. Yalçınbayır, a prominent liberal and the party's secretary-general at the time, agreed with critiques that they should have controlled the inappropriate conduct of their supporters. Yalçınbayır promised to have more respectful press conferences in the future. Erdoğan, in contrast, refused to back down. He claimed that the audience present at the press conference were not party members but "the people" – displaying his populist tendencies – and there was no reason to fear them.[70] In hindsight, this was an early sign of Erdoğan's troubled understanding of press freedom and his polarizing populism, which would become increasingly visible in the years to come.

Disagreements Surface

The early yet subtle fissures among the founders of the party only grew over time, and internal differences became more visible after the AKP came to power. The party ran on a liberal democratic platform in the 2002 national elections and registered a critical electoral victory only a year after its establishment. With 34.4 percent of the votes, the party won the majority of the seats in parliament, thanks to the 10 percent electoral threshold (one of the highest in the democratic world), and

---

[69] Derya Sazak's interview with Gül, *Milliyet*, August 27, 2001.
[70] Reported by Çakır and Çalmuk, *Recep Tayyip Erdoğan*, 215.

formed a single-party government. This victory also created an opportunity for Islamists to display their democratic commitments.

Liberals clearly had greater clout in the first AKP government. Gül served as the prime minister until Erdoğan's political ban – given in 1998 for inciting hatred and enmity among the people – was lifted in March 2003 and remained in the cabinet until 2007. Other liberals also occupied seats in the cabinet: Şener and Yalçınbayır served as deputy PM, Yakış became AKP's first foreign minister, and Beşir Atalay and Ali Babacan were ministers of state. The parliamentary group of the party also included several figures close to the liberal wing of the party. They used their weight on key issues such as European Union accession and economic governance, and Gül personally led the negotiations for Turkey's membership.

Thanks to liberals' predominance in the cabinet and the limited power of the electoralists in the parliamentary group, the AKP government conformed to political ideals defined in its platform. Displaying a clear commitment to democratic principles, the party took several steps to improve democracy and human rights, expand freedoms, and bring Turkey closer to accession to the European Union. In line with this purpose, the government passed several constitutional amendments and five packages to harmonize Turkish law with European Union standards. For instance, it abolished the controversial state security courts and made changes to the organization and responsibilities of the NSC,[71] narrowed the jurisdiction of military courts, accepted the supremacy of the European Court of Human Rights (ECHR) over domestic jurisdiction,[72] abolished the death penalty for all crimes, lifted the bans against broadcasting in languages other than Turkish, and facilitated instruction in native languages other than Turkish (a crucial step in recognizing Kurdish cultural rights in the country). The government also made it harder to ban political parties, broadened the freedom of association by lifting the obstacles to establishing and joining associations, and enhanced gender equality by amending the constitution and increasing the penalties for honor crimes committed against women. All these steps taken by the AKP in its first term in office not only improved Turkey's overall status in democracy indices (see Figure 6) but also convinced the European Union that Turkey was ready to start accession talks in 2005.

---

[71] One step was to appoint a civilian secretary to the NSC and replace the seats reserved for NSC-appointed members to the Board of the Higher Education Institute and the Higher Board of Radio and Television Broadcasting with civilians.

[72] This legislation acknowledged citizens' right to retrial in cases where the ECHR decides that a penalty given by the Turkish courts is in conflict with the European Act of Human Rights.

The Birth of the AKP and Its Internal Dynamics 103

Yet such progress was not devoid of conflict or inconsistencies. In certain instances, righteous majoritarianism of electoralists within the party crept in and clashed with more liberal tendencies. The reform of the penal code, for instance, reflected such disagreements. The new code, changed as part of the European Union accession process, significantly expanded civil liberties. Amid the reform process, then Prime Minister Erdoğan proposed to penalize adultery to protect the moral values of the Turkish people and strengthen families, a major concern for Islamists. He also justified this proposition by popular support in favor of this change.[73] His proposal, however, met with serious backlash from the European Union. Gül's team along with other leaders such as Cemil Çiçek, Ahmet Davutoğlu, and Mehmet Aydın convinced the prime minister to rescind his proposal and pass the new penal code without the adultery clause in September 2004.[74] Thanks to liberals' efforts, the amendment was shelved and the talks with the European Union ensued without interruptions. When Erdoğan revisited the issue of criminalizing adultery a decade later, he would call the decision to withdraw the proposal a major mistake.[75]

Liberals and electoralists also disagreed on intraparty democracy. Only a few months after coming to power, the AKP government led by Gül faced a major political dilemma. Turkey had to decide in early 2003 whether to assist the American war effort in Iraq. Gül decided to take the issue to parliament but refused to make a group decision that would bind the AKP deputies. He recognized the plurality of voices within his party and invited skeptics to raise their concerns. Erdoğan was in favor of the motion, yet his influence was limited since he was not a member of parliament at the time. In the end, Gül decided to hold a secret vote in parliament on March 1; such openness and respect for pluralism in his party at a very critical moment allowed ninety-seven AKP deputies to abstain or vote against the motion.[76] The motion was defeated. Erdoğan was quite displeased since he expected "loyalty and obedience" from deputies and, like Erbakan, was not willing to tolerate any form of internal debate or dissent.[77] Not

---

[73] Sever, *Abdullah Gül ile 12 Yıl Yaşadım, Gördüm, Yazdım*, 63–64.
[74] For details of this process of dropping the proposal to penalize adultery, see ibid., 63–68.
[75] "AKP 2004'te Suç Haline Getiremediği Zinayı Yeniden Gündemine Aldı"; Smith, "Turkey Wants to Make Adultery Illegal."
[76] Back in 1991 during the Gulf War, Turgut Özal, then prime minister, was in the same position as Gül later; unlike Gül, though, he took an open vote to ensure party discipline. The motion passed and Turkey provided substantial support to the American war effort against Iraq. I would like to thank one of the reviewers for pointing this difference out.
[77] Yavuz, *Secularism and Muslim Democracy in Turkey*, 129.

surprisingly, he interpreted this vote as an act of defiance and violation of his authority.[78] In retribution, he took most of the deputies who voted against the motion off the party's electoral lists in the 2007 elections, as will be discussed in the next section.[79]

These disagreements signaled the distance between liberals and electoralists in terms of their perception of democracy, intraparty pluralism, freedom of thought and expression, and social diversity. It was getting increasingly clear that Erdoğan had limited tolerance for democratic processes and debate.[80] Indeed, as Levent Gültekin, a columnist and liberal Islamist with access to the AKP's inner circles, has posited, Erdoğan has never been a reformist in the ideological sense of the term. He was a reformist in strategy but ideologically, he remained in tune with the Milli Görüş line. For Gültekin, the true leader of the reformists was Abdullah Gül. His group believed in deliberation and dialogue and respect for the other.[81] Subsequent developments would affirm the validity of Gültekin's assessment.

One could ask why Gül and other liberals joined forces with Erdoğan, given their ideological differences. Many indeed see the AKP as Erdoğan's party. My observations from the field and several interviews suggest otherwise. The founding members I talked to claimed that the AKP was in fact an initiative of the Ankara group, and they invited Erdoğan to join the new party.[82] The reason for this alliance was Erdoğan's organizational genius, popularity in the country, and name recognition as Istanbul's mayor. In other words, at the outset, the party was the party of liberal reformists. That is also why the AKP had three prominent leaders – Erdoğan, Gül, and Arınç – with no clear hierarchy among them, although Erdoğan was elected as party chairman. As Arınç posited in a televised interview several years later, at the time of AKP's establishment, Erdoğan was not "the" leader or the only choice for premiership; there were indeed several prominent names who could have served as the party chairman. Liberals, with their control over the party platform and the bylaws, thought that they could balance any party leader. The fact that, at the outset, Erdoğan's wing exercised limited control over the party reassured liberals. Yet internal dynamics of the party would change dramatically over the years.

---

[78] For details, see Sever, *Abdullah Gül ile 12 Yıl Yaşadım, Gördüm, Yazdım*.
[79] Interview with Ahmet Faruk Ünsal, June 24, 2014.
[80] Yavuz, *Secularism and Muslim Democracy in Turkey*.
[81] Interview with Levent Gültekin, January 1, 2017. Also see his book *Şatafatlı Mağlubiyet*.
[82] These claims are based on interviews I conducted with several founding members of the party between 2014 and 2017.

The Changing Balance of Power within the AKP

After his political ban was lifted by parliament in 2003 and he became prime minister, Erdoğan and his faction started to increase their influence over the party apparatus. This faction, unlike the liberal wing in the party, was essentially personalist, united around Erdoğan's leadership. In the ensuing years, this faction consolidated a dominant alliance through an intricate incentive structure to capture the party and sideline Erdoğan's rivals. Among them were prominent architects of the AKP. Arınç described this process in an interview in 2015 as the party's transition to personalism: "The party was about a collective, 'us'; then it turned into an organization of 'me' [referring to Erdoğan]," he said, "Only a few are left of that 'us' in the party."[83]

But how did the party transform in such a drastic fashion? How did Erdoğan manage to capture the organization established by liberal reformists and turn it into his personal machine? A key part of this process involved the growing power and resources of Erdoğan's faction. Specifically, Erdoğan's wing captured organizational resources such as rules, recruitment, finance, and internal communication, while liberals' control over these resources, with the partial exception of expertise, declined rapidly. Growing control over such key organizational resources allowed his faction to command the incentive structure, providing both collective and selective incentives to not only his supporters but also fence-sitters and rivals within (as well as outside) the party. Leveraging such organizational resources, Erdoğan's wing built a dominant alliance around electoralism and aligned the party's behavior with their righteous majoritarianism. The following section details this process.

Changing Organizational Rules

Traditionally, party leaders carry substantial clout over party organizations in Turkey.[84] As Heper and Sayarı assert, they possess great authority over their organizations through their tight control over the nomination of candidates for national and local elective offices as well as patronage distribution.[85] In short, Turkish party leaders managed

---

[83] *HaberTürk*, "Gül parti kurmaz ama bizi imtihan etmeye kalkmasınlar."
[84] Heper and Landau, *Political Parties and Democracy in Turkey*; Esmer, "At the Ballot Box: The Determinants of Voting Behavior"; Özbudun, *Contemporary Turkish Politics*; Rubin and Heper, *Political Parties in Turkey*; Heper, "Conclusion: The Consolidation of Democracy versus Democratization in Turkey"; Kabasakal, "Factors Influencing Intra-party Democracy and Membership Rights"; Arıkan Akdağ, "Candidate Selection Process as a Tool to Shape a Party's Dominant Coalition."
[85] Heper and Sayarı, *Political Leaders and Democracy in Turkey*.

to amass a great deal of personal power at the expense of organizational autonomy.[86]

The Milli Görüş movement was no exception. Necmettin Erbakan held the monopoly of power in all the movement's parties established from 1970 until his death in 2011. That is why the founders of the AKP, the Ankara group in particular, were quite wary of personal power and why they took several measures in the party statutes. These precautions in organizational design, however, fell victim to Erdoğan's maneuvers, which destroyed these safeguards through practical measures and formal changes to party rules.

At the outset, Erdoğan signaled his desire to control the party organization. At the time of its establishment in 2001, the party's founders elected the party chairman and the executive committees. The founders, together with members of central executive committees, formed the founders' council, which ruled the party and could change its rules until the first party convention.[87] Erdoğan took this transitional moment as an opportunity to place his supporters in key positions in the party.

In a smart move, he proposed to exclude former deputies of the FP from the party founders to "break" the continuity with the Milli Görüş movement; this, he suggested, would strengthen the party's defense against a possible closure case by the Constitutional Court.[88] What seemed like a reasonable demand at the time ended up weakening the Ankara group in the party governance. Several liberals within the group – among them were Gül, Arınç, and Şener, who had left Milli Görüş to establish the AKP – remained outside the list of party founders. In their stead, Erdoğan submitted several names close to him who became party founders. Thus, he reduced the weight of the Ankara wing in party governance.

This key development allowed Erdoğan's group to extend its power into the executive committees and later change party rules. In the first intra-party elections for executive committees in 2001, Erdoğan submitted a list of names with which he wanted to work. Because the bylaws required open-list elections for all committees, his motion was defeated after a two-hour-long discussion. Yet he refused to budge and circulated an informal list of names (which included some liberals) among the party founders before voting. In the end, most of the names on his list were elected to the executive committee; the only exception was Yalçınbayır,

---

[86] Ibid.
[87] See the AKP bylaws.
[88] Interview with Abdullatif Şener, June 24, 2014.

the only name off the list, who got elected as the party's first secretary-general, to Erdoğan's displeasure.

Only two years later, Erdoğan proposed to change the party bylaws to increase the leader's control over the organization. The amendments, if passed, were posed to mark a major shift toward leadership oligarchy, erosion of intraparty democracy, and the destruction of the checks and balances liberal reformists had installed. And they passed. Central lists replaced primaries for the nomination of candidates, closed lists replaced open lists in intraparty elections (at both national and local levels), and local administrators and delegates were to be elected through blanket lists. Such changes practically handed the entire party organization to the leader. Now the leader could pick nominees, members of the executive committees, local party branches, and the delegates.[89] Hence, the central leadership gained complete control over the incentive structure; all appointments and promotions in the party had to go through the party leader.

Again, one could ask why the executive committees agreed to these changes. The party leadership, Yalçınbayır explained to me in an interview, used scare tactics, intimidation, deterrence, scolding, and threats to streamline the party and curtail internal dissent. For instance, Erdoğan scared the members of the party with the threat that they may not be nominated if the party used primaries. Acting in a self-interested manner, the executive committee thus opened the door to Erdoğan's growing influence over the party. Such changes secured him a central position in the party organization and ever-greater control over the incentive structure.

Soon afterward, the leader's leverage over party rules also carried over to the party's parliamentary group. After the AKP won the 2002 elections, Erdoğan wanted to handpick party whips. Per party bylaws, however, deputies elected party spokespeople. In the first group elections, as he did in the election of executive committees, Erdoğan endorsed his allies, but the AKP deputies voted for other candidates.[90] Hence, the parliamentary group remained, in the words of Ahmet Faruk Ünsal (an AKP deputy between 2002 and 2007), participatory, pluralistic, and democratic with a strong sense of intraparty democracy. They discussed party decisions and legislation freely within the party group. Yet Erdoğan changed this rule, too, in 2003 and canceled elections for party whips, appointing them after the 2007 elections.

---

[89] Interview with Ersönmez Yarbay, June 24, 2014; interview with Ertuğrul Yalçınbayır, January 13, 2017.
[90] Interview with Ahmet Faruk Ünsal, June 24, 2014.

Changes introduced to party rules facilitated electoralists' infiltration of the party's executive committees in an expansive manner. As Akdağ finds in her study of the AKP's governing organs, the turnover rates in the executive committees at the party congresses in 2003 and 2006 were quite high.[91] In the first party congress in 2003, for instance, both Yalçınbayır and Yarbay, vocal critics of Erdoğan's leadership style, were taken off the executive committees. In their stead came names loyal to the party leader. The changes in executive committees in 2009 and 2012 were of lesser scope, which is indicative of electoralists' growing presence and consolidation of their power in the organization. Akdağ agrees that changing composition of the party's executive committees reflected the growing power of Erdoğan's faction at the expense of founding cadres of the party and other leaders such as Gül, Arınç, and Cemil Çiçek. In short, Erdoğan, upon changing party rules, maintained seats in executive committees as central pieces in his incentive structure, offering them selectively to reward his supporters or allure critics and rivals to build dominant coalitions. Building these dominant coalitions within executive organs, as Akdağ aptly puts it, allowed his faction to debilitate internal opposition to his policies.

Recruitment and Promotion

The changes to the nomination processes and parliamentary appointments passed in 2003 took effect for the first time during the 2007 elections. Subsequently, Erdoğan handpicked the members of the party's central committees in party congresses, its candidates in national elections, and the party whips in parliament. All positions in the party were now controlled by Erdoğan. Liberals had clearly lost control over party recruitment. For instance, when the party put together its electoral lists in 2007, Erdoğan and his close entourage remained in charge. Even the party's secretary-general, Yalçınbayır, was kept outside of this circle and learned the names on the party tickets from the press.[92] This was an excellent illustration of Erdoğan's growing monopoly of power.

Control over the party apparatus and electoral lists empowered Erdoğan at the expense of his rivals. For instance, several prominent figures with divergent views lost their seats in the 2007 elections, while those who contested Erdoğan's decisions were penalized. Erdoğan crossed off the names of Yalçınbayır (party's first secretary-general), Yarbay (the head

---

[91] Akdağ, "Candidate Selection Process as a Tool to Shape a Party's Dominant Coalition."
[92] Interview with Ertuğrul Yalçınbayır, January 13, 2017.

of AKP's Ankara branch), Yakış (AKP's first foreign minister in Gül's cabinet and one of the six authors of the party platform), and Ünsal (a leading human rights activist who opposed the war effort in 2003), among many others.

As a result, the AKP parliamentary group was filled with deputies who owed their political careers to Erdoğan. And once they were elected, their promotion in the parliamentary group also depended on their relationship with the leader. As Ünsal told me in an interview, after 2007 even the most symbolic positions within the parliamentary group remained at the leader's discretion.

Cabinet shuffles under Erdoğan's premiership also reflected his control over recruitment and the growing power of electoralists in the government. There were sixteen liberals with close ties to Abdullah Gül in the first AKP cabinet, most of whom were replaced by Erdoğan loyalists over the years. By 2011, there were only three ministers left from Gül's cabinet, and the rest were mostly from Erdoğan's team in the Istanbul municipality (1994–98). Among them, Binali Yıldırım, Mehdi Eker, Veysel Eroğlu, Ömer Çelik, Hayati Yazıcı, and Hilmi Güler served in many of Erdoğan cabinets.

Local party branches also received their fair share of Erdoğan's centralization efforts. Indeed, keeping tight control over the local branches was essential to winning vertical power games, a key stage in also winning horizontal power games and building dominant alliances. Over the years, the AKP, Kumbaracıbaşı observes, has become an increasingly centralized organization in a manner that clashes with its self-identified norms of intraparty democracy.[93] Recent studies on the AKP successfully document the centralization process during which the leader has come to select the entire cadre for every branch in the party, from the provincial level to the subprovincial. Thus, he maintains definitive control over the local organization, which plays a key role in intraparty elections. In the words of an AKP member whom Baykan quoted in his recent study of the party organization, "No one could remain within the organization, in central or provincial branches, against the will of Erdoğan."[94]

Such a tightly controlled structure alienated and marginalized liberals to a great extent and led to heavy recruitment of rank-and-file loyal to Erdoğan's faction. For instance, a successful businessman in Konya, a conservative city in central Turkey, joined the AKP to establish the party's local branch in 2001. He hoped that the AKP would meet the

---

[93] Kumbaracıbaşı, *Turkish Politics and the Rise of the AKP*, 154.
[94] Baykan, *The Justice and Development Party in Turkey*, 213.

needs of the people in a more participatory manner. By 2007, he was deeply disappointed with the top-down management style and lack of autonomy in local branches.[95] Realizing that the AKP was like "any other party" in its centralized decision-making, he resigned from his post and left the party.

Erdoğan's growing faction used its tight control over the party's local organization to sideline its rivals in vertical power games. More specifically, they employed regional rotation and liquidation of local branches. For instance, Şener's supporters in his hometown Sivas were purged and replaced with Erdoğan's supporters.[96] Similarly, Arınç lost his electoral bastion, Manisa, when Erdoğan decided to nominate him from another city (Bursa) where Arınç lacked local support. Without strong ties to their constituencies, these leaders were largely marginalized in the party. Şener, for instance, left the party in 2007, while Arınç stayed and continued to serve in government positions until 2015. He remained a vocal critique of party leadership and raised his objections to Erdoğan privately and publicly, with limited impact.

Gül's election as president in 2007 also facilitated Erdoğan's dominance in the party. The presidency was somewhat a symbolic and non-partisan position in the Turkish parliamentary system back in 2007. Upon his election, Gül had to resign from the AKP, losing his connection to the party base and leaving liberals in the party without a leader. Without a strong contender, Erdoğan strategically sidelined other liberal figures after 2007. Those prominent figures with significant expertise who were recruited by Gül, such as Yalçınbayır, Yakış, Atalay, and Ergin, among others, lost their positions in the party. Only Babacan and Ahmet Davutoğlu kept their positions and served in the cabinet until 2015 and 2016, respectively. Both finally resigned from the party in 2018 to establish their own parties.

In their place, Erdoğan recruited new members to strengthen his dominant coalition. Most of these figures were career politicians. Two of them are worth mentioning. Süleyman Soylu and Numan Kurtulmuş, two vocal critics of the government, had led their own, rather small, parties until 2012 when Erdoğan invited them to the AKP with promises of public office and top leadership positions. Both leaders hence received selective incentives to join Erdoğan's dominant coalition. Given substantial power, they accepted the invitation and changed their political positions accordingly. Since these figures owed their newfound positions to the leader, they had the incentive to remain loyal to him and execute his policies.

---

[95] Interview with a local businessman, November 14, 2007.
[96] Interview with Halil İbrahim Yenigün, June 4, 2014.

Gül, in the meantime, witnessed his shrinking influence over the party. Several prominent figures from the party were disillusioned and regretted Gül's election as president. For them, the party needed a strong leader who could counterbalance Erdoğan. Gül had performed this critical function until 2007, after which Erdoğan lacked any internal checks or balances over his authority. Witnessing the new direction of the party he had established with his colleagues, Gül also expressed his regret in becoming president and leaving the party.[97]

Some could argue that Gül enabled most of Erdoğan's policies during his term as president (2007–14). Indeed, Gül vetoed only 4 out of 800 items of legislation that his former party passed in parliament, including controversial legislation regarding the consumption of alcoholic drinks, internet regulations, and judicial independence.[98] Rather than indicating an ideological convergence between the two leaders, I suggest, Gül's conciliatory attitude shows three things. First, Islamist political culture in Turkey had been quite careful not to publicize internal disagreements in the party (unlike the center–left tradition in the country). Coming from this tradition and the ranks of the AKP, Gül preferred on multiple occasions to work behind closed doors to express his concern rather than publicly vetoing a legislative bill.[99] Besides, unlike Erdoğan, he often preferred conciliation over confrontation. Second, by the time such controversial legislation came before Gül after 2011, Erdoğan was already at the peak of his power. Gül's veto, therefore, would not have changed anything partly because his ties to the party were overwhelmed by Erdoğan's dominance, and partly because the president could only veto an item of legislation once. In the case parliament returned the bill without changing it, the president had to approve it or escalate the crisis by taking the bill to the Constitutional Court. In key pieces of legislation Gül left the final say to the court rather than confronting Erdoğan. Finally, Gül also received his fair share of collective and selective incentives under Erdoğan's leadership. Erdoğan agreed to nominate Gül as the AKP's presidential candidate in 2007 despite intense pressure from the armed forces and judiciary. When his election stalled due to an unwarranted interpretation of the voting process, the party called for early elections and came out victorious. Soon after, Gül was elected Turkey's first president from the ranks of an Islamist party, which was a major event in secular Turkey. One could claim that he served as the head of the Turkish state, thanks to the popularity of the AKP. All three factors probably

---

[97] Sever, *Abdullah Gül ile 12 Yıl Yaşadım, Gördüm, Yazdım*.
[98] *Cumhuriyet*, "İşte Gül'ün Köşk Karnesi."
[99] Sever, *Abdullah Gül ile 12 Yıl Yaşadım, Gördüm, Yazdım*.

played a role in Gül's presidential style. Yet given growing ideological differences between the two leaders, Gül could not remain silent longer, as I will discuss later.

After his term ended in 2014, Gül attempted to return to the AKP. Erdoğan, however, was not willing to share his power with Gül anymore. So he made sure the party congress convened before Gül's term ended. This move made it practically impossible for him to return to the party's leadership. After the congress, Gül's ties to the party were almost completely cut off. Despite being one of the founders, he was not even invited to the party's major events in subsequent years. The AKP had become a leader's party with Erdoğan, one of the three founders of the AKP, sidelining the other two.

In short, Erdoğan monopolized the recruitment (and promotion) process at different levels of the party and provided significant incentives to party members to join and then stay in his coalition. His faction's control over the incentive structure allowed it to build a dominant alliance using political positions in parliament, cabinet, municipalities, state bureaucracy, and the party apparatus as rewards for their supporters. Dengir Mir Mehmet Fırat, Erdoğan's close aide between 2002 and 2007, concurs:

> Erdoğan established dominance by way of appointing his team in the Istanbul municipality, close friends, and family members to executive committees and the parliament. This parliamentary group follows what Erdoğan orders to the letter. There are no more people left in the party to defend the party program or raise objections to the leader.[100]

In the end, as Yalçınbayır told me in an interview, "The party platform has been suspended ... [and] the party cannot go back to its basic principles due to self-interest. Deputies are interested in reelection, climbing up the ladder, maintaining their status and positions."[101]

Such close control over incentives (and disincentives through sanctions) allowed Erdoğan's faction to co-opt many members in the party and amass enough power to sideline liberals. That is how the AKP has fallen under his almost complete control.

Party Finance

Party finance also played a critical role in Erdoğan's rising dominance. From the outset, he commanded financial resources essential for the

---

[100] Ongun, "Fıratla söyleşi."
[101] Interview with Ertuğrul Yalçınbayır, January 13, 2017.

party's survival. In an interview, Yarbay underlined the significance of party finance for controlling the organization. When the party was established, Yarbay noted, it had two major financial sources: Erdoğan's personal contributions and state support for the parliamentary group.[102] Yarbay claimed that when the party rented its headquarters in Ankara, Erdoğan paid the rent in full. None of the seventy-three founders made any contribution.[103] Although it is still not clear how he amassed so much financial power, it is safe to assume that his tenure as Istanbul's mayor allowed him to build strong ties with private financiers, which he would bolster after 2003.

Liberals, in contrast, indirectly contributed to party finances. All political parties with a parliamentary group receive public funds to finance their electoral campaigns. Since liberals formed the AKP's parliamentary group, they facilitated the transfer of funds to the party. Yet it was still the party leader who had discretion over party finances. So although the party received funds, thanks to the liberals, it was Erdoğan who ended up allocating these resources. His already strong position in party finance hence became ever more pronounced, allowing him to strengthen his ties with local branches. For instance, Erdoğan allocated 30 percent of the party budget to local party organizations, creating a strong material incentive for local leaders to remain loyal to party leadership. Such positive material incentives, as Ayan asserts, helped consolidate Erdoğan's control within the party.[104]

Erdoğan's access to private resources only expanded over the years as the party turned into a dominant force in Turkish politics in successive electoral victories. The party, under his leadership, rapidly forged crony ties to businessmen.[105] As I discussed elsewhere, Erdoğan used his position as the prime minister to build a dependent business clientele through an elaborate system of rewards and punishment. The ruling party distributed public tenders and resources to its supporters in the business community in exchange for their loyalty and political support. Such contributions ranged from in-kind donations to the party to campaign finance.[106] Hence, he emerged as the interlocutor between the state and his cronies and amassed substantial financial power for his faction. Businesses in construction, energy, and media turned out to be key sectors in this process.

[102] Interview with Ersönmez Yarbay, June 24, 2014. And *Hürriyet*, "Hazine'nin aslan payı DSP'ye."
[103] Interview with Ersönmez Yarbay, June 24, 2014.
[104] Ayan, "Authoritarian Party Structures in Turkey."
[105] I have detailed these processes elsewhere with a co-author. See Esen and Gumuscu, "Building a Competitive Authoritarian Regime."
[106] For further details, see Esen and Gumuscu, "Why Did Turkish Democracy Collapse?" and Esen and Gumuscu, "Building a Competitive Authoritarian Regime."

It was not only the party's business cronies that received government largesse though. The members of Erdoğan's coalition also made handsome profits, thanks to their loyalty to the party leader. The graft probe of 2013 revealed some of the corrupt links ministers and mayors built via lucrative deals using their public office. Erdoğan, in short, promised appealing material incentives as well as political advancement to his supporters within and outside the party.

Of course, liberals also had access to financial support from outsiders, though such support remained limited since Erdoğan sanctioned business owners who supported his rivals through politicized economic bureaucracy such as the tax authorities. In the end, the fact that liberals did not directly control the party or state coffers deprived them of crucial resources. The control Erdoğan possessed over public and private resources, in contrast, fed a virtuous cycle of dominance for electoralists.

Communication within and outside the Party Organization

Internal and external communication prove equally significant in building a dominant coalition in political parties. Erdoğan's faction made critical advances in commanding both resources at the expense of liberals. As the party leadership subdued local branches, it also controlled internal communication. The party organs in charge of media and external and internal communication played a central role. Erdoğan often appointed his most trusted aides to such positions and relied on them to control internal communication. They, for instance, built a centralized computer system that integrated all local branches to the party headquarters. All campaign materials, regular party issues, directives regarding crises, and regular interaction with the party constituency were disseminated from the headquarters to local branches. The party also organized regular training for its cadres, whose content was designed by party leadership. That is why many conversations I had in the field with local party officials echoed Erdoğan's assertions almost verbatim.

Perhaps as important, if not more, for building a dominant coalition has been external communication, namely the national media. Erdoğan's growing control over the media, thanks to his deepening ties with the business world, did not just help him build political dominance in the country but also allowed him to sideline his rivals within the party.

Erdoğan's crony ties with businesses turned out to be essential in media capture. His faction wielded control over the media via two main routes.[107]

---

[107] Esen and Gumuscu, "Rising Competitive Authoritarianism."

The government overtook newspapers and TV stations from their owners due to their financial troubles in the aftermath of the 2001 crisis and subsequently arranged for their sale to pro-AKP businessmen. Several network stations and dailies, for instance, changed hands after 2002.[108] At times, the government even provided cheap credit to potential buyers from public banks.[109]

Then, the government utilized state bureaucracy to put political and financial pressure on media companies in the country. In a key development in 2009, for instance, the tax agency fined the Doğan Media Company a total of US$3 billion for tax evasion after its newspapers published corruption stories involving AKP officials. In response to these measures, Doğan Media agreed to sell two widely circulated and well-established newspapers, *Milliyet* and *Vatan*, to a pro-Erdoğan businessman. Soon after their sale, the company negotiated a settlement with the government. A few years later, when the company returned to its neutral broadcasting policy, the government exerted greater pressure on Aydın Doğan, the main shareholder in the company. Doğan finally sold the remainder of his news outlets to the same pro-AKP businessman in 2018. As a result, the mainstream media in the country fell under government control.

This growing control over national media affected horizontal power games in two respects. First, pro-Erdoğan media reinforced his popularity and consolidated the AKP's dominance in Turkish politics. The party's sustained electoral success made it increasingly harder for internal opposition to challenge a party leader with extensive popular support and public resources. Second, media control reinforced the leadership's command over internal communication in the party. When Erdoğan's opponents could not use the rules or internal mechanisms of communication to reach the party base, they tried to bypass the party machine by reflecting some of these disagreements onto the national media, often without much impact. Erdoğan's faction capitalized on its command over the media to both silence and intimidate its opponents. Pro-Erdoğan columnists, for instance, frequently attacked his rivals in the party. Arınç and Gül were among chief targets due to their prominence as founding leaders. Before Gül's term ended as the president, several columnists in progovernment media launched a smear campaign to discredit him. Gül maintained his silence, but his wife broke hers in a reception where she conversed with an independent reporter. She said: "They [pro-Erdoğan columnists] hurt us. Mr. Gül did not say much because

---

[108] Jenkins, "AKP Strengthens Its Hold on the Turkish Media."
[109] Yılmaz, "Çalık'ın Kullandığı Kredinin Koşulları."

he is a polite man... Our experience during the February 28 process when my headscarf was questioned [by the secular media] paled in comparison... The attacks from pious–conservative circles hurt us the most." And she ended on a harsh note: "I'll start the real *intifada* [uprising]."[110] Although her anger did not turn into an uprising of any sort – most likely because her husband asked her to keep her silence – this brief statement sufficiently revealed the internal conflict between Gül and Erdoğan.

Erdoğan's faction also ordered news outlets to sanction other leaders to keep them practically invisible. Hence, pro-Erdoğan media closed the only communication channel his rivals could use to reach the party base. Monopolizing both internal and external communication, the dominant faction severed the connection between their rivals and supporters. Arınç discussed these sanctions in a televised interview broadcast on an independent news channel.[111] He claimed that he was barred from the public broadcast station as well as other networks supporting Erdoğan's faction. Davutoğlu also received his share of character assassination from the pro-Erdoğan media (and social media trolls) after becoming a major contender during his tenure as prime minister from 2014 to 2016, as I discuss next.

A Failed Attempt at Capturing the Party

As soon as Erdoğan got elected as the new president in 2014, he had to resign from the party per the constitution. But he also made sure that the party remained loyal to him. His former advisor and foreign minister Davutoğlu replaced him as the chairman and prime minister. To Erdoğan, he was a placeholder until the transition to a presidential system, his long-time goal, was completed; Davutoğlu, in contrast, was eager to establish his control over the party organization and remain a powerful prime minister. This was also an opportune moment for the intraparty opposition to capture the party in "Erdoğan's absence." Davutoğlu's attempt at capturing the party illustrates how vertical and horizontal power games affect outcomes in intraparty struggles.

When Davutoğlu took over the government, the AKP was going through a fierce battle with its former ally, the Gülen movement.[112] The

---

[110] Yetkin, "Hayrünnisa Gül: Asıl intifadayı ben başlatacağım!"
[111] *Eğrisi Doğrusu*, 29 January 2016: www.youtube.com/watch?v=QIseBWB07fc&feature=youtu.be
[112] Fethullah Gülen, an Islamic preacher, formed his religious movement in the late 1960s. By the 1990s, Gülen's followers had reached positions of influence in the state bureaucracy, judiciary, and academia and were well-organized among businessmen and journalists.

two partners had a fallout soon after they successfully liquidated the secular establishment. Afterward, the AKP government sought to limit the power and influence of the Gülen movement, while Gülenists deployed their bureaucratic weapons against the party via graft probes.[113] The year 2014 became a year of crisis for the AKP, which tried to control the damage caused by its former ally.

Partly because of such strains and partly due to corruption scandals, the AKP lost its parliamentary majority in June 2015 elections for the first time since 2002.[114] The only way to stay in power was to form a coalition government. Davutoğlu proved to be more inclusionary than Erdoğan and signaled his willingness to form a coalition with the secular CHP. He soon started talks. Both Gül and Arınç supported this initiative. Arınç endorsed the values of pluralism, respect, and deliberation, echoing Gül in his support for a coalition government in the party's highest organs and cabinet meetings. Arınç argued that the voters had indeed expressed their preference for pluralism and deliberation.

Erdoğan, however, disagreed. He derailed the coalition talks between the AKP and the CHP, and pushed for snap elections. In November of the same year, Turkey had another general election. In between the two elections, electoralists in the party and their allies in the media marred coalition governments as essentially ineffective, meanwhile delegitimizing the opposition and polarizing society. A heightened security crisis in the country[115] also helped electoralists, who associated the deteriorating security situation with the AKP's waning power. Thanks to these factors, the party recovered its losses in November and formed a majority government.

Failed coalition talks showed Erdoğan's reluctance to let Davutoğlu take over the party. Davutoğlu, undeterred, attempted to form his own dominant coalition inside the party. In the party convention in September

---

[113] In retaliation for the Gülen movement's graft probes, the government ordered investigations of Gülen-affiliated media organizations, which then resulted in the arrests of several journalists and company CEOs, as well as business associations, firms, and banks. Erdoğan used his power and control over a set of key state institutions to cause significant financial losses to these companies.
[114] Özbey's interview with Davutoğlu, "Mesela Hakan Şükür Siyasi Ayaktı."
[115] The AKP started peace talks with the Kurdish insurgency in 2013 to end the conflict that had dated back to 1984. After several months of talks, the process collapsed due to disagreements in early 2015; in the summer of 2015, the two sides turned to violence, which quickly escalated. The Kurdish insurgency resorted to urban guerilla warfare and terrorist attacks in civilian centers, while the government started a military campaign against the Kurdish insurgency and punished supporters of the pro-Kurdish party through curfews and forced migration. For details, see Aydın and Emrence, "Politics of Confinement."

2015, he prepared his list for the executive committees. New central organs could hand Davutoğlu control of the organization. To expand his intra-party coalition, Davutoğlu visited estranged liberals and solicited the support of the party's founders, including Gül and Arınç. Although they had their differences, both leaders openly supported Davutoğlu's bid for leadership in the 2015 party congress.

Erdoğan, as expected, intervened. His strong grip over the party organization proved effective. In fact, before leaving the party in 2014, he had changed local branches in 40 cities and more than 300 districts.[116] He was still powerful in vertical power games. Using his personal clout over party delegates, he had his faction put together an alternative list for executive committees. Erdoğan then threatened Davutoğlu with a contested internal election unless he agreed to include Erdoğan loyalists in his lists. Since Erdoğan commanded the support of party delegates, Davutoğlu had to back down to maintain his position as the chairman. The new committee included Erdoğan's son-in-law, Berat Albayrak, among other loyalists and excluded several Davutoğlu supporters such as Ali Babacan, Sadettin Ergin, Mehmet Şimşek, and Beşir Atalay. Davutoğlu thus failed to capture the party. In the end, the AKP remained under Erdoğan's control.

Davutoğlu led the party for the next eight months. Yet his desire to follow an independent policy agenda and commitment to the parliamentary system clashed with Erdoğan's unfading desire to switch to presidentialism. To undercut Davutoğlu's resistance, Erdoğan loyalists lobbied to limit the chairman's prerogatives during an executive committee meeting in April 2016.[117] In the following weeks, a website called the Pelican Brief, likely on Erdoğan's orders, launched a smear campaign and attacked Davutoğlu's policies. The group that ran the site had ties with Erdoğan's son-in-law, who had recently joined the party's executive committee. Conceding defeat, Davutoğlu resigned from his post, leaving his place to a long-time Erdoğan loyalist, Binali Yıldırım.

Electoralists at the Helm: The AKP Pivots to the Milli Görüş Line

As the Ankara group lost its access to organizational resources in favor of Erdoğan's wing, the party's course changed dramatically. The AKP that had undersigned democratic reforms between 2002 and 2007 was gone; in its stead came an AKP that pursued majoritarianism, instrumentalism,

---

[116] Bulut, "AK Parti'de Büyük Değişim."
[117] Özbey's interview with Davutoğlu, "Mesela Hakan Şükür Siyasi Ayaktı."

exclusion, and polarization. Early political liberalism and pluralism left its place to blunt electoralism.

Many argue that the AKP under electoralists headed by Erdoğan is a populist party without an ideology. I disagree. The AKP's populism under Erdoğan's undisputed leadership is deeply embedded in Islamism. As Tuğal asserts, Islam – as interpreted by the party elite – actively shapes this populism and defines the boundaries of inclusion and exclusion.[118] Accordingly, those who primarily identify with Islam are the real "people," and others are the "heathen" elite who oppress Muslims. This same polarized worldview informed the Milli Görüş ideology. It also informed electoralists' vision, headed by Erdoğan, who after consolidating their power revived populist Islamism.

The party's practice of democracy hence aligned with "righteous majoritarianism." This sense of moral superiority stems from its self-identification with Islam. Electoralists deem their party as the protector of Islam in the country: As long as the AKP remains in power, the Turkish people could express their Muslim identity.[119] Yet to be a "true Muslim," one must also support the AKP. Otherwise, as Çaylak posits, one loses their faith. Since the AKP embodies Islam, supporting it becomes an expression of faith.[120] Criticizing the government, by way of contrast, means criticizing Islam; dissent means being unfaithful.

The AKP under electoralist (or Islamist populist) dominance aims to erect an Islamic society using the state's power without necessarily changing its fundamental structure. Democracy, or elections (as they see it), has remained both a key instrument toward this aim and a major source of legitimacy. Accordingly, the Turkish people are Muslim; Muslims compose the "true people" in the country, and the AKP is their true and only representative. Using state power to Islamize society, for electoralists, is therefore a democratic act.

So is limiting the power and presence of minorities (political or religious) and their representatives in the country. The opposition parties, electoralists deem, are illegitimate – not only because they keep losing elections but also because they represent "a rabid minority" (*azgın azınlık*). As such, they do not deserve tolerance, engagement, or equal treatment from the government. Because they carry ill intentions, their political rights and civil liberties can be limited without any "democratic repercussions." As the representative of the "real people," the AKP has no obligation to tolerate its opponents or commit to institutional forbearance.

[118] Tuğal, "Islamism in Turkey."
[119] Çınar, *Vesayetçi Demokrasiden "Milli" Demokrasiye.*
[120] Çaylak, "İslamcı Siyasette İktidar ve İtikat."

This hegemonic Islamism informs AKP's illiberal and authoritarian practices under electoralist rule. I now turn to details about the anti-pluralist, instrumentalist, and majoritarian practices of the AKP government. I will trace these attitudes as well as internal disagreements between different factions through the colonization of the state, constitutional reforms, Islamization efforts, and the party's treatment of the opposition.

Colonizing the State

The year 2007 was a fateful year for the AKP. President Sezer's term ended that year, and a new one had to be elected, as I discussed earlier. Although a mostly symbolic position, the president nevertheless had some say in top bureaucratic appointments and oversight over the government and parliament. Still suspect of the AKP's democratic commitments, the secular establishment, including the military and the judiciary supported by the main opposition party (CHP), wanted parliament to elect a nonpartisan president. Secular civil society mobilized in public protests to demand a non-Islamist candidate. Then the Chief of General Staff increased the pressure on the government, with a formal statement published on its website. The top brass, as the statement revealed, preferred "a genuinely secular president, not a fake one." In response, the AKP called for early elections. In July 2007, the party won 47 percent of the votes, registering a thirteen-point increase in its vote share. This victory handed the party a clear mandate to nominate its own presidential candidate. A couple of months after the election, Gül was nominated and elected as the next president of the republic.

Undeterred by the AKP's strong electoral showing, the following year the prosecutor general filed a closure case against the party for allegedly undermining the secular nature of the republic. The Constitutional Court refused to ban the party but agreed that the AKP had indeed been involved in antisecular activities. The severity of such actions, the court deemed, did not warrant party closure yet required financial sanctions.

In retribution, the Erdoğan government capitalized on its popular mandate to liquidate the veto players, specifically the military and the judiciary. Certainly, the civilianization of Turkish politics and marginalization of the military were welcome steps toward democratic consolidation. Both liberals and electoralists agreed on this goal. Judicial reform was more complex, though, and herein electoralists diverged from liberals.

For electoralists, elections provided the party with a mandate to run the country as they liked without much hindrance. That is why the

AKP did not stop once it neutralized the military. It soon moved on to court-packing to politicize the referees who should remain neutral for a well-functioning democracy. These referees formed the backbone of horizontal accountability, and their politicization killed any hope of attaining liberal democracy in the short run. The party's "democratic" crusade against the secular establishment as a result turned into an effort to conquer the state, as Somer aptly puts it.[121]

This was a clear return to the Milli Görüş vision, which instrumentalized democratic procedures to colonize the state with pious and loyal cadres. This desire partly stems from Islamism's institutional underdevelopment, which lends itself, as Roy suggests, to a political imagination that is based on individual virtue.[122] So building a proper Islamic polity depends largely on converting individuals to "true Muslims" and implanting them in the state bureaucracy. When pious Muslims take over the state apparatus, their proper behavior will remedy all ills. With this intention, over the years the electoralists have aimed to colonize the state bureaucracy to recruit their supporters to civil service.

At first, electoralists relied on the Gülen movement and its "pious" cadres to replace the bureaucratic corps that the government had inherited from its secular predecessors. The Gülen movement (or Hizmet as their members called it) was established in 1966 with the goal of fighting communism and raising a "golden generation" that would be pious, hardworking, and well-educated, with a strong sense of solidarity and "military-like discipline."[123] The leader of the movement, Fethullah Gülen, was wary of the secular regime's repression, rejected explicit political mobilization, and preferred to build a network of educational institutions, CSOs, media companies, and businesses motivated by Islamic principles. A chief, yet less publicized, objective of Fethullah Gülen remained colonization of the state bureaucracy with the members of the "golden generation" through the manipulation of bureaucratic recruitment processes.[124]

The AKP–Gülen alliance quickly purged secularist bastions in the state and silenced critics in the society. The Gülen movement was particularly fit for this quest, since they had been infiltrating the security

---

[121] For further discussion of the AKP's intention to conquer the state, see Somer, "Conquering versus Democratizing the State."
[122] Roy, *The Failure of Political Islam*.
[123] Yavuz, *Toward an Islamic Enlightenment*.
[124] These manipulative tactics included widespread cheating in centrally administered tests and lot-drawing in bureaucratic appointments.

bureaucracy and the judiciary since the 1980s. The Gülenist cadres in the judiciary and the police forces tried several people from the Turkish armed forces, CSOs, civil service, and the media in politicized trials.

During these trials, the judges and the public prosecutors – affiliated with the Gülen network – frequently violated the fundamental rights of the defendants. Prolonged pretrial detention became the norm. The prosecutors relied extensively on secret witness testimony and fabricated evidence, frequently violating due process. The courts also imposed a media blackout on these probes, thereby limiting public scrutiny over the cases. Such violations deteriorated Turkey's democracy scores in international indices; in its 2013 report, for instance, Freedom House lowered Turkey's civil liberties score. The report posited that a lower score was in order

due to the pretrial detention of thousands of individuals – including Kurdish activists,[125] journalists, union leaders, students, and military officers – in campaigns that many believe to be politically motivated. The conduct of the trials, together with mass arrests of Kurdish activists in other cases, prompted widespread concern about the government's commitment to civil liberties and the rule of law.[126]

In the meantime, the AKP government appointed its loyalists to key institutions that it cleared of secularists. As Yavuz reports, the AKP government had indeed ceded control of the ministries of education, internal affairs, and judiciary to the Gülen movement.[127] The AKP–Gülen alliance thus colonized the state by replacing merit with ideological and political criteria in bureaucratic appointments to remove the remnants of the secular establishment.[128]

Yet when the marriage between the two partners ended with an ugly divorce after 2012, the AKP turned to other religious orders to fill the posts left by purged Gülenists. Recent reports from bureaucratic recruitment processes reveal that the AKP seeks signifiers of religiosity or references from pro-AKP religious orders in job interviews as criteria for recruitment.[129]

---

[125] The Kurdish political movement was not spared from the widespread crackdown. In separate trials, thousands of activists were arrested and kept in prisons without a fair trial.
[126] Puddington, "Freedom in the World 2013."
[127] Yavuz, "Cemaatçiler savaşı kaybetmiş Naziler gibi! Hoca'ya karşı isyan var."
[128] Interestingly, more liberal figures such as Cemil Çiçek and Beşir Atalay in the party frequently complained and critiqued the Gülenists' increasing involvement in decision-making processes and presence in the state bureaucracy. For more, see Yavuz, *Toward an Islamic Enlightenment*, 218. Similarly, Bülent Arınç frequently voiced his concerns regarding prolonged pretrial detention in these trials.
[129] See Pehlivan and Terkoğlu, *Metastaz*.

Constitutional Reform: Institutionalization of Majoritarianism

Electoralists' righteous majoritarianism has also informed the party's handling of constitutional reform. Unlike Tunisia and Egypt, Turkey has not undergone a revolution, but it certainly went through a fundamental transformation. A central part of this transformation involved constitutional change that essentially redesigned the entire political system in two major referenda in 2010 and 2017. The first referendum, approved by 58 percent of voters, redesigned the entire judicial system. The second referendum, approved by a slim margin, replaced the parliamentary system with executive presidency. Both processes were quite exclusionary, and the goal was to capture control of the judicial branch and eradicate checks and balances over the executive. The new system entrenched majority rule and was perfectly democratic from the viewpoint of electoralists because it received the support of the people. The entire reform process, however, remained highly exclusionary and manipulative without much concern for pluralism and minority rights.

The 2010 Referendum: Capturing the Courts Indicative of electoralists' majoritarian tendencies and reluctance to pursue democratic consolidation was their insistence on redesigning the judiciary. Until 2010, Erdoğan had frequently complained about higher courts' decisions to overrule the AKP legislation. For him, courts prevented the government from doing its job. He had a clear aversion to judicial oversight. To construct a "friendly" judiciary, the AKP submitted amendments to change the structure of the higher courts and the Supreme Council of Judges and Prosecutors (HSYK), charged to manage the internal affairs of the judiciary. Basically, the amendments aimed to hand the government control over judicial appointments and drastically reduced judicial independence with a new incentive structure.[130]

Throughout the process, the AKP acted in a unilateral and exclusionary fashion without much input from the opposition or CSOs. The opposition remained deeply concerned with the amendments that restructured the judiciary and demanded separate votes for each amendment. The AKP ignored their objections.

A major and the possibly only noncontroversial change in the reform package involved individual citizens' access to the Constitutional Court. A welcome step in the right direction, the amendment was introduced in the package, thanks to then President Gül's efforts.[131] Later, this clause turned out to be a key mechanism for the restitution of plaintiffs' rights, which had been systematically violated by the Gülenists in politicized trials.

---

[130] Mert, "Iki kere hayır!"
[131] Sever, *Abdullah Gül ile 12 Yıl Yaşadım, Gördüm, Yazdım*, 118.

The party also chose to polarize society throughout the referendum campaign. For the AKP, there were only two camps: the forces of democracy (read: the AKP and the will of the majority) and the forces of autocracy. Those who criticized the government or opposed constitutional reform were all "coup plotters"; they were authoritarian, disrespectful, and dismissive of the will, norms, and values of the people.[132] There was no room for discussion. Everybody had to pick a side. Erdoğan even threatened the largest business association in the country, TUSIAD, which had expressed its reservations about the constitutional changes.[133] Amid such an environment of deep polarization, deliberation and engagement were the main victims.

The referendum passed with 58 percent of the votes in September 2010. Soon after, the electoralists along with Gülenists set to colonize the Turkish judiciary. In the first postreferendum HSYK elections, for instance, the bureaucrats of the Ministry of Justice prepared and circulated a list of candidates they wanted elected. This list included several bureaucrats who had been working closely with the government since 2002. Not surprisingly, every single name on the list was elected, while no other candidate supported by other groups joined the new HSYK. The new council ruled in favor of prosecutors and judges aligned with the government's position in highly politicized trials such as Ergenekon, Balyoz, and Denizfeneri.[134] Such decisions spurred debates on the independence of the judiciary. The then Chairman of the Constitutional Court Haşim Kılıç, known for his distance from the secular establishment, critically assessed these changes:

Rule of law is a very important instrument that transforms political, social, and cultural life. It is essential that the transformative power of this instrument is not used for a tutelary system that disciplines society but for distributing equality and freedom for all. It is critical that we avoid the mistake of using the ongoing reforms to take revenge for the past. We would like to believe that a true change, which excludes the continuation of the authoritarian–tutelary system with a new set of actors, is possible... [A] fast and effective judiciary insulated from all forms

---

[132] NTV's interview with Erdoğan: www.ntv.com.tr/turkiye/erdogan-hayir-diyen-darbecidir,bQHGDGasykazMmycFR3roA

[133] Erdoğan was deeply disturbed by the neutrality of the main business circles over the course of the campaign. Calling on TUSIAD, he warned: "If you do not pick a side, you will get disposed." See *Milliyet*, "Bitaraf olan bertaraf olur." Such pressures on CSOs, business associations, and trade unions, only increased after 2010.

[134] In Germany, a charity called Lighthouse, established and operated by Turks, was prosecuted and tried for embezzlement and fraud. During the trial, several ties to Lighthouse charity in Turkey and the AKP were alleged by the employees. An investigation was started in Turkey in light of this testimony.

of ideological and political influence is necessary for the happiness of our people and should be integral to our efforts for further reforms.[135]

Kılıç's position deepened the concerns that the constitutional reform compromised judicial independence. His warnings to the government fell on deaf ears.

As the president throughout this process, Gül insistently supported judicial independence. Arınç sided with this view, as well, and claimed that the Turkish judicial system was in chaos due to political influences. For Arınç, the AKP's original mission was to restore justice and the rule of law; revanchist attitudes – as exemplified by Erdoğan – were wrong and in violation of such principles. However, their criticisms were moot since neither of the leaders had real power anymore.

The 2010 referendum marked a turning point after which the judiciary became increasingly politicized. The momentum increased after electoralists and Gülenists parted ways in 2013. The AKP established complete control over the judicial branch to eradicate its former allies from the courts. Lawyers with close ties to the party were appointed justices, many also joining the higher courts. Rule of law was the main victim in this incentive structure. In its stead came a politicized judiciary and the rule of the majority.

Building a New Political System: From Parliamentarism to the Executive Presidency The colonization of the state was the first step toward the overhaul and redesign of the political system. In line with its hegemonic Islamism, the electoralists set to replace the parliamentary system with an executive presidency. Erdoğan was not particularly fond of the Turkish parliamentary system, which dated back to 1920. His faction wanted a "Turkish style" presidentialism, whose main features remained largely vague. As its details clarified, the system turned out to be a highly centralized presidency with weak checks and balances. Such a system boded quite well for majoritarian and winners-take-all politics. It also conformed to the Islamist political imagination, which rests on the centrality of a pious leader. The presidential system as envisioned by electoralists, I argue, carries an elective affinity with hegemonic Islamism and its righteous majoritarian tendencies.

Elected as the president with limited powers under the old system in 2014, Erdoğan's chief aim was to establish a presidential system with executive authority. To realize this goal, he needed the support of his party and allies in the media. He also needed a prime minister who would

---

[135] *Hürriyet*, "Siyasetin yargıyı kuşatmasına izin vermeyeceğiz".

agree with his goals. That was why his faction replaced Davutoğlu with Yıldırım in 2016. Only two months after this swap, the Gülen movement mobilized its cadres within the Turkish armed forces to stage a coup against the AKP government. The coup failed.[136] But it allowed Erdoğan to aggressively pursue his plans to transition to an executive presidency. The AKP government, now under Yıldırım's premiership and practically under Erdoğan's control, imposed a state of emergency and suspended civil liberties. The system thus turned into de facto presidentialism with no checks. Erdoğan started to lead cabinet meetings, sidelined parliament, and ruled the country singlehandedly through executive decrees. Using the putsch as a pretext, Erdoğan used decrees to purge more than one hundred thousand civil servants from the state and hundreds of academics. He closed tens of CSOs, broadcasting stations, newspapers, and websites. Electoralists in the parliamentary group kept extending emergency rule for months.

Abdullah Gül, with no official position in the state or the party after 2014, voiced his objections to prolonged emergency law. He repeatedly urged the government to go back to democratic rule as soon as possible. His calls were ignored. Remaining liberal figures in the party also opposed presidentialism. They too were ignored. Meanwhile, electoralists capitalized on emergency rule and submitted the presidential system to a referendum in April 2017. The constitutional redesign process was unilateral, imposed by the AKP's electoralists without much input from other stakeholders, and completed amid rapid democratic backsliding. Naysayers competed with the government and its nationalist allies on a quite uneven playing field and lost by a narrow margin.[137] De facto presidentialism was now institutionalized. In May, Erdoğan returned to the AKP as chairman. A year later, he was elected the first president in the new system and continued to rule by decree, as sanctioned by the amended constitution.

"Islamist Presidentialism" If the new executive presidency has an elective affinity with the AKP's hegemonic Islamism, which rests on electoralism and majoritarianism, this stems from the centrality of a virtuous leader in the Islamic political imagination. Electoralists' revived this ideal by establishing the rule of "a pious leader" in Turkey.

The political writings of Necip Fazıl Kısakürek, the chief ideologue of Turkish Islamism, from the 1940s to the 1970s were critical in this

---

[136] For a discussion of factors that led to the failure of the coup attempt, see Esen and Gumuscu, "Turkey: How the Coup Failed."
[137] Esen and Gumuscu, "A Small Yes for Presidentialism."

regard. Milli Görüş indeed received great inspiration from Necip Fazıl, and the AKP under electoralists' domination revived his imagination and implemented his ideas.

AKP's presidentialism strongly resembles Necip Fazıl's ideal political system, which he called *başyücelik*. In this system, all political power rests in the hands of a virtuous and pious leader, whom he calls *başyüce* (the exalted one). For Necip Fazıl, the *başyüce* is a symbol and embodiment of the nation; he is the most virtuous, knowledgeable, and reasoned member of his nation. His decrees serve as the law while all branches of the government, including the judiciary, operate and serve justice in his name. Necip Fazıl equates *başyüce* with what Islamic sources refer to as *ululemr*, discussed below.[138] The new presidential system enacted with the 2018 elections, with its highly centralized power structure and weak checks and balances, closely resembles Necip Fazıl's utopia.[139]

Erdoğan's growing personality cult with an increasingly Islamic quality also echoes Necip Fazıl's vision. To cultivate the image of a pious leader, Erdoğan has frequently displayed his religious credentials. He regularly attends Friday prayers or publicly recites verses from the Qur'an in Arabic during funerals, mosque openings and visits, cemetery visits, commemorations, school appearances, and even on his foreign trips. Progovernment media widely covers such stories to build Erdoğan's cult of personality as the pious leader of all Muslims.[140]

Such stories are largely welcomed by the party base. In 2015, I attended an AKP rally in Istanbul organized to celebrate the conquest of Istanbul by Mehmed II. The space was filled with posters carrying Islamic symbols and references. Many supporters showed up with banners calling Erdoğan "God's gift for the Muslim world." One banner read: "We elected you the president for the entire *ummah*." AKP officials at different ranks have also echoed similar sentiments. For one deputy, Erdoğan was God-sent and a second prophet; he was a leader who shares God's qualities. For another, it was an act of faith to touch him, and his presence required prayers to express gratitude to God for sending Erdoğan.[141]

This personality cult has gained a semi-messianic quality in the wake of the July 2016 coup attempt.[142] In order to evoke emotional and religious

---

[138] Kara, *Türkiye'de İslamcılık Düşüncesi*.
[139] Aybak, "The Sultan Is Dead, Long Live 'Başyüce' Erdoğan Sultan!" Yavuz, "A Framework for Understanding the Intra-Islamist Conflict between the AK Party and the Gülen Movement."
[140] *AHaber*, "Başkan Recep Tayyip Erdoğan Köln'de Kur'an-ı Kerim okudu"; *Yeni Akit*, "Erdoğan Özbekistan'da Kur'an okudu."
[141] Çaylak, "İslamcı Siyasette İktidar ve İtikat," 33.
[142] For more on the coup attempt, see Yavuz, "A Framework for Understanding."

sentiments among AKP supporters, the party's PR team appropriated an Islamist poet's verses into a slogan: "*Ne yapsalar boş, göklerden gelen bir karar vardır*" [Their efforts are futile; a decree has come from heavens], to imply divine intervention in favor of Erdoğan.

Erdoğan's status was hence exalted, in the eyes of both his voters and pro-AKP intellectuals, to a divinely sanctioned leader. Some religious scholars also called him the *ululemr*, the executive and social authority for Muslims (*içtimai irade ve icra makamı*).[143] In Islamic tradition, ululemr refers to "a believer-ruler." Muslims, according to a common reading of the Qur'an, should obey the *ululemr*'s orders as they follow God's and the Prophet's commands.[144] These scholars have hence suggested that, as *ululemr* of Muslims, Erdoğan deserves almost total obedience. Donned with Islamic legitimacy and qualities, Erdoğan's personality cult revolves around the myth of a virtuous and pious semi-messianic leader whose rule is sanctioned by the Qur'an. In short, Erdoğan embodies Islam.

Islamizing Society

Electoralists' return to the Milli Görüş line did not end with the erection of a presidential system supported by Islamic references. It also involved the Islamization of the society through instrumentalization of the education system and state-controlled Diyanet (Directorate of Religious Affairs). This, according to their argument, was necessary for the defense of Islam. For electoralists, their electoral victories mandated such Islamization.

The Ministry of Education and Diyanet took the center stage in these efforts because the two agencies have worked to impose Islamic morality through (1) a dramatic expansion of the Diyanet's scope of activities and the politicization of its message and (2) making Imam Hatip schools central to the education system with the aspiration of raising "pious generations." These two mechanisms deserve further attention.

The Diyanet was established in 1924 to meet the demand for religious clerical personnel after the new republican elite abolished the Islamic institutional infrastructure inherited from the Ottoman state. The Diyanet has always played an important ideological role in serving the state.[145] Yet this mission was mostly above party politics and the institution remained loyal to republican principles. The AKP colonized the

---

[143] Karaman, "İtâat"; Hatipoğlu, "Ulu'l emre itaat nedir?"
[144] While this verse is open to different interpretations, the orthodox view is that the verse invokes total obedience to *ululemr*.
[145] For a detailed discussion, see Öztürk, "Turkey's Diyanet under AKP Rule."

Diyanet and transformed it into a political instrument as well as one of top-down Islamization. The Diyanet's growing prominence and politicization have practically ended Turkish secularism.

Accordingly, the Diyanet's budget, resources, personnel, and scope of activities have rapidly increased, particularly after 2010 when the AKP replaced the prosecular Ali Bardakoğlu with revisionist Mehmet Görmez as the head of the Diyanet. A new piece of legislation, passed the same year, expanded its organizational mission and strengthened its administrative capacity. Marking a key moment in its transformation, this legislative framework allowed the Diyanet to perform religious services outside of mosques, establish a new TV station, and expand its operations abroad.[146] To accommodate such changes, the AKP government allocated substantial resources to the directorate. Its personnel increased from 93,000 in 2009 to more than 140,000 in 2020[147] and its budget has increased seven-fold since 2006, surpassing several ministries and public agencies like the National Intelligence Agency.

A key target group for Diyanet's expanding scope includes children. Thanks to the AKP's education reforms, hundreds of Qur'an courses were opened for kindergarteners. Erdoğan personally supported the efforts to reach children: "It is essential that the Diyanet takes steps to pull children into the mosques," he said, "This is an army of 140,000. [...] If we are to build the future, we must strongly encourage a life centered around the mosque today, as we did yesterday."[148]

The Diyanet has also become increasingly politicized over the last decade and adopted, Öztürk finds, an ideological line synchronized with the ruling party's discourses and actions.[149] The changing content of the *khutba*s (sermons recited during Friday prayers) delivered by the directorate attests to this fact. Öngür, in his study of 1200 *khutbas*, finds that the Diyanet under AKP rule serves to build a religious identity that takes the Ottoman past as its reference point.[150]

The Diyanet's increasing politicization became evident during the coup attempt in July 2016. As the government tried to thwart the coup, the Diyanet deployed thousands of religious personnel in more than 80,000 mosques to mobilize the people against the coup.[151] Diyanet personnel recited the *sala* – customarily recited before funerals and Friday prayers – throughout the night all over the country, lending Islamic legitimacy to

---

[146] For more on the Diyanet's activities, see its website: www.diyanet.gov.tr/tr-TR
[147] NTV, "Artık bu yanlış tabuların yıkılması lazım."
[148] Ibid.
[149] Öztürk, "Turkey's Diyanet under AKP Rule," 620.
[150] Öngür, "Performing through Friday Khutbas."
[151] Esen and Gumuscu, "Turkey: How the Coup Failed."

the progovernment resistance to the coup. The mosques also invited ordinary people to resist the putschists by evoking Islamic sentiments. The Diyanet continued its unwavering support for the government after the faithful night. Its personnel attended daily democracy vigils and performed sermons in support of the government. In a vigil I attended in Kısıklı, Istanbul, on July 24, 2016, a religious official led a communal prayer that went as follows:

> We dedicate our prayers to our martyrs who lost their lives for democracy, the nation, *Islam*, and the flag on the night of July 15. Dear God, do not let those traitors hurt our homeland; eliminate the threats and traps posed against our *commander in chief*, our *ululemr*, our nation's and *the Muslim world's source of pride* Recep Tayyip Erdoğan. Dear God, we believe and have complete faith that Erdoğan is the hope of our nation and region, and of the *entire Islamic world*. Dear God, do not disappoint the hope of the *ummah*. Damn those who set traps and those who divide the *ummah* and the *infidel of Pennsylvania* [a reference to Gülen in his American exile], who is a traitor, who lacks honor, and who has *no faith or religion*. [...] He has no land, no nationality, *no faith or religion*. [...] In the past, coups would silence the call to prayers and *sala*s. Thanks to the will of God, the orders of our commander in chief and the chairman of the Diyanet, *sala*s and calls to prayer silenced the coup. There is no greater honor. [...] And I want you to continue attending the Democracy Vigils until our commander in chief ends them. [emphasis added]

As the excerpt from this sermon shows, Diyanet personnel have become a party to the political conflict between the ruling party and its former ally, both of which hold an Islamic orientation. Its officials also lent Islamic legitimacy to the AKP government and Erdoğan by calling him the *ululemr* and leader of the Muslim world while excommunicating Erdoğan's enemy Gülen.

Another key component of the AKP's efforts to Islamize society concerns education. The AKP seeks to instrumentalize the state apparatus to establish Islamic normativity in the society. In a public speech he delivered in 2012, Erdoğan declared that the AKP's primary goal as a political party is to raise "pious generations." These generations, he argued, would carry computers in one hand and the Qur'an in the other.[152] The goal was to raise the ideal youth, pious and moral – a youth who would defend Islam.[153]

To raise pious generations, Erdoğan followed the Milli Görüş prescription and treated Imam Hatip schools as a key means toward this end. Accordingly, the number of Imam Hatip schools under the AKP

---

[152] Erdoğan, "2012 Speech at AKP Weekly Meeting."
[153] Lüküslü, "Creating a Pious Generation," 640.

rule increased fourfold between 2002 and 2020, displaying a rapid uptick after 2011. In the same period, the number of students enrolled in these religious vocational schools increased tenfold to more than six hundred thousand. The government also changed the system so that thousands of students were forced to attend Imam Hatips, restricting their access to other schools. Only students with better academic performance could enter the national placement tests and pick distant schools listed by the Ministry of Education.[154] The government also allocated more resources to religious schools to improve the quality of facilities and to make them more appealing. In 2018, for instance, 23 percent of the government's education budget went to Imam Hatip schools, which hosted only 11 percent of the high school student cohort.[155]

For electoralists, the measures to Islamize society are perfectly compatible with democracy. The majority of the Turkish people are Muslims, and they supposedly demand a greater role for Islam in the society through their support for the party. Besides, the republican regime, they surmise, had undermined religious liberties for decades, so the government's measures count as normalization rather than top-down imposition. Such measures, hence, advance the rights and freedoms of "the real people" and, therefore, democracy. In 2018, Erdoğan clearly summarized this righteous majoritarianism and rather narrow conception of civil liberties:

> We freed our education system from tutelary policies. Our children are no longer discriminated on the basis of their belief, attire, outlook, and we *established freedom in our country*. [...] In the past 16 years, only the *terrorists'* and their supporters' *scope of activity has narrowed*. [...] No one has witnessed any erosion in their liberties or any intervention in their lives. [...] We will continue to develop democracy and expand freedoms and rights.[156] [emphasis added]

Yet the democracy and civil liberties scores reported by different institutions indicated otherwise. Rule of law and civil liberties declined rapidly after 2011, along with liberal democracy scores, following some improvement in AKP's first term in office, as Figure 6 shows.[157] The next section details how exactly these scores deteriorated.

---

[154] Çepni, "Her yer imam, her yer hatip! MEB imam hatipleri kılavuzda 'nitelikli' yaptı."
[155] Butler, "With More Islamic Schooling, Erdoğan Aims to Reshape Turkey."
[156] Erdoğan's speech at the opening ceremony of TÜGVA (Türkiye Gençlik Vakfı) Center: www.youtube.com/watch?v=y-DIk-p-JOo
[157] For more details on deteriorating rights and liberties, see Esen and Gumuscu, "Rising Competitive Authoritarianism in Turkey."

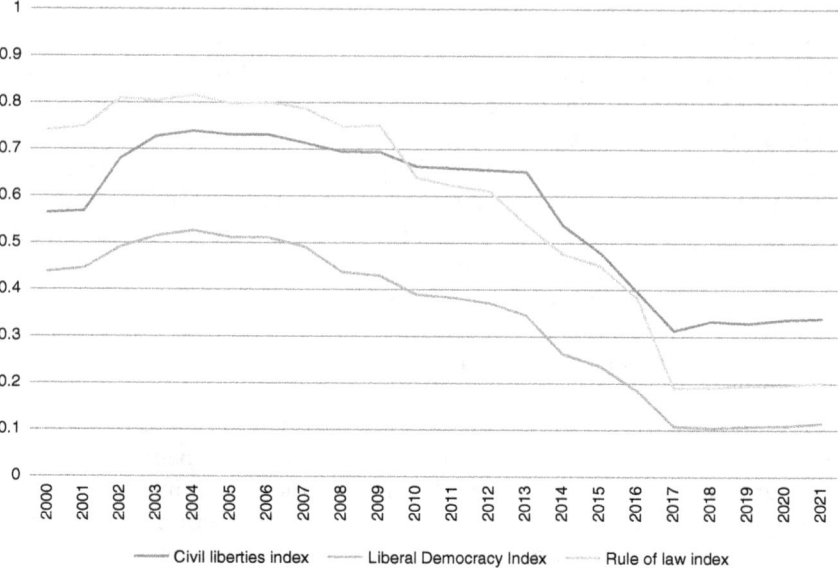

Figure 6 Liberal democracy in Turkey, 2002–2021
Source: Compiled by the author using V-Dem 12.0 data

Antipluralism: Silencing Critiques within and outside the Party

The electoralists' righteous majoritarianism precluded political pluralism, deliberation, and democratic engagement, and instead involved delegitimization of the opposition, polarization, and systematic violation of civil liberties: freedom of expression, press, assembly, and association (see Figure 6). As electoralists went in an increasingly hegemonic direction, liberals, now in a much weaker position, raised their objections to such authoritarian practices. Ergün, a prominent liberal voice who had also served as AKP deputy and minister, claimed that the party returned to the ideological line of the Milli Görüş and embraced its Islamic and communitarian character, while Erdoğan had become a leader of jihad much like Erbakan and the party platform had come to be based on a religious mission.[158] Yet the liberals were now too weak to impact the party trajectory. Soon, many of them left.

---

[158] Bora, *Cereyanlar*, 506; see also Ergün's memoirs, *Adım Adım Siyaset*. After resigning from the AKP in 2019, Ergün joined the DEVA Party established by liberal members of the AKP in 2020.

Delegitimization of the Opposition Electoralists eschewed political pluralism through delegitimizing dissent. To discredit all forms of opposition, the Erdoğan wing evoked Islamic sentiments, popular will, and nationalism. Per populist Islamism, as discussed earlier, the AKP constituency formed the real "people," and the rest were groups that had been Westernized and alienated from Turkish society and its cultural, religious, and historical realities. As such, they had illegitimate lifestyles and political preferences. This discourse severely undermined political pluralism in the country and exacerbated polarization. Eventually, polarization and delegitimization reached new heights with Erdoğan's faction calling the opposition "traitors," "terrorists," and the "enemy of the people," as illustrated by the quote above.

The CHP, Turkey's main opposition party, has been the primary target of electoralists' delegitimization campaign. The AKP leadership framed the contemporary CHP as a descendant of an authoritarian and elitist political tradition that is dismissive of the Islamic values of the Turkish society.[159] As such, the CHP is often presented as an anti-Islamic force in politics. Specifically since the 2011 elections, Erdoğan regularly depicted the CHP as the party that banned Islamic religious practices, used mosques as barns, and spoiled the call to prayer by translating it into Turkish.[160] He also leveraged the sectarian cleavage in the society by identifying the AKP with Sunni Islam and making frequent references to the Alevi origins of CHP's leader.[161]

A similar dismissive and delegitimizing attitude targeted the Kurdish movement. Unlike its relationship with the secular CHP, however, the AKP had a more complicated relationship with pro-Kurdish parties. On the one hand, the party competed with them over Kurdish support. On the other hand, the AKP attempted a few times to resolve the long-lasting Kurdish issue in collaboration with the Kurdish movement.[162]

---

[159] For examples of the AKP's framing of the CHP, see Erdoğan's various speeches during the 2009 municipal electoral campaign.

[160] See, for instance, Erdoğan's rally speech in Sivas in 2011: www.youtube.com/watch?v=iveRNyzlGt8. *Yeni Şafak*, "Dün nerede iseler bugün de oradalar."

[161] For a discussion of Erdoğan's discourse on the Alevi identity of his main opponent, see Ergin, "Erdoğan and CHP Leader's Alevi Origin" and Al Jazeera, "Erdoğan Slams CHP as Opposition March Nears Istanbul." As the AKP, under electoralists' influence, switched to majoritarianism and polarization, the CHP began to pursue a prodemocratic agenda. The party made alliances with other opposition parties and defended political rights and civil liberties against the AKP's systematic violations.

[162] The Turkish Republic is a centralized state based on Turkish nationalism. The legal framework of the republic does not recognize any ethnic groups other than Turkish national identity. Kurds form the largest ethnic minority in the country without any legal recognition. A Kurdish insurgency sought independence starting in the 1980s and has claimed more than 40,000 lives.

Specifically, the party initiated two peace processes in 2009 and later in 2013 and followed an accommodationist policy toward Kurds. Both processes were marked by inconsistencies and ambivalence, thanks to AKP's instrumentalism, pragmatism, as well as sharp pivots throughout.

The ideological underpinnings of the AKP's approach to the Kurdish question were also embedded in Islamism; Islamic solidarity not only recognized but also superseded ethnic differences and served as the social cement that would bind both Turks and Kurds. Erdoğan followed this formula to resolve the issue. In return, he expected Kurdish support for the presidential system. Yet by early 2015, the Kurdish movement grew wary of Erdoğan's rather narrow conception of Kurdish rights – limited to some cultural rights melted within an Islamic pot – and demanded official status for the Kurdish language, the right to instruction in their mother tongue, and recognition of Kurdish identity in the constitution. Erdoğan was not willing to give any of these rights. In the meantime, trust between the two parties rapidly eroded, as the Turkish government stood by as the Islamic State of Iraq and Syria (ISIS) placed a siege on a Kurdish region, Kobane, in Northern Syria.[163] In the June 2015 elections, the pro-Kurdish HDP clearly stated that they were against presidentialism. By the summer of 2015, the peace talks had come to an end; soon afterward, Erdoğan cracked down on the Kurdish movement.

After the AKP abandoned the peace process, it pivoted to an Islamist-nationalist line, reminiscent of the Milli Görüş's alliance with Turkish nationalists in the 1970s and 1990s. Erdoğan adapted a more belligerent rhetoric and worked hard to delegitimize the pro-Kurdish HDP. Islam constituted an important point of reference in such efforts. So he denigrated the pro-Kurdish party as unIslamic to appeal to conservative Kurds. For instance, in a 2016 rally in a predominantly Kurdish city, Erdoğan asked, "Haven't they [the Kurdish movement] destroyed your mosques? They are atheists! They are Zoroastrians!... They do not follow our values."[164] In the meantime, the state cracked down on the Kurdish movement; several Kurdish deputies, including the party chairman Selahattin Demirtaş, were imprisoned for years without a conviction; the party organization was debilitated, and the Kurdish movement's electoral fortunes in the local elections of 2014 and 2019 were overturned by Interior Ministry without court rulings. Clearly, as evidenced by this sharp authoritarian turn, electoralists were motivated

---

[163] For an excellent overview of the Kurdish question after 1923 and Kurdish political attitudes, see Karakoç and Özen, "Kurdish Public Opinion in Turkey." For the AKP's approach to the Kurdish question, see Çiçek, "Elimination or Integration of Pro-Kurdish Politics."

[164] *Cumhuriyet*, "Bunlar ateist, bunlar Zerdüşt."

by instrumentalism instead of democratic principles and pluralism in their handling of the Kurdish question.

Electoralists were not willing to recognize political pluralism within Islamism either. So Islamic organizations and parties that refused to submit to AKP rule faced sanctions with different levels of severity. Besides the conflict between the government and the Gülen movement, the fate of the Islamic human rights organization MAZLUMDER, with a much more prodemocratic agenda than the Gülen movement, is another example of the cost of insubordination against the AKP. Soon after the AKP ended the peace process with the Kurdish movement and reignited the conflict in 2015, MAZLUMDER closely observed Kurdish regions and released a report on human rights violations in conflict zones a year later. Erdoğan was furious. He targeted the organization, denounced the report, and threatened the members with prosecution.[165] In 2017, a court order appointed a trustee to the organization, who called for a legally contested congress. In the congress, pro-Erdoğan members closed sixteen local branches active in Kurdish cities and elected an Erdoğan loyalist to replace Ahmet Faruk Ünsal, a long-time human rights activist and former AKP deputy.

The AKP government also placed greater pressure on the Islamist Furkan Foundation, whose leader criticized the government's domestic and foreign policies. The leader, Alpaslan Kuytul, spent months in prison during his ongoing trial. He was charged with defaming the president, supporting the Gülen movement, and abusing religion for criminal purposes, among other offenses.[166] The Internal Ministry also appointed a trustee to the foundation, basically ending its operations, and has kept its members under close surveillance and pressure by law enforcement since 2018. As Çavdar, a prominent expert on Islamist movements, states, the AKP (i.e., Erdoğan's faction) would not accept any kind of competition from among Islamist circles.[167]

Another Islamist movement, which has received its share of government pressure albeit lighter, is, interestingly, the final political iteration of the Milli Görüş movement: the SP. The party took a liberal democratic turn after the AKP pivoted toward hegemonic Islamism. The change partly emanated from leadership change, with Temel Karamollaoğlu becoming the chairman of the party in 2016. From then on, the SP has become a vocal critic of the government's erosion of the rule of law, human rights abuses, and the violation of civil liberties. The party also opposed Turkey's transition to a presidential system in

---

[165] *Bianet*, "Erdoğan'dan STK'lara."
[166] He was acquitted from some of these charges while there were four ongoing court cases at the time of writing.
[167] *DW*, "Furkan Vakfi neden gündemde?"

2017 and formed an electoral alliance with the secular opposition to defeat the constitutional referendum. The SP leaders called for inclusion, engagement, and deliberation with all parties. Electoralists in the AKP reacted by reclaiming Erbakan's legacy and invited the SP to join forces with the AKP. When Karamollaoğlu refused to join a system that is basically unaccountable, the government attempted to divide the SP by appealing to Erbakan's son. The pressure bore fruit when Fatih Erbakan established a new party and claimed the headquarters of the SP, which had to move elsewhere. Similarly, to silence the party, state officials under government directives repeatedly took SP's political ads off the air.

Violation of Civil Liberties Such pressures on the opposition to the AKP's hegemonic Islamism (from secular and Islamist circles alike) evoked reactions from different parts of the society. Electoralists under Erdoğan's leadership responded with frequent violations of freedom of expression, information, association, and assembly, whenever different social groups pushed back against hegemonic Islamism.

Freedom of the Press For electoralists, the media has been a battleground wherein journalists have either been for or against the government. So, from the outset, Erdoğan's faction aimed to build a government-friendly media.[168] They pressured major media companies to hire pro-AKP columnists, employed defamation lawsuits and punitive measures to silence journalists, and transferred ownership of major newspapers and broadcasting stations to their supporters, as I discussed earlier. Liberal voices within the party objected to such measures, yet they were too weak to make a difference.

On several occasions, Erdoğan openly suggested that critical columnists hurt the interests of the nation by creating instability in the country; he also called on the media bosses to hire their staff according to these interests and fire those who do not follow a malleable editorial line.[169] The owners of these corporations then either fired critical voices or asked them to self-censor. Those journalists who remained critical and maintained their independent perspectives were purged in several waves. One major wave struck when the Turkish air force bombed and killed 34 unarmed cross-border traders mistaken for Kurdish insurgents in December 2011.

---

[168] Esen and Gumuscu, "Rising Competitive Authoritarianism in Turkey"; Esen and Gumuscu, "Building a Competitive Authoritarian Regime."

[169] See Erdoğan's speech in his party group, *Haber7*, "Yazarını Erdoğan'a şikayet eden medya patronu."

Several prominent columnists of liberal and Islamic convictions criticized the government's handling of the incident and lost their jobs as a result. A second major wave hit with the Gezi Park protests in the summer of 2013, discussed below, when the mainstream media refrained from reporting on one of the most wide-scale protests in Turkish history. After critical voices were silenced, even objective reporting on critical developments became intolerable for electoralists, so they have increasingly resorted to media blackouts to silence the media at times of crisis.

The party has also supported and defended criminal investigations of journalistic activities. During his long tenure as premier, Erdoğan has publicly defended the detention of journalists and likened them to terrorists and their journalistic activities to acts of terrorism. In his speech to the Council of Europe in 2011, for instance, Erdoğan approved of the detention of two journalists (Ahmet Şık and Nedim Şener) for writing books: "It is a crime to use a bomb," Erdoğan said, "but it is also a crime to use materials from which a bomb is made. [...] Some books are indeed more effective than bombs."[170]

The pressure on the media has not been limited to conventional press. It has also targeted social media. Several social media sites, including YouTube, Twitter, Facebook, and Wikipedia, were banned at different times to silence critiques and regulate the information flow. After lifting these bans, the government continued to monitor the internet. Thousands of sites are blocked every year, a great majority by a government-controlled agency (BTK) citing obscenity, defamation of Islam, promotion of atheism, and terrorism as reasons.[171]

By way of contrast, liberals such as Gül displayed great respect for the freedom of expression and information, which he deemed the pillars of a true democracy. As Erdoğan expanded his crackdown on the media after 2009, Gül publicly objected to the arrests of journalists, exposing the growing rift among party leaders. In 2011, Gül released a statement rebuking Erdoğan's view likening books to bombs: "I cannot interfere with the affairs of the judicial branch," he wrote, "Yet it is my contention that there are certain developments that the public conscience would not accept. This situation hurts the achievements Turkey has made so far. I'm deeply concerned. I expect that the prosecutors and courts act with the utmost care not to undermine the rights and honor of certain individuals."[172] A year later in his keynote speech in the opening ceremony of parliament, Gül reinforced his position on the freedom of the press:

---

[170] Quoted in "Turkish PM Rebuffs Criticism over Press Freedom"; "Erdoğan: bazı kitaplar bombadan daha tesirli."
[171] *Freedom House*, "Freedom on the Net 2019 Turkey."
[172] Sever, *Abdullah Gül ile 12 Yıl Yaşadım, Gördüm, Yazdım*, 100–3.

It is a source of prestige for a country for its authors, thinkers, and philosophers to share their views without fear. It is essential that journalists and reporters do not face any obstacles when they serve to deliver news to the public. No one should be imprisoned for their thoughts or sharing their opinions in the media. We need to clearly separate those who incite violence from those who express their opinions.[173]

Quite disturbed by purges in the media, Gül frequently urged reporters to resist political pressures.[174]

Arınç also joined Gül in his criticism of such political pressures and defended freedom of the press against Erdoğan's encroachments. In a televised interview, in reference to the tax fine the government charged to Doğan Media Company (as discussed earlier), he called it quite unfair.[175] Arınç also objected to the media blackout on the Gezi Park protests. He repeatedly expressed that freedom of speech and information and political criticism was essential to democracy.

Liberals' interventions proved ineffective. As a result of electoralists' pressures, press freedom in Turkey has quickly declined over the years. In 2002, Turkey ranked 99th for press in the freedom index; in 18 years, it declined by 55 and ranked 154th in 2020.[176] Internet freedom rapidly deteriorated, as well. Freedom House categorized Turkey as a non-free country in net freedom in 2016 and has not changed its status since then.

Protests and Freedom of Assembly As the electoralists monopolized power in the country, democratic, liberal, secular, and republican forces in the society pushed back through popular mobilization. Electoralists rallying around Erdoğan responded with increasing authoritarianism, polarization, and exclusion by way of systematic violations of freedom of assembly and heavy crackdowns on popular protests. For electoralists, protests were not a legitimate expression of political demands. The only legitimate political expression for them was the ballot box. Democracy, as electoralists saw it, was simply elections.

Gül's differences with Erdoğan over the meaning of democracy became starker and more evident as Erdoğan amassed greater power and used this power to shrink the political space. An incident in 2012 signaled fundamental disagreements between the two. On the Republic Day of October 29, the secular CHP wanted to march in the capital and visit Atatürk's mausoleum. The police halted the march on Erdoğan's orders. In defiance, President Gül ordered the security forces to lift the barricades, so they did.

---

[173] Ibid., 112–13.
[174] Ibid., 114.
[175] *Eğrisi Doğrusu*, January 29, 2016: www.youtube.com/watch?v=QIseBWB07fc&feature=youtu.be
[176] Reporters Without Borders (RSF), "2020 World Press Freedom Index Ranking."

Erdoğan ranted that the police failed to do their job, while Gül defended his intervention by his presidential authority over the police for a calm and safe celebration of Republic Day. This was only a preview of what came next.

Less than a year later, in May 2013, hundreds and thousands mobilized throughout the country to protest the government's authoritarian practices and demand its resignation. The spark that ignited the uprising was a public park (Gezi Park) in downtown Istanbul; the government planned to destroy the park to build a shopping mall. When independent CSOs organized a sit-in to stop the construction, they faced a heavy police crackdown. Frustrated by the police's harsh treatment, many more protesters joined the sit-in, and the police responded with greater force, punishing the protesters on site, as I discussed earlier.

Erdoğan flexed his majoritarian muscles throughout the crisis. For him, protesters were a small minority without any political import. They did not represent "the people," who indeed sided with the AKP. For Erdoğan, the ballot box was the sole venue of political participation; all other forms of political participation were antidemocratic and illegal. So he ignored the protestors' demands to stop the construction and insisted that a shopping mall would be constructed regardless. For him, popular mobilization represented the antidemocratic impulse of those who could not defeat the AKP at the polls; the Gezi Park protests were nothing more than a "coup attempt."

To delegitimize and dismiss extensive popular mobilization, Erdoğan employed a discourse based on animosity and denigration. He took on a belligerent tone and vilified the protesters instead of engaging with them. Protesters were looters, terrorists, atheists, and coup plotters, he suggested, and Gezi Park protests were attempts to impose the will of the minority on the majority (the AKP constituency).[177]

To show that "the real people" supported his party, Erdoğan capitalized on polarization and countermobilization in public rallies, under the theme of "respecting the will of the people."[178] In these rallies, he evoked fears and hatred among his supporters by invoking their Islamic sentiments. He depicted protests as attacks on Islam because they were against the AKP government. In these rallies, "They [protesters] entered mosques with their shoes on carrying beer bottles," Erdoğan roared, "They attacked my veiled sisters!"[179] He was alluding to a news story circulating in pro-AKP media about a young, veiled woman and her baby who were allegedly attacked by a group of half-naked men wearing leather pants in the midst of the protests. The story alleged that the men shoved

---

[177] *Sabah*, "Başbakan'dan Gezi Parkı açıklaması."
[178] *TRT Haber*, "Milli İradeye Saygı mitingleri devam ediyor."
[179] NTV, "Erdoğan: Başörtülülere Saldırdılar."

the woman and her baby around and urinated on them in daylight in one of the busiest spots in Istanbul. The police investigation and closed-circuit cameras revealed no evidence of such an incident. Yet Erdoğan maintained his accusations for months. The imam of the mosque where protesters took refuge from the riot police also denied Erdoğan's allegations and stated that no one consumed alcohol inside. His statement did not alter the government discourse, but he lost his position in the mosque and was demoted to a small village on the outskirts of Istanbul.

In short, Erdoğan managed to present a historic popular protest in Turkey as if it were an antireligious, anti-Sunni, antidemocratic challenge to the "will of the people" (read: Sunni Muslims voting for the AKP).[180] So the government reacted to protests with fervor and a heavy crackdown. The riot police used brutal force with impunity, killing 5, blinding 15, and injuring more than 8,000 protesters. An increasingly politicized judiciary followed up with terrorism charges against CSOs, professional syndicates, and football fans who joined the protests. The charges were at first dismissed, yet the case was reopened after the failed coup attempt of 2016. The trial ended in April 2022, with Osman Kavala, a famous philanthropist and businessman, given a life sentence and seven other defendants eighteen years.

Gül and other liberal leaders, in contrast, had a very different take on the protests. As president throughout the events, Gül called police brutality against activists a mistake, instead of owning and encouraging it, as Erdoğan preferred to do.[181] He also urged for mutual respect for different political views, tendencies, and beliefs. Gül legitimized protests as a form of political expression and claimed that democracy was more than elections; it was a system that allowed for political participation in different forms and styles.[182] For him, there was nothing more natural than expressing objections to government policies through peaceful protests like the ones in Gezi Park. He also recognized the demands of the protesters as justified and promised to do whatever necessary to meet their demands.[183] In line with this belief, using his authority as the president, Gül ordered the police to back down, allowing protesters to occupy the park taking advantage of Erdogan's absence during a trip abroad. A few

---

[180] *TRT Haber*, "Milli İradeye Saygı mitingleri devam ediyor"; for an analysis of the AKP after Gezi protests, see Yenigün, "Turkish Islamism in the Post-Gezi Park Era."
[181] For Gül's statement, see *HaberTürk*, "Cumhurbaşkanı Gül'den flaş Gezi Parkı açıklaması." Interestingly, Gül's statements were taken off the presidency's website after Erdoğan's election as president. *Cumhuriyet*, "Erdoğan, Abdullah Gül'ün Gezi Parkı açıklamasını sildirdi."
[182] *Hürriyet*, "Cumhurbaşkanı Gül'den Gezi Parkı açıklaması."
[183] Ibid.

years later during a televised interview, Gül also contested Erdoğan's claim that the Gezi protests were a coup attempt and suggested that the government's mishandling of the criticisms aggravated the crisis.[184]

Similarly, Arınç, the cabinet spokesperson at the time, joined Gül in a more conciliatory approach and acknowledged the concerns of the protesters. He apologized for police brutality and promised to resolve the crisis in a civil and democratic manner. He recognized diverse political views as richness, expressing respect for the opposition and peaceful dissent.[185]

Gül and Arınç raised their liberal objections to Erdoğan's majoritarianism, with limited impact. Erdoğan finally agreed to meet with CSOs and wait for the court ruling to decide the fate of the park. In the short run, the park was saved, but freedom of assembly was lost for good. Electoralists took every measure after the Gezi Park protests to make sure a similar mobilization would never recur. The waning influence of liberals in the party was already evident, as electoralists explicitly declared that a new era had begun in the country. The new AKP would no longer be inclusionary, they claimed. A high-level AKP official's candid statement in 2013 was particularly revealing of what was to come:

Those groups, like liberals, who walked with us in the previous decade, will not do so in the next 10 years. In the past, we worked together to replace the former regime in the name of freedom, rule of law, and justice, but the future is about building a new system. This new system we'll build is not in line with their demands. Therefore, they will not walk with us because the system and the future that we will erect will be unacceptable to them.[186]

And so, it was.

Conclusion

The AKP was established as a coalition of different groups with different perceptions and practices of democracy. Those with greater commitments to liberal democratic norms carried greater weight at the outset, only to lose their power and influence to electoralists. In its first term in power, the AKP government carried out critical reforms that put Turkey on the path of European Union accession. Leading figures such as Abdullah Gül, Bülent Arınç, Abdullatif Şener, Ali Babacan, and Beşir Atalay

---

[184] NTV's interview with Gül: www.youtube.com/watch?v=tDw2gLwRzF4

[185] For Arınç's statements, see *Milliyet*, "Bülent Arınç'tan 'Gezi Parkı' açıklaması" and *Hürriyet*, "Bülent Arınç ilk gün için özür diledi."

[186] *T24*, "Babuşcu: Gelecek 10 yıl, liberaller gibi eski paydaşlarımızın arzuladığı gibi olmayacak." Babuşcu was certainly referring to the liberal allies the party had in its first terms in power. But liberals within the party were also sidelined in the meantime and had lost all of their influence over the government's direction at the time of this statement.

had major influence over the direction of the government. However, their influence began to wane after 2007, when Erdoğan exerted greater command over organizational resources. Building an extensive incentive structure, he formed a dominant coalition in favor of electoralism and sidelined liberals.

Erdoğan's coalition had a majoritarian understanding of democracy, treated other political parties as enemies and illegitimate actors, and disrespected minority rights and civil liberties. The new regime also gained an Islamist quality as electoralists instrumentalized the state apparatus to Islamize the Turkish society in a top-down fashion.

As electoralists entrenched their control of the party, the government capitalized on a discourse of polarization and exclusion. Social groups outside of the AKP constituency have been treated as inauthentic parts of the Turkish society and, therefore, undeserving of political rights and civil liberties. Increasingly, these groups came to be treated as terrorists by the authorities. As the government systematically violated the political rights and civil liberties of those who refused to vote for the AKP, the country descended into an authoritarian regime. Liberals within the AKP frequently criticized the path the party took after 2007 and defended freedom of expression, information, and assembly. However, their weakened position in the party has prevented them from making a real impact on the party and the government.

As Turkey descended into authoritarianism under electoralists' rule, liberals recognized that they could not effect change within the party. So they left. Several liberals with Gül's support left the AKP to establish a center-right party in 2020 under Babacan's leadership. The Democracy and Progress Party (Demokrasi ve Atılım Partisi, DEVA), as it is called, recalled the AKP in its earlier years. Davutoğlu left the AKP, too, to establish his own political organization, namely the Future Party (Gelecek Partisi, GP), in 2020 with a more conservative agenda. Both parties have a clearly liberal democratic agenda defending pluralism, civil liberties, and deliberation. Their departure left the AKP to electoralists' absolute control.

The AKP's shifting trajectory along with its political dominance pushed the country over the authoritarian brink. In the end, Turkish democracy collapsed not because Islamists were in power but because liberal Islamists within the party lost the power struggle against electoralists – hence the political roller coaster in Turkey's recent history from democratic reforms to democratic collapse. What about other Islamist parties? How did they act in government? Next, I turn to the experience of the Muslim Brotherhood in Egypt.

4 Electoral Islamism and Killing the Dream of a Democratic Muslim Brotherhood

The revolutionary fire that started in Tunisia in late 2010 quickly spread to Egypt when hundreds of thousands of Egyptians showed up in Tahrir Square in Downtown Cairo to demand freedom and dignity. They wanted Hosni Mubarak's thirty-year-old regime to fall. Their persistent calls for eighteen days bore fruit on February 11, 2011, when Mubarak stepped down. Thus began Egypt's transition to democracy.

With the transition progressing to civilian rule and elections, thanks to the pressure of the youthful revolutionaries, the most organized political forces – not necessarily revolutionaries – capitalized on the opportunity. Islamists were chief among them.

Prior to the revolution in 2011, which ended Mubarak's thirty-year reign, the Muslim Brotherhood had been the main opposition against the regime. For the almost three decades since Mubarak's limited political opening of the 1980s, Brothers had had abundant opportunities to participate in legal politics. In the process, they adopted a new political vocabulary and conformed to the legal parliamentary framework. In parliament and professional associations, where they gained prominence in the 1980s and 1990s, Brothers called for free and fair elections, a civil and independent judiciary, presidential term limits, and the expansion of civil liberties. In their political activities, they embraced concepts such as the civil state, citizenship, freedom of expression and association, and human rights.

Those who subscribe to the inclusion-moderation thesis claimed that the Brothers learned the value of democracy in their encounters with their ideological rivals and through participation in formal politics even under a semi-authoritarian regime.[1] Others, in contrast, pointed at the limits of this ideological change by highlighting the Brotherhood's

---

[1] For an excellent example, see El-Ghobashy, "The Metamorphosis of the Egyptian Muslim Brothers" and Wickham, "The Path to Moderation."

ambivalence on sharia rule, as well as minority and women's rights.[2] Surely, the authoritarian political setting pushed Brothers to cooperate with the secular opposition and demand the democratization of the system. Yet it was unclear how widespread such democratic commitments were within the movement. Only after the fall of Hosni Mubarak in 2011 did we obtain the opportunity to observe Brothers' varying commitment to democratic principles.

The Muslim Brotherhood took center stage after the revolution in 2011. Its superior mobilizational capacity handed the movement a significant advantage in electoral politics, as it did in the case of the AKP. After eighty-four years of struggle, the Brothers prevailed in both parliamentary and presidential elections and took the driver's seat for Egypt's democratic transition. Mohamed Morsi's victory in the 2012 presidential elections was a groundbreaking achievement for the movement. On the night of his election, Morsi promised to unite all Egyptians – Muslim and Christians, men and women – and to advance the revolutionary cause for democracy, human rights, and dignity. Over the next 365 days, rather than uniting and democratizing his country, he alienated large segments of the population through polarization, monopolization of power, "Ikhwanization" of the state, and violating civil liberties in a systematic manner. Morsi became the president of the Brotherhood and instrumentalized state power to carry out its ideological agenda, as Erdoğan did in Turkey.

The sense of alienation, exclusion, and disappointment with Morsi's performance triggered popular mobilization against his rule. Two years after Mubarak's ouster, protestors were this time calling for Morsi's resignation and renewed presidential elections. Morsi rejected these calls, belittled the massive popular mobilization, and dismissed the demands of the protesters. Instead, he countermobilized his supporters. The Egyptian armed forces used growing tensions as a pretext and ousted Morsi on July 3, 2013, thus ending the short-lived democratic experiment in the country.

Why did the Brotherhood follow righteous majoritarianism and polarization instead of mutual tolerance and institutional forbearance after coming to power? This chapter seeks to solve this puzzle by way of unpacking the Brotherhood's internal power dynamics and differences regarding democratic politics. This exercise reveals Muslim Brothers' rather complicated relationship to democracy.

---

[2] Hamzawy, Ottoway, and Brown, "What Islamists Need to Be Clear About"; Brown, *When Victory Is Not an Option*.

The events after 2011 have indeed revealed the extent to which the Brotherhood had internalized democratic politics over the years. The dominant faction in the movement, known as the old guard, took electoral procedures very seriously, campaigned effectively, and mobilized their supporters and resources for elections. Once they attained power, they resolutely defended the popular legitimacy that came with electoral victories. Yet their understanding of democracy remained strictly majoritarian and largely instrumentalist because elections, for them, mandated the Islamization of the society and state. This was simply an electoralist understanding of democracy, which led the Brotherhood to pursue righteous majoritarianism, polarization, and exclusion, as did the AKP in Turkey.

The old guard, which dominated the organization before and after the transition, still encountered significant opposition from within. In fact, the movement had included several figures with clear democratic commitments and pluralist attitudes, which distinguished them from the old guard. Widely known as "reformists" – or, as I call them, liberal Islamists – these figures committed to pluralism, engagement, civil liberties, and equal rights for religious and political minorities. They called for mutual tolerance and forbearance, perceiving Islamism as compatible with liberal democratic principles. Despite their sustained efforts, they failed to capture the organization.

Again, as in the case of the AKP, organizational resources played a central role in the old guard's dominance and liberal Islamists' weakness. The former gained control of rules, promotion and recruitment, finances, and internal communication at the expense of the latter, and such monopoly over the incentive structure allowed the old guard to carry their hegemonic posture to the executive office with Morsi's election. A tight-knit circle, the old guard built an extensive incentive structure that favored them in both vertical and horizontal power games over their liberal rivals.

To understand the roots of the Brotherhood's internal dynamics, however, we need to revisit the political evolution of the movement. I begin with a short historical account, tracing its changing relationship to politics and emerging splits within. Then, I turn to the shifting power balance between the old guard and liberal Islamists, and how the former sidelined the latter. Three moments are critical in this discussion: the Wasat Party initiative of 1996, the 2009–10 internal elections, and the post-2011 purge of the liberal Islamists. Tracing these key moments show that, unlike the course of the AKP in Turkey, the old guard had already sidelined liberals within the movement before coming to power in 2012. Then they chartered the course of the Brotherhood in line with their electoralist and majoritarian understanding of democracy.

A Brief History of the Muslim Brotherhood: Islam, Islamism, and Politics

The British ruled over Egypt indirectly from the 1880s to the 1950s in collaboration with the local elite. During British rule, the country evolved into a constitutional monarchy, and new political forces emerged on the scene with the rise of Arab nationalism. In the meantime, the Egyptian society underwent transformation on multiple fronts as the process of modernization gained speed. Westernization in social, political, and economic life reached all corners of the country, while secularization in state affairs and the decline of the role of Islam in daily life became visible. These trends concerned pious Egyptians who desired to maintain Islam's role in everyday life to save their society from the grips of secularization and Westernization.

Hassan al-Banna, a school teacher in the small city of Isma'iliyya, was one of those deeply concerned by declining religiosity in his country as well as continued British influence and missionary activities.[3] He was also disturbed by Al-Azhar's seemingly negligent approach to the creeping secularization of the Egyptian society.[4] When Banna established the Muslim Brotherhood[5] in 1928, he defined it as a movement that mobilizes Muslims and encourages their return to faith. Unlike any other religious society which existed in Egypt at the time, he believed that the country had been undergoing a severe societal crisis, and Islam was the solution. The Brotherhood under Banna argued that Muslims should reject the narrow interpretation of Islam, which had pushed it into the private sphere, and expand it to include politics.[6] For him, "a Muslim [would] never become a real Muslim if he [was] not political and [had] a view for affairs of his people."[7] He thus turned politics into an indispensable part of Islam.

In 1932, Banna moved to Cairo, where the organization quickly grew into a popular movement, thanks to his charisma and the power of his message of reviving Islam. The movement sought to keep Islam a central

---

[3] For more on the Brotherhood's anti-missionary orientation, see Baron, *The Orphan Scandal*.
[4] Mandaville, *Islam and Politics*, 76.
[5] Political Islam displays greater diversity with regard to political objectives and tactics in Egypt than in Turkey. Despite the diversity of actors, the Brotherhood had more or less monopolized the terrain of political Islam and become its mainstream expression in Egypt until the 2011 revolution. Radical groups such as Jamaat al-Islamiyya (the Islamic Society) made the headlines often in the 1970s and 1990s with assassinations and attacks on tourists and Coptic Christians, yet they remained mostly insignificant and fragmented within broader Islamism. See Bayat, *Making Islam Democratic*, 40.
[6] Lia, *The Society of the Muslim Brothers in Egypt*, 75, 202.
[7] Quoted in Lia, *The Society of the Muslim Brothers in Egypt*, 202.

part of everyday life by preaching and teaching the Islamic message, also known as *da'wa*. Throughout the 1930s, the Brotherhood became increasingly politicized and prioritized ousting the British from Egypt alongside Islamic revival. In this period, Muslim Brothers turned into an organizationally advanced religiopolitical movement that rejected any separation between Islam and politics.

Banna believed that Islam regulated every aspect of life.[8] It was "all-inclusive, encompassing the affairs of the people in this world and the hereafter [...] a faith and a ritual, a nation and a nationality, a religion and a state, spirit and deed, holy text and sword," and that is why it was capable of curing the ills of the society and providing Muslims with "complete and total truth."[9] The Brotherhood's mission was to return to this truth.

As Banna defined it, the movement's ideology centered on antiimperialism, social justice, Islamic unity, and rejection of political parties. The movement aimed to "release Egypt from western influence and apply Islamic jurisprudence, Islamic military spirit, Islamic health traditions and scientific studies, Islamic morality, and an Islamic economic system."[10] All of these goals would be reached when an Islamic society and state that fully conforms to sharia is established.[11] He suggested:

> We are calling you to Islam: government is part of it, and freedom is one of its religious duties. If someone should say to you: this is politics! Say: this is Islam, and we do not recognize such divisions. [...] We are agents of the truth and of peace in which we believe and which we exalt.[12]

In this respect, the Brotherhood's ideology was based on an all-comprehensive perception of Islam which Banna summarized in two precepts: Islam was *din wa dawla* (religion and state) and was *huwa-l hal* (the solution). Because Islam was an indivisible truth, the task of Islamization encompassed all aspects of life, including religion, politics, and economics. Thus, the Brotherhood had to remain active in all spheres of life. For its members, their movement was

> [A] *da'wa* from the Qur'an and the *Sunna* of the Prophet Muhammad; a method that adheres to sunna; a reality whose core is the purity of the soul; a political association; an athletic association; an educational and cultural organization; an economic enterprise; and a social concept.[13]

---

[8] Al-Banna, *Five Tracts of Hasan Al-Banna (1906–1949)*, 46.
[9] Al-Banna quoted in Mitchell, *The Society of the Muslim Brothers*, 232–33.
[10] Al-Banna, *Five Tracts of Hasan Al-Banna (1906–1949)*, 31–32; Sullivan and Abed-Kotob, *Islam in Contemporary Egypt*, 45.
[11] Mitchell, *The Society of the Muslim Brothers*, 232–36.
[12] Al-Banna, *Five Tracts of Hasan Al-Banna (1906–1949)*, 36.
[13] Sullivan and Abed-Kotob, *Islam in Contemporary Egypt*, 45.

So the movement sustained activities in the political, economic, social, and cultural spheres directed toward the same goal: the Islamization of the society. Its members ran hospitals, evening schools, and social cooperatives.[14] The Brothers believed that the best course toward an Islamic order was through reformist gradualism. Islamization started with the individual, and *da'wa* formed the basis of this gradual change toward an Islamic order. For Banna, a nation could achieve its goals and aspirations only through the education of souls with strong ideological consciousness centered on political and national aims.[15] That is why the reform began with the individual. Then came the creation of the Muslim family, the Islamic society, and the Islamic state.

Despite the method of incremental reform, the leaders of the movement also recognized the potential of the nation-state in building an Islamic society. So the Brotherhood required its members work within the existing political system to disseminate their message to wider audiences, including policymakers. Banna stressed the need to "bring the Islamic mission to the rulers [...] and make [it] known to them." For him, this was the most useful and efficient method of achieving the Islamic mission.[16]

With that intention, Banna ran in the parliamentary elections of 1942. Five years later, he reached out to King Farouk in a public letter. There he identified a series of policies required to give the Egyptian society an Islamic direction and urged for changes in all aspects of life, from politics to personal matters. For instance, Banna called for a single-party system and full conformance to Islamic legislation in state affairs as well as the personal conduct of all state employees. He also proposed bringing up Islamic youth and designing separate curricula for boys and girls. His letter also recommended strict moral codes in the society by penalizing prostitution, gambling, and drinking, banning loose behavior (particularly for women) and dancing, and surveilling beaches and cafes. He also urged heavy censorship of cultural output such as films, songs, and books, and supported penalizing infringements upon any Islamic doctrine – such as breaking the fast in Ramadan, willful neglect of prayers, or insulting the faith.[17] In short, in his letter to the king, Banna rejected the separation of the public and private spheres and demanded strict regulation and control of personal matters such as marriage, recreation, religious practices, and clothing. Such demands conformed to his

---

[14] Mitchell, *The Society of the Muslim Brothers*, 285. Baron discusses the influence of missionaries on Brotherhood's evolving mission in great detail in *The Orphan Scandal*.
[15] Lia, *The Society of the Muslim Brothers in Egypt*, 67.
[16] Ibid., 249.
[17] Al-Banna, *Five Tracts of Hasan Al-Banna (1906–1949)*, 126–29.

vision of Islam as a total order. Interestingly, this letter also marked the movement's departure from exclusively bottom-up reformism. Banna recognized the power of the state to "make society Islamic again."

The Brotherhood's gradualism and instrumentalism kept its politics mostly ambivalent. Clearly, establishing an Islamic state and society was more important than the means that it took to attain that end. It could be through any political system, monarchic or republican. So the contours of the Islamic system remained largely vague, except for two main pillars: Islamic law and a pious ruler.[18] The state's conformity with the Islamic law mattered more than the particular political system in which it functioned, for it was Islamic law along with a pious ruler that would guarantee the prevalence of justice and the proper functioning of the political system. When asked about the details of this political system, the Brothers chose to leave the specifics to the time, place, and needs of the people.[19]

The movement was most specific about the ruler. For the Brotherhood, he had to "be Muslim, male, adult; he [had to] be just, pious, virtuous, and knowledgeable in Muslim jurisprudence."[20] He was supposed to establish and maintain Islam and execute its laws to generate general welfare. In the process, the ruler was expected to consult with an *ahl al-shura* (consultative assembly),[21] suggesting that consultation (*shura*) constituted another important pillar of the Islamic state.[22] Yet this consultation was neither democratic nor binding. The leader was the ultimate decision-maker and the *shura* only played an advisory role. Thus, it remained unclear how the leader would be selected or how he would be accountable before Islamic law.

Banna's position on democracy remained ambiguous. And the movement's emphasis on a qualified ruler in the realization of the Islamic state raised issues of accountability. In the end, the Brotherhood flirted with political reality and refrained from committing to a particular political

---

[18] Butterworth, "Prudence versus Legitimacy," 95.
[19] Mitchell, *The Society of the Muslim Brothers*, 245. By leaving the details of an acceptable political system unspecified, the Brotherhood remained ambivalent about democracy. Yet they have been clear about the issue of theocracy. Although unspecified, the political system that the Muslim Broterhood advocates would not be theocratic, which they argued was unlikely in Islam. There were two reasons why. First, there is no religious class or clergy in Sunni Islam, and second, authority in Islamic political organization derives from men, not God; the people give this authority to the ruler because he will obey the Islamic law.
[20] Mitchell, *The Society of the Muslim Brothers*, 246.
[21] According to Banna, the members of the *ahl al-shura* should be elected among jurists and men practiced in leadership.
[22] Ibid., 248.

system. As such, its ideology long remained an amalgam of different political ideas, including elements of democracy, totalitarianism, and monarchy. Despite this ideological fuzziness, the Brothers carried on with their mission of reform. Indeed, the Brothers' insistence on gradualism as the primary method of attaining an Islamic society and state allowed them to work within the Egyptian political system whenever they obtained the opportunity.

By the onset of World War II, the Brotherhood was already an important force to reckon with and a significant political contender to the dominant Wafd Party. Several factors empowered the movement, including the training of young, dedicated preachers; the use of modern forms of propaganda, education, and organization; and a strong interest in political and national issues pertaining to the interests of the lower middle classes.[23]

Eventually, a secret apparatus was also formed to complement the organization's activities in religion, politics, and the economy. This secret apparatus training for an armed movement emerged as a response to increasing internal pressures, particularly from the youth, who demanded increased political activity, greater equality with other political bodies that had paramilitary forces, and a more prominent role in the Palestinian crisis.[24]

The Brotherhood's growing popularity and militarization, however, prompted state repression. King Farouk outlawed the organization in 1948. Prime Minister Mahmoud Fahmy El Nokrashy's assassination by a Brother further exacerbated the tension between the movement and the state. A year later, Banna was assassinated by the secret police in retribution.

Driven underground, the organization supported the Free Officers Movement led by Colonel Gamal Abdel Nasser to overthrow King Farouk in 1952. After a few years of peaceful coexistence, Nasser, unhappy with Brothers' religiopolitical demands, outlawed the movement and launched a major clampdown.[25] Between 1954 and 1967, thousands of members of the organization were imprisoned, tortured, and executed, including a major Brotherhood leader and ideologue, Sayyid Qutb.

Qutb's writings proved to be influential among Islamist circles. His emphasis on two major themes was particularly powerful. First was the emphasis on the un-Islamic nature of existing regimes and the need

---

[23] Lia, *The Society of the Muslim Brothers in Egypt*, 57, 280.
[24] Ibid., 177–81.
[25] As a pretext for this repression, Nasser used an attempt on his life made by the Brotherhood in 1954.

for a holy struggle (i.e., jihad). Second was the need for a vanguard to establish a proper Islamic state and society. These ideas inspired several young activists who gravitated toward radical militant organizations in the late 1960s and 1970s in reaction to intense state repression. For them, the Egyptian regime was infidel and the Brotherhood's gradualism unacceptable.

The leaders of the Brotherhood remained cautious and insisted on gradualism. In 1969, then General Guide (the leader of the movement) Hassan al-Hudaybi, along with other prominent names, distanced themselves from Qutbian radicalism and renewed their commitment to gradual and nonviolent reform of the society.[26]

The Brotherhood had to persevere until Nasser's decline to recover from repression. Egypt's defeat in the 1967 war with Israel shattered his charisma and provided the remnants of the movement with some breathing room. After Nasser's death in 1970, Anwar Sadat became the new president and recognized the movement as a potential ally against his leftist and Nasserist opponents. Sadat did not legalize the Brotherhood but allowed for the publication of its periodical *al-Da'wa* and for Islamic activism on college campuses. During Sadat's presidency between 1970 and 1981, the Brotherhood hence began to recover from the repression of Nasser's regime. During this period, the movement, under Umar al-Tilmisani's leadership, continued to reject the militant activism of less powerful Islamist organizations.[27] Tilmisani proclaimed that the Brotherhood neither approved of revolutionary change nor desired to capture power:

> The Brethren do not consider revolution, nor do they depend on it, nor do they believe in its utility or its outcome. As for rule, the Brethren do not request it for themselves. If they find among the nation one who can handle this burdensome responsibility, who can rule following Islamic mores, the Brethren will be his soldiers, his supporters, and his assistants.[28]

Thus, the Brotherhood projected the message that the ultimate objective of establishing an Islamic order was more important than the acquisition of power. It would willingly assist any ruler who would use the state apparatus to Islamize the society. While Tilmisani assured Sadat that the Brotherhood was not a threat to his regime, he also sought to revive the

---

[26] For a detailed analysis of Hassan al-Hudaybi's role in the Brotherhood, see Zollner, *The Muslim Brotherhood*.
[27] Jihad and Jamaat al-Islamiyya were the two prominent militant organization in the 1970s. An excellent study on radical Islamism in Egypt is Kepel, *Muslim Extremism in Egypt*.
[28] Quoted in Sullivan and Abed-Kotob, *Islam in Contemporary Egypt*, 324.

organization by reaching out to Islamist university youth. He was largely successful, as hundreds of college students joined the Brotherhood in the 1970s. These students would politicize the movement from the early 1980s onwards and form the core of the liberal faction in the movement.[29]

Many Islamists, in contrast, chose militant activism and established jihadi groups. One of these militant organizations assassinated Sadat in a public ceremony in 1981. His death carried his vice-president, Hosni Mubarak, to power. Soon after, Mubarak promised political liberalization and called for multiparty elections in 1984. The Brotherhood, under Tilmisani's leadership, took advantage of the political opening and pursued participation in formal politics, marking a major turning point in its political evolution.

Since it was still an illegal organization, the Brotherhood could run for seats in the parliament only through alliances with other parties or as independents. In 1984, they allied with the secular Wafd, winning seven seats in the parliament. In 1987, they decided to ally with the Labor Party and gained thirty-five seats. In the late 1980s and 1990s, Brothers also added professional associations to their areas of outreach. College students who joined the movement in the 1970s were active members of professional associations by the 1980s. They recognized the relatively open space in these unions compared to the rest of the political system and achieved overwhelming success in elections in syndicates for engineers, doctors, teachers, lawyers, pharmacists, and journalists.[30]

The Mubarak regime soon reversed the political liberalization process in the face of increasing pressures from the opposition calling for further democratization. The opposition, including the Brotherhood, boycotted the 1990 elections for its undemocratic, unsupervised, and nontransparent procedures.[31] At the same time, militant Islamists, emboldened by their jihadi experience in Afghanistan in the 1980s, returned to Egypt. Several local jihadi groups carried out terrorist attacks on tourist sites, killing several foreigners and Egyptians. Mubarak used this new wave of violent Islamist activism as a pretext to crack down on the nonviolent and gradualist Brotherhood. Hundreds of Brothers were arrested prior to the 1995 elections, and the courts sentenced prominent figures among the middle generation, including Essam el-Erian and Abdel Moneim Aboul Fotouh, to several years in prison.

---

[29] For a detailed account of the Brotherhood's recovery and revival after the 1970s, see Carrie Wickham, *Mobilizing Islam*.
[30] For Brotherhood's participation in professional syndicates, see Fahmy, "The Performance of the Muslim Brotherhood in the Egyptian Syndicates."
[31] Cowell, "Mideast Tensions."

The regime's heavy hand eased after 2000, although bursts of repression and imprisonment resurfaced during election cycles toward the end of the decade. Thanks to the renewed liberalization of the system, the Brothers ran in the 2000 and 2005 elections and registered critical successes. In 2000, the Brotherhood won seventeen seats in the parliament, forming the largest oppositional bloc to Mubarak's National Democratic Party. In 2005, the movement reached its highest representational capacity ever, winning 88 seats in the 444-seat parliament. This success triggered a harsh response from Mubarak in the 2010 election, when the regime resorted to extensive electoral abuse and voter intimidation. Such extreme measures wiped out the opposition, including the Brotherhood, in the parliament.

The Brotherhood's sustained participation in the political system starting in the 1980s, although punctuated by occasional repression, encouraged Brothers to refine their political preferences and define their relationship to democracy. They articulated what Islamism meant in Egypt and what an Islamic state and society should look like in a new era. A key outcome was that, in response to changing opportunities in Egyptian politics, the Brotherhood embraced electoral politics. In the meantime, the movement increasingly approximated a political party. Yet this process also brought internal disagreements and strife. While some Brothers accepted electoral politics without internalizing liberal norms, others committed to liberal democracy.

The year 2010 was the last election for the Mubarak regime. Just in a few months, the long-time dictator fell, and the Brotherhood rose to the helm after eight decades of political struggle. Before I discuss how the Brotherhood handled this historic opportunity, let us turn to the rise of different factions and their struggle for power, which would inform the movement's trajectory before and after the 2011 revolution.

The Muslim Brotherhood's Janus-Faced Political Evolution and Growing Internal Rifts

Following Nasser's death in 1970, the Brotherhood underwent a process of revival and reconstruction. The movement's political vision became more nuanced during its second founding in the early 1980s.[32] Umar al-Tilmisani, as the General Guide from 1972 to 1986, spearheaded this process by opening greater space within the movement for university youth. In this period, different groups pushed and pulled the movement in different directions as it went through renewal and reorganization. These groups aspired to shape Brotherhood's trajectory at this critical juncture.

---

[32] For an excellent study of Brotherhood's second founding, see Willi, *The Fourth Ordeal*.

The new generation of activists – also known as the "middle generation" – formed the liberal wing and pushed the movement in an increasingly political direction. The liberal Islamists primarily included those who had joined the Brotherhood when they were still university students in the 1970s. Figures such as Aboul Fotouh, Abu al-Ela Madi, Essam el-Erian, Essam Sultan, and Mohammed Habib were among the leaders of this growing faction. Inspired by Tilmisani's leadership, they rejuvenated the movement in the 1970s and became the engine of its politicization in the 1980s. The group came to be known as "reformists" for their political activism and critique of Brotherhood's methods and internal workings. They mostly came from urban centers and were predominantly part of the professional middle classes. Later in the 1990s and 2000s, urban-educated youth concentrated in Cairo and Alexandria would join the middle generation in their demand for democracy within the Brotherhood and in Egypt.

Islamic youth injected new blood into the movement in the 1970s and 1980s. When they joined, Madi told me in an interview, the Brotherhood seemed like a big empty home; their generation had to complete the building and furnish the house.[33] With the liberalization of the regime during Mubarak's early years in power, the university youth of the 1970s, who became the young professionals of the 1980s, started to shape the trajectory of the Brotherhood through active political participation. Tilmisani, whom Madi called their spiritual father,[34] supported their efforts wholeheartedly. He was considerably open-minded and allowed liberal Islamists to expand within the movement.

Following Tilmisani's death in 1986, these liberal Brothers faced a backlash from the old guard, most of whom had joined the Brotherhood in its early decades and lived through the turbulent years of Nasser's regime. Their aim was to preserve the movement as a religiopolitical entity, prioritize its survival over all else, and keep it under the control of a vanguard. The old guard included a variety of groups: figures from the first generation of Brothers, the Qutbists (or the 1965 organization),[35] and Salafis.[36] The first generation of Brothers were among the founders of the movement and companions of Hassan al-Banna. Qutbists were those inspired

---

[33] Interview with Abu al-Ela Madi, July 2, 2007.
[34] Wickham, *The Muslim Brotherhood*, 52.
[35] For more on the Qutbists within the organization, see Pargeter, *The Muslim Brotherhood*; for more details on Qutb's ideas, see Quṭb, *Milestones*.
[36] Led by Jamal al-Din al-Afghani and Muhammad Abduh, *Salafiyya* (return to the ancestors) advocated a return to the Islamic fundamental texts (the Qurʾan and the Sunnah) and reopening of the right to *ijtihad* (individual interpretation of the founding texts). This reinterpretation of the founding texts would enable Muslims to respond to the political, cultural and scientific challenges of Westernization and modernization, since Islamic heritage was compatible with modern ideas and institutions. Rashid Rida, a

by Sayyid Qutb, who argued for the necessity of a vanguard to guide the society toward Islam, much like Prophet Muhammad did in the seventh century. Unlike radical Qutbists in jihadi organizations though, Qutbist in the Brotherhood advocated a gradual and peaceful vanguard movement vested in socioreligious change. Salafis in the movement, on the other hand, were often less political and more social in their orientation, focused more on the proper Islamic outlook, from attire to gender relations, and maintained a strictly literalist interpretation of sharia. Many members that belonged to this wing had a rural background, and several of them had been exposed to quite conservative Salafism in Saudi Arabia.[37] Figures such as Mustafa Mashhur, Ma'mun al-Hudaybi, Mahmoud Ezzat, Mohammed Badie, and Khairat el-Shater formed a tight-knit circle around these ideals. Later Saad El-Katatni and Mohamed Morsi joined them in the vanguard, as I will discuss later.

Upon Tilmisani's death, the old guard sought to recapture the movement, clashing with the liberal Islamists, who aimed to turn the Brotherhood into a political party. As fruits of their growing activism, the movement released election manifestos and party platforms and campaigned in multiple elections. The old guard agreed on the necessity of political activism, but they tended to see it as a new form of outreach and a protective shield against regime repression. So they expanded Brotherhood's activities into the parliament and the syndicates. Ma'mun al-Hudaybi even expressed the movement's readiness to establish a party in 1993.[38]

Sustained political participation required greater political sophistication, and Brothers could no longer postpone key political issues to an indeterminate future. The liberal Islamists, through their work in parliament and professional associations, ignited a debate on democracy, human rights, religion, and politics within the movement.[39] As the internal debate continued, differences between two main groups crystallized. They diverged with respect to their understandings of democracy and

---

student of Abduh, made a conservative turn in Salafiyya thought by emphasizing the comprehensiveness and self-sufficiency of normative Islam more strongly than had Abduh. It is Rida's conservative version of Salafiyya that inspired al-Banna and the Brotherhood. For more, see Esposito, *Islam and Politics*, 49, 62–66.

[37] A sizable Salafi trend also existed outside the purview of the Brotherhood. These Salafi movements were politically quiet and focused on charitable work and religious activism (*da'wa*). They deemed the Brotherhood too political for their taste and "light" in their Islamic practices. Only after the 2011 revolution did some of these Salafi movements enter politics by establishing political parties. Chief among them was the Nour Party.

[38] Quoted in Sullivan and Abed-Kotob, *Islam in Contemporary Egypt*, 328–29.

[39] For more on this middle-generation and their activism in professional syndicates, see Wickham, *Mobilizing Islam* and Fahmy, "The Performance of the Muslim Brotherhood in the Egyptian Syndicates."

the movement's identity. The old guard believed Islam to be "the truth" and the Brotherhood to be the embodiment of the Islamic message. Their understanding of democratic politics rested on instrumentalism and righteous majoritarianism. The liberal Brothers, in contrast, considered the Brotherhood and Islam not to be the same thing, as the former, unlike the latter, was certainly fallible. For them, democracy was a game among equals and a system that promised peaceful turnover in power and conflict resolution. Hence, they committed to a more pluralist and liberal understanding of democracy. In an interview, Madi told me that his wing of the movement dramatically diverged from the old guard whose aim was self-preservation and Islamization of the society. Madi and his colleagues, in contrast, set democratic principles as their compass, while the old guard held onto Islam as "the solution."

Political disagreements between the old guard and the liberal Islamists crystallized from the 1980s onwards. Each pulled the movement in different directions, producing several contradictions in the Brotherhood's political documents and interactions with other actors. An early incident in 1994 revealed fundamental disagreements and the coming internal clash. Prominent names such as Abu al-Ela Madi and Essam Sultan engaged in nationwide talks for democratic reform in Egypt. As Madi recalls:

> In 1994 Egypt's professional syndicates held two conferences on national dialogue and civil society. As a result, a committee was formed to draft a national reconciliation document. The document was completed in 1995 and signed by leading opposition figures, including Fouad Serageddin, Khaled Mohieddin, and myself.[40]

This document marked a historic moment, whereby the Brotherhood joined other opposition forces for the first time to demand the democratization of the regime. In a serious blow to such efforts, Ma'mun al-Hudaybi, who served as the official Brotherhood spokesman in the same committee, refused to sign the national reconciliation document. He engaged in heated debates with the secular members of the committee because they refused to make any reference to religion or sharia in the document. In the end, all other members of the committee, including liberal Brothers, signed the document except for al-Hudaybi, who called it an "atheist national charter."[41] For him, any call for democratic reform had to include reference to sharia.

Political rifts within the movement further deepened in the first half of the 1990s. Despite rising pressure from liberal Islamists, as this incident

---

[40] Madi, "Decades On."
[41] Wickham, *The Muslim Brotherhood*, 86.

shows, the old guard remained eager to control the movement, as I will discuss later. In line with their political convictions, they cultivated a strong culture of obedience and refused to tolerate any internal dissent, which was seen as a threat to the movement's survival. The liberal Islamists, who had demanded that the Brotherhood pursue democracy, legality, greater cooperation with the secular opposition, and internal democracy within the organization, accused the old guard of being "autocratic, ideologically rigid, and obsessed with internal unity and discipline."[42]

The Wasat Party Initiative

After a decade of internal struggle, a group of Brothers such as Madi and Sultan established an independent political party in 1996. This party, appropriately named Wasat (Center), rejected the old guard's political vision and formulated a democratic framework.

The Wasat Party differed from the Brotherhood in three key respects: the perception of Islam and its role within the polity, its adherence to democratic principles, and its stance on minorities and women. The party distanced itself from the old guard's authoritarianism and scriptural dogmatism and sought to build a new polity around a civilizational conception of Islam that was more inclusive and pluralist than the old guard's. Islam, for the Wasat, was not religion and state (*din wa dawla*).[43] Nor was it the solution to society's problems (*huwa'l hal*). Like the old guard, the Wasat Party called for the application of sharia while endorsing a modern and democratic interpretation of the fundamental principles of Islamic law. Sharia, for the new party, was not the only source of legislation, as the old guard insisted. It was rather a source of principles, part of a peaceful and tolerant political culture. The founders of the party rearticulated Islam as a culture, which included all

---

[42] Wickham, *Mobilizing Islam*, 217.
[43] Stacher, "Post-Islamist Rumblings in Egypt"; Wickham, "The Path to Moderation." Wickham points to the experience of the Brothers in professional associations as the source of change in their attitudes. Accordingly, the middle generation in the Brotherhood cooperated with ideological rivals against the state's authoritarianism and took over responsibility in governing these associations. This whole process, for Wickham, represented a period of political learning in that the Brothers came to realize the value of democratic processes and principles. Assuming that it was indeed the learning process that created a group of moderates among Muslim Brothers, this explanation does not tell us why these moderates failed to transform the movement and gain support from the broader constituency of Islamists, or why the political learning has indeed remained an individual experience without diffusing to the rest of the movement.

components of the Egyptian society, irrespective of their religious creed. Replacing the perception of Islam as *din wa dawla* with a civilizational conception also meant that Islam was no longer a fixed truth frozen in time but a living phenomenon articulated and rearticulated by Muslims and non-Muslims both. In other words, the Wasat Party offered a national–cultural interpretation, rather than a religious interpretation of Islam. This national framework allowed for the endorsement of principles of egalitarian citizenship. For the Wasat Party, for instance, all adult citizens had a right to hold public office, including the presidency and prime ministry.[44]

Because Islam was no longer an ideology for the Wasat Party, its program rarely made references to religion. Instead, the platform offered secular solutions to concrete societal problems. For instance, the party program frequently mentioned the high level of corruption in Egypt. But unlike the Brothers who urged moral reform and Islamization of the individual to address the problem of corruption, the Wasat Party endorsed transparency and accountability within a better functioning legal system.[45]

The Mubarak regime denied legal recognition to the party, despite its repeated efforts. The old guard disowned the Wasat Party initiative and joined the Mubarak regime to discredit its founders, as I discuss later. Without substantial resources and organizational stamina, the party turned into a marginal actor. The old guard was relieved, but only for a moment. For there were still several liberal voices – like Aboul Fotouh, Habib, and Erian – who preferred to stay in the movement to pursue *"wasatization"* (moderation) from within instead of joining the Wasat Party. Thanks to their sustained activism and growing outside pressure on the movement to clarify its political vision, internal disagreements resurfaced in the late 1990s and early 2000s.

Such disagreements became increasingly visible in Brotherhood's official documents released to elaborate its economic, political, and social visions.[46] These platforms detailed the movement's understanding of the proper relation between religion and politics, democracy, human rights and freedoms, women's rights, minorities, and citizenship. Overall, the movement was moving in a democratic direction. Yet what various groups made of democracy differed significantly.

---

[44] Wasat Party, "Party Program," 7.
[45] Ibid., 9.
[46] These documents included the "Political Testimony" in 1994, "Statement on Democracy" in 1995, "An Initiative for Reform" in 2004, the electoral program of 2005, and the draft party platform of 2007.

Islam, the Brotherhood, and Politics

Political differences between the liberal Islamists and the old guard generated ambivalence in the Brotherhood's political platform and produced several contradictions. The electoral program of 2005, for instance, specified that the Brothers wanted to establish "a civil state with an Islamic frame of reference." The political system in this civil state would be a republican, parliamentary, and constitutional system under the umbrella of the principles of Islam.[47] The term "civil state" implied that officeholders would be civilians and not Islamic scholars or clergy. The Islamic frame of reference, on the other hand, referred to the idea of establishing a state that is in full compliance with sharia. This meant that the nation had the authority to build its institutions, although it had to follow the rules set by God. In other words, the contours of the law of the state were predetermined by Islamic law. But what the Brothers meant by sharia was unclear, and who would decide on the conformity of legislation with sharia remained uncertain.

In an interview in 2007, Aboul Fotouh, a prominent liberal Islamist, claimed that sharia did not contain any details in terms of political matters because it was a philosophy rather than a codified law.[48] For him, implementing sharia meant establishing human welfare and dignity, not enforcing traditional criminal punishments (i.e., *hudud*).[49] The purpose of the sharia was more important than its letter, he argued, echoing Rached Ghannouchi, as will be explained in greater detail in Chapter 5. Aboul Fotouh's take existed in clear contrast to the old guard's understanding, which echoed the literal Salafi interpretation.[50] Al-Hudaybi, a staunch member of the old guard, challenged Aboul Fotouh's view:

> Sharia includes texts relating to systems which nowadays are considered to be an integral part of politics. We, the Muslim Brotherhood, demand that *these particular Islamic injunctions* be adhered to and acted upon. They cannot be disregarded, neglected, or their application and enforcement ignored.[51] [emphasis added]

When it came to mechanisms of compliance, there was no consensus either. Mohammed Habib, another liberal Brother, for instance, claimed that the Constitutional Court and regular judges would make sure that legislation complies with sharia.[52] The Brotherhood's old guard begged

---

[47] The Muslim Brotherhood, "The Muslim Brotherhood's Program for the Parliamentary Elections of 2005."
[48] Interview with Aboul Fotouh, July 18, 2007.
[49] Aboul Fotouh, "Democracy Supporters Should Not Fear the Muslim Brotherhood."
[50] For example, Salafis endorsed strict implementation of criminal punishments delineated in Islamic sources.
[51] Wickham, *The Muslim Brotherhood*, 95.
[52] Interview with Mohammed Habib, July 19, 2007.

to differ. They released a statement to clarify their position in 2007 in response to the criticisms of the Brotherhood's ambiguity regarding the mechanics of applying sharia in a democratic state by Hamzawy and others. In this official statement, they specified that there should be a council of religious scholars to oversee the legislative function of parliament and oversee compliance with sharia. This council, reminiscent of the Iranian system, would hold veto power over the elected parliament. The old guard, in other words, envisioned a state with both democratic and theocratic features. This dual nature radically departed from the liberal Islamists' conceptualization of "a civil state with an Islamic frame of reference" and confused outsiders.

The Brotherhood's position on elections and political pluralism included similar contradictions. On the one hand, thanks to the push by liberal Islamists, the movement advanced a liberal democratic agenda and demanded that elections be free and fair, that multiple political parties compete for political power, and the freedoms of belief, expression, and association be fully recognized. On the other hand, the old guard insisted on an instrumentalist view of democracy and prioritized Islamization over democratization. Mahdi Akef, the movement's General Guide between 2004 and 2010, clarified its priorities. "The final goal of the Muslim Brotherhood [in entering] parliament, elected councils, syndicates, and all civil society establishments," Akef declared, "is to [erect] the Muslim society."[53] And he imprinted this view in the 2005 electoral program:

Spreading Islam as a whole guarantees stability, development, revival, prosperity, honor, sovereignty, peace, security, safety, truth and justice for the nation. All these will be achieved *only* by Islam, as it is indeed *the* solution for all our problems, and it is the way to achieve all what we need and wish in all fields, economically, politically, culturally, socially, and educationally for the sake of the homeland.[54]

The old guard received its inspiration from Banna. Islam, for them, was more than a religion; it offered the only and comprehensive truth, and it regulated all aspects of life. Brothers' mission was to revive Islam through peaceful means. The members of the Brotherhood were, then, "*Islamic preachers* who use[d] wisdom and [...] preaching to apply Allah's law as He ordered through the available peaceful means, [such as] existing constitutional institutions and the fair ballot boxes."[55] Democracy was a

---

[53] The Muslim Brotherhood, "The Muslim Brotherhood's Program for the Parliamentary Elections of 2005."
[54] Ibid.
[55] Ibid.

peaceful means, but not an end in itself. As the Milli Görüş movement in Turkey deemed, the true end was to establish an Islamic society.

At the same time, the Brotherhood, for the old guard, was an indispensable actor of Islamic reform in the Egyptian society and a guarantee of the preservation of Islam. Islam and the Brotherhood were one and the same. This sanctification of the movement informed the political preferences of the old guard and their followers: (1) the survival of the movement was an utmost priority, since without it there was no future for Islam in Egypt; (2) because Islam is an all-encompassing religion and the Brotherhood is the guardian of the Islamic method, separation of the religious and political functions of the organization violated the main tenets of Islam, and both *da'wa* and political activities complemented each other to attain this broader objective of Islamic reform; and (3) other political actors lacked this moral strength and could not be proper partners for the movement's mission; therefore, cooperation and engagement with such ideological rivals for political reform were not preferable, but if they become necessary, such partnerships should be short-term and strategic in nature.

With respect to democracy and political freedoms, the old guard thus adopted an instrumentalist and antipluralist position. Democratic politics provided the Brotherhood with outreach efforts and saved it from regime repression. For the old guard, the purpose of formal politics "was not to effect a transition to democracy but to prepare the way for Sharia rule."[56] "Either you have God's law or you don't," Ma'mun al-Hudaybi (speaker of the Brotherhood's parliamentary bloc at the time) remarked. "There is no middle ground between them."[57] Brothers entered parliament, as their leaders argued, "to utter the word of Truth at all times."[58] In short, neither democratization nor cooperation with other political actors were of import for the old guard. Islamization came before everything else, and democratization was just another stage in this process.

Aboul Fotouh and other liberals contested this instrumentalism. Aboul Fotouh, for instance, claimed that Islamic discourse was not holy; instead, it was the product of human understanding. Democracy, moreover, was more than a means of reaching power; it was a unique fruit of human experience that had intrinsic value.[59] Democracy, hence, was an end in itself. He also rejected the religious component of democracy as envisioned by the old guard; for him, democracy signified rule by the people, not rule by the law of Allah.

---

[56] Wickham, *The Muslim Brotherhood*, 58.
[57] Ibid., 54.
[58] Interview with Hudaybi in 1988, cited in Wickham, *The Muslim Brotherhood*.
[59] Elad-Altman, "Current Trends in the Ideology of the Egyptian Muslim Brotherhood," 3.

The middle generation also differed from the old guard in their commitment to political pluralism. They valued democracy and human rights and collaborated with other stakeholders of different ideological backgrounds toward democratic reform, seeing them as partners and equals. When it came to the movement's identity, they did not perceive the Brotherhood to be one and the same as Islam. Instead, their political activism was a fallible human attempt to improve the social and economic conditions in Egypt; they were not charged to deliver "the Truth." Their goal, therefore, was to advance human rights and freedoms, and the movement was an instrument toward this goal.

Separating Religious and Political Activism

Such disagreements carried important implications for the trajectory of the Brotherhood as an organization. The liberal Islamists and the old guard clashed over its identity and organizational principles. Because the old guard saw Islam as an inseparable whole, separating religious activity from political activity was indeed in violation of the principles of Islam. For them, the Brotherhood's political branch was an integral part of the broader movement. The liberals challenged this conviction and called for functional differentiation and complete autonomy of political activities from the religious mission.

In 2005, the General Guide Mohammed Mahdi Akef released a statement reaffirming Banna's vision for the Brotherhood. "[This] is a community of Muslims dedicated to the rule of Allah's law," Akef claimed. "[They] seek to revive Islam and to establish an Islamic state that will follow Islam's rules, implement its social order, and propagate its principles."[60] Separation of religion and politics, for Akef, was impossible:

> This great religion must be taken as one integrated whole, each part of which can function only with the other. [...] It is absolutely impossible to separate religion from politics, or religion from the state, or the acts of devotion from [political] leadership. This is the Brotherhood's faith.[61]

The liberal Islamists pushed back by challenging the old guard's view of an all-comprehensive Islam, summarized in the motto "Islam is the solution." Aboul Fotouh responded to Akef when I interviewed him in 2007:

> Some say of Islam is the solution, [but] what is the opinion of Islam to solve the traffic problem? It is not a rule of Islam; parliament legislates on the matter. We ask

---

[60] The Muslim Brotherhood, "The Muslim Brotherhood's Program for the Parliamentary Elections of 2005."
[61] Ibid.

the Islamic law to be *marja'iyya*, cultural reference for us when we legislate when we make our laws. [...] We believe in Islam as a civilization. It does not interfere in different details but provides general principles in economics, politics, etc.[62]

So the liberals called for the separation of the Brotherhood's religious functions from its political activities and demanded the establishment of an independent political party with no organic ties to the religious movement.[63] Such a separation would give the party autonomy from the old guard and allow for the democratization of membership by removing the existing barriers for women and non-Muslims. A prominent moderate liberal Islamist Essam el-Erian elaborated on the necessity of separating different functions of the movement: "The Brotherhood agreed upon separating the functions of preaching from politics," he said and continued: "The Muslim Brotherhood is a general Islamic organization fully concerned with Islam [in politics]. It is as a civil party with an Islamic authority *that is open to all citizens*. [...] Such a party will be conservative in nature, civil in practice, and political in style.[64] [emphasis added]

Women's and Minority Rights

The separation of political and religious functions of the movement had direct implications for minority rights and inclusion. The presence of a sizable Coptic Christian minority (roughly 10–15 percent of the population) in Egypt made the Brotherhood's approach toward minority rights even more pertinent. The old guard's understanding of democracy proved to be deeply majoritarian when their attitudes toward the Christian minority or heterodox Muslim groups such as Baha'is, Shi'a, and Sufis[65] were taken into consideration. Their perception of women was also deeply hegemonic and patriarchal, denying women their rights. The liberal Islamists, in contrast, displayed clear liberal leanings with respect to both religious minorities and women.

In 2004 and 2005, the movement proclaimed in its electoral program that Copts should be equal citizens with equal rights and duties as Muslims.[66] "Citizenship is the basis of life in a democratic society," Aboul Fotouh claimed. "Every citizen is equal to all others, regardless of doctrinal differences. Citizens should choose their government through free

---

[62] Interview with Aboul Fotouh, July 18, 2007.
[63] El-Erian, "Towards the Renaissance."
[64] Ibid.
[65] On the relationship between Sufism and the Brotherhood, see Elsässer, "Sufism and the Muslim Brotherhood."
[66] The Muslim Brotherhood, "The Muslim Brotherhood's Program for the Parliamentary Elections of 2005."

and fair elections." The old guard, in contrast, justified equal status for Copts not through democratic principles of equal citizenship but through Islamic law, which demands "fair treatment" of non-Muslims. While liberal Islamists pushed for equal citizenship in Egypt, the old guard proposed discriminatory policies on different occasions. For instance, in 1996, Mustafa Mashhur, the General Guide at the time, declared that the special tax on non-Muslims (*jizya*) had to be reinstated in Egypt. Similarly, the draft party platform of 2007, in clear violation of the liberal line, included a discriminatory proposition to bar non-Muslims (and women) from running for the highest executive office in the country.

Along with the rights of religious minorities, the status of women has been another area of contention among the Brothers. Women, for liberal Brothers, were equal with men and were entitled to full political and social rights.[67] "Islam want[ed] women to put their minds and efforts at the service of society," Aboul Fotouh declared in an interview in 2005. He also commented on the much-contested topic of women's bodies and proper clothing. For Aboul Fotouh, women's attire had no import and should not even be a subject for debate; the *hijab* "was merely a question of identity and belonging, just as saris [were] for Indians."[68]

The old guard, by way of contrast, proved to be quite conservative on women's freedoms and rights. For them, men and women were not equal. They were different, with different rights and duties. Women were first and foremost mothers, rather than individuals with liberties. Preservation of their sanctity and family care were among women's chief duties. They could enjoy certain rights only if they fulfilled these duties. For instance, women could participate in elections and in public life only if they preserved their honor and dignity. Their social and educational life would also be shaped by these priorities. The old guard, therefore, advocated an educational program specifically designed for women so they could better fulfill their functions within the family. A special curriculum would teach girls proper childcare, household management, and motherhood.[69] Because women were essentially emotional creatures, the old guard deemed, they could not compete for high executive offices.

The Brotherhood's 2007 draft party platform raised such concerns. This draft was much less liberal in orientation than the 2004 party platform and retreated from many of its ideals. Most critically, the new platform suggested barring women and religious minorities from running

---

[67] El-Erian, "Towards the Renaissance."
[68] Aboul Fotouh, "The Islamic Path to Reform."
[69] The Muslim Brotherhood, "The Muslim Brotherhood's Program for the Parliamentary Elections of 2005."

for the highest offices in the country. Thus, it undermined the principle of equal citizenship and instead sought male Muslim supremacy. Prominent figures within the old guard, such as Mahmoud Ezzat and Rashad al-Bayoumi, were basically reverting the liberal direction of the movement in 2004 platform.[70] We know from liberal Islamists' criticism in the aftermath that the old guard had not consulted them in the preparation of the new document. The old guard – and the official narrative of the Brotherhood – proclaimed that the platform was written by a group of Brothers, legal experts, and religious scholars; then, it was opened to debate within the Guidance Bureau, local offices of the Brotherhood, and the Shura Council. Aboul Fotouh, still a member of the Guidance Bureau at the time, stated in several interviews that a debate on the draft platform had never occurred. Similarly, Gamal Heshmat, then the leader of the Brotherhood's parliamentary group, claimed that the views of the parliamentarians were not taken into consideration.[71]

Still, liberal Brothers challenged such discriminatory provisions for both women and religious minorities. In an interview I conducted in 2007, el-Erian expressed his opposition to the clauses that barred women or Copts from running for executive office; he had voiced his concerns within the movement but had failed to convince others (read the old guard).[72]

It was increasingly clear from such contestations that the Brotherhood was divided. Besides, their political and ideological positions seemed irreconcilable. The old guard was eager to control the movement and get rid of liberal Islamists, whom they had long perceived as outsiders. And they succeeded. The next section explains how.

Purging the Liberal Islamists within the Brotherhood

By the time Morsi got elected the new president of Egypt in 2012, the old guard had secured absolute control of the organization. And their understanding of democracy informed the Brotherhood's trajectory in power. How did the old guard manage to capture the organization?

The short answer is that the old guard prevailed by capturing key organizational resources. They exercised substantial command over organizational rules, recruitment and promotion, internal communication, and the movement's finances to build a dominant coalition. These resources allowed the old guard to dictate the incentive structure for rank and file Brothers in vertical power games. Deprived of such resources,

---

[70] Kandil, *Inside the Brotherhood*, 136.
[71] Hamzawy, "Regression in the Muslim Brotherhood's Platform?"
[72] Interview with Essam el-Erian, July 17, 2007.

the liberal Islamists gradually lost the horizontal power games and failed to withstand the competition.

The old guard neutralized them in three major waves. The first wave hit with the Wasat Party initiative in 1996. A second wave came with the 2009 internal elections that many contested as fraudulent. The final showdown came with the 2011 revolution. The old guard took the political opening as an opportunity to purge or subdue the remaining liberal Borthers within the organization.

Rules and Structure of the Organization

The Brotherhood's organization is like a pyramid with a strict hierarchy. The smallest organizational unit of the movement is a cell (*usra*) that includes five to six members who meet weekly to discuss Islamic topics as well as local activities. Cells unite to form local branches (*shuʿba*), and local branches unite to form regions (*mantiqa*). In each governorate, the movement also has an administrative office (*maktab al-idari*). At the peak of the pyramid overseeing the local organizations are three key organs: the General Guide (*al murshid al-ʿam*), the Guidance Bureau (*maktab al-irshad*), and the Shura Council (*meclis al-shura*).[73]

The Shura Council, with more than a hundred seats, performs legislative functions for the Brotherhood, and its decisions remain binding for all. Ninety members of the Shura Council are elected in internal elections from each governorate, with a specific number of seats reserved for them in the council. Another fifteen members are appointed by the Guidance Bureau. The Guidance Bureau has fourteen to sixteen members, elected by the Shura Council, and serves as the highest executive organ of the movement. Its members are charged with the execution and implementation of the Shura Council decisions and day-to-day affairs of the movement. The General Guide, elected by the Shura Council, is the spiritual and operational leader of the movement. He holds the authority to oversee all branches and keep them accountable. He can also change the charter and the bylaws of the movement or make unilateral decisions with only four members of the Guidance Bureau.[74] His powers are practically unlimited, yet he is also theoretically accountable to the Shura Council, which can replace him if he fails to fulfill his duties, a prerogative the council has never exercised.[75]

---

[73] Interview with Abdelrahman Ayyash, January 11, 2016. Also see al-Anani, *Inside the Muslim Brotherhood*.

[74] For details, see *Muslim Brotherhood*, "Bylaws of the International Muslim Brotherhood" and Kandil, *Inside the Brotherhood*, 68–69.

[75] *Muslim Brotherhood*, "Bylaws of the International Muslim Brotherhood."

In theory, the Shura Council seems to be the most important of the three since it is elected by active members of the Brotherhood, holds both the General Guide and the Guidance Bureau accountable, and performs budgetary oversight.

This is at least what Brotherhood's bylaws specified for each organ. In reality, the Shura Council rarely exercised its powers. In fact, the council lost its authority to the Guidance Bureau, which ended up controlling not only the entire organization but also its budget and external relations. The Bureau often assumed legislative functions and ruled without convening the Shura Council for most of the 1990s.

The centralization of power in the Guidance Bureau stemmed from the old guard's desire to monopolize power. So they manipulated the rules of the organization to serve their interests. First, the old guard conveniently took advantage of the precarious political context within which the movement operated to rule the movement single-handedly.[76] This close-knit circle kept the movement's bylaws secret for many decades, citing security reasons. No members could access the rules of the organization until 2010. In the aftermath of contentious internal elections in 2009, the youth of the Brotherhood pressured the senior leadership to make the bylaws public. Only then did the executive office publish the bylaws.

Second, the old guard arbitrarily amended the bylaws a few times until 2010 to guard their power in the organization. Thanks to these changes, the rules remained flexible enough to hand greater power to the General Guide and the Guidance Bureau. Indeed, the elections for the Guidance Bureau were supposed to be every four years. Yet the old guard amended the rules to extend the Bureau's term when the security situation impeded elections, and they repeatedly postponed internal elections citing the security concerns as a pretext. According to Madi, they took advantage of the illegality of the movement to operate in secrecy and avoid accountability and transparency inside the organization.[77] Indeed, the Shura Council met only twice to elect the Guidance Bureau, once in 1995 and later in 2009. Without the council electing the guide or members of the bureau, the old guard dominated both offices, appointing their own to key positions without internal elections.

With limited accountability in the organization, figures in the Guidance Bureau entrenched their power. They formed a tight-knit circle and rarely allowed anyone to penetrate their lines. Their followers also climbed up the organizational ladder much faster and remained in their

---

[76] Al-Anani, *Inside the Muslim Brotherhood*.
[77] Interview with Abu al-Ela Madi, July 2, 2007.

seats longer. For instance, Mustafa Mashhur was quickly promoted to the first deputy to the General Guide following Tilmisani's death. His election as the new General Guide after the death of Muhammad Hamid Abu al-Nasr in 1996 proved to be quite contentious. The Qutbists within the Guidance Bureau elected Mashhur without consulting the Shura Council.[78] Mashhur remained the guide until his death in 2002. Similarly, Ma'mun al-Hudaybi became the official spokesman of the movement upon his return from exile in 1986. Hudaybi was promoted to the first deputy General Guide and succeeded Mashhur. Other seats were occupied by Ezzat, Shater, and Akef, among others, for most of the 1990s and 2000s.

After Tilmisani's death, the old guard treated the middle-generation as outsiders to the organization and set the hardships that the former generations encountered under state repression as the criteria for senior positions in the movement.[79] Their dominant position blocked liberal Islamists from rising to leadership within the movement and curbed their impact. Only a few figures among these younger generations could join the Guidance Bureau. One such figure was Aboul Fotouh, who joined the bureau in 1985 under Tilmisani's leadership, a seat he would keep until the 2009 internal elections. Others in the bureau were Mohammed Habib and Essam el-Erian, who served shorter terms than Aboul Fotouh. These liberal Islamists pressured the old guard to make such processes transparent and decentralize power within the movement. Habib, for instance, often complained of the secretive and hierarchical style that allowed the Qutbists to dominate the Guidance Bureau through such organizational maneuvers and sidelining the Shura Council in the 1990s.[80]

Whatever limited power liberal Brothers had in the movement's executive branches ended for good in the internal elections of 2009,[81] when amendments to the bylaws bore fruit. In what many called an "internal coup," the old guard eliminated their opponents in the highest executive branch and entrenched their command over the organization. Aboul Fotouh was ousted; Habib was sidelined; Erian was co-opted. Meanwhile, Khairat al-Shater, favored by the old guard, kept his seat despite being in prison.[82] The old guard also managed to elect another general guide among their ranks, namely Mohammed Badie, in January 2010. Badie was Qutb's prison mate and a loyal follower. The

---

[78] El-Ghobashy, "The Metamorphosis."
[79] Wickham, *The Muslim Brotherhood*.
[80] Habib quoted in Al-Awadi, "Islamists in Power."
[81] Lynch, "Conservative Gains in Muslim Brotherhood Elections."
[82] Tammam, *Abdel-Monem Abu El-Fotouh*, 27–28; Kandil, *Inside the Brotherhood*, 137.

new guide appointed three close allies as his deputies: Mahmoud Ezzat, Rashad al-Bayoumi, and Gomaa Amin.[83] Ezzat, coming from a rural background, was known as the mastermind behind the coup against the liberal wing. He served as Brotherhood's secretary-general for many years before becoming Badie's deputy. Exercising close control over the movement's organizational structure and finances for years, he was dubbed the "iron-man" by the members of the movement. To many, he became the most powerful man in the movement in the absence of a charismatic General Guide after Tilmisani's death.[84] With his close associate Shater, the duo amassed significant organizational power.

Recruitment and Promotion

Unlike the AKP in Turkey, recruitment in the Brotherhood was highly selective and a long process with multiple stages. Not everybody could join the movement; those who were sympathetic to its cause had to go through a rigorous socialization and vetting process before becoming a member. Membership also had its stages, and each stage had accompanying duties and rights, creating an intricate incentive structure. Prospective members were called sympathizers and supporters, and they could attend the weekly meetings in the cells. Once they were vetted after months of scrutiny and training, they were accepted to the organization and could become "real Brothers." Only then they unlocked a set of privileges members enjoyed. Yet they still could not vote in internal elections at this stage and had to attain "regular" membership to do so. Regular members could attend meetings at the local level and vote in the elections but had to wait until they became "active" members to run for the Shura Council or the Guidance Bureau.[85] When a regular member became an active member, they took an oath to express their loyalty to the movement and obedience to its leaders:

I pledge allegiance to the Almighty Allah to constantly uphold and safeguard the principles of Islam, to fight in the cause of Allah, to adhere to the terms and duties of the Brotherhood's membership, showing as much as possible obedience to the just leaders in sorrow and in joy as long as it does not involve disobedience to Allah, I pay allegiance and may Allah be my witness.[86]

In short, it took years to join the movement, during which potential members were subject to intensive indoctrination (*tarbiyya*) and were

---

[83] *Al-Ahram Weekly*, "Mohammad Badie Appoints Conservative Voices after Being Elected the Guide."
[84] Interview with Abdelrahman Ayyash, January 11, 2016.
[85] Ibid. See also Al-Anani.
[86] Muslim Brotherhood, "Bylaws of the International Muslim Brotherhood."

expected to show a high level of commitment to the movement and obedience to leadership. Without fulfilling these requirements, one could not join or remain a Brother. The flip side was that whoever disobeyed the leaders and generated dissent was sanctioned and even kicked out of the movement. The threat of such sanctions obviously created a strong disincentive to criticize the leadership after spending years to join the movement. After all, losing membership also meant losing the wide Brotherhood social network and its resources. The Wasat Party initiative is a good case in point. When sixty-two Brothers established the party in 1996, the Guidance Bureau threatened the founders of the party with expulsion and asked them to rescind their party membership. Several of them eventually did, presumably due to fear of losing their social capital within the organization. Only sixteen founders, among them Madi, chose to resign from the Brotherhood.

Both material and immaterial incentives to join and remain in the organization combined with recruitment and promotion criteria based on loyalty and obedience cultivated a very strong hierarchy among the Brothers. This strong hierarchy was, in fact, the old guard's doing.

Hence, they remained particularly invested in the movement's organization (*tanzim*) and discipline.[87] They controlled the entire organization and shaped its incentive structure in vertical power games. The liberal Islamists, in contrast, pursued political activism outside of the organization, engaging with Brotherhood's rivals and pushing for reform in Egypt. Because they advocated the separation of religious and political activism, they pursued the latter while leaving the *da'wa* and recruitment to the old guard.[88] This allowed the old guard to control the "backbone of the organization and enabled them to *steal* the younger generation" from the liberal wing.[89] Many liberal Brothers in retrospect called this a mistake on their own part.

Central to the old guard's recruitment strategy was what Tammam calls "ruralization."[90] From the movement's second founding in the 1980s, the Guidance Bureau pursued rural recruitment and ruralized all levels of the movement, from local chapters to the Guidance Bureau. Recruits from rural governorates proved to be more socially and politically conservative and overtly hostile in their attitude toward Copts. They were also more loyal to and less critical of the old guard compared to recruits from urban centers such as Cairo and Alexandria, where

---

[87] Kandil, *Inside the Brotherhood*, 137.
[88] Interview with Abu al-Ela Madi, July 2, 2007.
[89] Wickham, *The Muslim Brotherhood*, 93. Emphasis added.
[90] Tammam, "Ruralization of the Muslim Brotherhood."

the youth, in particular, were attracted to the liberal Islamist' ideals. Primarily concerned with *daʿwa* and the Islamization of the society, the rural members were eager to submit to the authority of their leaders, while urban youth demanded greater transparency and democracy within the movement following the middle generation.

Recruits from rural backgrounds, perhaps more so than others, benefited from the Brotherhood's material and collective incentives. The movement provided a strong sense of identity and a vast network armed with significant resources. As Hussein Kazzaz summed it up in an interview, many Brothers joined the movement's student organizations in college; married someone from the movement; found jobs in Brotherhood-affiliated companies; and received services from Brotherhood clinics, schools, and kindergartens.[91] They could easily lead lives almost completely isolated from the rest of the society.[92] For recent migrants from rural areas, the Brotherhood's networks provided a sense of safety and belonging in the vast city life.

Often, the old guard built nepotistic relations with rural recruits, which fortified their incentive structure as well as their organizational dominance. They relied heavily on rural Brothers to man positions in mid-level leadership, the Shura Council, and the Guidance Bureau. Whoever remained loyal to the leadership was rewarded. The Guidance Bureau appointed members to the Shura Council, overrode local election results, and suspended administrative offices to keep a strong grip over local chapters and promote their supporters.

As Madi notes, the members of the Guidance Bureau filled "the strategic posts in the group's regional and local branches with individuals beholden to them and vested in their conception of the group's mission."[93] The case of Sabri Arafa is a good example. As Kandil reports, Arafa, supported by the old guard, lost the elections in his province; still, he kept his seat in the local and national Shura Council and was later elected to the bureau. When members inquired about his promotion that clearly violated the bylaws, the bureau members advised, "Not questioning your Brothers is a sign of faith" and "A good Muslim is the one who minds his own business."[94]

By the mid-2000s, middle-ranking leadership positions were dominated by Brothers from rural centers such as Asyut, Minya, Dakahlia, and Sharqiyya.[95]

---

[91] For a brilliant work on the Brotherhood's social services and their beneficiaries, see Clark, *Islam, Charity, and Activism*.
[92] Interview with Hussein Kazzaz, January 6, 2017.
[93] Kandil, *Inside the Brotherhood*, 68–69.
[94] Ibid.
[95] Tammam, "Ruralization of the Brotherhood."

The old guard also made sure that loyalists of rural backgrounds carried greater weight in the Shura Council. The process started in the 1990s and reached a peak in 2008. In the 2008 Shura Council elections, more seats were allocated to rural governorates such as Dakahlia, Sharqiyya, and Gharbiya (twenty-five seats) than heavily populated Cairo and Alexandria (eleven seats), a traditional home to liberal Islamists and one-third of the Egyptian population.

These changes also ruralized the Guidance Bureau. Cairo's dominance in the highest executive organ of the movement ended by 2009; if the seats were proportionately allocated, nine out of sixteen members should have come from Cairo, yet only three were from major cities.[96] Several new members with provincial backgrounds replaced liberal Islamists from major urban areas in 2008 and 2009. Morsi, the future president from Sharqiyya, and Sa'ad al-Katatni, the future chairman of the FJP from Minya, were among them.

The liberal wing and their allies among the urban youth reacted to ruralization and "radicalization" of the movement. They deemed that the 2008 and 2009 elections were not proper. In a public statement, leaders of the urban youth rejected the internal elections as undemocratic and nontransparent because the members of the Shura Council could not meet in a single location to elect the members of the Guidance Bureau for security reasons. "The absence of elections in such circumstances is a trick designed to hide the undemocratic behavior of the movement," they declared, claiming that the Brotherhood was "supposed to be the finest example of democracy for the nation."[97] They called for new elections where women could also vote and proposed their own list for the Guidance Bureau.[98] Not surprisingly, the list mainly consisted of liberal Islamists. In the end, their call fell on deaf ears. Clearly, the urban youth was now a minority in the Brotherhood. The rank and file were dominated by provincial members with more conservative tendencies, thanks to the old guard's strategy of rural recruitment and promotion.

Internal Communication, Socialization, and Indoctrination

For the old guard, internal communication was of critical importance, since the culture of obedience was a direct result of the heavy indoctrination that marked the backbone of internal communication within the

---

[96] Kandil, *Inside the Brotherhood*, 32.
[97] *Egypt Independent*, "Brotherhood Youth Criticize Group's Structure."
[98] Their list included Mohamed Ali Beshr, Khairat al-Shater, Abdel Moneim Aboul Fotouh, Essam el-Erian, Mohammed Habib, Gamal Heshmat, Abdel Rahman el-Bar, Abdel Hai el-Faramawi, Ibrahim el-Zaafarani, Mohammed al-Baltagy, Ahmed Abdel Rahman, Mohamed Abdel Ghani, Mustafa el-Naggar, Ibrahim al-Hudaybi (representing the youth) and Amal Khalifa (for women).

movement and complemented the guard's recruitment and promotion strategy. The old guard controlled the organization and its entire internal communication, from grassroots activism to the literature assigned for the recruits. So the movement became responsive to their message.

In each stage of membership, Brothers had to go through a process of instruction and socialization run by an office within the Guidance Bureau. This is how the staged membership system, al-Anani observes, enabled the Brotherhood to shape its members, their worldviews, and behaviors; this is how the leadership tightened its grip on the movement.[99] The old guard closely monitored and controlled the office in charge of instruction and indoctrination[100] and created its curriculum. In Madi's words, the old guard had thus brainwashed the new generations and cultivated their own way of thinking among the youth.[101]

The curriculum was designed to convey several messages and build a collective incentive structure.[102] The first and most important message was that the movement and Islam were the same. All the teachings in the Brotherhood's curriculum, according to its leaders and members, are not ideological indoctrination but religious instruction. The movement taught its members how to be – and how to live as – good Muslims. Working for the Brotherhood was working for Islam; being a brother meant being a proper Muslim; leaving the Brotherhood meant leaving Islam. As a brother told al-Anani in stark terms: "[When you leave the movement,] you are renouncing your faith not an ideology; you are abandoning God not Hasan al-Banna."[103] Hence, the members, if they internalized this message, were incentivized to stay in the movement and remain loyal to the leaders.

Second, both Islam and the Brotherhood had enemies, and these enemies worked hard to destroy them both. Working for the Islamic mission (and by implication the Brotherhood) required complete dedication, loyalty, solidarity, and obedience. This ongoing war required vigilance and solidarity. It also required following the ten pillars of Banna's teachings: understanding, sincerity, action, jihad, sacrifice, obedience, perseverance, resoluteness, brotherhood, and trust. Unquestioning and total obedience to the leaders were must. They were the leaders of Muslims in the absence of a caliph and would direct the *ummah* to salvation. Because Islam and

---

[99] Al-Anani, *Inside the Muslim Brotherhood*, 98.
[100] Ibid., 86.
[101] Interview with Abu al-Ela Madi, July 2, 2007.
[102] For a comprehensive overview of Brotherhood's curriculum, see Chapter 2 in Kandil, *Inside the Brotherhood*.
[103] Al-Anani, *Inside the Muslim Brotherhood*, 50.

the Brotherhood were one and the same, dissent within the movement also signified a sinful act, or was at the least an expression of weak faith. Hence, the leaders were sanctified and beyond reproach.

Despite this heavy indoctrination centered around complete obedience to leadership, when some challenged the leaders and questioned their decisions, the old guard made sure to confine their impact within the movement. A well-known target was the liberal Islamists. When a group of Brothers established the Wasat Party in 1996 without approval, the old guard threatened the party founders with expulsion, but not all members budged. Then the leaders discredited them through accusations of embezzlement and fired them.[104] As the leadership joined the Mubarak regime to discredit the Wasat Party and the Brotherhood's lawyers made a case against Wasat's legalization in the court,[105] the old guard circulated an internal document to reaffirm that Islam was an all-encompassing religion and it was a duty of faith for all Brothers to respect one's elders, while allegiance was an obligation "grounded in the morals of [Islamic] faith."[106] In other words, Wasat Party members violated Islamic duties and had questionable faith.

Once the first wave of liberal Brothers was purged with the Wasat Party initiative, the old guard kept the remaining liberals invisible in the organization and prohibited them from engaging with the rank and file.[107] The leaders practically monopolized the line of internal communication and made sure that liberals' message did not trickle down to the movement's base. Figures like Aboul Fotouh, el-Erian, and later Mohammed al-Baltagy were cut off from the local offices. Ezzat, for instance, as the secretary-general of the movement for most of the 1990s, isolated Aboul Fotouh from the base. He was also consistently demonized and discredited in the eyes of the younger members. Whenever Aboul Fotouh raised his criticisms against the old guard, the leadership, using the internal communication channels, warned the members that Aboul Fotouh was recruited by Americans; he only remained in the Guidance Bureau so the senior Brothers could keep an eye on him.[108]

The old guard did not only control the local offices, their indoctrination, and the curriculum but also proactively monopolized new and emerging venues of communication. For instance, with the onset of widespread use of the internet, Shater established the *Ikhwanweb*, the

---

[104] Kandil, *Inside the Brotherhood*, 135.
[105] Wickham, *The Muslim Brotherhood*, 82.
[106] Ibid., 93–94.
[107] Interview with Abdelrahman Ayyash, January 11, 2016.
[108] Kandil, *Inside the Brotherhood*, 135.

Brotherhood's official English website, in 2004. So the old guard entered cyberspace. In an age when online fora and blogs became popular among Egyptian youth, the old guard kept an online channel with a centralized and unified message for its internal and external audiences.

The Organization's Finances

Finances also played a key role in bolstering the power of the old guard. Brotherhood's revenue primarily came from its members' dues. Once an individual becomes an associate member, they contribute a certain share of their income to the movement. More affluent members pay up to 7 percent of their income, while less affluent members pay around 1 percent. In addition, members are also encouraged to make donations and pay their *zakat* (religious alms) to the movement. With hundreds and thousands of members – the actual number is not known since the movement does not keep records for security reasons – the Brotherhood commands substantial financial resources.

Whoever controls the movement's finances also wields power within the organization. In theory, it is the Guidance Bureau that controls finances and reports to the Shura Council that approves the movement's budget. However, as Sayyid al-Melegi claims, the Guidance Bureau took over and has had control over the council's power on budget and financial resources since the 1990s.[109] Two figures within the Guidance Bureau, Shater and Ezzat, remained in charge of the movement's finances.

Shater, a close associate of Ezzat, along with several others left Egypt in the 1970s for self-imposed exile in the Gulf to avoid regime repression. He stayed in the Gulf for years, where he engaged in entrepreneurial activity. Soon after his return to Egypt, he partnered up with a long-time brother, Hasan Malek, to start new businesses. Shater then quickly ascended within the organization and joined the Guidance Bureau in 1995, thanks to his familial connections, financial clout, and ideological proximity to the old guard. As a prominent figure in the bureau, he took over the movement's finances and invested members' dues in scores of small and medium enterprises in a wide range of sectors from pharmaceuticals to car dealerships.[110] These enterprises financed Brotherhood activities for decades. His financial wizardry also invited repression when the Mubarak regime arrested Shater and his partner in 1992 for financing the movement. Upon his release several months later, Shater continued to control the

---

[109] Al-Anani, *Inside the Muslim Brotherhood*, 114.
[110] Ibid.; Kandil, *Inside the Brotherhood*, 79.

Brotherhood's finances while building his own wealth. With such immense power, as Henry told me in an interview, Shater established extensive patronage and sustained significant influence within the movement.[111] He went so far as to build a parallel organization within the Brotherhood that was loyal to him over anyone else, including the General Guide.[112] Morsi, the future president, for instance, was one of his proteges.[113]

In short, the old guard's control of the leadership in a strictly hierarchical organization with an authoritarian and paternalist culture allowed them to sideline liberals within the movement. Commanding the selective and collective incentive structure through their control over the rules of the organization, recruitment and promotion processes, internal communication and indoctrination, and finances played a critical role in the old guard's dominance. That is how, when the revolution took off in 2011, the old guard was firmly at the helm of the organization. Then, they used their power in the movement to shape Brotherhood's trajectory.

The Brotherhood after the Revolution: The Old Guard Sidelines the Liberal Islamists

The Mubarak regime fell in just seventeen days following thirty years of rule.[114] Inspired by their counterparts in Tunisia, Egyptian youth mobilized to end the authoritarian practices of the government on January 25, 2011. The popular mobilization quickly gained a revolutionary character, and the Supreme Council of Armed Forces (SCAF) sided with the revolutionaries to oust Mubarak on February 11. Thus began a political transition that would last less than three years.

Brotherhood's urban youth had been working with other political groups prior to the revolution, and they unsuccessfully pushed the leadership to engage with prodemocracy movements and dissident groups such as Kefaya, Kulluna Khaled Said, and the April 6th movement. The old guard, however, prioritized Brotherhood's interests over democratic coalition-building and followed a cautious path before they were convinced that Mubarak was certain to fall. Their hesitance attracted significant reaction from the youth, some of whom defied the orders and joined the protests. The Brotherhood youth in urban centers built a broad revolutionary front for eighteen days until Mubarak's ouster, and the old guard joined

---

[111] Interview with Clement Henry, January 28, 2013.
[112] Reported by several former and current Brothers, al-Anani, *Inside the Muslim Brotherhood*, 153.
[113] Kandil, *Inside the Brotherhood*, 79.
[114] For excellent accounts on the Mubarak regime and its resilience, see Brownlee, *Authoritarianism in an Age of Democratization* and Blaydes, *Elections and Distributive Politics in Mubarak's Egypt*.

the revolutionary momentum in late January. As Yasser Fathy, a prominent student leader at Alexandria University and a former Brother, told me in an interview, the youth lost the initiative to the leaders thereafter because they lacked an action plan and organizational power. They were later dispersed within the Brotherhood, as I discuss below.[115] In the end, the leaders reasserted their authority soon after Mubarak's removal.

The split within the movement boiled down to the way different factions approached the transition. For the old guard, the transition provided new opportunities to advance the mission of the Brotherhood. It also introduced new challenges that required careful steering. Amid political turbulence, the old guard aimed to keep the movement intact, secure its survival and gains, and leverage the democratic process to accomplish its long-standing goals, that is, Islamization. So they took advantage of new opportunities to maximize the movement's power and influence over the transition. The best strategy to attain such goals, for the leadership, was electoral politics. The institutional path included several stages of establishing a political party, running in elections, drafting a new constitution, and cooperating with existing powerholders, including the armed forces, if need be.[116] Given the movement's superior mobilizational capacity and traditional emphasis on gradual reform, it came as no surprise that the old guard pursued electoralism over revolutionary alternatives.

The liberal Islamists, including the urban youth, had their priorities elsewhere. They desired democratic change instead of maximizing the Brotherhood's partisan gains and perceived the movement as a means toward this greater end. So they supported greater engagement and collaboration with the non-Islamist opposition to pursue revolutionary change instead of electoral victory. They also pushed for greater transparency and internal democratization within the movement, arguing that the new political context rendered Brotherhood's secretive and hierarchical organization obsolete.

Yet the balance of power within the movement was in favor of the old guard. As Fouad explained in an interview, the youth could hardly reach the leaders and raise their concerns. The rigid hierarchy and obedient culture that the old guard had deliberately built throughout the 1990s and 2000s meant that whatever decision the Guidance Bureau made would be followed by all levels down to the local level.[117] In fact, the old guard imposed several controversial decisions in a top-down fashion throughout the transition.

---

[115] Interview with Yasser Fathy, August 9, 2017.
[116] Interview with Khaled Fouad, August 8, 2017.
[117] Ibid.

In February, for instance, the Guidance Bureau decided to push for a rapid transition to civilian rule by holding parliamentary and presidential elections before drafting a new constitution. It was clear that the leadership desired to capitalize on the movement's discipline and mobilizational capacity to surpass other actors, who needed time to build their organizational capacity. This would give a significant head start to the Brotherhood in elections and in drafting the new constitution. They contended that a political party, as the movement's organic extension, would be a suitable instrument for this goal and secretly met with the SCAF to negotiate the terms of the legalization of the Brotherhood's political wing. For the liberal Brothers, making deals with the military was unacceptable.

At this stage, the old guard also promised that it would follow a path of "participation, not domination." They promised that they would not field a presidential nominee or contest every seat in the parliament. Despite this early position, the movement rapidly changed course and sought to obtain power and shape the transition process to their liking through electoral politics.[118]

Again in February, the Brotherhood carved out a seat in the constitutional committee to impact the transition process. The goal was to have parliamentary elections prior to the drafting of the constitution and hand the Brotherhood leverage over the new foundational document and the regime in the making. It got what it wanted when a pro-Islamist judge, Tarek El-Bishry, proposed a set of amendments to the constitution to regulate the presidential and parliamentary elections and specify procedures for drafting a new constitution.[119] Accordingly, elections would precede the drafting of a new constitution, and a newly elected parliament would select a Constituent Assembly (CA) charged with drafting the text. The Brotherhood enthusiastically supported the proposal, presumably counting on its mobilizational advantage in the founding elections. Yet many within the revolutionary forces demanded the drafting of a new constitution before the elections. The liberal Brothers agreed.

The old guard refused to reconcile and pushed for a fast-track transition to civilian rule via elections. The constitutional amendments were taken to a referendum in March. The movement pulled its entire weight behind the "Yes" vote and ran a campaign filled with exclusionary and polarizing propaganda. As the International Crisis Group has documented, the Brothers deeply Islamized their campaign to invoke Islamic sentiments and evoke fear among pious Egyptians. For instance, the

---

[118] Pargeter, *The Muslim Brotherhood*.
[119] International Crisis Group, "Lost in Transition: The World According to Egypt's SCAF."

Brothers on the campaign trail frequently warned their supporters that "opposing the amendments would be tantamount to rejecting Article II of the 1971 constitution, which describes Islamic Sharia as the principal source of legislation."[120] In other words, rejecting the amendments was tantamount to rejecting Islam. The amendments passed with 77 percent voting in favor. And the old guard got what they wanted.

The next step was to establish a political party. In April 2011, the Brotherhood formed the Hizb al-Hurriya wal-Adala (FJP) as a nominally independent party with strong ties with the mother organization.[121] In a quite controversial move, the General Guide Mohammed Badie prohibited the Brothers from joining other political parties.[122] The aim was to preserve the political unity of the movement under the old guard's leadership and maximize its electoral gains. The leaders drafted the entire party platform and its bylaws. They also selected the party's leadership among the conservative members of the Guidance Bureau. Mohamed Morsi became the chairman and Sa'ad al-Katatni became the secretary-general. Both came from rural backgrounds. Essam el-Erian, a liberal voice co-opted by the old guard, became the party's official spokesman. The old guard's control over the party did not end there. They determined the number of seats the FJP would contest in the parliamentary elections as well as its nominees.[123] Hence, they extended their control over the emerging incentive structures in the new party. The Guidance Bureau also continued to monitor the FJP's parliamentary work and political strategy over the course of the transition. The party's top leaders – Morsi, Erian, and Katatni – held weekly "coordination" meetings with the prominent figures in the bureau, Khairat al-Shater, Mahmoud Ezzat, Mahmoud Hussein, and Mahmoud Ghozlan.[124]

As the leadership continued to single-handedly design the political trajectory of the movement, the internal rifts reached an irreconcilable level. Particularly contentious was the establishment of a Muslim Brotherhood party and its relationship to the mother movement, relations with other actors including the SCAF and revolutionaries, and the decisions regarding elections.

There was no debate within the movement as to the necessity or the nature of a political party. Struck by the absence of internal discussion, Hussein Kazzaz, a veteran member of the movement, recalls asking why

[120] Ibid.
[121] The Brotherhood submitted a formal application on May 18, 2011.
[122] *Egypt Window*, "Hizb Al-Hurriyya Wa-l-'adāla."
[123] El-Hennawy, "Defying Leadership, Brotherhood Youth Form New Party"; Brown, "The Muslim Brotherhood as Helicopter Parent."
[124] Trager, *Arab Fall*, 111.

members had not deliberated on the matter. The leaders told him that they had already decided on the issue in the 1990s, hinting that a new discussion was unwelcome. So the old guard's decision two decades prior stood intact, even though the political context was fundamentally different after the revolution.[125]

The liberal Islamists contested the decision. Aboul Fotouh rejected the idea of establishing an official party of the Brotherhood, claiming that this decision was not taken by the Shura Council. For Aboul Fotouh, the fusion of religion and politics in an official Brotherhood party would be a threat to the nation.[126] Haythem Abou Khalil, who had been leading the "reform front" that emerged in reaction to the purge of leading liberals in the 2009 internal elections, agreed with Aboul Fotouh. Khalil's group demanded greater political pluralism and freedom within the Brotherhood, a clear separation of religious and political functions, while also rejecting some of the key decisions of the leaders such as endorsing a "Yes" vote for the constitutional amendments in the March 2011 referendum. Frustrated with their lack of impact on the leadership, the group, led by Ibrahim Zaafarani and Abou Khalil, left the Brotherhood to establish the liberal democratic Renaissance (Nahda) Party in March 2011. Their party platform focused exclusively on economic issues and rarely referenced Islam.

In reaction to the tight control movement's leaders extended over its members' political activities, liberal Islamists who had not yet joined Khalil insisted on separating the religious and political functions of the Brotherhood. Hoping that they could change the movement from within, they organized an independent conference in March and called for the complete separation of religion and politics in the Brotherhood. The separation, they hoped, would politically emancipate them and secure the independence of the FJP. Student leaders from Alexandria, Cairo, Mansoura, Al-Azhar, and Ain Shams universities also agreed that the Brotherhood should not work with the SCAF but should ally with the revolutionary forces. They penned long letters to the leadership, criticizing how the leaders had managed the transition process, and warned that the Brotherhood could win in the short run but would lose in the long run and cause the revolution to fail.[127] Resolute to maintain discipline and strict hierarchy even under a more open political environment, the leaders refused to tolerate such dissent and threatened to expel the Brothers who participated in the conference. It was clear that the old guard would not tolerate internal pluralism even under a democratic system.

---

[125] Interview with Hussein Kazzaz, January 6, 2017.
[126] Hasan, "Aboul Fotouh: Arfaḍ Ta'sīs Hizb Li-l-Ikhwan al-Muslimin Fi Masr."
[127] Interview with Yasser Fathy, August 9, 2017.

When the young Brothers finally realized that the old guard would not budge, they left to form their independent party, Hizb al-Tayyar al-Masry (The Egyptian Current Party). They rejected Islamism as an ideology and did not refer to sharia in their platform. "We cannot refer to the Islamic Sharia because this is not an Islamist party and it is not a party for the Muslim Brotherhood youth," said Mohammed Shams, a twenty-four-year-old cofounder of the party.[128] Unlike the old guard, they engaged with other political groups in the country and prioritized democratic change over partisan interests.

A few months later, Aboul Fotouh established his own political party, Masr Kawiya (Strong Egypt Party), and joined those liberals who decided to operate outside of the Brotherhood's political framework. Back in March, he had broken ranks and declared his political independence from the leadership, saying he would run as an independent candidate in the upcoming presidential elections. He was expelled from the Brotherhood in June 2011 for violating the organization's initial decision not to field a candidate in the elections (which was rescinded later) and froze the membership of 4,000 Brothers who had been working for Aboul Fotouh's campaign.[129]

This final purge of liberal Islamists within the Brotherhood in the aftermath of the revolution left the movement under complete control of the electoralist old guard. Having monopolized power within the organization, they were now ready to monopolize power in the country.

The Old Guard at the Helm

Electoralism dictated the old guard's perception of democracy; for them, electoral victories signified clear mandates to shape the transition process and rule as they deem fit. So the Brotherhood, under the old guard's uncontested control, adopted righteous majoritarianism, treated their political rivals as illegitimate entities, and instrumentalized democratic procedures to begin the Islamization of the society and state. With liberals purged or sidelined within the organization, there was no political voice left to demand inclusive politics and engagement with other political actors. Instead, exclusion, polarization, and hegemonic Islamism characterized Brotherhood's political style throughout the democratic transition.

---

[128] El-Hennawy, "Defying Leadership, Brotherhood Youth Form New Party."
[129] *Al-Masry Al-Youm*, "Arba'at alf min shabāb al-Ikhwan yanḍammūn li-ḥamlat da'm «Abu al-Futuh» wa-l-jama'a tujemmid 'uḍwiyyathim." The Wasat Party supported Aboul Fotouh in presidential elections. See *Al-Ahram*, "al-wasaṭ yu'ayyid Aboul Fotouh bi-intikhābāt al-ri'āsa."

These attitudes became evident starting with the parliamentary elections which were scheduled for November 2011. Although the old guard promised otherwise, as elections approached, they reversed course and the FJP contested the majority of seats in parliament in the November elections. Once it captured the plurality of seats, the FJP sought to dominate both the CA and the legislative committees in parliament to draft the new constitution and dominate the legislative agenda.

Brotherhood's Electoral Platform and Campaign

Prior to the elections, the FJP released its electoral program, which gave certain clues with respect to the system Brotherhood's leaders envisioned. Overall, the document was a major improvement over the draft party platform released in 2007. It offered guarantees for universal rights and liberties, equal citizenship, and a political system based on the separation of powers without any tutelary authority. Besides, there were no clauses discriminating against religious minorities. Yet the document also maintained some of the grey zones of the draft platform by keeping sharia central to its political vision:

> The State envisaged in our program is the national constitutional *Islamic modern democracy*, based on Sharia as a frame of reference. By its nature, Sharia nurtures aspects of faith, worship and morality, and also regulates various aspects of life for Muslims and their non-Muslim partners in the homeland. However, in few cases, Sharia regulates these aspects through definitive texts with direct relevance and significance. It can also regulate through *general rules and principles*, leaving details for interpretation and legislation as suits different times and environments, in the service of justice, righteousness and the interests of the homeland and citizens. *This is to be entrusted to legislative councils, while the Supreme Constitutional Court is charged with monitoring the constitutionality of resulting legislation.*[130] [emphasis added]

Thus, the FJP signaled that it would keep certain injunctions of the Islamic law (i.e., *hudud* punishments, inheritance, divorce, and so on) intact and make sure that future legislation conformed to them. Apparently, these injunctions would be the red lines of the regime the Brotherhood envisioned. Yet what the party referred to as general rules and principles of sharia remained largely vague. How secular parties and CSOs would operate under this system remained unclear. And the political implications of the full implementation of sharia law remained ambiguous.

---

[130] Freedom and Justice Party, "Election Program – Parliamentary Elections 2011."

A closer look at the platform also revealed discriminatory policies geared toward women. In line with its Islamizing mission, the party established "moral development" of the Egyptian society as its major goal. Such moral development centered on the sanctity of the family and preserving the chastity of women with immediate implications for the rights and duties of women. As stated in its platform, the FJP aimed to "[e]nsure women's access to all their rights, *consistent with the values of Islamic law*, maintaining the balance between their duties and rights" [emphasis added]. The FJP also openly rejected the Convention on the Elimination of All Forms of Discrimination against Women (CEDAW) signed by the Mubarak regime, which called for the legal equality of men and women and an end to all forms of discrimination based on sex. The FJP argued that the convention "control[led] the most private of the marital relationship details," which, the party claimed, should be under the purview of sharia. The party also perceived the National Council for Women and the National Council for Childhood and Motherhood as "the intelligence arm of the international players in Egypt." The party proposed to:

Integrate traditional family values in education curricula, consolidate the values of chastity and modesty in the media, in education curricula, and in street advertisements, reviewing labour laws, to allow mothers with new-born children to spend more time with their children, so as not to limit their role in raising and upbringing their young, as much as possible, reviewing personal status laws, ridding them of materials destructive to the family, and endeavoring to make personal status laws comply with Islamic law, while reserving the right of Copts to their own personal status laws.[131]

Hence, the FJP signaled that they would sustain their religious mission, the Islamization of society starting with the family and the education system, on a grander scale. Overall, the electoral platform revealed that the party was eager to design Muslim life and politics in a fundamental fashion and would not tolerate social pluralism and diversity among Muslims.

To realize these goals, the Brotherhood had to win the parliamentary elections. So the old guard fully mobilized the political machine for elections scheduled for November 28, 2011.[132] Breaking its earlier promise of not dominating politics, the FJP-led bloc ended up contesting all of the seats in multimember districts.[133] But it did not stop there. It also supported

---

[131] Ibid., 25.
[132] Voting began on November 28 and ended on January 3, 2012.
[133] The constitutional amendment divided the seats in parliament into two groups: two-thirds of the seats would be open to political party competition in closed lists, while the rest would be allocated to individual contenders. El-Hennawy, "Brotherhood Contests over 50 Percent of Parliamentary Seats."

several independents (presumably with similar ideological standing) in single-member districts.[134] The aim was to dominate the new parliament.

As the political party with the strongest network of committed supporters, the FJP emerged with a victory in the ballot box with 37 percent of the votes. It won 216 out of 508 seats (43.4 percent), while its closest contender, the Islamic alliance composed of conservative Salafi parties, obtained 125 seats. The secular liberal Wafd received forty-one, and the secular center–left Egyptian Bloc got thirty-four seats. The rest of the parties received ten or less seats, while independents got twenty-five seats in total.[135]

The leaders of the Brotherhood took this modest electoral victory as a clear mandate for their Islamist platform. In a strong expression of righteous majoritarianism, Khairat al-Shater claimed that the elections had proven that Egyptians were demanding "an explicitly Islamic state" and "the people are insistent [that] all institutions should revise their cultures, their training programs and the way they build their individuals in the light of this real popular choice."[136]

Shater's interpretation of the election results displayed the hegemonic and majoritarian tendencies of the old guard and precluded power-sharing arrangements and engagement with political parties with lesser support. So, with a plurality of the seats in parliament, the FJP sought to dominate legislative committees. The speaker of the house and several committee heads were elected among the FJP deputies, who were reluctant to share these positions with their rivals.[137] Such a hegemonic posture alienated other parties in the parliament and some of them, such as the liberal Wafd, ended up boycotting the committee elections. The Brotherhood was not willing to just participate; it desired to dominate.

The Constituent Assembly Elections: The Muslim Brotherhood Seeks Conflict over Compromise

The new parliament was also charged with selecting 100 members for a CA that would draft a new constitution. The FJP adopted the same majoritarian attitude in the CA elections on March 24, 2012. The party leveraged its parliamentary plurality to shape the CA and, by extension, the new constitution. In a series of negotiations, the FJP and Salafist parties agreed to elect half of the CA among members of parliament,

---

[134] Trager, *Arab Fall*.
[135] Carnegie Endowment for International Peace, "2012 Egyptian Parliamentary Elections."
[136] Kirkpatrick, "Keeper of Islamic Flame Rises as Egypt's New Decisive Voice."
[137] El-Gundy, "Freedom and Justice Party Heads Most of Egypt's Parliamentary Committees."

to the dismay of non-Islamist deputies.[138] For the rest of the assembly, which would come from different parts of society, the Islamist bloc favored figures sympathetic to their ideology. When the elections were complete, 64 out of 100 members either came from Islamist parties or had ties to Islamist movements.[139]

Every single name on Brotherhood's list was elected to the CA; among them were both members of parliament and representatives from different social and professional segments. For instance, the only student representative, Mohamed el-Rakibi, was Mohamed Morsi's nephew. The only diplomat in the assembly, former ambassador Mohamed el-Tantawi, was well known as an Islamist sympathizer.

In reaction, liberal voices within the CA walked out in boycott, claiming that the assembly was not representative of the Egyptian society. Liberal Islamists like Essam Sultan, deputy chairman of the Wasat Party, joined non-Islamists and called for consensus and a common understanding among its members before the assembly resumed its activities. Instead of seeking consensus and exercising institutional forbearance, the FJP and its allies went ahead with further procedures. They elected Katatni as the chairman of the new assembly with a quarter of CA members missing. Sultan also walked out in protest of Katatni's election.

For electoralists in the Brotherhood, such calls for consensus and greater inclusion of all segments of the society were undemocratic. The assembly was perfectly legitimate because its members were elected by the people's representatives. From a procedural and majoritarian point of view, the Brotherhood was right. Yet it was also clear that they were not willing to follow democratic norms of engagement, deliberation, and institutional forbearance. The goal was to maximize the movement's power using electoral procedures. The FJP reacted harshly to the claims that the CA was not representative. Party leaders such as Sobhi Saleh accused those seeking wider consensus within the assembly of seeking a "dictatorship of the minority." He warned that the assembly would not be beholden to this dictatorship and the meetings would continue irrespective of any boycotts.[140] Katatni, then the speaker of the assembly, doubled down and threatened the boycotters

---

[138] *Ahram Online*, "Brotherhood Raises MP Ratio for Constituent Assembly Seats ahead of Saturday vote."

[139] *Ahram Online*, "Islamists Reserve 65 Seats on 100-Member Constituent Assembly"; Revkin, "Parliament Names Constituent Assembly Members, but Many Refuse Their Seats."

[140] Essam El-Din, "Islamists Attack 'Dictatorship of the Minority.'"

by replacing them with reserve members, which included many more Islamists with sympathy for the Brotherhood.

One way to establish the legitimacy of the assembly was to delegitimize its critiques. In that vein, the Brotherhood leaders resorted to polarization and further exclusion. For them, the boycotters were traitors and autocrats: "a *disloyal* minority of Christians and secularists conniving with the old regime."[141] These exchanges clearly conveyed Brotherhood's electoralism, majoritarianism, and its lack of tolerance for dissent, criticism, and minority demands. Also noteworthy was their rather narrow political toolkit, which mostly included balloting – because they were good at it. Compromise, deliberation, and negotiation were not part of that toolkit, given the Islamist majority in the parliament. Boycotters refused to concede. They took the case to the High Administrative Court to annul the assembly elections. The court ruled in their favor, citing a prior judicial ruling which prohibited deputies from self-selecting to electoral bodies.

Presidential Elections

In the meantime, the Brotherhood sought to maximize its influence in the executive. In March 2012, soon after the parliamentary elections, parliamentary speaker Katatni threatened the acting government with a vote of no confidence to extract concessions from the SCAF. Katatni met with General Tantawi to increase the FJP's seats in the cabinet, but the negotiations broke down when the old guard deemed SCAF's offer of four unimportant cabinet seats unacceptable.[142] The Brotherhood wanted more power.

It was clear from these meetings that the military would not give the Brotherhood executive power over the course of the transition. Frustrated with the persistent pushback from its non-Islamist rivals and the military, electoralists eager to dominate the transition decided to field a candidate in the presidential elections. The proposal to field a candidate was quite contentious and was discussed in the Shura Council for thirty-three hours in an extraordinary session in March 2012. Many members with extensive political experience, including el-Erian, al-Baltagy, and Heshmat, opposed the idea of having a Brotherhood nominee. They reasoned that such a drastic reversal would ultimately discredit the movement. They also argued that the Brotherhood was not ready to govern. Most of those who pushed for a yes vote, in contrast, had

---

[141] Pahwa, "Pathways of Islamist Adaptation," 1076.
[142] Interview with Osama Soliman, June 5, 2017.

backgrounds in *tarbiya* (religious education and *da'wa*) and argued that they, as the representatives of Islam, had an obligation to govern Egypt. For the Brotherhood, Islamic reform had four stages. The movement had been investing time and energy in the first two stages, namely individual reform and social reform. The revolution, according to yea-sayers, initiated the third stage: Islamic government. In their view, no movement or party was a better fit for this task than the Brotherhood, which spent decades defending Islam in Egypt. Besides, they believed, Egyptians handed them a popular mandate for an Islamic government. Other actors, however, precluded it from carrying out this popular mandate; to pass to the stage of Islamic government, they argued, the Brotherhood had to compete for the executive office.[143]

According to a Shura Council member who was present in this discussion, the leadership was adamant about reversing the earlier decision to not dominate the transition. Brothers were skeptical though. In the first vote, the motion failed. Reportedly, Ezzat and Morsi asked for a repeat vote, in clear violation of internal rules.[144] In between the two votes, the old guard held separate meetings with council members to convince them. The motion to field a presidential nominee finally passed with a small margin (52 percent in favor). In the same meeting, the council also designated Khairat al-Shater as its presidential nominee.

This was a major reversal for the Brotherhood and one that sent conflicting messages to the society at large and generated rifts within the movement. Once again, the electoralist old guard dictated key organizational decisions. This vote also revealed the FJP's total submission to the mother movement, as it was Brotherhood's Shura Council, and not the party's organs, that made the decision to contest the presidential elections and selected its nominee.

In April 2011, however, the Supreme Constitutional Court disqualified Shater from the presidential race along with two other nominees, citing his prior prison term. In response, the Brotherhood nominated their second choice, Mohamed Morsi, a member of the Guidance Bureau and head of the political branch. Morsi, coming from a rural background, was a firm believer in the movement's organizational hierarchy and culture of obedience. He also vehemently defended Brotherhood's right to rule Egypt.

On the campaign trail, Morsi capitalized on polarization to woo voters. He revived the traditional Brotherhood slogan, "Islam is the

---

[143] Interview with a Shura Council member.
[144] Willi, *The Fourth Ordeal*, 267.

solution" and self-identified as the real Islamist candidate in the race. For Hamid, the increased Islamist tone was due to the unexpected Salafist victory in the parliamentary elections, which presumably pushed the movement toward the far-right.[145] Yet the connection was suspect, since Salafis, after their candidate failed vetting, decided to support liberal Islamist Aboul Fotouh in the presidential elections. Thus, one can safely claim that Morsi's real rival was Aboul Fotouh, who synthesized liberal democratic commitments with Islamic credentials. The Morsi campaign aimed to discredit Aboul Fotouh with claims that a Fotouh victory would be the end of Islam and he would ban mosques like Atatürk and Nasser had done in Turkey and Egypt, respectively. The Brotherhood complemented this rhetoric with scare tactics among its members to prevent them from voting for Aboul Fotouh.[146]

Despite shifting rightward and embracing the slogan "Islam is the solution," Morsi received only 24.8 percent of the votes. Although he won the plurality and secured the second round, this was still a clear decline in Brotherhood's electoral fortune compared to the 37 percent that the FJP bloc received in the parliamentary elections. The second runner-up was Ahmed Shafik, Mubarak's former prime minister, with 23.6 percent of the votes. Their closest rival, the center–left Hamdeen Sabahi, received 20.7 percent, while liberal Islamist Aboul Fotouh came in fourth with 17 percent. In the end, only a quarter of Egyptians voted for Morsi, while millions voted for other nominees.

In the second round, the Egyptian people were caught between an autocratic rock and an Islamist hard place. Recognizing the untenable choice people had to make, liberal Islamists tried to pull Morsi closer to a more participatory, inclusive, and pluralist understanding of democracy. In such an attempt, liberal Islamists with former ties with the Brotherhood such as Aboul Fotouh, Ibrahim al-Hudaybi, Fahmy Howeidy, and Heba Raouf Ezzat invited Morsi to sign a charter for a civil and democratic state.[147] Although Morsi agreed to meet with these figures, he refused to make any formal commitments. In other words, instead of opting for compromise, consensus, and coalition-building through deliberation, the Brotherhood once again went for electoralism and majoritarianism in clear contrast to Ennahda, as I discuss in the next chapter.

[145] Hamid, *Temptations of Power*.
[146] Interview with Abdelrahman Ayyash, November 27, 2016.
[147] Wickham, *The Muslim Brotherhood*, 260, fn 45.

Morsi's Year in Power: "Ikhwanization," Polarization, and Exclusion

Morsi came out victorious with 51.7 percent of the votes in a quite competitive second round and became Egypt's first freely elected president on June 24, 2012.[148] Morsi's year in power was marked by his attempts to maximize his power and Brotherhood's impact on the Egyptian state. Echoing AKP's contention that effective governance required the fusion of powers, the Brotherhood frequently complained of the hurdles posed by the remainders of the Mubarak regime. Mostly such complaints were legitimate, for pushback from the former regime sought to impede democratization. Soon, however, Morsi's actions revealed that, like his counterpart in Turkey, his goal was to capture the state instead of democratizing it. His main strategy for this task centered on electoralism and partisan mobilization, instead of building cross-ideological democratic coalitions among revolutionary forces. In other words, Morsi deployed Brotherhood's political machine to win elections and conquer the state.

Morsi rushed to impose the Brotherhood's control over different parts of the state and the society through "Ikhwanization" (in reference to Brotherhood's Arabic name, Ikhwan) including Al-Azhar, the media, judiciary, and trade unions through politicized appointments and presidential decrees. In the end, his term was characterized by exclusion, polarization, and unilateralism, as he alienated significant parts of the society that had voted for him. In a series of interviews that I conducted in Cairo in January 2013 with actors across the political spectrum, I recorded their statements of disillusionment after giving Morsi the benefit of the doubt. For several respondents, his policy of "Ikhwanization" was a major source of disappointment. Emad Shahin, one of his former advisors, confirmed that Morsi remained under the influence of Mahmoud Ezzat and Khairat al-Shater.[149] Many agreed that Morsi acted as "the president of the Brotherhood" and failed to become the president of all Egyptians. That is, his loyalty remained with the old guard instead of charting his independent course.

So what did Egypt's first freely elected president do in office? This section analyzes Morsi's one year in power and how he undermined basic freedoms and alienated broad segments of the society.

At the time of his election, major uncertainty defined Egypt's political transition. There was no constitution (other than Mubarak's) and no

---

[148] International observers such as the Carter Center reported some irregularities in both rounds, though they concluded that such irregularities did not favor one candidate over another. For further details, see the Carter Center's full report on Egypt's presidential elections.

[149] Interview with Emad Shahin, January 29, 2013.

parliament. A few days before the presidential elections on June 14, 2012, the Supreme Court declared parliamentary elections unconstitutional because parties contested seats reserved for individual candidates. On June 17, the SCAF dissolved parliament and expanded its authority at the expense of the future president.[150] Both the judiciary and the military signaled to the Brotherhood that they would not let it monopolize power.

On August 12, only two months into his term, Morsi released a presidential decree and assumed all executive and legislative authority. Adamant to draft a new constitution, Morsi annulled SCAF's June 17 declaration and handed himself the right to appoint a new CA in case there emerged any setbacks in drafting the new constitution.[151] As he attempted to monopolize power presumably for the sake of the revolution, Morsi failed to rule inclusively and share power with the revolutionary forces. Indeed, Morsi's entire presidential team was made up of Brotherhood sympathizers,[152] thus frustrating the expectations of non-Islamist revolutionary forces in the society.

Morsi also attempted the "Ikhwanization" of the state. In September, he appointed four Muslim Brothers and a Brotherhood sympathizer to ten governorates in Egypt.[153] This would be the first of many more partisan appointments in key bureaucratic posts. It was clear to many observers that Morsi did not want to reform state bureaucracy or the judiciary but to conquer it, exactly like his counterparts in Turkey.[154]

Again echoing the AKP, controlling the media also became a priority for the Brotherhood under Morsi's presidency. A crucial difference was that the media remained largely controlled by the state in Egypt. So, unlike Erdoğan, Morsi did not need to build an elaborate clientelist network to control the media through private owners. Appointing partisan figures to the state-run press would suffice. And that is what he did. Instead of democratizing the Egyptian press, Morsi took advantage of the authoritarian institutions he inherited from Mubarak. The Ministry of Information was one of these institutions that had exercised substantial control over Egyptian media. The opposition pushed hard for its reform and demanded a nonpartisan Ministry of Information along the BBC model in the United Kingdom.[155] Morsi dismissed the proposal and appointed a long-time Brother, Salah Abdel Maqsoud, as the new minister in early August.

[150] *Egypt Independent*, "SCAF Expands Its Power with Constitutional Amendments."
[151] *Ahram Online*, "Morsi's Constitutional Declaration."
[152] Specifically, fifteen of twenty-one members of his team were Islamists, and a plurality were affiliated with the Brotherhood. Aboulenein, "Morsy Appoints Islamist-Dominated Presidential Team."
[153] Trager, *Arab Fall*, 165.
[154] Interview with Amr Chobaki, January 29, 2013.
[155] Ibid.

In another partisan move, Morsi authorized the Islamist-dominated upper house to appoint new editors to major state-run newspapers – namely *Al-Ahram, Al-Gomhuria*, and *Al-Akhbar*. The new editors were quite controversial, with suspect commitment to religious freedoms. Abdel Nasser Salama, the new editor of *Al-Ahram*, had lost his column for writing anti-Christian articles, whereas Gamal Abdel-Rahim, appointed to *Al Gomhuria*, had shut down a conference on religious freedoms for Baha'is and incited hatred against the Baha'i community.[156] After taking over these papers, the recently appointed editors started a purge in their new homes; they fired some columnists and forced others to retire while replacing them with columnists sympathetic to the Brotherhood.[157] Egyptian media was becoming increasingly Ikhwanized.

In the meantime, liberal Islamists who parted ways with the Brotherhood forcefully criticized Morsi's actions. Aboul Fotouh, as chairman of his new party Masr Kawiya, remained highly critical of Morsi's disregard for the opposition and his dependence on the Brotherhood loyalists for administrative appointments and cabinet shuffles.[158] In an interview, Aboul Fotouh told me that Morsi was elected as the president of all Egyptians, yet his ties to the Brotherhood did not permit him to act as one; in fact, Aboul Fotouh posited, Morsi meshed Islam and politics, thus polarizing society by juxtaposing Islam against secularism, which was a grave mistake. Aboul Fotouh called for a clear separation of religion and politics and a more inclusive and transparent government that would build consensus among the revolutionary forces.[159] Because Morsi failed in these respects, Aboul Fotouh openly called and campaigned for new elections for several months following Morsi's November decree.

On November 22, Morsi released a presidential decree that placed his existing and future decisions above judicial review and annulled all pending court rulings against his previous decrees.[160] The decree also included a vague and broad provision that "the President may take the necessary actions and measures to protect the country and the goals of the revolution," practically donning him with powers even Mubarak had not acquired.[161] Thus, the president monopolized legislative and executive power in his office and eliminated any judicial oversight over his decisions.

---

[156] El-Gundy, "Egypt Shura Council Announces New Heads for 3 State Papers."
[157] Blumenthal, "The Muslim Brotherhood's War on Egyptian Media."
[158] *Reuters'* interview with Aboul Fotouh, November 24, 2012.
[159] Interview with Aboul Fotouh, January 30, 2013.
[160] The same day he released this decree, Morsi also appointed Talaat Abdullah as the prosecutor general overstepping the authority of the Supreme Judicial Council. For Chobaki, this was an excellent instance of Brotherhood's aim to conquer the state. Interview with Amr Chobaki, January 29, 2013.
[161] *Ahram Online*, "Morsi's Constitutional Declaration."

As expected, the decree ignited nationwide protests. A new bloc – the National Salvation Front (NSF), composed of liberal and center–left figures – spearheaded this wave of mobilization against the decree that handed Morsi "dictatorial powers." Liberal Islamists also joined the protests. "The Muslim Brotherhood needs to understand that democracy is not just a way to gain power but an end in itself," Aboul Fotouh exclaimed.[162] Instead of compromising or engaging with the opposition, Morsi dismissed, belittled, and delegitimized these protests by calling them enemies of the revolution. He chose the course of polarization and countermobilization. Standing behind its president, the Brotherhood soon weighed in. In response to ongoing popular protests, the movement organized "a million-man march to support legitimacy and sharia" on December 1 and framed protesters as un-Islamic.

As the crisis escalated and Morsi refused to back down, anti-Morsi protesters began a sit-in in front of the presidential palace on December 4, calling on Morsi to rescind his decree. Again, Morsi resorted to countermobilization. On December 5, pro-Morsi supporters attacked the protesters to disperse the sit-in. Ten were killed and hundreds were injured in the clashes, while reports of Brothers torturing protesters spread widely. Once again, Morsi chose to delegitimize protests instead of mitigating the crisis. He claimed that the protesters were "hired thugs" paid by Mubarak loyalists, and they had ties with "foreign interests determined to thwart the revolution."[163]

In the meantime, a group of pro-Brotherhood lawyers filed a complaint against the leaders of the NSF. General Prosecutor Talaat Abdullah, appointed by Morsi in a controversial decision, acted upon the complaint and ordered an investigation into the three NSF leaders with high treason, an attempted coup, and conspiracy against the legitimate government.[164] Morsi's efforts to conquer the state had begun to give its first harvest. The prosecutor dropped the charges a few weeks later, yet the message was clear. Morsi had a majoritarian understanding of democracy, had no tolerance for popular protests, and was unwilling to engage with his opponents. Besides, he did not hesitate to deploy Mubarak's authoritarian tools to subdue political opposition when necessary.

Obviously, Morsi equated democracy with elections and majority rule, leaving little room for engagement, compromise, and negotiation. Morsi's conception of democracy blatantly excluded political minorities and their rights. He also perceived protests to be illegitimate, although

---

[162] Daragahi, "In Power, Egypt's Muslim Brotherhood Remains Secretive."
[163] Kirkpatrick, "Morsi Turns to His Islamist Backers as Egypt's Crisis Grows."
[164] *USA Today*, "Egypt's Opposition Leaders under Investigation."

the Brotherhood mobilized its supporters several times to put pressure on the SCAF over the course of the revolution. In short, Morsi and the Brotherhood remained committed to "righteous majoritarianism," as their movement was superior to other political actors both ideologically *and* electorally. Ideological superiority rendered other actors and their demands illegitimate, while their electoral weakness meant that these groups were "undemocratic."

Nevertheless, Morsi had a political crisis with which to contend. He refused to resolve it through negotiation and deliberation. After all, he was the elected president, and his movement had significant mobilizational capacity. Electoral odds were in their favor. So once again he relied on electoral tools. Amid popular mobilization and countermobilization, Morsi rushed the CA to complete the constitution and unilaterally called for a referendum on December 15. This step poured gas on fire, rather than putting the crisis out.

The new constitution clarified several issues that the electoral platform of the FJP, discussed above, had left ambiguous. With such clarifications, many provisions in the draft platform ended up echoing the Brotherhood's controversial 2007 draft platform. The new constitution established a presidential system and guaranteed separation of powers, rule of law, and civil liberties. It also, thanks to the Islamist-dominated assembly, established Islam as the main frame of the constitution and took measures to ensure full implementation of sharia. For instance, in addition to Article 2 which established sharia as the principal source of all legislation, which was inherited from the 1971 constitution, the draft also specified the principles and sources of sharia in Article 219.[165] It also designated Al-Azhar in Article 4 as the authority to be consulted on such principles. Hence, the Islamic ulama became a legal authority overseeing the constitutionality of all legislation in the country. This marked a clear departure from the FJP's electoral platform, which did not foresee a tutelary authority over the legislative branch.

Equally disconcerting was the issue of minority rights. As the party platform promised, Article 3 of the draft constitution recognized the religious autonomy of Jews and Christians. These two were the only religious communities the constitution recognized. Without mentioning Baha'is and Shi'a living in Egypt, the assembly subjected non-Sunni Muslims to the rather discriminatory practices of Sunni orthodoxy. In this way, it confirmed the Brotherhood's limited tolerance for religious and social

---

[165] Article 219 read as follows: The principles of Islamic Sharia include general evidence, foundational rules, rules of jurisprudence, and credible sources accepted in Sunni doctrines and by the larger community.

pluralism among Muslims. In line with the movement's mission, Articles 10 and 11 of the draft constitution also authorized the state to safeguard public morality and foster religious values in the society. Along these lines, it set religious education as the core of tertiary education (Article 60) and prohibited insulting prophets and religious messengers (Article 44). Hence, the Brotherhood's mission of Islamizing society was institutionalized in the new constitution.[166]

The draft constitution clearly imposed hegemonic Islamism over Egyptians. Religious minorities, women's rights organizations, human rights activists, and journalists argued that the new constitution was neither inclusive nor democratic because the CA failed to represent the diverse Egyptian society and the new constitution restricted civil liberties. Several parties called for a boycott, while Aboul Fotouh's Masr Kawiya asked his supporters to vote against the draft constitution. Some Salafi groups refused to vote in favor, arguing that the constitution was not Islamic enough. Disregarding the opposition, Morsi hurriedly pushed for the ratification of the foundational document in a popular referendum. He presumed that a new constitution would end the political crisis.

The Brotherhood once again mobilized for an electoral victory. On the day of the referendum, only 33 percent of Egyptians showed up at the ballot box, of which 64 percent voted in favor. This meant that the new fundamental law of the country was supported by a mere 20 percent of the entire society. Besides, yea-sayers were mostly concentrated in rural areas, whereas the majority of Cairenes (56 percent) voted against the new constitution. In a highly centralized state like Egypt, this was a disconcerting sign.[167] Yet this "victory" sufficed for the Brotherhood as a clear popular mandate. After all, the old guard's rivals had once again been defeated in the electoral game.

However, the crisis did not fizzle out. Liberal Islamists, now mostly purged from the Brotherhood, sustained their critique of Morsi and the FJP's majoritarian practices and called for renewed elections. Aboul Fotouh continued the campaign he started against Morsi after the November decree, and other liberals joined him in his call. Fahmy Howeidy, an independent Islamist intellectual, also called for early presidential and parliamentary elections in late January.[168]

---

[166] For the full text of the Egyptian Constitution (2012). It is worth noting that while the draft secured the establishment of an Islamic state, it also ensured military autonomy, signaling to the Egyptian armed forces that the Brotherhood would respect their interests.

[167] I would like to thank Georges Fahmi for raising this point.

[168] *Masress*, "Akhbār Mohamed Morsi: Fahmi Huwaydi Yadʿū Mohamed Morsi Li-Intikhābāt Riʾāsiyya Mubekkira."

In the meantime, Morsi continued Ikhwanization at full thrust. In a quite controversial move, he appointed ninety new members, mostly Islamists, to Egypt's upper house right before the constitutional referendum.[169] He inherited the right to appoint members to the upper house from the Mubarak regime. The reason he rushed these appointments was twofold. First, the new constitution, once ratified, required the transfer of legislative authority from the president to the upper house until a new parliament was elected. Second, the new constitution also limited the number of presidential appointees in the upper house to twenty. So with these last-minute appointments, Morsi prolonged Brotherhood's dominance in the legislative branch using Mubarak's authoritarian practices.

Morsi then continued with revisions in the cabinet. In two government shuffles in January and May, he replaced several ministers with members of the Brotherhood, leaving only a handful of seats for technocrats.[170] Then, in June, Morsi appointed seventeen new governors, divided between brothers and former military officers. Among them was the leader of the Jamaat al-Islamiyya, Adel al-Khayat, appointed as the new governor of Luxor. Al-Khayat's appointment spurred strong public reaction because the militant Islamist organization that he joined as a student had killed fifty-eight tourists in a 1997 terror attack in Luxor.[171] The new governor resigned due to intense controversy over his appointment, yet Morsi once again displayed his desire to build an exclusively Islamic coalition to penetrate the ranks of the administration.

Civil Liberties

In the meantime, Morsi's righteous majoritarianism increasingly encroached on civil liberties. His plans to redesign the media extended well beyond publicly owned press and broadcasting stations. He also put pressure on privately owned media. Due to its critical coverage, a particular target was OnTV, owned by Coptic billionaire Naguib Sawiris.[172] Prompted by these actions, Washington DC-based watchdog Freedom House reported in 2013 that Morsi's rise to presidency

---

[169] Trager, *Arab Fall*, 190; the upper house had 270 seats.
[170] *Ahram Online*, "Who's Who: Egypt's New Ministers."
[171] *France 24*, "Egypt's Luxor Governor Resigns after Controversy."
[172] The government placed a travel ban on Sawiris' father and younger brother for evading taxes in a 2007 sale of one of their ventures, a move that echoed Erdoğan's instrumentalization of state authority to penalize his critics.

led to several negative developments for the media during the latter half of 2012, including increased polarization between pro- and anti-government outlets, a heightened use of defamation laws against the press, and physical harassment of journalists by nonstate actors with the tacit support of the authorities.[173]

According to the Committee to Protect Journalists (CPJ), seventy-eight assaults against journalists occurred during Morsi's year in office. In most cases, the attacks were committed by his supporters during street clashes with opponents. Taking things to a whole new level, and adamant to stop critical coverage of Morsi's presidency, his supporters even laid siege to Media Production City, where Egypt's private satellite stations are located, in December 2012 and March 2013, demanding the "purification" of the media from those who "marred" the image of the Brotherhood.[174] The protesters threatened the lives of employees and attacked journalists with impunity.

The new constitution drafted by the Brotherhood also failed to establish safeguards for freedom of the press. Many Mubarak-era practices crept into the document. For instance, Article 215 replaced Mubarak's Higher Council for Journalism with the National Media Council (composed of government appointees), which was charged to "establish controls and regulations that ensure the commitment of the media to adhere to professional and ethical standards" and "observe the values and constructive traditions of society."[175] This vague provision left considerable space for political interference in editorial decisions in the media.

At the executive level, like Erdoğan has done in Turkey, Morsi evoked self-censorship through defamation lawsuits against journalists. He reportedly filed twice as many lawsuits for insulting the president as Mubarak had done in his thirty-year reign.[176] His new prosecutor general Talaat Abdullah also ordered arrests of journalists and media professionals for defaming Morsi, reporting false news, and inciting violence against the Brotherhood.[177] In a much-publicized case, Islamist lawyers filed a lawsuit against Bassem Youssef, a famous political satirist, for insulting the president (and Islam) on his show by printing Morsi's photo on a pillow.[178] As a result of such developments, Freedom House changed the status of the press from partly free to not free under Morsi's presidency.

---

[173] Freedom House, "Freedom of the Press 2013 – Egypt."
[174] *Middle East Monitor*, "Islamists Besiege TV Channel HQ for Disseminating False Information."
[175] Committee to Protect Journalists, "Proposed Egyptian Constitution Would Limit Media Freedom."
[176] *Ahram Online*, "More 'insulting President' Lawsuits under Morsi than Mubarak."
[177] Committee to Protect Journalists, "CPJ Condemns Siege at Cairo's Media Production City."
[178] *Ahram Online*, "More 'insulting President' Lawsuits under Morsi than Mubarak."

Morsi's majoritarian stance not only undermined the freedom of the press but also threatened the freedom of expression, thought, and association. The main target was acts that violated "public morality," as defined by the old guard. During Morsi's year in power, the number of prosecutions for blasphemy, insults against religion, and offenses against public decency increased dramatically, mostly targeting non-Islamist citizens, journalists, and media personalities.[179]

After the constitutional referendum, Morsi also submitted a law to the upper house to "regulate" CSOs. Although the draft included some improvements over the Law of Associations (2002) inherited from the Mubarak regime, it still maintained key restrictions to the freedom of association, including government controls over the activities and funding of foreign and local CSOs. Accordingly, government-controlled "coordination committees" would oversee and limit the activities and funding sources of all CSOs through centralized licensing and would dissolve or penalize them if need be.[180] Amr Darrag, then Minister of Planning and International Cooperation, defended the proposal:

> On the one hand we'd like to empower civil society and allow *innocent* funding for different activities to get through. On the other hand, we don't want the country to be open to financing that supports something that *does not benefit the country*. There has to be some sort of monitoring of foreign funding in order to make sure it is *compatible with the national agenda*.[181] [emphasis added]

Obviously, concepts such as "national agenda" and "innocent funding" were quite vague and allowed for partisan interpretations of the law while handing the ruling party substantial power over civil society.

Delegitimizing the Opposition and Undermining Political Pluralism

In the meantime, the Brotherhood continued to delegitimize the opposition, further eroding the freedom of expression and assembly. Echoing the Milli Görüş movement and electoralist Islamists in Turkey, several Brothers delegitimized main opposition figures by questioning their Egyptian identity and authenticity. For them, the secular opposition was Western-orientated and at odds with the Islamic faith. Pro-government media proved to be essential in this task. For instance, FJP's official newspaper *Freedom and Justice* and Brotherhood's broadcasting

---

[179] Freedom House, "Freedom of the Press 2013 – Egypt."
[180] Shea, "Egypt's Morsi Continues Pursuit of New Civil Society Restrictions."
[181] Middle East Institute, "A Conversation with the FJP's Amr Darrag."

station *Misr25* actively vilified the non-Islamist opposition as disgruntled members of the old regime, thugs, or infidels.[182] They were not merely Brotherhood's political rivals, they were its "enemies."[183]

Others went so far as to suggest that Brotherhood's opponents were indeed opponents of Islam. For instance, Khaled Amayreh, a Palestinian journalist, in an essay published on Ikhwanweb claimed that political Islam and Islam were the same thing: "One cannot reject political Islam as a matter of principle, without rejecting Islam itself," he posited and continued, "Political Islam is not the invention of the Muslim Brotherhood or other Islamists. It is rather solidly rooted in Islam and its holy scripture, the Qur'an."[184] Thus, rejecting Brotherhood's political agenda was the same as rejecting Islam itself; criticizing Islamism was tantamount to criticizing Islam. By treating Islam and the Brotherhood as one and the same, the old guard closed the door to political pluralism and imposed their own ideology as "the truth." Hence, they forced Egyptians to make a choice between their faith and political preferences.

The electoralists' exclusionary, hegemonic, and polarizing attitude alienated the opposition, while Morsi's slow progress in improving the living standards of Egyptians eroded his broader political support. Unemployment and inflation continued to rise under his rule. For sure, the remnants of the Mubarak regime in the state and certain segments of the society rooted for Morsi's failure. And at times they used their clout to make life harder for ordinary Egyptians by withholding security, transportation, and garbage-collection services.[185] Yet it is also true that Morsi refused to build a coalition with revolutionary forces to counteract such hurdles. Instead, he hoped that he could keep power by sustaining the privileges of the armed forces and continue to rule single-handedly without making compromises to his non-Islamist rivals. He was mistaken. As Shahin explains, Morsi lost the youth and the urban poor, who had played a key role in Mubarak's ouster and was left with his hard-core supporters. It was in this context that a new opposition movement, Tamarod (Rebellion), started to mobilize hundreds of thousands against Morsi's presidency. Tamarod petitioned for renewed

---

[182] Freedom House, "Freedom of the Press 2013 – Egypt."
[183] Interview with Khaled Fouad, August 8, 2017. It should be noted that the Brotherhood's relationship with Salafi parties were more complicated than its relationship with non-Islamists. At times, the Brotherhood made critical compromises to Salafi groups to receive their support.
[184] Amayreh, "Egypt's Unreasonable Opposition."
[185] Willi, *The Fourth Ordeal*, 292.

presidential elections and claimed to collect millions of signatures. To end their campaign with a popular showdown, they called for a major rally on June 30, the anniversary of Morsi's election. They were presumably supported by anti-Brotherhood forces of the ancien régime. A few within the movement even demanded the armed forces intervene in their favor to put the revolution back on its track.

In the meantime, Morsi and the Brotherhood countermobilized their base to show where popular support indeed resided. The Brothers decided to organize a counterrally on June 28 in support of Morsi, who belittled the extent of popular mobilization against his rule and refused to engage with protesters or acknowledge their demands. In numerous conversations I had with Brothers afterward, they told me that the leadership failed to grasp the significance and the depth of popular rage against Morsi.[186] For the Brotherhood, its electoral victories implied a strong mandate. They believed that elections provided them with unshakeable legitimacy. In line with this understanding, Morsi accused protesters of being undemocratic. This entrenched electoralism, as was the case in the AKP, deemed popular protests, even if they were peaceful, as extrademocratic. Legitimate political expression in democracies, they argued, was confined to the ballot box.

Morsi's dismissal of protests and his countermobilization efforts further escalated the situation. Tamarod held the largest protest in Egyptian history on June 30, exacerbating the ongoing political crisis. Aboul Fotouh's party also participated in the protests, calling on Morsi to step down while distancing itself from both the armed forces and their supporters. Madi, the leader of the Wasat Party, in contrast, not only joined the Brotherhood's rally on June 28 to endorse its electoral legitimacy but also recognized the legitimacy of peaceful protests under the Tamarod banner.

The simultaneous mobilization of thousands of Brothers and their opponents created an explosive mix. Morsi poured gas on it with his fiery rhetoric, which depicted the opposition as the enemy of the Brotherhood. The leadership continued to belittle mass mobilization as el-Erian called the protests "photoshopped."

The clashes between pro-Morsi and anti-Morsi protesters in the final days of June left eleven dead and hundreds injured. The armed forces released an ultimatum on July 1, urging Morsi to resolve the crisis. Madi, a leading liberal Islamist, urged Morsi to compromise:

---

[186] Based on field observations and interviews conducted in Summer 2017.

The [Wasat] party still believes in the legitimacy of a democratically elected president with preservations on the fact that Morsi's government is not responding to the ambitions of the people. We ask all political forces to come together for dialogue to reach a conclusion that serves the demands of the Egyptian people, making sure that the military does not interfere in reaching and making of conclusive policies.[187]

The president ignored such calls and delivered a speech on July 2 to defend his electoral legitimacy. In his speech, Morsi uttered the word "legitimacy" fifty-six times: "We have to prove to the world that we are capable of democracy [...] peacefully, we protect [democratic] legitimacy," he said, "Legitimacy is our only safeguard from future faults. [...] I do not accept anyone saying anything or taking any steps against legitimacy; this is completely out of the question."[188]

Although in the same speech he signaled he could make a few concessions, these were too little too late.[189] The opposition, still dissatisfied, insisted that he resigned. Morsi declined. He and the old guard chose to remain committed to electoral legitimacy. The Egyptian armed forces intervened on July 3 to oust him.

Immediately after the coup, leaders of the Brotherhood, including Morsi, Shater, Badie, el-Erian, and Baltagy were arrested. Morsi's supporters stayed in Rabia Adawiya Square to defend the elected president. A few weeks later, the armed forces dispersed the sit-in in a bloody crackdown. Hundreds of people, including women and children, were killed. In the months and years that followed, the Brotherhood's leaders and thousands of activists were imprisoned and placed under inhumane conditions, denied most basic rights and access to medical care. Hundreds of Brothers received death sentences in sham trials, including Badie, Morsi, and Baltagy. Hundreds, including children, were executed.[190] Facing multiple charges, Morsi spent six years in prison without proper medical care, although he had several chronic illnesses. The first freely elected president of Egypt died in prison in 2019 after a court hearing.

The new authoritarian regime under Abdel Fattah el-Sisi, the leader of the coup, did not spare liberal Islamists or secular revolutionaries either. The regime cracked down on political parties, CSOs, and activists, including Tamarod. Both Madi and Sultan were arrested after the coup for inciting criminal activities. Aboul Fotouh was arrested in 2018 for leading and financing a terrorist group and is still in prison at the time of writing; like others, he has been denied medical care despite having had multiple heart attacks.

[187] Wasat Party, "bayān ḥizb al-wasaṭ ʿan al-azma al-ḥāliyya."
[188] BBC News, "Morsi's Defiant Speech Stresses 'Legitimacy.'"
[189] El-Sharnoubi, "Egypt's Morsi Defies Calls to Step Down."
[190] International Bar Association, "Egypt Increases Use of Capital Punishment to Crush Dissent."

This is how Egypt's democratic transition ended, with the Brotherhood falling into disarray.[191]

Conclusion

As this chapter showed, like their Turkish counterparts, the old guard in the Brotherhood internalized electoral politics without committing to democratic norms. They capitalized on electoral legitimacy to justify their majoritarian, unilateral, and polarizing politics. In the process, they strongly committed to "electoral procedures" and institutions to translate their organizational capability into political hegemony.

In the parlance of the inclusion-moderation thesis, the old guard participated in the legal political framework for strategic reasons. For them, democracy remained an instrument for establishing an Islamic government but not an end in itself or a source of principles that would safeguard human rights, civil liberties, minorities, and political pluralism. So, as Hamid suggests, the Brotherhood committed to illiberal democracy, but not because Islamism is inherently authoritarian, hegemonic, and incompatible with liberal democracy, as he argues.[192] Liberal Islamists who populated the movement since the 1980s proved otherwise. They pushed the Brotherhood toward greater transparency and democracy before and after the revolution. For them, democracy was an end in itself. They attempted to change the organization multiple times, but their efforts were frustrated, thanks to the organizational resources the old guard enjoyed. This internal balance of power in favor of the electoralist voices, as Trager also underlines,[193] determined the course of the movement in power. Brotherhood's conflict with elements of the old regime or political rivalry with Salafi parties[194] came secondary to internal forces. The old guard made certain choices every single step of the way and reacted to external impetus in line with their perception of democracy.

What would have happened if liberal Islamists had been at the helm of the movement? We will never know – although Aboul Fotouh's willingness to work with the secular opposition is suggestive of more pluralist possibilities. But we know how their counterparts in Tunisia made a major difference. It is to their story we now turn.

---

[191] For a detailed discussion of the disintegration of the Brotherhood after the coup, see Willi, *The Fourth Ordeal*, Chapter 7.
[192] Hamid, *Temptations of Power*.
[193] Trager, *Arab Fall*.
[194] Hamid, *Temptations of Power*.

5   Ennahda's Path toward Liberal Islamism

On December 17 in 2010, Mohamed Bouazizi, a twenty-eight-year-old street vendor, set himself on fire in Sidi Bouzid, a small town in Southern Tunisia. He was selling fruit to feed his family when the municipal officials confiscated his cart. He acted to protest the local authorities who had humiliated him by taking his only means of income. This act of dignity set the revolutionary fire in the country – as well as in the region – that took down the twenty-five-year Ben Ali regime in just thirty days.

The revolution opened the doors to a democratic transition while strengthening the Islamist movement in the country. The wave of momentous political change allowed Islamists in exile to return and unite with their brothers and sisters after two decades of separation and repression. The very first elections after Ben Ali's demise, perhaps unsurprisingly, handed political power over to Ennahda, the most organized political force in the country at the time, despite being under heavy repression of the ancien régime since 1990.

On the night of the election, Rached Ghannouchi, the charismatic leader of Ennahda, vowed to uphold the revolutionary goals of building a free and prosperous Tunisia.[1] And his party kept this promise, unlike its counterparts in Turkey and Egypt. The party, thanks to its electoral dominance, largely designed the Tunisian democratic transition along with other stakeholders. In the process, Ennahda adhered to democratic principles in power and became a force for compromise, deliberation, and engagement. In close collaboration with its political rivals, the party turned Tunisia into a democratic country, the only democracy in the Arab world, at least until President Kais Saied's power grab in the summer of 2021.

Why did Ennahda adhere to democratic norms, whereas the AKP and the Brotherhood did not? This chapter argues that since the 1990s, liberal Islamists within the party apparatus pulled Ennahda toward

---

[1] Al Jazeera, "Ennahda Wins Tunisia's Elections."

democratic commitments not only when they were in opposition but also after coming to power in 2011. As in the case of other Islamist parties, Ennahda has never been a monolith, and so liberals' dominance in the party was not a foregone conclusion. Competing political visions have coexisted within the party apparatus since its establishment in the 1980s. In fact, radicals pulled the movement toward a confrontational line in the late 1980s and the early 1990s at the expense of liberal Islamists.

From its inception to the 1990s, the Islamic movement in Tunisia was divided between democrats, on the one hand, and radicals, on the other. The latter group preferred to confront the regime rather than work through the system. They also rejected democracy. Democrats, in contrast, headed by Ghannouchi and Abdelfattah Morou, embraced democracy as their ideal system and aimed to work through existing institutions to establish a democratic polity. Radicals fizzled out as they confronted the regime in the early 1990s in exile and under the heavy repression of Ben Ali. Ennahda took a different turn in the 1990s; overall, the party moved closer to democracy. While some embraced a more liberal conceptualization of democracy, others (led by Sadeq Chorou and Habib Ellouze) approached a majoritarian understanding. The latter group–electoralists, as I call them – also prioritized the religious functions of the movement over its political mission (i.e., the democratization of Tunisia) and disagreed with the party leadership on priorities. A few even prioritized the survival of the movement and were ready to compromise with the regime if need be. As such, they echoed the old guard of the Brotherhood – both in terms of their instrumentalist understanding of democracy and the urgency they placed on organizational coherence and survival.

In the aftermath of the 2011 revolution, the same groups pursuing hegemonic Islamism through electoral means pushed again for a more maximalist line to leave their ideological imprint on the new system in the making, much like the old guard did in Egypt. The balance of power proved to be in favor of liberal Islamists this time around. Despite broader social factors in electoralists' favor, such as the rise of Salafism and religiosity in the 2000s, liberals maintained organizational control and resources and managed to sideline electoralists within.

As was the case in Turkey and Egypt, organizational resources mattered greatly in the distribution of power within Ennahda. Thanks to their ever-increasing control over the incentive structure through recruitment, promotions, rules, and finances, liberal Islamists prevailed in horizontal power games and dominated the party organization after the revolution. And this dominant alliance in turn allowed them to charter the course of the party in a liberal democratic direction.

The liberal wing did not enjoy a secure hold over party resources at the time of the revolution though. Instead, the Tunisian democratic transition and liberals' growing control over the party unfolded simultaneously during the party's second founding in 2012. Two factors played an important role in this process. First, the revolution and the ensuing democratic transition empowered Ghannouchi and his faction, which had been pushing for a prodemocratic agenda in the party, and bought them time to capture party resources. Second, Ghannouchi's heavy weight in the party leadership allowed them to extend their influence through organizational resources and liquidate electoralists in horizontal power games. Ghannouchi's strong showing in vertical games in the party empowered liberals over their rivals, providing them with greater presence in leadership positions through recruitment and promotion in the 2014 elections and again in the 2016 party congress. His control over party finances throughout this period also amplified his faction's hold.

So Ennahda remained committed to democratic norms during and after the transition. Despite being a dominant political force in a fragmented political scene, the party drafted a liberal and democratic constitution with other stakeholders, agreed to resign from government amid popular pressure – unlike Morsi in Egypt – and, most importantly, left power in 2014 in a peaceful manner. Until President Kais Saied's (a political outsider) power grab in 2021, the give and take of democratic politics has become habitual for Ennahda. The recent crisis, however, brought rifts in the party – this time, among liberal Islamists – once again revealing the significance of intraparty politics.

As this chapter shows, the case of Ennahda reaffirms the centrality of intraparty dynamics in accounting for party behavior and reveals the limits of existing theories of Islamist change stressing external forces. Without unpacking these internal mechanisms, one cannot ascertain the impact of external impetus (inclusion, exclusion, repression, and so on) on a party. To explain this process, I first turn to the origins of the Islamist movement in Tunisia and its political and ideological evolution over time. A thorough analysis requires focusing on Ghannouchi's philosophical contributions, the party's founding documents, and intraparty dynamics captured by interviews with the leaders and members of the movement. After conducting this analysis, I turn to the shifting balance of power among factions and factors determining this balance with a specific emphasis on organizational resources. As I do so, I unpack differences of political attitudes between different factions within Ennahda.

Political Evolution of the Islamist Movement in Tunisia: The Origins of Ennahda

As outlined in Chapter 1, Bourguiba's reforms upon independence significantly curtailed the impact of religion in everyday life and confined Islam to the private lives of Tunisians. A few incidents of dissent notwithstanding, such changes in social life did not trigger a significant reaction until the 1970s. One of the first organized attempts to revive Islamic practices among Tunisians was the Association for the Preservation of the Qur'an. Established in 1970 by figures sympathetic to Islam within the regime and several Zaituna shaikhs, the association aimed to spread piety among Tunisians.

A new generation of preachers maintained their distance from this state-sanctioned association and chose instead to form a loosely organized group, called the Islamic Society (Jamaat al-Islamiyya) in 1971.[2] The members of this group, led by Hmida Ennaifer, Morou, and Ghannouchi, held discussions and seminars on social, cultural, and moral issues to spread Islamic teachings.

In the early 1970s, Islamists in Tunisia, inspired by the Brotherhood in Egypt, strived for an Islamic revival to defend Islam against Bourguiba's top-down secularization. The Islamic Society published a journal titled *Al-Maarifa* (Knowledge) in 1972 to reach a broader audience. Like the Brotherhood, their utmost concern was *da'wa* and the reform of the Muslim individual and family. Thanks to its increasing visibility and activism in mosques and university campuses, the society started to build an underground organizational network after 1976.

It is safe to call the 1970s the golden decade of Islamic revival in Tunisia. In the 1970s, the regime was pivoting toward neoliberal economic policies accompanied by an authoritarian turn as Bourguiba entrenched his rule even deeper. This double shift triggered a formidable resistance from left-wing movements. As the leftist opposition preoccupied the government, the ruling elite relaxed its grip over religious networks and lent tacit support to Islamic revival, like the ruling elite did in Egypt in the 1970s and in Turkey in the 1980s. The Bourguiba regime accommodated religious expressions in the public sphere and rallied Islamic symbols to restore its popularity. This political context allowed Islamists to increase their appeal among discontent Tunisians.

Throughout the 1970s, the Islamist movement expanded rapidly while taking an increasingly political direction. Three crucial factors affected the change. First, the clashes between the regime and the left reached

---

[2] McCarthy, *Inside Tunisia's al-Nahda*, 21.

an unprecedented level by January 1978. On what is known as "Black Thursday," security forces killed almost 500 civilians. The leaders of the Islamic movement could not remain indifferent to the ongoing political conflict in the country, although they initially sided with the regime against their perennial enemy, the left.[3]

Second, with the growing influence of the Brotherhood, new preachers in the movement increasingly discussed not just proper Islamic behavior but also social and political problems. The Brotherhood's literature dominated conversations in Islamists' study circles. Activists read the writings of Sayyid Qutb, Mohammed al-Ghazali, Abul A'la al-Maududi, and Yusuf al-Qaradawi.[4] As one activist from Sousse, a major coastal city in Tunisia, described to McCarthy:

There were sentences from the hadith of the Prophet, and memorizing of the Qur'an, and a commitment to Islamic behavior, and the requirements were more educational than anything... In addition, there were some other indications – the questions of freedom in the country, of oppression, dictatorship, the one-party system.[5]

The movement's monthly publication *Al-Maarifa* also engaged the broader Islamist literature and became increasingly political in this period.[6] Such engagement marked a fundamental change in activists' conception of Islam and its relationship with politics: Islam was now an ideology for the movement's leaders. Echoing the Brotherhood, Ghannouchi argued in several pieces published in *Al-Maarifa* that "Islam [was] not just spiritual *da'wa* but creed, and worship, and a comprehensive political and social system which does not differentiate between the material and the spiritual."[7] For him, as Banna claimed, "There [was] no room to differentiate between religion and politics, and religion and the state." Islam was "the only *ideology* capable of leading the deprived and oppressed peoples"[8] [emphasis added]. True Islam, he concluded, represented a comprehensive system and a way of life (or a civilization with an ideology) and was more than just a religious sentiment and a set of traditions and rituals.[9] It was a solution to Tunisia's problems.

Finally, the Islamic revolution of 1979 in Iran proved to many Muslims, Sunni and Shi'a alike, that Islamism was a real political force and could change the course of history. So it convinced many Islamists in

---

[3] Waltz, "Islamist Appeal in Tunisia."
[4] After the revolution in Iran, Khomeini and Baqir al-Sadr were added to Tunisian activists' reading list. Ibid.
[5] Quoted in McCarthy, *Inside Tunisia's al-Nahda*, 37.
[6] Hermassi cited in Waltz, "Islamist Appeal in Tunisia."
[7] Quoted in McCarthy, *Inside Tunisia's al-Nahda*, 37.
[8] Quoted in ibid., 42.
[9] Tamimi, *Rachid Ghannouchi*, 22.

Tunisia, as it did elsewhere in the Muslim world, that Islamic political action was not fruitless.

In contrast to Iran though, the majority of Tunisian Islamists did not seek revolutionary activism. Instead, they began to pursue legal action and political participation starting in the early 1980s. In August 1979, Ghannouchi and Morou converted Jamaat al-Islamiyya into a political organization and called it Harakat al-Ittijah al-Islami (Islamic Tendency Movement, hereafter MTI for its French acronym). The MTI, as opposed to its predecessor, was explicitly political since its leaders believed Islam to be a comprehensive religion with clear guidelines for all aspects of life.[10] As such, the MTI followed the Brotherhood line and framed Islam as *din wa dawla* (religion and state). Its formal structure also replicated the Brotherhood's organizational hierarchy connecting local cells to national leadership. Hence, what started as a religious revival movement organized around the notion of *da'wa* turned into an ideological party in the span of a decade.

The Islamic Tendency Movement

In June 1981, the MTI held its first press conference seeking legal recognition from the regime. The MTI's founding statement identified the problems Tunisia faced. The Tunisian society, the document claimed, had been in a state of crisis for decades. Tunisia was backward and dependent on Western powers. This dependence, echoing the Milli Görüş movement in Turkey, was the making of the existing regime and a natural result of its inauthentic character and project of secularization and alienation from its Islamic identity. The remedy, for Islamists, was (1) to end Tunisia's alienation and backwardness through the restoration of its Arab–Islamic identity, (2) the revival of Islam as a political force in Tunisia and elsewhere in the Muslim world, (3) restoring people's right to self-determination by ending internal tutelage (of the Bourguiba regime) and external domination (by Western powers), and (4) the reconstruction of the country's economic life on the basis of Islamic principles for more equitable distribution of wealth. Ghannouchi was "convinced that Islam was the spirit of this *ummah*, its maker and the builder of its glory, and its only hope for victory and progress."[11] In short, Islam was the solution for Tunisia.

---

[10] Figures like Ennaifer and Selahaddin Jourchi were not on the same page with Morou and Ghannouchi with respect to the necessity of political activism. Instead, they endorsed intellectual revival and established the group Progressive Islamists with the intention of reviving intellectual traditions in Islam. As such, the Islamic movement of the 1970s gave birth to two main groups. The latter turned to intellectual revival, while the MTI took a more political path. See the interview with Ennaifer in Keddie, "The Islamist Movement in Tunisia."

[11] Quoted in Tamimi, *Rachid Ghannouchi*, 21.

The way to achieve these goals for the MTI was through nonviolent activism in intellectual, cultural, and political realms. More specifically, the MTI promised to place the mosque (i.e., Zaituna) at the center of worship and mass mobilization. It sought to build a contemporary system of Islamic governance, rather than following secular politics. As part of the process of reviving Tunisia's authenticity, the movement also promised to Arabize the education system (to clear away French colonial influence). On the political front, the movement vowed to fight together with other national forces against authoritarianism and for freedom of expression and assembly. It also expressed a desire to work in solidarity with workers and peasants to advance social Islam, which would end injustice and economic inequalities in the country.[12]

The MTI largely echoed the Brotherhood in Egypt and the Milli Görüş movement in Turkey, with one key difference. The Islamic movement under Ghannouchi's leadership refrained from self-identifying with Islam. The MTI's 1981 statement read: "The 'Islamic Movement' does not present itself as an official spokesman in the name of Islam in Tunisia and does not ever aspire to be attributed to it. It recognizes the right of all Tunisians to engage in honest and responsible relations with religion." In other words, the fact that they represented the Islamic current in Tunisia did not mean that they spoke for Islam.

The objectives and means that the MTI identified, however, required legal recognition and participation in formal institutions. Because the secular regime had precluded the establishment of religious parties, MTI's demand to establish a political party was ignored. A month after its press conference, the authorities arrested the leaders of the MTI, including Morou and Ghannouchi. Under regime repression, both leaders maintained their commitment to democracy and prioritized legal political activism to establish an Islamic democracy. The movement released a joint statement in 1982, with three other opposition parties requesting general amnesty for political prisoners, revision of the laws governing associations, and the repealing of the press code. These "democrats" were willing to engage with the moderates in the Bourguiba regime and argued that the best course of action for their movement was to participate in formal politics. With that intention, Morou met with then Prime Minister Mzali in 1984 in prison.

---

[12] MTI, "The Founding Statement of the Islamic Trend Movement."

Rifts inside the MTI

Not everybody in the MTI agreed with Ghannouchi or Morou on the primacy of democracy or the notion of Islamic democracy, however. In fact, like other Islamist movements, the MTI hosted factions with divergent political preferences.[13] Internal disagreements pertained to three major issues: (1) the nature of the movement with respect to the separation of religious and political activism, (2) the movement's political objectives, and (3) the strategy the movement should follow to attain its political goals.[14]

One group preferred to keep both the religious and political functions of the movement intact. This group, led by Salah Karker and his close associates Sadeq Chorou and Mohammed Chammam, rejected democracy; they instead called for an Islamic state based on the literal reading of the sacred texts without any room for independent interpretation. As such, their Islamism remained distant from pluralism and democracy. Their political practice was also nonpluralist, since they rejected multiparty politics and cooperation with secular forces such as leftist organizations. For Karker, for instance, democracy and party pluralism were un-Islamic;[15] thus, along with his followers among the youth, he refused to legalize the movement and desired to remain a socioreligious organization with underground political activities. The group also advocated for confrontation with the regime and desired to overthrow Bourguiba in the 1980s and capture political power instead of turning into a formal political entity. They thought that the best strategy to do so was to wage war against the autocratic regime.

As Waltz and Wolf both suggest, regime repression caused the rise of an antidemocratic wing in the movement in the mid-1980s. As Morou points out, the balance of power turned in favor of such radical groups in the 1980s. When the regime cracked down on the MTI, it was mostly the democratic leaders who remained behind bars, thanks to their visibility and willingness to legalize the movement. Ghannouchi and Morou's prison sentence from 1981 to 1984 left the political space wide open for antidemocratic forces, as Morou claimed in an interview. In their absence, Karker rose to prominence in the movement in the 1980s, along with his close associate Chorou.[16]

---

[13] This section draws on the excellent works of Hermassi, Dunn, Wolf, Boulby, Camau, and Geisser.
[14] For more details on these divisions, see McCarthy, *Inside Tunisia's al-Nahda*, 81.
[15] Wolf, *Political Islam in Tunisia*, 53.
[16] Ibid., 61.

MTI's third national convention in November 1984 displayed radicals' increasing influence in the movement. Ghannouchi's position was growing weaker, and Karker, with his growing presence, was ready to exclude prodemocratic figures. As a former MTI member reported to Wolf:

> Karker strongly rejected my unconditional support for democracy, women's rights, and other western concepts. [...] He thought this was against the spirit of Islam. He threatened to exclude me and like-minded people from the movement. Ghannouchi tried to mediate between us; he often talked to us and claimed that he understands our point of view [...] but ultimately he did little to defend us and we left the movement.[17]

Ghannouchi's inability to stop such purges affirmed his increasing weakness within the movement, even though he was elected chairman in the 1984 convention.

Radicals gained significant traction among the youth on college campuses; they clearly played the vertical games better than their rivals. The causes of Islamic revival were manifold. As both Boulby and rightfully point out, economic hardships of the 1970s and 1980s and high levels of unemployment led to frustration among the working classes and the youth. This frustration heightened, as college graduates also realized that educational attainment had not delivered the much-anticipated social mobility. Political disillusionment with Arab nationalism and socialism also pushed these social groups to search for new alternatives.[18] Economic and political factors cannot tell the whole story though. The search for an identity in these circumstances also played a role in the increasing appeal of Islamism on Tunisian campuses in the 1980s. Islamist networks within and outside of college campuses provided the disillusioned with what McCarthy calls a "transcendent motivation" and an embrace of a new community offered by religious faith and morality.[19]

Radicals' increasing popularity among youth turned the MTI into a key player in the 1984 bread riots. The regime responded with brutal force, killing several protesters. Then Prime Minister Mzali also recognized the mobilizational prowess of the MTI; perhaps recognizing the splits within the MTI, he started talks with some of the reformist leaders and released them from prison in August 1984. The regime, however, still denied the movement legal recognition and dismissed all veiled students from teachers' colleges in 1985.

---

[17] Quoted in ibid.
[18] See Boulby, "The Islamic Challenge" and Anderson, "Political Pacts, Liberalism, and Democracy."
[19] McCarthy, *Inside Tunisia's al-Nahda*, 26.

In an interview with Nikki Keddie in June 1985, Morou claimed that their task as Islamists was to build the political institutions that preserved the rights of all citizens, as in Europe. His wing did not only demand elections but also endorsed freedom of the press and association, as well as other human rights.[20] Such differences certainly led to tensions in the movement between different wings. Morou often targeted radical MTI members and forced some of them to resign from the movement in the mid-1980s. He elaborated on such internal rifts in the same interview:

> I do not hide from you the fact that in our movement there are people who are not for democracy. They are for dictatorship in our movement as in all existing movements. [...] After our imprisonment they had an open field. The government pushes youth to look for a revolutionary path. Until now it has not tried to understand these movements. It has not tried to talk with or authorize these movements. I personally press always for the democratic path, the path of dialogue, but when a youth come[s] to me, he says, "You push for the democratic path, but the government is against democracy. It is trying to kill us. Why do you want us to be for the democratic path? The inevitable path is the path of revolution." As the Islamists in Iran did. And sometimes I say to myself: Those young people are right sometimes. I think it is the governments of Islamic countries that have pushed Islamists to revolution. The Shah in Iran pushed the lslamists to become what they are. And I fear the other governments have not learned that lesson.

In fact, as Morou suggested, the regime's repressive measures frustrated several activists who insisted on confronting it. Convinced that the best strategy to deal with the regime was confrontation, Karker and Chammam started to devise the secret apparatus – an underground armed wing – in the mid-1980s.[21] At MTI's convention in Menzah in 1986, a harder and more centralized party line was formalized.[22]

In February 1987, the regime cracked down on the Islamist student union (UGTE) and arrested Ghannouchi in March 1987 for delivering an unauthorized speech in a mosque. By then, Islamists had replaced leftists as the weighty danger for the regime. The bombing of four hotels in August by radical Islamists exposed the MTI to further repression. The regime responded with brutal force and arrested more than 1,000 MTI members, 90 of whom were charged with conspiring to overthrow the regime. The regime sentenced Karker and Ghannouchi along with several other MTI members to death. Karker and several others went to exile and assumed leadership of the movement from afar. They decided it was time to overthrow the government with the aid of their secret apparatus in December 1987.

---

[20] Keddie, "The Islamist Movement in Tunisia," 32.
[21] Ibid.; Dunn, *Renaissance or Radicalism?*
[22] Hermassi, "The Rise and Fall of the Islamist Movement in Tunisia," 108.

Before they could carry out their plans, though, in November 1987, then Prime Minister Zine El Abidine Ben Ali swiftly removed Bourguiba from power in what many called a "doctors' coup."[23] The new president promised democratic reforms and expanded freedom of the press and allowed for the establishment of new political parties. To solidify its commitment to democracy, the government released a new national charter and scheduled parliamentary elections for April 1989.[24]

Following through with his promise for political liberalization, Ben Ali released political prisoners, including MTI, members and dropped charges against 60 Islamists, including Ghannouchi, and allowed exiled leaders like Morou to return to Tunisia. This opening allowed the democratic wing to return to the party with a renewed sense of hope for political inclusion in a more competitive system.

They welcomed Ben Ali's coup as a new opportunity to gain legal status and renamed their movement Harakat al-Nahda (Ennahda) in 1989. By dropping "Islam" from the movement's official name, they hoped to circumvent the political party law and the National Pact of 1987, which prohibited the formation of religious parties, and secure legal recognition from the state. Ben Ali defied such expectations and denied a legal permit to Ennahda. Despite this setback, the democratic wing convinced the rest of the movement to run in the 1989 elections as independents.

Ennahda's Platform and Brief Experience with Formal Politics

Due to the impact of inclusion in formal politics, Ennahda's platform turned out to be more specific than the MTI's. Like the Milli Görüş and the Brotherhood, the party accepted a procedurally democratic political system where the power of the state would be deployed to cultivate an Islamic society. The new party platform was clearly written by democrats, who left their pluralist imprint.[25]

Accordingly, the party had four clusters of goals: (1) *Politically*, the party adhered to (a) republican principles of popular sovereignty, *shura* (participation/consultation), and strong civil society; (b) the establishment of communal and individual freedoms and human rights; and (c) an independent and nonaligned foreign policy in cooperation with Arab and Islamic countries against oppression in Palestine and colonialism in the

---

[23] The term "doctors' coup" refers to the medical report that dubbed Bourguiba senile and unfit for government.
[24] For details, see Anderson, "Political Pacts, Liberalism, and Democracy."
[25] Wolf, *Political Islam in Tunisia*, 69.

Arab region, as well as the rest of the world. (2) *Economically*, Ennahda sought (a) self-sufficiency and satisfaction of basic needs; (b) regional economic integration in the Maghreb, as well as in the Arab and the Islamic world; (c) integration of the public and private sectors; and (d) a more humane and equitable distribution of resources based on man's right to enjoy the fruits of his labor by way of eliminating disparities resulting from exploitation, hoarding, monopolies, and other illicit practices. (3) *Socially*, Ennahda endorsed (a) social rights and universal access to food, health, education, housing, and so on; (b) preservation of the family as the basis of a healthy society, supporting marriage and childcare; (c) promotion of the status of women without "degeneration" so that they could preserve their "dignity"; and (d) provision of education and employment to the youth. (4) *Culturally*, the party aimed to (a) instate Arab–Islamic identity in the country's constitution and laws; (b) start a comprehensive intellectual and scientific renaissance based on the foundations of Islam to end the state of decay, underdevelopment, dependence, and alienation; (c) adopt Arabic as the language of education, administration, and cultural production; (d) endorse scientific research to achieve growth and independence; (e) create an independent and fair media that contributes to the progress of the country and supports its identity; and (d) spread "virtue" and support the foundations of a renaissance.

The party also made key concessions; it unequivocally accepted the personal status code (discussed in Chapter 1), a key issue for gender equality, while its more radical members disengaged from security forces.[26]

Radicals, skeptical of this political strategy, agreed to it with one condition: Ennahda would seek the greatest electoral gains in elections. Chorou, the leader of the party at the time,[27] wanted to compete for all seats in the parliament in the 1989 elections. For him, elections would be an instrument for capturing the state. In contrast, Ghannouchi adopted a more lenient approach and preferred to compete for fewer seats. In the end, Chorou prevailed and Ennahda contested the majority of seats. In short, radicals pulled the party toward an electoralist, majoritarian, maximalist position.

The tug-of-war between radicals and democrats within the movement continued during the election cycle and produced an ambiguous

---

[26] Hermassi, "The Rise and Fall of the Islamist Movement in Tunisia," 110.
[27] It is not clear when exactly Chorou replaced Ghannouchi. Some sources claim that Chorou became the leader of the party in 1988 and would occupy this position until 1991. Hermassi claims that the change of leadership occurred in 1989 at a secret convention in Sfax.

and contradictory campaign in the 1989 elections. On the one hand, democrats retained a moderate stance in defense of democracy, human rights, and women's rights. In sharp contrast, radicals like Sheikh Mohammed Lakhoua advocated the establishment of an Islamic state, instatement of sharia and *hudud* (corporal) punishments, annulment of the secular personal status code (which the party had officially accepted), and confinement of women to their homes. Other radical Nahdawis echoed the old guard in the Brotherhood and Milli Görüş and equated Islam and Ennahda; for them, the elections would separate believers from nonbelievers.[28]

Despite such contradictions, Ennahda ran a vibrant campaign and dominated the opposition, emerging as a political force to be reckoned with. The official count put the party's vote share at 14 percent (and as high as 30 percent in some districts in major cities), though Ennahda officials estimated their support to be much higher.

While Ennahda emerged as the largest opposition party in the elections, secular parties remained quite weak. In some districts, Ennahda received four times the combined vote of its secular rivals. The party's fortune at the polls, however, did not translate into parliamentary seats. Because the electoral system favored larger parties, all seats were allocated to the ruling party, Ben Ali's Democratic Constitutional Rally, known by its French acronym RCD.

The democrats in Ennahda were defeated. The 1989 elections not only failed to deliver its promises of formal recognition and representation, but the party's ambiguous messages on the campaign trail also inflamed fears among seculars. With his prodemocratic strategy defunct, Ghannouchi left for self-imposed exile in protest of the electoral outcome. He was frustrated that the electoral process had failed to deliver meaningful democratization. Ben Ali, wary of the party's success, banned Ennahda along with six other opposition parties from running in the local elections scheduled for June 1990.

Ghannouchi's departure weakened the democratic faction within the party. In his absence, the radical wing of Ennahda took over. Soon after the elections, with Ghannouchi gone and Ben Ali shrinking the political space, Chorou, who had always believed that there was no politics without force,[29] sidelined Morou and confronted the regime. In an alleged attack, Nahdawis set the RCD office in Bab Souika on fire in March 1991, killing a guard and injuring another. In protest of the violence committed by their fellow party members, prominent democrats such

---

[28] Hermassi, "The Rise and Fall of the Islamist Movement in Tunisia," 117.
[29] Wolf, *Political Islam in Tunisia*, 76.

as Morou, Fadhel Beldi, and Benaissa Derni froze their membership in 1991.[30] "Some young people from the Ennahda movement were involved in the [Bab Souika Affair] with the agreement of certain leaders," the trio claimed in their statement, and continued, "Violence was rejected by the precepts of our religion and is contrary to the values of our civilization."[31]

These attacks marked the death knell of Ennahda, as Ben Ali moved to disband the movement after October 1991. The authorities arrested and charged 300 Ennahda members with a plot to overthrow the government. By 1992, thousands of Nahdawis were either in prison in Tunisia or in exile. Those who were not lucky enough to leave the country suffered humiliation, rape, torture, and isolation in prison cells until the early 2000s.[32] Several of them died in detention.

The lucky ones spent years in exile. Ghannouchi went to London, while Chorou, Karker, and Habib Mohni ended up in Paris together with forty of their followers. Hundreds of others were scattered across different countries in Europe and the Middle East.

Ennahda, in the end, had to weather regime repression with two parallel organizations, one in exile and one in Tunisia. The local organization remained quite weak, thanks to sustained regime pressure, while Ennahda in exile was fragmented with sustained internal rifts. Only after the 2011 revolution were the local and the exile branches could unite once again.

Ennahda's Transformation in Exile: The Rise of the Liberal Democrats

In exile, the balance of power shifted in favor of the democrats. Disturbed by the intense regime repression and violent activism of their peers, democrats put greater pressure on radicals to conform to the democratic and nonviolent line of the movement. Their growing control in party leadership, internal communication, and indoctrination allowed them to chart the course of Ennahda. They got to shape the party platform, the party's political objectives, and its strategy in the 1990s and 2000s.

In this period, democrats' perception of democracy also matured and approximated liberal democracy. This shift in thinking can be clearly observed in Ghannouchi's writings, which increasingly shaped Ennahda's platforms. In a nutshell, democracy became a priority for Ennahda, as its leaders rearticulated Islamization as democratization, while openly

---

[30] Dunn, *Renaissance or Radicalism?*
[31] Quoted in Wolf, *Political Islam in Tunisia*, 76.
[32] For a detailed account of Nahdawis' prison experiences, see Chapter 4 of McCarthy, *Inside Tunisia's al-Nahda*.

embracing pluralism and civil liberties. This was a dramatic rearticulation of the party's Islamist orientation. In line with this shift, the party leaders increased their collaboration with secular democrats against the regime. This section details how this transformation occurred.

Ben Ali's crackdown on the movement was a critical turning point for Ennahda. It triggered a leadership struggle between democrats and radicals in exile. Radicals, mostly located in France, adhered to the Qutbian line and deemed violence as necessary in their struggle against the regime. The group based in the United Kingdom and headed by Ghannouchi, in contrast, distanced themselves from violent factions and pursued democratic activism.

A major step in the democratization of Ennahda was Karker's marginalization in the movement. After he left Tunisia in 1988 for exile, Karker started to flirt with violent resistance in Afghanistan and later in Algeria. His involvement with Islamic militants did not help Nahdawis who were seeking a haven in Europe in the early 1990s following Ben Ali's crackdown on the movement. In 1995, Karker was placed under house arrest in France for pursuing militant activism. Then heading the executive bureau of Ennahda in exile, Ghannouchi along with other senior leaders invited Karker to denounce violence.[33] He agreed to abandon violent activism in Tunisia but defended violence as a legitimate tool for Algeria. Unconvinced, the executive bureau decided to freeze his membership. Karker lost his clout in the movement.

Despite the opposition of the radicals in France, Ghannouchi reassumed party leadership in the party convention in December 1995 with 52 percent of the delegates' votes.[34] As democrats regained organizational power in exile, Ennahda showed clear commitment to democratic norms and principles. After 1995, the party's official line approximated Ghannouchi's position on Islamic democracy.

Ghannouchi provided substance to Ennahda's political agenda in several of his writings. Unlike Hassan al-Banna or his successors in the Brotherhood or leaders of the Milli Görüş movement in Turkey, he combined the identities of a political leader and thinker. His background in theology and philosophy allowed him to produce texts on Islamism as an ideology and provide substance for the political system his movement envisioned.

During his prison sentence between 1981 and 1984 and later in exile, Ghannouchi penned several articles and books on the nature and principles of Islamic governance. In his early writings, his focus remained

---

[33] Ibid., 94.
[34] McCarthy, *Inside Tunisia's al-Nahda*, 81.

on the need for an Islamic government: "Islam is a complete and comprehensive way of life that encompasses economic, social, spiritual, moral, political, diplomatic, and penal aspects,"[35] Ghannouchi posited. Because, echoing the Brotherhood, Islam is "a faith, a code of conduct, and a set of guidelines for a system of government," he maintained, "A state is an essential requirement; for without it an Islamic way of life cannot be fully established."[36] For him, it was incumbent upon all Muslims to strive for Islamic governance.

But what did he mean by Islamic government? An Islamic government, Ghannouchi thought, merged Islamic ideals such as shura and sharia with democratic tools. This formulation, on the surface, seems to echo the political vision of the Brotherhood and other mainstream Islamist movements. Yet Ghannouchi's conceptualization of sharia significantly diverged from other Islamists as early as the 1980s. Sharia, for him, was not a body of laws fixed in word and content (as Salafis assert) but a set of broad guidelines and principles, and a source of human liberties.[37] The principles of sharia included viceregency (the idea that humans are God's representatives on earth), equality, dignity, justice, and freedom of choice, belief, thought, and expression. Whether or not a government was Islamic depended on its compliance with such principles, rather than a literal application of the Islamic law. This was a key difference between Ghannouchi and the Brotherhood's old guard.

Such principles transcended the limits of time and space, yet their translation into practical measures in everyday matters required reasoned interpretation (*ijtihad*). Unlike Qur'an and sunna, Ghannouchi deemed, these interpretations were not divine and were debatable and could be accepted or rejected by the *ummah*. In an Islamic state, parties with different interpretations of Islamic principles competed for the people's trust. No party held a monopoly over Islam, its authority, or the meaning of the sacred text. By accepting pluralism in Qur'anic injunctions on everyday matters, Ghannouchi also rejected Salafi proclivities and thus created a space for Islamic democracy. Religious pluralism hence formed the basis of political pluralism within Islamism. In an Islamic democracy, he posited, sovereignty resided with the *ummah* (including both Muslims and non-Muslims) who legislated to apply sharia principles and guidelines through shura and delegated their authority to an executive (*imamah*) with a revocable contract.

---

[35] Tamimi, *Rachid Ghannouchi*, 93.
[36] Ibid., 94.
[37] Ibid., 91.

Despite its more pluralist core, Ghannouchi's Islamic democracy in its earlier formulations was still an exclusionary republic. In a society with no religious minorities, the system could be quite democratic, given assurances for fundamental freedoms, human rights, pluralism, rule of law, and accountability in the system. Still, Islamic democracy carried majoritarian tendencies. Ghannouchi's conception of two-tiered citizenship, which separated Muslims from non-Muslims, was noteworthy in this regard. While Muslims enjoyed all political rights and liberties in this Islamic democracy, non-Muslims would abstain from holding high political office because they rejected the objectives of an Islamic democracy.[38] In other words, citizens, while enjoying the same civil liberties, were discriminated against on the basis of creed.

In his later writings, however, Ghannouchi reframed Islamic democracy as an ideal-typical system that could be actualized only under certain conditions. He argued that Muslims had to let go of this ideal when they were in the minority, when they lived under dictatorships (because Islamic movements cannot topple these dictatorships alone), or when they were under colonial control. These three preconditions also rested on a majoritarian logic. In his fourth condition, however, Ghannouchi went beyond majoritarianism and set universal consensus as the precondition to establishing an Islamic democracy. Ghannouchi maintained that Muslims, even if they were in majority, could not erect an Islamic democracy if the system incited opposition from within or from other countries.[39] He practically declared Islamic democracy unachievable: "According to our faith," he stated, "an ideal is only accomplishable in the Hereafter. In this world, what matters is that we quest for the ideal."[40]

Given the impracticality of an Islamic government, what should Muslims strive for then? For Ghannouchi, the second-best option after an Islamic government was secular democracy. Despite its shortcomings, he argued, Western democracy "[was] still a thousand times better than despotism"[41] and "it [was] the duty of the Muslim as individuals and communities" to share noble objectives with those who do not share the same faith or ideology. The noble objectives, he suggested, included the achievement of good and avoidance of evil, serving the interests of mankind, prevention of injustice and oppression, protection of human rights, and recognition of the authority of the people.[42]

---

[38] Jawad, "Democracy in Modern Islamic Thought," 333.
[39] Ghannouchi, "The Participation of Islamists in Non-Islamic Government," 59–61.
[40] Rached Ghannouchi quoted in Tamimi, *Rachid Ghannouchi*, 103.
[41] Rached Ghannouchi quoted in ibid., 88.
[42] Ibid., 58–59.

In short, Ghannouchi identified liberal democracy as the best form of government. For him, a secular democratic system was preferable to a religious nondemocratic order. The choice was, therefore, between democracy and dictatorship, not between Islamic and non-Islamic governments. After all, Islam, Ghannouchi argued, aimed to fulfill essential requirements of human life, such as human rights, basic security, and freedom of expression and belief. When a secular democratic order fulfilled these requirements, the country became *dar al Islam* (the land of Islam), even if it lacked an "Islamic government." This implied that liberal democracy and Islam were inseparable, and democratization, for Ghannouchi, would bring societies closer to Islam.

Ghannouchi's interpretation of political Islam clearly diverged from other Islamists. Unlike Qutb, for instance, he perceived democracy not as an un-Islamic system but as a political system fully compatible with Islam.[43] Ghannouchi expressed his skepticism of wholesale rejection of Western institutions as part of a false dichotomy and argued that liberal democratic institutions constituted the best safeguards for human rights and against despotism available in human history. Neither was democracy an instrument toward building an "Islamic government," as Brotherhood's old guard assumed.

A year after its first convention in exile, Ennahda released a statement to celebrate the fifteenth anniversary of the founding of the Islamist movement.[44] The statement reflected the ongoing self-criticism in the party and unequivocally affirmed its commitment to democracy and nonviolence. Ennahda demanded freedom of expression, assembly, and the press; respect for the right of the majority to govern through elected institutions; minority rights; and establishment of an independent judiciary. The party explicitly denounced violence and adopted dialogue, peaceful political participation, and pluralism as its main method.

One could suggest that the party thus approached the Brotherhood and the Milli Görüş line. Unlike these two movements, however, Ennahda rejected majoritarianism. The party defined persuasion, dialogue, and tolerance among different elements in the society, along with elections as essential parts of a political system. Islamists, even if they won most of the votes, the statement elaborated, had to include other parties in government. In an instance of self-reflection, Nahdawis also confessed that

---

[43] Although Ghannouchi describes democracy as compatible with Islam, he also identifies the conditions of such coexistence. Accordingly, democracy neither undermines Islam nor imposes restrictions on those who work to establish an Islamic system, creating certain tensions that echo the paradox of democracy.
[44] Ennahda, "The Lessons of the Past and the Problems of the Present and Future Aspirations."

they made a mistake by not cooperating with other political forces in the 1989 elections. This realization would later inform Ennahda's strategy before and after the 2011 revolution.

In its seventh party congress in April 2001, Ennahda delegates reaffirmed these principles and their commitment to democracy and freedom. Both the party statement and internal elections pointed at Ghannouchi's growing power in the movement, who was reelected as chairman with 75 percent of the delegates' votes. Ennahda's statement echoed Ghannouchi's views on Islam and democracy:

> One of the tasks that the Movement aspires to achieve is to restore the legitimate right of the masses to self-determination away from any internal guardianship or external domination and reject the principle of monopolization of power. This includes the right of all popular forces to exercise freedom of expression and assembly and other legitimate rights.

The statement of 2001, like the declaration of 1996, also qualified Ennahda's relationship with Islam, echoing Ghannouchi's religious and political pluralism: Ennahda was not "the representative of Islam" in politics; rather, its interpretation of "Islamism" constituted one possible take among many. The movement adhered to the Islamic tradition and affirmed Islam as its ideological ground, but it had no aim to monopolize Islamic politics. As such, Islam formed a source of inspiration for the party's political, economic, and social vision. The movement, hence, recognized Islamic pluralism and distanced itself from Islamist groups that prioritized Islamization over political reform. This was a clear departure from the position of the Brotherhood and Milli Görüş, both of which self-identified with Islam.

Ennahda's understanding of the relationship between Islam and democracy under the leadership of democrats specifically marked a clear departure from the Brotherhood line. For electoralists in the Brotherhood, and for radicals in Ennahda, Islamization of society was the foremost priority, while democracy was neither necessary nor sufficient for an Islamic state. For them, democracy could serve as an instrument of Islamization. Ennahda under liberal democrats' influence, in contrast, prioritized democracy over Islamization and went further to define democracy as an indispensable aspect of Islam. For them, Islamization required democratization. This view of Islam and democracy also informed Ennahda's democratic struggle in cooperation with secular forces.

It should be noted that the transformation of Ennahda in a liberal direction occurred mostly in exile, where the party had a much smaller organization. However, democrats also ascended within the local party organization in Tunisia, albeit at a slower pace and with limited scope. Starting in the mid-2000s, some Nahdawis pushed for a similar ideological transformation in the local party structure. The rethinking of the project, as McCarthy asserts, emerged from internal debates in Tunisia. One of the most progressive democrats, Ajmi Lourimi, called for a substantial shift in the movement's vision toward human rights advocacy and democratization. In 2009, he declared:

> The goal of the movement became not taking power but participation, and so began the slogan of joint work with the opposition and serious, comprehensive national reconciliation instead of the slogan of complete Islamization and of taking power, and it moved to the call for mutual recognition and to considering the project as the task of society as a whole not the task of an individual party, and it became clear it was impossible to return to the first stage of Islamization and that it was impossible to continue the second stage of taking power.[45]

Lourimi's call would find its audience, and the party would embrace democratization over Islamization after the revolution.

Democrats also increased their power within the local party organization in Tunisia at the expense of radicals, although it took longer for them to recover from the heavy repression of the regime. Ben Ali, in the mid-2000s, released prominent figures from prison. Among them were second-generation Islamists like Hamadi Jebali, Ali Laarayedh, Ajmi Lourimi, and Abdelhamid Jlassi. These democrats led the efforts of rebuilding the local party organization. Hamadi Jebali in Sousse and Ali Laarayedh in Tunis worked together to construct Ennahda's local infrastructure mostly in a clandestine fashion due to ongoing regime repression. Since the Ben Ali regime had wiped out the Islamist network in the country in the previous two decades, these local leaders revived the movement base almost from scratch.

Laarayedh placed particular emphasis on student recruitment on college campuses and met regularly with students, as Wolf reports.[46] Interestingly, Ennahda's main rival on campuses were no longer leftists; it was Salafis. Salafism, as a strictly conservative interpretation of the Qur'an, was on the rise in the country and appealed to disenfranchised youth. Ennahda preferred to compete with Salafis, rather than aligning with them, and attempted to convert them to democratic political Islam.

In contrast to the party's experience in the 1980s, democrats this time exerted greater influence over the student movement in the 2000s. Their prominence in the party created a distance between Ennahda and the rising Salafism on Tunisian campuses. Local leaders refrained from filling their base with Salafis. When Nahdawis met with

---

[45] Quoted in McCarthy, *Inside Tunisia's al-Nahda*, 120.
[46] Wolf, *Political Islam in Tunisia*, 120.

a Salafi, they encouraged him to reconsider his Islamic understanding before joining Ennahda.[47] They offered a peaceful and democratic alternative to Salafism's rigid worldview that revolved around scripturalism, *takfir* (excommunication), and rejection of political participation. Ennahda's desire to compete with Salafism, instead of recruiting its base, was a clear contrast to the Brotherhood's old guard, which deliberately kept the ranks of the movement open to Salafi youth in the 1990s and 2000s.

Nahdawis also revised the party's curriculum and engaged with ideologues of democratic political Islam – including Fahmy Howeidy, Tarek El-Bishry, Mohammad Salim Al-Awa, Burhan Ghalioun, Yusuf al-Qaradawi – to achieve "intellectual immunity against the rigidity of Salafism," in the words of an activist.[48] As McCarthy finds, these activists "crafted a new vocabulary of contention, embracing liberal ideals of democracy, a civil state, equality, and freedom of conscience. They took advantage of new opportunities for cross-party cooperation and discussion. And they pressed the senior leadership to acknowledge the changing political climate and to address the mistakes of the past."[49]

Local leaders of Ennahda, including Jebali and Laarayedh, strongly expressed Ennahda's political vision in terms of human rights advocacy and democracy.[50] Laarayedh, who pursued civil society activism upon his release in 2004, played a key role in Ennahda's participation in the October 18 movement, which rallied democratic political actors against the Ben Ali regime.[51] With democrats now dominating the party leadership, Ennahda worked with its ideological rivals (i.e., secular parties) within and outside of Tunisia to call for democratization because they believed that democracy and Islam were inextricably linked.

The October 18 movement originated from a month-long hunger strike of eight opposition leaders in 2005. The purpose was to draw attention to the systematic violation of human rights before the UN World Summit in Tunis. Once the strikes ended, the participants agreed to organize their efforts into a collective. In their words:

The 18 October collective in Paris [was] a framework for the fight for freedoms and rights, a space for reflection and debate on the conditions for a democratic transition in Tunisia. It [brought] together political parties, associations and independent figures of different tendencies and sensitivities who advocate[d] for

---

[47] McCarthy, *Inside Tunisia's al-Nahda*.
[48] Ibid., 110.
[49] Ibid., 120.
[50] Wolf, *Political Islam in Tunisia*, 116.
[51] For more details, see McCarthy, *Inside Tunisia's al-Nahda*.

freedom of expression and the press, freedom of association and organization, and promulgation of a law of general amnesty and the release of all political and opinion prisoners.[52]

Both exiles and local Nahdawis played a crucial role in this collaboration. Ali Laarayedh, Mohammed Nouri, and Zied Doulatli joined the collective and participated in two years of discussion and debate on critical issues that had created a wedge between Ennahda and secular forces in the past. These concerned women's rights, gender equality, and freedom of opinion and conscience. Following these meetings, participants of the October 18 collective declared their commitment to democratic principles and the common political ground they established in their discussions. As a signatory, Ennahda affirmed its adherence to the equality of all citizens, nonviolence, gender equality, and the advancement of women's rights, including the preservation of the personal status code, as well as freedom of conscience and belief. All political actors in the collective "gathered around the recognition of the need for a real democratic break with the dictatorship," while the party expressed its strong desire to work with other stakeholders toward this objective. This willingness and collaboration marked another key difference between Ennahda and the Brotherhood, which refrained from joining forces with the secular opposition against the Mubarak regime before the revolution.[53]

Liberal democrats' views did not go unchallenged in the movement though. Several within the party critiqued these political goals. "Elitists," as Pargeter calls them, questioned democrats' antiregime attitudes and raised the possibility of negotiating with the Ben Ali regime instead of pushing for democratic change with other forces.[54] Presumably, they desired to protect the movement from destruction due to its openly antiauthoritarian position. Instead, they sought compromise, accommodation, and peaceful coexistence with the regime, much like the old guard of the Brotherhood did under Mubarak. This internal split reflected different preferences regarding Ennahda's goals and identity.

---

[52] *Collectif 18 Octobre*, "Textes du Collectif 18 octobre Pour les Droits & les Libertés en Tunisie à Paris."

[53] Furthermore, Ennahda's eighth congress in 2007, held in exile, affirmed these trends in its final statement. The movement deemed itself as a moderate and democratic alternative to extremist and violent tendencies (i.e., Salafism) and reaffirmed its commitment to human rights, equal citizenship, fundamental freedoms such as freedom of expression and information, and the "organization of political life based on true democratic changes and reforms." The statement was prompted by an incident in 2006 when a jihadi movement known as the Soliman group conspired to overthrow the Ben Ali regime but they were caught before they could carry out their plans.

[54] Pargeter, *Return to Shadows*.

Therefore, liberals' supremacy in the party was not certain, as I will discuss later. In fact, as Pargeter argues, many within the local organization wished to revert to the Brotherhood line of self-preservation and abandon the political goals of the movement: namely to democratize Tunisia.[55]

Ennahda's ideological evolution toward democracy under Ghannouchi's leadership in the 1990s and 2000s was also met with skepticism by secular quarters of Tunisian society. Much like secular forces in Turkey, they suspected that the party's democratic activism was self-serving and obscured by dissimulation. In their view, Ennahda would instrumentalize democracy to establish an Islamic state in Tunisia. There was, however, no way to test this claim before 2011. So it remained an open question whether Ennahda would commit to democratic principles when and if they came to power. Developments during and after the 2011 revolution provided the party with ample opportunity to prove its democratic commitments. In this period, the liberal democrats in Ennahda secured their control over the party organization. As their tenuous hold over a split movement turned into a firm grip, Ennahda became a force for democracy in Tunisian politics.

The Revolution and Ennahda's Rise to Power

Mohammed Bouazizi was not the first person to self-immolate in the region. Yet it was his act that sparked local protests in his hometown which quickly spread to the rest of the country – as well as the region. By January 11, the entire country was beholden to widespread protests against a seemingly stable autocratic regime. Obviously, Tunisians begged to differ. They held deep grievances, and Ben Ali had failed to address them. Economic conditions played a key role in fueling the revolutionary fire. Unemployment was rampant (particularly among the youth); economic growth stagnated, and whatever growth occurred mostly benefited Ben Ali's cronies. Regional inequalities had widened, corruption was widespread, and there was no political outlet to release such grievances. So when Bouazizi killed himself, the Tunisian people rose with demands for dignity and better living standards. Ben Ali, the leader of one of the most repressive regimes in the region for twenty-four years, failed to diffuse the revolutionary fire with a government shuffle and emphatic speeches. On January 14, he left the county and his regime collapsed.

Unlike the Brotherhood in Egypt, Ennahda lacked a strong local organization at the outset of the revolution; thus, the party did not play a

---

[55] Ibid.

central role in popular mobilization. Regardless, the momentous political change allowed the party to quickly recover from decades-long repression under Ben Ali. First, on January 30, Ghannouchi returned to Tunisia amid cheers after twenty-two years in exile. Hundreds of other Nahdawis followed suit. Soon Ennahda was legalized: the party's democrats finally reached their longtime objective. The party began to rebuild its local organization by giving speed to its previously clandestine attempts. Jlassi opened 2,064 offices after the revolution all around the country, including the poorer provinces in the south and wealthier coastal cities in the north. With its organizational capacity unmatched by other political actors, the party quickly turned into the most organized political force in the country.

Different factions within the party sought different trajectories for Ennahda in the postrevolutionary era. They held three fundamental disagreements concerning: (1) the nature of the movement, (2) its political objectives, and (3) the appropriate method to attain these objectives. Former radicals now embraced electoralism. For figures like Chorou and Ellouze, who led this group, Ennahda was first and foremost a religious movement with inextricable political goals. These goals included the Islamization of the society through the establishment of an Islamic state and instatement of sharia. They deployed both preaching (*da'wa*) and political activism to attain these objectives. For them, democratic institutions could serve to maximize the party's influence in the society and spread its message; democracy was, thus, a means toward the establishment of an Islamic state. They believed, Ennahda should maximize its political gains over the course of the transition to attain majority support and enshrine sharia rule. As such, they echoed the old guard in the Brotherhood.

For democrats, who increasingly articulated their perception of democracy in liberal terms, Ennahda was exclusively a political movement seeking democratization. Democracy was not an instrument toward an Islamic state but an indispensable part of Islam and an end in itself. For this faction, democracy was more than elections and majority rule; it signified pluralism, inclusion, and deliberative engagement. Ennahda, they believed, should not dominate the transition, it should work closely with other political actors in this process.

The two factions, as expected, displayed diverging attitudes during the transition. While liberal democrats insisted on deliberation, consensus-building, inclusion, and pluralism, electoralists sought the maximization of Ennahda's political gains for the sake of Islam. As Tarek Kahlaoui, an expert on Tunisian Islamism, observed, the wing headed by Jebali and Ghannouchi advocated political alliances with other political actors; the other wing headed by the conservative Chorou, in contrast, preferred to form cultural coalitions primarily with Salafis – as the Brotherhood did in Egypt.[56] Electoralists rejected liberals' ideas and accused them of compromising the true Islamic identity of the movement, as I detail below. Yet because they were in a much weaker position, electoralists failed to chart Ennahda's course during the revolution. This time it was the liberals who called the shots, as the next section shows.

Democrats under Ghannouchi's leadership had growing influence over the party in exile with the support of the rank and file who critiqued the confrontational attitude of radicals in the 1990s. In this process, Ghannouchi's radical competition was either sidelined, as in the case of Karker, or in prison, as in the case of Chorou. Meanwhile, Ben Ali's ongoing repression well into the 2000s prevented the development of an extensive party organization in Tunisia outside the control of the exiled leadership. In the aftermath of the revolution, the liberal leadership entrenched its position, a topic I will return to later in the chapter.

Ennahda's Democratic Commitments during the Transition

Upon Ben Ali's ouster, Tunisia steered toward a political transition. The revolution's popular spirit and demands for dignity placed the country on a democratic course. After Ben Ali left Tunisia on February 11, the speaker of the house became the interim president and oversaw the transition. To set the terms of the transition, a commission was formed (widely known as Ben Achour Commission) on February 18. The commission scheduled the Constituent Assembly (CA) elections on October 23, disqualified Ben Ali's party (RCD) from running, established the Higher Authority for Elections, and set the gender parity rule.[57] The CA was charged to draft a new constitution for a democratic Tunisia and govern the country until the next elections. Therefore, the stakes of the first election were quite high, as was the case in Egypt.

Despite such high stakes, Ennahda adopted reconciliation and inclusion over domination and exclusion, thus refraining from taking a hegemonic posture vis-à-vis its rivals. At the outset, the party expressed its commitment to the principles of the October 18 movement and vowed to collaborate with all stakeholders in the new democratic system in the making. Ennahda's electoral platform accepted

---

[56] Interview with Tarek Kahlaoui, June 28, 2012.
[57] The parity rule required all parties to nominate equal number of male and female candidates alternating on electoral lists.

[t]he Republican system as the best guarantee of democracy and best use of the country's wealth for the benefit of the people, as well as the guarantor of the essentials of a dignified life, including employment, health, education, respect for human rights without discrimination on the basis of sex, color, belief or wealth, and the affirmation of women's rights to equality, education, employment and participation in public life.

Specifically, Ennahda aimed "to establish a democratic system that breaks with tyranny, founded on the basis of citizenship, freedoms, dignity, the supremacy of the Constitution, rule of law and all standards of good governance"; to provide full employment for all Tunisian men and women and balanced regional development; and to "build a modern, balanced society, steeped in solidarity and rooted in its identity." For the party, Islam served as a supreme point of reference for the democratic republic.[58] However, what this meant for future institutions of the country remained vague.

It was Ghannouchi who clarified the guiding principles of a democratic state. He posited that Ennahda's principles were the principles of the October 18 collective,[59] including a democratic civil state and fundamental human rights – freedom of belief and conscience and gender equality.

Such principles did not remain on paper as they did in the case of the Brotherhood. They, indeed, informed and shaped Ennahda's choices leading up to the elections and its aftermath. These choices affirmed that the party did not seek hegemony or perceive democracy as a means toward an Islamist end. For Ghannouchi, the transition required cross-party partnership, including coalitions, consensus-building, crisis management through dialogue, compromise, and inclusion. Along these lines, Ennahda advocated proportional representation over plurality system to increase representation, inhibit majoritarian tendencies, and induce coalitions among political actors.[60] Similarly, the party distanced itself from presidentialism and endorsed a parliamentary system, which would "guarantee public and private freedoms, independence of the judiciary, freedom of information and alternation of power through a balanced, dynamic distribution of powers between the various state institutions and through free pluralistic elections." Also, before the elections, the party leadership vowed to form a coalition government and share power with other parties, irrespective of the electoral outcome – a promise they kept after the election.

With these institutional preferences, Ennahda rejected domination and majoritarianism despite being the most organized political force in the

---

[58] *Ennahda Electoral Program* 2011 (translated in Wolf, *Political Islam in Tunisia*).
[59] Ghannouchi, "Ennahda's Democratic Commitments and Capabilities."
[60] Ibid.

country.[61] It also expressed support for pluralism and inclusion regardless of the identity and ideology of its rivals. Such attitudes clearly contrasted with the trajectories of the Brotherhood and the AKP (after electoralists captured these organizations). The Brotherhood pushed for a majoritarian system early on during the transition to capitalize on its mobilizational capacity, while the AKP under electoralists' leadership abolished the parliamentary system to instate an executive presidency embedded in winners-take-all logic. Of course, as the AKP experience has shown, democratic promises made before coming to power can later be abandoned, as I discussed in Chapter 2. So how did Ennahda fare in government?

Ennahda in Power: The Tug-of-War between Liberals and Electoralists

On October 23, 2011, in the first free and fair elections in Tunisian history, Ennahda won a landslide victory with 37 percent of the votes and 41 percent of seats in the assembly.[62] The rest of the seats were divided among eight parties. The total vote share of these eight parties following Ennahda reached a bare 35 percent. Its closest followers, the liberal Congress for the Republic (CPR after its French acronym) and social–democratic Ettakatol (the Democratic Forum for Labor and Liberties), received 8.7 percent (29 seats) and 7 percent (20 seats), respectively. Hence, there emerged a major gap between Ennahda and other political parties and an excellent opportunity to observe Nahdawis' democratic commitments.

Ennahda's perception and practice of power, attitudes over the constitutional process, and management of political crises after the election revealed its inclusionary, pluralist, and deliberative attitude. Although the party dominated the political scene, it resisted majoritarian tendencies and hegemonic politics. Instead, Nahdawis shared power with other political actors, often at Ennahda's expense.

After the October election, the party built a coalition government – known as the Troika – with two secular parties, the CPR and Ettakatol. Ennahda thus kept its promise of coalitional politics and power-sharing. With this arrangement, it retained the prime minister's position along with fourteen ministries, including the interior, justice, and foreign affairs, while the remaining sixteen seats were shared among the CPR, Ettakatol, and independents. The assembly also elected the CPR's Moncef Marzouki, a renowned human rights advocate, as the president, and Ettakatol's Mustapha Ben Jaafar became the speaker of the assembly.

---

[61] Stepan, "Mutual Accommodation," 54.
[62] BBC, "Tunisia's Islamist Ennahda Party Wins Historic Poll."

One could argue that Ennahda formed coalitions and made compromises because it was electorally weaker (compared to the Brotherhood, for instance). Ennahda's dominance in parliament, however, challenged such claims. As the senior partner in the coalition government, Ennahda was clearly the dominant actor in the cabinet, as well as in the assembly. In fact, soon after the formation of the Troika, several Ettakatol and CPR deputies left their parties, further weakening the junior partners in the coalition. Furthermore, Nahdawis in the assembly had high party discipline and attended all sessions, while others rarely attended meetings. This discrepancy among parties handed substantial control to Ennahda during the transition.[63]

Besides, as Marks aptly puts it, Ennahda's minimalism and inclusive politics were not due to its weak electoral gains; rather, the party's comparatively lesser electoral gains were the party's own doing.[64] Ennahda's insistence on proportional representation and coalitional politics constituted self-imposed limits and diluted its electoral power. As Stepan estimated, under a first-past-the-post system, Ennahda would have captured 90 percent of the seats.[65] Alternatively, a modified proportional representative system with a high electoral threshold could have also secured the party a comfortable majority in the parliament. Even after the elections, as Kahlaoui observed, Ennahda could have easily formed a majority government with the independent deputies of the assembly; yet the leadership deliberately chose to form a coalition government with two secular left-wing parties.[66]

It was clear that liberal Nahdawis in the party leadership did not seek to dominate politics. That is why they refrained from maximizing their political gains through their institutional and political choices (in clear contrast to the Brotherhood during the transitional period in Egypt) and unwaveringly followed institutional forbearance.

Some groups in the party, however, objected to such self-imposed limits, since they desired to maximize partisan benefits on religious and revolutionary grounds, like electoralists did in the Brotherhood. Some youth members, in particular, demanded radical action from the party leaders in favor of the Islamization of the state and society.[67] In the meantime, more liberal voices within Ennahda, like Lotfi Zitoun, pushed for

---

[63] Interview with Youessif Cherif, June 20, 2012.
[64] Marks, "Purists vs Pluralists," 109.
[65] Stepan, "Tunisia's Transition and the Twin Tolerations."
[66] Interview with Tarek Kahlaoui, June 28, 2012.
[67] Boubekeur, "Islamists, Secularists and Old Regime Elites in Tunisia"; Barrie, "Ninth Conference: Ghannouchi Remains Leader as Ennahda Denies Any Conflict within the Movement."

greater inclusion. Ghannouchi's chief of staff since 1992, Zitoun claimed a year after the revolution that Ennahda should have expanded its coalition and included other actors in the transition process:

> We had previously decided in the movement not to monopolize the power, even if we collected 60 percent of the votes. Our position was to form a national unity government. The fact is, we have been victims of the seduction *"ighra"* of power. And when two political parties agreed to form this coalition, we did not look any further. We have not been convincing enough and have not made the effort to convince the recalcitrant. [...] The agreement of 18 October is a consensus on the most contentious issues, the personal status code, the question of women, the place of religion, democracy. [...] It is not enough to have the majority to make the country work. [...] For the democratic transition to continue and not to fall into the chaos or the rule of a single party. The danger exists with one of the two options, there must be big coalitions and we are moving towards that.

It would be liberal voices like Zitoun's that would chart the course of the party.

Islam and Politics in the New Era

Maybe the governing coalition did not expand as Zitoun desired, but Ennahda did not fall into the trap of political dominance either. Thanks to liberals' greater power within the party, Ennahda made crucial compromises during the drafting of the constitution. One key issue concerned the relationship of Islam and politics in the new era with three immediate questions: the inclusion of sharia in the new constitution, freedom of conscience, and protection of the sacred.

In its platform, to the dismay of electoral Islamists, Ennahda did not seek the establishment of sharia rule. Soon after the elections, though, both Ennahda's electoralists and religious conservatives in the society demanded Islamic law to form the basis of all legislation in the new regime. On March 16, 2012, tens of thousands called for sharia in a demonstration before parliament.[68] Among them were Nahdawis such as Habib Ellouze, who maintained close ties to the Salafi currents and led Ennahda's radical youth in their call for sharia rule.[69]

Ennahda leaders could have mobilized this support and polarized the society to attain a hegemonic position. Indeed, there existed strong societal support for instatement of Islamic law, with polls showing 56 percent of Tunisians in favor.[70] Despite such popular demand, the leaders of

---

[68] *Ahram Online*, "Thousands Rally Demanding Sharia Law in Tunisia."
[69] Wolf, *Political Islam in Tunisia*, 138.
[70] Pew Research Center, "The World's Muslims: Religion, Politics and Society," 46.

the party, primarily Ghannouchi, thought that the issue of sharia was divisive. Instead of opting for polarization, as the Brotherhood did, he pushed for conciliation. For him, the Tunisian society included different ideas and beliefs; the people held different interpretations of Islam, and all of them were acceptable. Democracy and secularism together would guarantee freedom of faith for *all* citizens.[71]

The party leadership, after some discussion, renewed its commitment to a civil democratic state, as defined by the 1959 constitution, in a public statement on March 26.[72] The statement also passed with an overwhelming majority in the party's Shura Council, with only twelve members out of eighty voting in favor of sharia rule. The vote attested to the weight of liberals in the party.

Electoralists within Ennahda remained undeterred. They aspired to charter an explicitly Islamist line for both the party and the new constitution. In August, ten Ennahda deputies joined six others to propose the criminalization of attacks on the "sacred," specifically God, the Qur'an, and the Sunna.[73] The party leadership refused to debate the proposal within the party or the assembly, and electoralists had to shelve their demands until the final vote on the constitution in January 2014, as I will discuss briefly.

Political Crisis Erupts

As the constitutional process unfolded, an assassination in February 2013 threw the country into political turmoil. Chokri Belaid, a prominent secular and left-wing politician, was murdered by radical Salafi groups that had surfaced in the 2000s and became visible after the revolution.[74] Groups like Ansar al-Sharia and Hizb ut-Tahrir appealed to the Tunisian youth and managed to capture more than 500 mosques that had been previously under state control.[75] Ongoing civil wars in Libya and Syria further emboldened jihadi Salafis in Tunisia. Some established links with Al-Qaeda in the Islamic Maghreb (AQIM), stationed in Libya, and committed acts of political violence against civilians and political activists in the months to come.

---

[71] Interview with Rached Ghannouchi, July 4, 2012.
[72] BBC News, "Tunisians Edge Away from Sharia"; Reuters, "Tunisia's Ennahda to Oppose Sharia in Constitution."
[73] Human Rights Watch, "Tunisie: De la prison et des amendes pour les «offenses au sacré»."
[74] For Salafism in Tunisia, see Marks, "Youth Politics and Tunisian Salafism."
[75] Interview with Asma Nouria, June 20, 2012.

The opposition accused the Troika, specifically Ennahda, of being lenient on Salafi violence. Ennahda's initial reaction to Salafism in fact was based on inclusion and dialogue. Convinced that political exclusion would breed radicalism, the Troika government licensed Salafi parties in early 2012. Ennahda desired to socialize these parties into democracy, and as Asma Nouria, of the University of Tunis, claimed, the government even appointed a Salafi to the Ministry of Religious Affairs.[76] The party's approach to Salafi movements, however, changed after September 2012 Salafi attack on the US Embassy in Tunis.[77] Soon the party leadership realized that they had underestimated the severity of the problem and decided to eradicate Salafi violence with tough measures.

The Salafi threat rapidly polarized Tunisian politics. Beji Caid Essebsi, former interim prime minister and a prominent figure under the Bourguiba regime, had formed the Nidaa Tounes (NT) Party in 2012 to unify fragmented secular parties against the "Islamist threat." Essebsi capitalized on his Bourguibist credentials and fears of an Islamist takeover to woo middle-class secular voters. Such tactics would ring hollow if it were not for Ben Ali's strategy of fear-mongering during his reign. Indeed, Ben Ali had presented his dictatorial regime as a safeguard against Islamism and forced secular middle classes in these countries to acquiesce to his corrupt regime. The Bourguibists made a comeback via this secular–Islamist cleavage, which had been running deep in Tunisia.

Ennahda leadership was thus stuck between a secular rock and a Salafist hard place. The secular extraparliamentary opposition demanded Ennahda to step down in favor of a technocratic government, while Ennahda's electoralists and youth deemed the party's electoral victory as a mandate for their Islamist mission. Liberals' conciliatory attitude and concessions frustrated both; one found them too little and the other found them far too excessive.

The leaders of the party had a hard time balancing these two extremes. Some prominent figures like Morou and Jebali pushed for greater compromise. Morou, for instance, called on his party to step down after Belaid's assassination because the crisis necessitated a unity government to overcome political differences.[78] Then Prime Minister Hamadi Jebali agreed with Morou and resigned from his post, calling for a technocratic government. Electoralists such as Chorou and Ellouze, in contrast,

---

[76] Ibid.
[77] Interview with Radwan Masmoudi, July 21, 2017. Also see Khalil, "Ennahda Distances Itself from Salafists."
[78] Interview with Abdelfattah Morou, July 24, 2017.

rejected any compromise and desired to retain power to carry out their ideological agenda.[79] The party leadership, supported by its coalition partners, decided to hold onto power with some compromise. For them, the Troika as a democratically elected government could preside over the transition until the constitution was complete. In the end, Ali Laarayedh replaced Jebali, and to address the concerns of the opposition, the new prime minister appointed independent figures to ministries of defense, justice, and interior.

Such concessions failed to calm down the opposition outside of parliament. In the following months, they continued to call for the dissolution of the CA. For them, the constitutional process – which had been quite transparent, democratic, and inclusive by universal standards – was illegitimate. They were emboldened by the rise of the Tamarod movement in Egypt against the Brotherhood. As Marks notes, the unelected leaders of NT sensed an opportunity in Egypt's crisis and hoped to corner the Troika for more concessions. While NT aimed to attain extensive popular mobilization to force Ennahda from power, not all opposition parties were on board. Leaders like Ahmed Najib Chebbi, the leader of the Republican Party, perceived the constitutional process as legitimate and democratic, and sought consensus among the political elite. Chebbi supported the completion of the constitution while calling Ennahda to make compromises.

Popular Mobilization Intensifies

The crisis further deepened after a second assassination in July 2012. Radical Salafis killed prominent Arab nationalist Mohamed Brahmi, triggering nationwide protests. As sixty deputies walked out of the assembly in protest of Brahmi's assassination and popular mobilization gained further momentum, Mustafa Ben Jaafar suspended the CA in early August. Ennahda thus encountered a formidable political front as well as growing popular dissent. Instead of mobilizing its supporters against the protestors, as Morsi did in Egypt, or resorting to repression, as Erdoğan did in Turkey, Ennahda sought deliberation and engagement.

Later that month, Ghannouchi met with Beji Caid Essebsi in Paris to resolve the crisis. In an interview, Ghannouchi told me that the meeting with Essebsi was a personal decision.[80] Given the heightened polarization in the country, his decision was a dramatic attempt at reconciliation and strong commitment to mutual tolerance. Soon after, Ennahda agreed to

[79] Ibid.
[80] Interview with Rached Ghannouchi, July 26, 2017.

form a consensus committee in the CA where it would carry only one vote irrespective of its seats in parliament, a major compromise for a predominant party. Ennahda also agreed to hold talks with main civil society actors in late September. Four major organizations – Tunisian General Trade Union (UGTT), Tunisian Business Association (UTICA), the Bar Association, and the Tunisian League of Human Rights – known as the National Dialogue Quartet – agreed to facilitate the peaceful resolution of the political gridlock. Ennahda leaders met with the UGTT representatives to discuss their proposals. A few days later, Ennahda accepted the roadmap that the Quartet delivered. The roadmap entailed: (1) the completion of the constitutional draft, (2) resignation of the Troika government upon the ratification of the constitution, (3) establishment of a technocratic government until the parliamentary and presidential elections, and (4) formation of a commission to oversee the elections.[81]

Hence, a grave threat to Tunisian democratic transition was averted, thanks to Ennahda and its partners' willingness to compromise and engage with the civil society and the extra-parliamentary opposition. A key factor was the dominance of liberals in the party who self-distanced from majoritarian, exclusionary, and hegemonic Islamism. Their pluralist predisposition and commitment to engagement and compromise allowed the party to weather severe political crises over the course of the transition.

Morou, known for his liberal democratic tendencies, commended the compromises his party made while shunning electoralists' hegemonic and majoritarian tendencies within party ranks:

It is wrong to believe that the majority allows you to rule because they can make you reach power; it will not allow you to stay there, because staying in power depends on the legitimacy of your achievements on the ground. Had we stepped down earlier, we could have avoided several negative things. [...] Reaching power is only a stage, not the goal. I think the Islamists should realize that if they reach power, that *doesn't allow them to monopolize power*. They should learn to live with the rest of the political currents in the country, as happened in Tunisia. *Making concessions doesn't mean the weakening of the movement*, but rather the mastering of the mechanisms of political coexistence for the country's interest. So, I say that the Islamists must face reality and realize the challenges they face, and I mean economic development first and foremost. This will not be achieved by slogans, but by competence.[82] [emphasis added]

Morou's words proved how far the party leadership was from a majoritarian understanding of democracy, hinting at the weakness of the electoralists within while affirming the difference between Ennahda, on the one hand, and the AKP and the Brotherhood, on the other.

---

[81] See Stepan, "Mutual Accommodation" for details.
[82] Al-Monitor, "Ennahda Leader Says Compromises Serve Tunisia's Interests."

Electoralists Strike Back

Electoralists, as one might guess, strongly disapproved of the compromises made by party leadership. For them, Ennahda held an electoral mandate and had a right to rule the country as it deemed fit. Thus, it was a grave mistake to accept the roadmap the National Quartet proposed. However, Ghannouchi's leadership prevented them from reversing the party's course. Still, they strived to shape the draft constitution.

When the final draft came before the assembly for promulgation on January 4, they proposed a series of amendments to leave their ideological imprint on the founding document. They proposed to add "the Qur'an and the Sunna as the principal sources of legislation" to draft Article 42.[83] This proposal practically sought to enshrine sharia in the constitution, as the Qur'an and the Sunna formed the fundamental sources of Islamic law. When taken to a vote, only twenty-one Ennahda deputies voted in favor, while thirty-seven abstained – in line with the party line – and seventeen voted against. The amendment was defeated.

Next, electoralists attempted to change other Articles with implications for religious freedoms. One such target was Article 6, which read: "the state is the guardian of religion. It guarantees freedom of conscience and belief, the free exercise of religious practices, and the neutrality of mosques and places of worship from all partisan instrumentalization. The state undertakes to disseminate the values of moderation and tolerance and the protection of the sacred, and the prohibition of all violations thereof." Ennahda's seventeen deputies proposed to strike "freedom of conscience" from the text, opening up the possibility of penalizing blasphemy, a key demand for electoral Islamists. The motion was again rejected by the assembly; seventeen Nahdawis voted in favor, thirty-five voted against, and twenty-seven abstained.[84] Ironically, electoralists did not only fail to strike freedom of conscience but also caused a dramatic change in the Article when Ellouze called Mongi Rahoui, a secular deputy, an apostate.[85] Liberal Nahdawis worked with their secular colleagues to amend the Article and add a state guarantee against *takfir* (excommunication) and the incitement of violence and hatred. The final text passed with overwhelming support of Ennahda deputies; only twenty voted against. Electoralists were once again defeated by their fellow Nahdawis in collaboration with their secular rivals. In short, Ennahda, although it had a dominant position in the assembly, avoided a hegemonic Islamist agenda while in power.

---

[83] For the CA vote tally on sharia, see Marsad, "Vote sur un amendement n°42 de l'article premier."

[84] Marsad, "Vote sur un amendement de l'article 6: Supprimer la liberté de 'conscience.'"

[85] *L'Express*, "Constitution tunisienne: l'accusation d'apostasie interdite."

The fact that liberals precluded the establishment of an Islamic state, despite the pressure from within the party and the streets, did not mean that the draft constitution was flawless. For instance, Article 31 guaranteed all fundamental freedoms in line with liberal norms, while Article 49 delimited them to prevent violation of the rights of others or the requirements of public order, national defense, public health, or public morals.[86] The vague language left significant space for judicial discretion in the courts.

Still, the final version of the new Tunisian constitution proved to be quite liberal and secular, in striking contrast to the constitution the Brothers dictated in Egypt.[87] In fact, representatives of organizations such as Human Rights Watch and the Friedrich Boll Stiftung commended the legislative process for its inclusivity toward religious minorities and civil society and for passing the most progressive law of the associations in the region.[88] Equally critical, the process itself turned out to be inclusive, pluralist, and transparent, unlike constitutional reforms in Turkey under the AKP and in Egypt under Morsi.

On January 27, 2014, the CA ratified the constitution with 94 percent of the deputies' votes. Soon after, the Troika government stepped down. A technocratic cabinet took over to take the country to parliamentary and presidential elections scheduled for November and December 2014. With the new constitution, according to Ghannouchi, the conflict over Tunisian identity was over – Ennahda had fulfilled its mission.[89]

Beyond the Transition

Ennahda carried its conciliatory attitude well into the 2014 elections and beyond. In March 2014, the Shura Council decided to limit the number of elected positions Ennahda sought in the cabinet and public administration.[90] In accordance, the party decided not to field a candidate in the presidential election in December 2014. This decision sharply contrasted with Brotherhood's approach in Egypt, which sought to maximize their political gains through elections. Ennahda, instead, opted for a minimalist position and signaled its desire to share power with other stakeholders.

---

[86] For a detailed analysis of this fine balance and its implications for freedom of expression, see McCarthy, *Inside Tunisia's al-Nahda*.
[87] For the final text of the constitution, see *Constitute Project*, "Tunisia's Constitution of 2014."
[88] Interviews with representatives between June 27 and July 2, 2012.
[89] Interview with Rached Ghannouchi, July 27, 2017.
[90] Boubekeur, "Islamists, Secularists and Old Regime Elites in Tunisia," 120.

The two contenders for power were Essebsi and Marzouki. Rather than allying with either candidate, Ennahda leadership declared its neutrality and let its supporters decide. Electoralists within the party, such as Chorou and Ellouze, criticized this decision and warned against future splits and resignations from the party. Chorou explicitly endorsed Marzouki in his open letter to party supporters, who viewed Marzouki as a more sympathetic figure toward political Islam.[91] For Ghannouchi, "the country's security and stability [were] more important than any of the candidates' victory in the elections."[92] So he mediated between the candidates during the campaign and persuaded Marzouki to follow a more conciliatory approach.[93]

The party's electoral lists were also filled with progressive names and liberals, who replaced several electoralists serving in the CA, as I discuss below. On the campaign trail, the party leaders refrained from polarizing discourse and focused exclusively on economic and security issues, and remained silent on Islam and sharia. In fact, the only party that did not talk about religion on the campaign trail was Ennahda.[94]

The election results were, however, quite disappointing for the party, whose vote share dropped 10 percentage points. It came in second after Nidaa Tounes (NT). There were several reasons why. Three years after the revolution, Tunisians still suffered from economic hardships, and the Troika government had hardly delivered any meaningful results. To make things worse, revolutionary upheaval in the region destabilized the security situation in Tunisia. Many people held the Troika responsible. Furthermore, Ennahda's concessions and rejection of sharia rule throughout the constitutional process alienated significant segments of its base. Many young Nahdawis demanded a greater role for Islam in their country, and by 2014 it was clear that Ennahda would not deliver what they wanted. Most of them ended up joining Salafi movements. Others had wanted Ennahda to act more assertively in power and fulfill its popular mandate. Frustrated with Ennahda's compromising attitude during the transition, many of its supporters did not go to the polls in 2014.[95] Despite these drawbacks, Ennahda still retained some of its core supporters, receiving more than 30 percent of the vote.

Soon after the election, Ennahda conceded defeat and expressed its willingness to join a future coalition government with NT. Both Chorou

---

[91] *Business News*, "Habib Ellouze et Sadok Chourou préparent l'explosion de la cocotte d'Ennahdha."
[92] Ibid.
[93] Bin Mahfouz, the head of the Tunisian Bar Association, praised Ghannouchi's efforts for his role in overcoming the political crisis. Al-Fathali, "Ennahda's Ghannouchi Plays Mediator in Tunisia."
[94] Wolf, *Political Islam in Tunisia*, 156–58.
[95] Interview with Ali Laarayedh, July 24, 2017.

and Ellouze denounced the talks between the two parties, claiming that NT was practically the continuation of the former regime and would bring injustice and corruption to Tunisia.⁹⁶ Liberals proceeded despite such criticism. When the two rival parties agreed to form a grand coalition, Ennahda accepted the limited ministerial portfolios NT had offered. In the first cabinet formed after the elections, Ennahda held only one ministerial (out of twenty-eight) and four secretaries of state positions (out of fifteen), all with limited political influence. Given the fact that Ennahda had only twenty seats less than NT, the cabinet arrangement was a major concession for Ennahda. Ellouze fiercely objected once again, but to no avail. Interestingly, the party maintained its position even after NT lost its parliamentary plurality when several deputies resigned from the party by January 2015. Ennahda, then the largest party in the parliament, conceded power to its secular partner and accepted having few ministerial positions in the successive governments. The driving factor behind these decisions, as Ghannouchi formulated, was the fact that Ennahda prioritized democratic commitments over partisan gains.⁹⁷

What Drives Ennahda's Democratic Commitments?

As this democratic transition period in Tunisia clearly shows, Ennahda, in Marks' words, "adopted a number of farsighted, participation-oriented positions that evinced a much thicker understanding of democratic politics"⁹⁸ than its counterparts in Turkey and Egypt. Dialogue, engagement, and compromise topped the tendency to polarize the society for partisan purposes and monopolize power through exclusion and majoritarianism. So what drives Ennahda's commitment to democracy?

Wolf suggests that political change in Ennahda was strategically motivated and stemmed from internal and external pressures on the party.⁹⁹ For her, the internal pressure of Tunisian civil society and the fear of secular opposition, and, Western pressure left no choice for Ennahda but to compromise.¹⁰⁰ Netterstorm also argues that Ennahda leaders compromised due to their fear of a counterrevolution and to protect and advance the constitutional process.¹⁰¹

---

⁹⁶ The Economist Intelligence Unit, "Former Prime Minister Resigns from Hizb Al-Nahda."
⁹⁷ Stepan, "Mutual Accommodation," 62.
⁹⁸ Marks, "How Egypt's Coup Really Affected Tunisia's Islamists."
⁹⁹ Wolf, *Political Islam in Tunisia*, 96–97.
¹⁰⁰ Ibid., 141.
¹⁰¹ Netterstrøm, "The Islamists' Compromise in Tunisia."

Fear of a counterrevolution driven by popular protests only partly explains Ennahda's behavior, since this fear was not shared by all groups within the party, and there emerged serious disagreements with respect to the best course of action in response to popular mobilization. Certain groups in Ennahda insisted on dismissing the protests and external pressures in general, instead maximizing their partisan gains as the old guard in the Brotherhood did. Liberals within Ennahda, in contrast, prioritized the constitution and the democratic transition over partisan interests and reconciled with the extraparliamentary opposition instead of polarizing society, as I discussed above. Clearly, the party had other strategies available, but the party leaders chose the strategy based on mutual tolerance and institutional forbearance.

As Wolf describes, after the revolution, liberals remained in charge of the organization, held internal discipline, and eschewed a revengeful attitude.[102] Their dominance in the party, I argue, is the determining factor in Ennahda's commitment to democracy and deserves greater attention. Thanks to liberals' preeminence in the party, Ennahda remained on the course of liberal Islamism and acted as a prodemocratic force, despite internal opposition, during the transition.

But where do liberal Islamists come from? For some, Ennahda's repression under Ben Ali is a key factor. For McCarthy, for instance, Ennahda's democratization was a product of Nahdawis' long-term political exclusion and their prison experience that exposed them to long debates with leftists.[103] Cavatorta and Merone also highlight exclusion under Ben Ali to claim that Nahdawis' political and social marginalization induced their ideological moderation.[104] Similarly, Nugent draws attention to the experience of repression under authoritarian regimes to explain the level of polarization and compromise during democratic transitions.[105] She suggests that Ben Ali's blanket repression of leftists and Islamists reduced the political distance between the two and facilitated their collaboration after the revolution.

As I discussed in Chapter 1, such analyses are noteworthy because they offer plausible explanations for individual-level change. But again, as we see in the case of Ennahda, not all prisoners became liberals during their time in prison or due to exposure to indiscriminate repression at the hands of the regime. Key figures in the case of Ennahda to whom these two explanations do not apply include Chorou and Ellouze.

---

[102] Wolf, *Political Islam in Tunisia*, 132.
[103] McCarthy, *Inside Tunisia's al-Nahda*.
[104] Cavatorta and Merone, "Moderation through Exclusion?"
[105] Nugent, *After Repression*.

Interestingly, liberals within Ennahda also contest such explanations. To justify their efforts to include Salafists in democratic processes, they argued that exclusion leads to radicalization. Indeed, the Islamist youth of Ennahda radicalized in the 1980s when first Bourguiba and later Ben Ali cracked down on the movement. Besides, inclusion was no guarantee for moderation either. The Salafi trend, which gained momentum in the 2000s under Ben Ali's rule, continued to grow during the democratic transition. Neither repression nor accommodation of Salafi organizations inhibited radicalization. In fact, many young men and women joined Salafi movements *after* the revolution.

Grewal, in his study of Ennahda's parliamentary activity, finds limited evidence for the role of prison experience.[106] Instead, for him, time spent in a secular democracy affected ideological moderation and secularization among Nahdawis. Tracking the voting records in the CA, for instance, Grewal finds that those Islamists who spent time in a secular democracy tended to vote more moderately as opposed to others who remained in Tunisia or were in exile in another country in the Middle East.

Lotfi Zitoun, in support for Grewal's argument, told me in an interview that exile has left a crucial impact on Ghannouchi's thinking. Not only were exiles exposed to democratic processes in Western countries, but they also engaged in long debates on the movement's successes and failures.[107] Yet, as Grewal also acknowledges, secular democratic experience does not always induce democratization. A dramatic instance is Sayyid Qutb, who was disillusioned with racism during his stay in the United States in the 1940s. The same goes for some Nahdawis such as Salah Karker, who resisted democratization despite spending time in a secular democratic country, or jihadi groups in Europe, who exploited the liberal democratic environment to pursue their radical agenda.

As this discussion reveals, repression, inclusion, exile, or engagement with the political other might impact individuals in quite different ways. Some Islamists embraced democratic norms as a result of Ben Ali's blanket repression of leftists and Islamists in prisons, their engagement with each other in the process, and their democratic learning in secular countries. Meanwhile, others remained skeptical and embraced electoral procedures without internalizing democratic norms.

To understand the course of Ennahda, we need to tackle the question of aggregation – that is, how individual experiences aggregate to transform the party line. For our purposes, we need to know why and

---

[106] Grewal, "From Islamists to Muslim Democrats."
[107] Interview with Lotfi Zitoun, July 27, 2017.

how liberals in Ennahda succeeded in changing the party, whereas their counterparts in Turkey and Egypt failed.

Liberals' Growing Control over Organizational Resources

In contrast to the Muslim Brotherhood, within which electoralists commanded control over the organization before the 2011 revolution, liberals secured their position within Ennahda during the democratic transition. This was partly because the party members were either in exile or under constant regime pressure before 2011. It was soon after the revolution the party had its second founding: Tunisian democratic transition and Ennahda's party re-formation went hand in hand. The revolution was, thus, a critical juncture as Nahdawis redesigned their movement.

At the outset, liberals did not have a clear dominance within the party, but they rapidly captured it. A few factors helped them. First, the revolutionary conjecture created a context that made liberals' prodemocratic agenda viable for the first time since 1981. The skeptics in the party who prioritized survival over democratization hence lost clout with the decline of the Ben Ali regime. Second, the leader of the liberal wing, Ghannouchi, was a party leader who commanded great respect from different groups within the party organization. He was not only a party chairman but also a spiritual and political guide for Nahdawis. Even though he received pushback on several issues, he intervened in critical moments during the transition that empowered the liberal wing, as I discussed earlier. Third, such interventions reinforced and expanded liberals' control over key organizational resources, allowing them to establish their dominance in the party.

Specifically, the liberal leadership leveraged recruitment and promotion, party finances, and internal communication throughout the transition to build a dominant alliance in the party. These resources were critical in the vertical power games which helped the liberal wing overcome the electoralists in horizontal power games. Both collective and selective incentives played a critical role in this process. Selective incentives through recruitment and promotion served to co-opt fence-sitters with rewards while sidelining opponents with sanctions. The party's election lists and internal promotion mechanisms were central in these efforts. The leadership also used collective incentives by redefining party identity and expanding its support among the rank and file. Internal communication channels helped spread their message among the skeptical members of the organization and expand their coalition within the party.

The change in organizational rules fortified these efforts. Armed with key organizational resources in the 2016 party congress, liberals managed to amend party bylaws and strengthen their grip on the highest organs of the party. They also purged conservative electoralists in leadership positions by separating the religious and political functions of the party. Finally, the increasing access to public resources – as well as control over party finances – that accompanied electoral victories buttressed liberals' position by expanding their incentive structure. As such, Ennahda has resembled the AKP rather than the Brotherhood. Unlike the AKP, however, Ennahda's electoral fortunes have declined over the years. Yet the party still managed to win a plurality of the seats in a deeply fragmented parliament and has turned into an indispensable coalition partner. Despite its relative decline, liberals sustained their dominance in the party and kept it on a democratic path. The shrinking resources for the party, however, weakened the selective incentives, while the party's collective incentive structure, based around democracy and liberalism, disillusioned hegemonic Islamists, who left the party for Salafi movements. I detail these processes in the next section.

Ennahda's Organizational Structure

Ennahda's organizational structure closely resembles that of the Brotherhood. The Shura Council forms the legislative authority and makes key decisions for the organization, while the executive bureau and the party leader implement the council's decisions. Local branches complement this organizational structure. Unlike the Brotherhood and like the AKP, though, the majority of the Shura Council, the entire executive bureau, and party chairman are elected in the party's national congress.

The Shura Council consists of 150 members, two-thirds of which are elected by the party congress. Elected members of the council, in turn, elect the rest of the council among different sectors of youth, women, members abroad, and so on in its first session. The council is charged with devising the general orientation of the party and its major policies, overseeing the budget, and selecting party nominees for elections.

Although the Shura Council holds significant power on paper, the executive bureau carries greater weight within the party organization. The bureau is charged with approving party lists for the parliamentary, regional, municipal, and other elections after collecting nominations from the party's various branches and organs. It can change the lists as it sees fit. The bureau also exercises substantial control over the party organization, since it can establish and close regional branches at will. In other words, by controlling recruitment and promotion, the bureau commands the party's selective incentive structure.

The chairman is elected in party's national congress and can serve only two terms, as decided in the 2012 party congress. They are a natural candidate for the highest position in the state unless the chairman decides to nominate someone else on the Shura Council's recommendation. After the 2016 party congress, the party leader also obtained greater authority in selecting the members of the executive bureau – a prerogative that was formerly reserved for the members of the Shura Council, as I explain below.

Recruitment and Promotion

In the 2012 party congress, when exiled and local Nahdawis were reunited after twenty years, Ghannouchi was reelected with 73 percent of the delegates' votes. Even before the expansion of the power of the party leader in 2016, Ghannouchi had already carried great weight in the party. His unequivocal support for democracy played a crucial role in building liberal dominance in the party. In neither the AKP nor the Brotherhood have we seen as strong a leader with such philosophical training and intellectual capital.[108]

Ghannouchi's leadership and intellectual depth with respect to Islam and democracy had tilted the playing field in favor of liberals since 1991, when he was reelected as the chairman. Such power and respect within the movement handed Ghannouchi significant discretion over key issues. His March 2012 intervention in the strife regarding sharia rule among Nahdawis is a case in point. In a closed-door meeting among leaders of the party, a slim majority voted in favor of invoking sharia in the new constitution. Then Ghannouchi intervened, as Feldman reports, and threatened to step down if the vote was not retaken with a different result. This time, a slim majority voted against invoking sharia, and the party leadership endorsed the party's secular democratic line.[109] Later, amid the political turmoil of summer 2013, Ghannouchi decided to meet with Beji Caid Essebsi in Paris to resolve the crisis. It was not the party organs but Ghannouchi himself who made the decision.[110] During our interview, Ghannouchi stated that he met with Essebsi to end the confrontation between the government and the opposition and to accept the national dialogue led by the Quartet. He signed the roadmap

---

[108] A crucial exception in the case of the Brotherhood could be Sayyid Qutb, who employed his intellectual depth to mobilize supporters for an antidemocratic ideology. But Qutb did not serve as the General Guide of the Brotherhood. Of course, Islamist intellectuals with democratic commitments existed in both countries, such as Ali Bulaç and Yusuf al-Qaradawi, among others, yet none were in a leadership position.
[109] Feldman, *The Arab Winter*, 139
[110] Interview with Rached Ghannouchi, July 27, 2017.

(leaving power in favor of a technocratic government) in this meeting without the approval of the party's Shura Council and assumed personal responsibility. He admitted that it was not easy for his party to accept this concession, but he convinced his colleagues that freedom in the country was more important than staying in power. He promised to step down if his compromise failed to deliver the desired outcome.[111] This critical intervention marked a key turning point in Tunisia's transition and shaped the party's future interactions with its rivals.

Yet, as Pargeter claims, Ghannouchi's hold over the party was not absolute prior to the revolution.[112] A growing group within Ennahda was demanding reconciliation with the regime rather than persistence on democracy. Democratic transition, however, provided both Ghannouchi and the liberals with an expanding pool of resources and a new political context that allowed for the construction of collective incentives. The expanding incentive structure at the behest of the liberals allowed them to incentivize Nahdawis to join their alliance.

One key addition to party ranks was Morou, a prominent liberal and cofounder of the movement. Upon Ghannouchi's invitation, Morou rejoined the party, much to the dismay of electoralists, whom Morou relentlessly criticized.[113] Soon Morou would become one of the most prominent figures in both the party and CA.

While more liberal voices were recruited by the leadership, electoralists also made a comeback with the second founding of the party and commanded significant support from the delegates. Sadeq Chorou, for instance, was elected to the Shura Council with the highest number of votes (more than 70 percent). Yet Ghannouchi pulled his weight behind the liberals for leadership positions. As Grewal notes, the executive bureau, using its discretion after the revolution, largely sidelined conservative voices and removed them from leadership roles in the party.[114] The election of Fathi al-Ayadi, a former exile, as the head of the Shura Council is a case in point. Clearly, Ghannouchi held substantial power in the organization. As a young Nahdawi complained to Wolf, no one could succeed within the party without his support.[115]

Not only top positions in the party but also seats in the cabinet were mostly given to liberals. In the first and second Troika governments, for instance, prominent liberals like Hamadi Jebali, Ali Laarayedh, Rafik

---

[111] Ibid.
[112] Pargeter, *Return to Shadows*.
[113] Interview with Abdelfattah Morou, July 24, 2017.
[114] Grewal, "Where Are Ennahdha's Competitors?"
[115] Wolf, *Political Islam in Tunisia*, 137.

Abdessalem (Ghannouchi's son-in-law), and Abdellatif Mekki occupied seats reserved for Ennahda. The liberal leadership meanwhile closely surveilled its parliamentary group. When necessary, as Boubekuer reports, the leadership wielded power over the deputies in controversial votes.[116] In an interview with Grewal, Noureddine Arbaoui, the head of Ennahda's political bureau, admitted that they called their deputies ahead of particularly contentious votes. A key instance occurred in January 2014 when the CA began to vote on the draft constitution. When electoralists submitted multiple amendments to insert a greater role for Islam in the constitution, liberals pulled the strings to defeat these motions. Indeed, the party headquarters threatened those deputies who were going against the party line with nonnomination in subsequent elections.[117]

Party rules allowed central committees to exercise such discretion over the party's electoral lists and, hence, selective incentives. Each local branch of the party selected its nominees and submitted names to the executive bureau for approval. Although more democratic than the AKP's highly centralized practice, this process still handed substantial power to the party's central committees, which could veto candidates.

So party leaders vetoed conservative voices of the CA in the 2014 parliamentary elections and replaced many of them with liberal candidates. Grewal finds, for instance, that of the deputies who voted in favor of the amending Article 1 of the draft constitution in a more Islamist direction, only 9 percent were renominated, compared to 47 percent of those who voted against or abstained. Nahdawis who voted in favor of sharia or ban against blasphemy were entirely taken off the party lists. Eighteen of the most conservative figures, including Nejib Mrad, Ahmed Smiai, Bechir Chammen, Sadeq Chorou, and Habib Ellouze, failed to receive renomination, while more than half of the most liberal names, including Zied Ladhari, Amer Laarayedh, Latifa Habacci, and Osama Saghir, were renominated in 2014.[118]

Liberals did not only control electoral lists but also other political and administrative positions that rapidly expanded with Ennahda's electoral victory in October 2011. They used such positions as incentives for their supporters to join the liberal coalition. More specifically, as the senior partner in the Troika government, Ennahda appointed fourteen

---

[116] Boubekeur, "Islamists, Secularists and Old Regime Elites in Tunisia," 120.
[117] Grewal, "From Islamists to Muslim Democrats."
[118] Grewal, "Where Are Ennahdha's Competitors?"

ministers, including the prime minister, twenty-four out of twenty-six governors, and an overwhelming majority of new appointments to civil service.[119]

Party Finance

The leadership also controlled party finances. All Ennahda members have to make regular financial contributions set by the executive bureau.[120] Ali Bouraoui, a member of the executive bureau in 2012, claimed that members contributed at least 5 percent of their income to Ennahda. In addition to members' contributions, the party had also relied on the contributions of Tunisian businessmen. Bouraoui also added to this list in-kind donations made by associations for social assistance. The party received such donations, that is, school supplies for kids, funds for young people who need assistance in marriage ceremonies, and food baskets for poor families, directing them to those in need.[121] All of these contributions strengthened the party's finances.

In 2019, the party budget totaled $2.5 million, an increase of half a million dollars since 2018. Ennahda also received limited public funds from the state like all other political parties. Although the Shura Council oversees the budget, it is the party chairman and the bureau that control party funds. All funds accrue to the party center and remain subject to the discretion of the party leadership. Most of these funds, reportedly controlled by Ghannouchi, are allocated in line with the interests of liberals within the party organization. For instance, most of the funds were spent on political activities instead of religious activism and preaching (da'wa).[122] Hence, the liberal democratic wing enjoyed greater access to party finances, while the religious activists within the movement (most of them electoralists) were deprived of such resources.

In short, in kind or in cash, such funds trickled down to the rank and file and helped the party leaders sustain their support. The private funds of the movement, before the revolution, and both public and private resources afterward bolstered their dominance. The party leadership used these funds to provide material and selective incentives to party members.

---

[119] The Union for Neutrality in Public Administration reported that new appointees in the civil service came from the ranks of Troika, and 90 percent of those were Nahdawis. Many viewed this as Ennahda's attempt to colonize the state. Weslaty, "Nominations Dans Le Secteur Public."
[120] See Ennahda's bylaws.
[121] Schneider, "Tunisie."
[122] Meddeb, "Ennahda's Uneasy Exit from Political Islam."

Party Rules and Liberals' Expanding Control over Selective Incentives

The party congress in May 2016 further entrenched liberals' – including women's – power in the party. Two issues were of critical importance: first, party bylaws, and second, longtime internal disagreement in terms of the identity and objectives of the party.

Liberals first pushed for changes in the rules. They proposed the party leader appoint all members of the executive bureau and the Shura Council vote on each member. The proposal created a lot of contention, with half of the delegates demanding a direct vote on the executive bureau by the council. Ghannouchi intervened in favor of the proposal, which would increase his discretion in the selection of the highest executive body of the party. In the end, the motion passed with 58 percent of the delegates' votes.

As a result, the leader's prerogatives expanded significantly, and Ghannouchi's informal weight within the party became institutionalized. Specifically, the new bylaws allowed the leader to appoint a general secretary, deputy, and members of the executive bureau, submitting the list to the Shura Council for approval. Hence, the power of the Council was reduced significantly, while liberals ended up controlling all key offices within the party and its incentive structure.

Liberals, after this fundamental change, renewed both the executive bureau and the Shura Council. Not surprisingly, most liberal and progressive figures in the party, young members and women, in particular, moved up in the party organization. Half of the executive bureau were newcomers, while the number of women increased by 25 percent.[123] Zied Ladhari, a prominent liberal, was elected as the new secretary-general. Another well-known liberal, Morou, became the first deputy chairman of the party, while Ali Laarayedh and Noureddine Bhiri were appointed as second and third deputies to the leader. Women's presence also increased in the executive bureau: Wassila Zoghlami, Sayida Ounissi, Meherzia Labidi, Aroua Ben Abbes, Yamina Zoghlami, and Farida Laabidi were given seats in the highest party organ.

Women's increasing prominence in the party fortified liberals' dominance. Their strong presence made a significant difference over the course of the transition. Grewal, in his study of voting records in the CA, found that gender, along with time spent abroad, were the two factors that explained progressive and liberal voting among Nahdawis.[124] In fact, women within Ennahda advanced democratic politics by working

---

[123] Zineb, "Ennahda Brings Fresh Blood to Party's New Executive Bureau."
[124] Grewal, "From Islamists to Muslim Democrats."

alongside their secular colleagues to improve the rights of Tunisian women. Most of these women had a strong sense of individualism and refused to act as men's shadow in the party. Their presence was not simply window-dressing, as has been the case lately in the AKP, or a byproduct of the parity requirement in the electoral law. The prominence of women in Ennahda also contrasted with Brotherhood's practices, where women were mostly absent from formal politics.[125] In fact, Ennahda women frequently criticized the Brotherhood for keeping women invisible in the movement and urged Egyptian women to stand next to men, not behind them.[126]

Women in Ennahda also formed a strong counterbalance to the conservative wing in the party. Tunisian electoralists, like their counterparts in the Brotherhood, often defy gender equality. Some even defend banning women from holding public office. Yet liberal Islamist women were keen on defending their rights. For instance, when electoralists contested the personal status code as a violation of sharia and aimed to remove progressive provisions on divorce and polygamy, the women of Ennahda defended the code and even took steps to improve the existing legislation. According to Bochra Belhaj Hmida, a secular feminist activist and veteran politician, Ennahda worked hardest among the parties in the parliament to pass legislation against domestic violence; Meherzia Labidi and Imen Ben Mohammed spoke loudest to improve the legislation and convince more conservative figures among their ranks to vote in favor of the bill.[127] And they succeeded.

The second big issue in the 2016 congress concerned the identity of the party. The delegates voted to rearticulate the party's identity and its functions. They separated the party's religious and political functions[128] and banned its officials from preaching and leading religious organizations. Thus, Ennahda fashioned itself exclusively as a political party and left *da'wa* (religious activism) to the civil society, a task the liberal Brothers failed to accomplish in Egypt.

This revision had multiple implications for both selective and collective incentives in the organization. First, those who were keen on sustaining

---

[125] It should be noted that the Brotherhood had a parallel organization for women under the label the Muslim Sisterhood. Although these women were active in Brotherhood's outreach activities, they did not play an important role in the movement's leadership.
[126] Interview with Meherzia Labidi, July 5, 2012; November 9, 2017; and April 15, 2020.
[127] Interview with Imen Ben Mohammed, July 26, 2017.
[128] Nahdawis preferred the concept of *takhassus* (specialization) instead of separation. More than 80 percent of the delegates voted in favor of separating political and religious works of the movement, and more than 87 percent approved of the new political vision of the party. The father of this vision, Ghannouchi, was reelected to the party leadership with 75 percent of the votes.

their religious activism and preaching, like Chorou or Ellouze, could no longer hold seats in the party's decision-making organs such as the Shura Council or the executive bureau, even if they had delegates' support. In addition, as the identity of the party changed, so did its membership criteria. The party dropped the morals (*akhlaq*) from its membership criteria, and it no longer sought two references among Nahdawis to admit new members. Imed Khemiri, spokesperson for Ennahda, explained that their aim was to make Ennahda a party of all Tunisians.[129] After 2016, Ennahda started to follow an even more liberal path in recruitment. Access to Ennahda ranks increased to include Tunisians with different backgrounds. With the party identity changing, many more conservative members in the rank and file ended up leaving the party to join Salafi organizations.

New recruitment gained further momentum with the 2018 local elections. The party opened its lists in municipal elections to independent candidates from different political backgrounds and invited professionals and technocrats to join its lists. Around 4,000 people responded to this call. Ennahda won 30 percent of municipal council seats in the elections, and half of its 2,139 municipal council positions were filled by independent members who had no formal ties to the party.[130] So the party became a new hub for careerists desiring to build political expertise. Public positions that accompanied electoral success hence allowed Ennahda's liberals to recruit politicians with no connections to conservative electoralist wing in the party.

Finally, the party's funds would be entirely allocated to political activities from the 2016 congress on. Religious activists with a hegemonic Islamic agenda were thus denied crucial resources. They had to raise their own funds from the society.

Internal Communication and Changing Collective Incentives

The 2016 party congress also solidified new collective incentives for the party and its supporters. These incentives, according to liberals, concerned Ennahda's democratizing mission, which replaced its Islamizing mission after the revolution. Many within the party remained skeptical.

The party leadership leveraged its grip over internal communication to rally the party's rank and file around its new mission. One of its key instruments was the academy of training and leadership qualification that was charged to conduct internal trainings within the party

---

[129] Author interview with Imed Khemiri, July 17, 2017.
[130] Meddeb, "Ennahda's Uneasy Exit from Political Islam."

organization. Its director was appointed by the party leader and remained directly accountable to him. Aside from routine trainings, the liberals also organized frequent workshops to reach out to the rank and file and gain their support.

Instead of imposing most of their key decisions and ideas in a top-down fashion, like electoralists in the AKP or the Brotherhood have done, liberals discussed these issues with their base to convince them of the necessity of such changes. Sometimes, the leadership made its decision and then began a conversation about its underlying rationale. In the process, liberals offered new collective incentives to the rank and file. For instance, many Nahdawis opposed their party's partnership with NT. Every weekend, Ennahda leaders visited local offices to convince the local activists and explain the logic behind this partnership.[131] As Marks observes, such discussions rested on two premises: (1) strategic self-interest and (2) Islamic principles and religious sources.[132] From a strategic point of view, the leaders argued that the transition to democracy required huge compromises and sacrifices. Some leaders even suggested that if Ennahda had not compromised, Tunisia would have been the same as Iraq, Syria, Libya, or Yemen.[133]

Liberals also justified their decisions by the changing political context that ultimately transformed the meaning and objectives of Islamism. They argued that Ennahda had had to fuse preaching and political activism before the revolution not because Islam required it but because the political context necessitated it. Under an authoritarian rule that repressed religious rights, Islamists had to merge the two functions to defend their rights.[134] They no longer needed to do so, liberals argued, since Tunisia was now a democracy and the new constitution secured both the Arab–Islamic identity of the country and basic freedoms. Ennahda, as a defender of Tunisian Islam, had fulfilled its mission when the CA ratified the new constitution in 2014 because the new constitution protects religious freedoms, which former regimes readily violated.

Other liberals went further and claimed that Islamism was an ideology of opposition and unfit for a governing party. Imed Khemiri, a high-ranking member of Ennahda, for instance, claimed that their Islamism was in fact "oppositional Islam," characterized by opposition to despotism, a call for democracy and freedom, and never by instatement of sharia.[135] Rafik Abdessalem also affirmed that it was easy to be

[131] Interview with Meherzia Labidi, November 9, 2017.
[132] Marks, "Purists vs Pluralists," 111.
[133] Interview with Ali Laarayedh, July 24, 2017.
[134] Interview with Abdulkarim Harouni, July 19, 2017.
[135] Interview with Imed Khemiri, July 17, 2017.

in the opposition, but being in power required time to reconcile their aspirations with geopolitical reality (raison d'etre).[136] These prominent Nahdawis hence rearticulated Islamism as a fight for political freedoms and suggested that the Islamist mission had been completed with the democratization in Tunisia.

In the 2016 congress, the dominant liberal faction formalized this discourse and declared its departure from political Islam. They rebranded Ennahda as a Muslim democrat party, akin to the Christian Democrats of Europe. The main aim was to highlight the party's commitment to democracy and separate it from other Islamist groups. When I interviewed high-ranking Nahdawis a year after the congress, they unanimously voiced their objection to the concept of political Islam and claimed that Ennahda is an Islamic democratic movement that does not speak in the name of Islam.

By abandoning "political Islam" and separating the religious and political functions of the party (*takhassus*), liberals simply shelved the mission of comprehensive (*shumuli*) Islam. This sharply contrasted with electoralists' conception of Islam as *din wa dawla* (religion and state). In his remarks before the 2016 party congress, Ghannouchi summarized his party's journey:

> Ennahda has changed from an ideological movement engaged in the struggle for identity to a protest movement against the authoritarian regime and now to a national democratic party. We must keep religion far from political struggles.[137]

Liberals also provided Islamic justification for their position by developing a particular understanding of Islamic rule which rested on *maqasid al-sharia* (objectives of sharia). These objectives included, first and foremost, freedom, justice, solidarity, and dignity.[138] According to this interpretation, if a political system fulfilled these objectives, then it would be considered Islamic, even if it was secular in orientation. Following this reasoning, the Tunisian constitution, liberals argued, was truly Islamic – even though it had no reference to sharia – because it was designed to meet these objectives.

Such arguments generated significant tension within the party. Several members thought that this change amounted to abandoning Islam, which they believed to be inherently political.[139] For them, Ghannouchi's reinterpretation of Islamic governance along the lines of *maqasid al-sharia* violated

---

[136] Interview with Rafik Abdesselam, July 28, 2017.
[137] Quoted in Souli, "Why Tunisia's Top Islamist Party Rebranded Itself."
[138] Interview with a member of the executive bureau, July 17, 2017, and interview with Meherzia Labidi, November 9, 2017.
[139] Netterstrøm, "The Islamists' Compromise in Tunisia," 120.

Islamic law. Some left the party. Liberals relentlessly worked to convince party members and succeeded to a considerable extent. Some of my interviews with young Nahdawis confirmed this success. A young Nahdawi from Tunis expressed his disagreement with Ellouze and suggested that a party should not represent a religion, which was a private matter between believers and God. For this young activist, if the party lost members because it refused to represent Islam, then so be it. Another young Nahdawi argued that religion was not only a private matter; it carried certain values such as justice and freedom. For her, Ennahda did not surrender these values. Although the party lost the support of its pro-Salafi members, she thought that Ennahda was on the right path because its goal was to set up a system that ensures equality of opportunity for all; on this path, losing Salafis' support was for the better.[140]

Ennahda's limited media presence with its more liberal editorial line complemented liberals' internal communication channels. Unlike the AKP and the Brotherhood, Ennahda has not built an extensive media power to reach its constituency and shape public opinion. This is partly because Ennahda has only recently returned to Tunisia and did not have enough time or opportunity to build its media empire. Still, the party newspaper, *Al-Fajr*, and private network stations close to the party helped the liberal leadership advance their agenda.

Before the revolution in 2006, Azzam Tamimi established a network station in London – Al-Hiwar – to spread Ghannouchi's ideas of Islamic democracy.[141] Again before 2011, Ghannouchi's son-in-law, Rafik Abdessalem, served as the director of Al Jazeera's Research Center, which wholeheartedly supported the uprisings in the region. Right after the revolution, Ennahda reestablished its newspaper *Al-Fajr*, whose editorial line has remained quite close to Ghannouchi's vision. One could also add the public station to this list – at least until 2014, when Ennahda lost power – whose director was appointed by the Troika after the revolution.

Furthermore, two private network stations – Zitouna TV and Zitouna Hidaya – have supported the party agenda. These stations are co-owned by a pro-Ennahda businessman, Sami Essid, and Osama Bin Salem, a member of the Shura Council and son of a former Ennahda minister.[142] The two partners claimed that they follow Ennahda's vision of moderation in their editorial line but have an independent broadcasting policy.[143] Despite their modest viewership, they nevertheless extended the reach of liberals' political message.

[140] Interview with a young Nahdawi, July 18, 2017.
[141] McCarthy, *Inside Tunisia's al-Nahda*, 104.
[142] Media Ownership Monitor Tunisia, "Zitouna TV."
[143] Auffray, "Zitouna TV, Islam de Fond."

In short, liberals' grip over internal communication helped them buttress their dominant alliance. Those who rejected the new identity of the party were marginalized. When they realized the difficulty in steering the party in a hegemonic Islamist direction, many of them left.

Conclusion

Liberals' firm grip over organizational resources allowed them to chart Ennahda's course toward deliberation, engagement, and compromise, rather than polarization, exclusion, delegitimization, and zero-sum conflicts.[144] In contrast to both the AKP in Turkey and the Brotherhood in Egypt, Ennahda remained strongly committed to democratic principles before and after coming to power. Despite heavy state repression in the 1990s, Ennahda leaders started to build democratic coalitions with other actors against the Ben Ali regime as early as the 2000s. After coming to power in 2011, the party sustained its inclusive politics and shared power with others.

At times, its internal rifts generated tensions and skepticism with respect to the "true" nature of the party; however, the party's liberals consistently warded off electoralists while building bridges with their political rivals across the ideological aisle. Their rejection of sharia rule and the criminalization of blasphemy in the constitution were crucial instances of such cooperation. The party also made a series of key concessions, to the dismay of electoralists, by agreeing to step down in 2014. Hence, liberals committed to inclusionary practices, shared power with their ardent opponents, and worked hard to overcome polarization in the Tunisian society. For them, democracy signified inclusion, deliberation, and compromise, instead of majority rule and maximization of partisan interests.

Liberals remained eager to apply these principles to intraparty affairs as well. As the party's eleventh congress approached in 2020, Ghannouchi loyalists signaled that he could stay another term as party leader. Many liberals contested Ghannouchi's unwarranted third term. As

---

[144] These liberals also remained critical of the Brotherhood over the course of the revolution. They claimed that the Brotherhood committed major political mistakes, such as overrelying on electoral legitimacy and denying any political space for those who lost the elections. Before the military intervention in July 2013, liberal Islamists in Tunisia had already concluded that the Brotherhood was on the wrong path by not sharing power with others. More recently, Ennahda also distinguished itself from the AKP, despite their early references to the party as a model Muslim democratic organization. During our interview, Rafik Abdessalem qualified Ennahda's experience as consensual democracy while he suggested that the AKP had built a majoritarian system. Interview with Rafik Abdessalem, July 28, 2017.

defined by Article 31 of the party bylaws, the party chairman can serve only two terms (as decided in the 2007 party congress). Starting a clean slate after the revolution, party members counted Ghannouchi's election as the party chairman in 2012 as his first term. In 2020, he, thus, had completed his two terms. One hundred prominent figures in the party, including several liberal voices and a few electoralists, invited Ghannouchi to abide by party rules and step down in the 2020 congress. They argued that democratic principles such as deliberation, accountability, and institutional forbearance also applied to their party organization.[145] They argued that changing party rules and getting rid of term limits were tyrannical measures. Ghannouchi first rebuffed such claims; later, however, he agreed to follow the party rules in the next party congress, which was postponed due to the pandemic, practically extending Ghannouchi's term.

In the meantime, the Tunisian economy, which was already in poor shape, further deteriorated during the pandemic, and the short-lived and weak coalitional governments proved to be ineffective in solving the country's problems. This vulnerability culminated in an existential threat when President Kais Saied, elected in 2019 as a political outsider, grabbed power in the summer of 2021 and put the country on an authoritarian path. Saied's power grab threw already divided Ennahda into turmoil. Holding Ghannouchi to account, more than a hundred members of the party, including former ministers and deputies, mostly liberals, resigned from Ennahda.[146] They demanded a stronger reaction to Saied's power grab, greater intraparty democracy to set party policies, and greater focus on social policies. The party thus lost significant blood over the principles it has cherished for so long.[147]

At the time of writing, the future of both Ennahda and Tunisian democracy is still uncertain. Yet one thing is sure: Ennahda turned Islam into a source of values such as justice, liberty, solidarity, and dignity. Although they do not like the label of "political Islam," liberals in Ennahda invented their liberal Islamism. As such, they proved the compatibility of Islam, Islamism, and democracy. They showed that when liberals dominate an Islamist party, it becomes a force for inclusion, deliberation, and pluralism.

---

[145] Sadiki, "Intra-Party Democracy in Tunisia's Ennahda"; Wolf, "Is Rached Ghannouchi Ennahda's President for Life?"

[146] For a complete list of signatories, see *Tunisie Numerique*, "La liste des 100 dirigeants d'Ennahdha."

[147] Liberal figures such as Morou, Zitoun, Jelassi, and Mekki, among several others, left the party over the course of two years.

Conclusion

Common perception takes political Islam as a violent and authoritarian monolith. As this book shows, that is not the case. It is true that jihadi organizations often with a Salafist bend mobilize hundreds of young men and women for violent struggle. Yet they form the minority voices within the broader chorus of political Islam. Mainstream Islamism, in contrast, works through the political system to enact its political agenda, however it is formulated.

This book shows that Islamism is not an inherently antidemocratic ideology either. Instead, Islamist parties have found in electoral politics a fundamental solution to their long-lasting ideological dilemmas surrounding leadership selection. As such, elections have filled a crucial institutional void in the Islamic political imagination. And many, if not all, Islamists have incorporated not only elections but also democratic norms into their ideological outlook. Going beyond the procedural understanding of democracy, they have embraced liberal norms such as pluralism, deliberation, and engagement.

In this book, I have focused on three Islamist movements that came to power after decades of political struggle. The experiences of the AKP, the Brotherhood, and Ennahda in government significantly diverged not only from jihadists but also from one another. While the AKP followed a mixed course in power, initially committing to liberal democracy and later pivoting to majoritarian Islamism, the Brotherhood remained on a majoritarian trajectory throughout its brief tenure. Ennahda, by way of contrast, has committed to liberal democratic norms since rising to power in 2011.

All three parties, despite their differences, have accepted elections as the most legitimate method of selecting decision-makers. One reason, to be sure, has been their organizational and mobilizational superiority over their political rivals. If elections were a numbers game, they had the numbers. Although this formulation had a clear majoritarian ring to it, it still advanced the will of the disenfranchised and included them in the political system, instead of inviting them to wage war against it, as jihadis often do. Moreover, even when electoralists built a majoritarian rule, which they reduced to elections, they still gave the people the option to vote them out of power. That said, democracy, I contend, is not majority rule. It requires the protection of minorities and their right to become a majority in future elections. It also requires the protection of individual rights and liberties regardless of a person's ideology, ethnicity, religion, or gender. Without such protections, elections are hardly free or fair, and the option of voting Islamists out of power becomes arduous. That is why Islamists' (or any other political actors') commitment to the fundamental features of democracy – including pluralism and the protection of minorities and civil liberties – is crucial.

Despite accepting elections as the main path to power, not all three parties agreed on the content of democracy. In truth, each held a different vision of democratic rule and displayed a diversity of political attitudes and preferences in power. To unpack this puzzle, the book advanced an account of factional politics. This account, built on existing studies of factional differences within Islamist movements, offered a systematic analysis of intraparty politics through an in-depth study of factional alliances, studying their organizational resources and incentive structures. As such, this account has attempted to correct for hindsight bias – the post hoc rationalization of party strategies – that dominates the study of Islamist parties. As the preceding chapters illustrated, all three Islamist parties had multiple strategies available to them when faced with external constraints. No strategy was an obvious choice for the entire party. In fact, different factions advanced competing rationalities within the party as they reacted to various constraints and incentives.

The course of the party in power, therefore, has largely been shaped not by external factors but by internal power struggles among different factions. Each factional bloc, that is, liberals and electoralists, attempted to chart the course of their organization and impose their understanding of democracy and what they thought was the best course of action in a particular context. Those factions that managed to build dominant alliances imposed their rationality on the party organization as *the* correct strategy. Thus, explaining party behavior via external factors in a retrospective fashion has proved faulty. The pluralism of positions and internal disagreements within parties over the best course of action has required a closer look at intraparty politics to explain why a party adopts a particular strategy in a particular context.

A key takeaway of the book, therefore, is that external factors come secondary in determining the path of Islamist parties (or any other political party) in power. That is, electoral considerations, changing power

Conclusion

balances, and international and regional forces have not dictated any particular behavior in the Islamist parties studied here. That is why when an external constraint or incentive prompted a variety of responses from different factions, these Islamist parties seemed incoherent, inconsistent, and even self-contradictory to observers. In the end, the impact of external forces was filtered through intraparty politics before inducing a reaction from the organization.

When, for instance, protests broke against the incumbents in these countries and CSOs lent support to the protests, various factions adopted different courses of action with significant disagreement over the best strategy. All factions operated within the same context and faced similar institutional constraints and incentives, yet they arrived at competing rationalities. In general, electoralists in all three parties wielded electoral legitimacy and deemed popular mobilization against their elected governments as illegitimate. So they opted for polarization and countermobilization. Liberal Islamists, in contrast, concurred that popular mobilization was as democratic and legitimate as elections and therefore required compromise. And they pushed for conciliation and engagement instead of confrontation.[1] Intraparty dynamics, therefore, mattered greatly.

Overall, when liberals had the upper hand, such as in Ennahda after 2011 and the AKP between 2001 and 2007, Islamist parties embraced deliberation, consensus, and engagement with other actors. In other cases where electoralists predominated, as in the case of the Brotherhood after 2011 and the AKP after 2007, Islamist parties have turned democracy into majority rule, delegitimized the opposition, and polarized their societies.

If dominant factional alliances chartered the course of the party, then access to organizational resources determined which factions could form dominant alliances. These resources – party rules, recruitment and promotion, finances, and internal communication – allowed factions to provide incentives to party members to join their alliance. Whoever controlled these key resources had the upper hand in intraparty struggles.

To capture a party, factions had to control recruitment and promotion. Changing or exploiting existing rules of the game also helped factions capture other resources. Party rules, recruitment, and promotion, along with party finances, formed the backbone of organizational incentives. Through recruitment and promotion, a faction could draw

---

[1] At this point, liberals within the Brotherhood had already left the movement and established their own organizations, as discussed at length in Chapter 4.

organizational boundaries and reward their supporters while sanctioning their opponents. A stark contrast between the Brotherhood and Ennahda, for instance, emerged with respect to their approach to recruiting Salafis. While Ennahda refrained from filling up its ranks with Salafis after 2005, the old guard in the Brotherhood targeted the Salafi youth as reliable recruits starting as early as the 1990s. As a result, the Brotherhood rank and file turned out to be quite conservative compared to Ennahda's.

Recruitment and promotion mattered also because they formed the basis of the incentive structure. Through the control of key positions, a leading faction could build extensive coalitions and sustain them. Erdoğan in the AKP, for instance, used such mechanisms quite effectively to sideline his rivals while building a sizable coalition within the party. Similarly, liberals in Ennahda and the old guard in the Brotherhood utilized internal mechanisms to capture the organization's executive organs.

Whoever controlled the party finances also exercised critical discretion over the party's trajectory. Erdoğan, in the case of the AKP, was the chief financier of the party, partly thanks to resources he had accrued during his mayoral term in Istanbul between 1994 and 1998. In the Brotherhood, Khairat al-Shater played a key role along with Mahmoud Ezzat, who had discretion over the organization's finances and investments. Ennahda had raised funds from its members in a more democratic manner, yet the control of those funds still rested in the party leadership – in this case, Ghannouchi since 1991.

Once these parties rose to power, the leadership also gained access to public resources. Cabinet and parliamentary seats, bureaucratic appointments, mayoral positions, all became a key part of the expanding incentive structure. Incumbency also strengthened the party's ties to those in civil society and the private sector who were willing to work with the government, expanding the resource pool for party officials. Thanks to increasing public and private resources, the rising faction could co-opt party members more easily and build larger coalitions within. Erdoğan, for instance, proved to be particularly competent in elite management. He co-opted and bought off some of his rivals by nominating them as deputies or mayors, or appointing them as advisors, ministers, university rectors, board members in public banks, or trustees to Islamic foundations, businesses, or municipalities. The same was true for the Brotherhood and Ennahda while in power. However, the Brotherhood remained in power only for a year, while Ennahda enjoyed this access until 2014 when it formed a coalition with secular NT and handed over most of the public positions to its partner. Still, liberals co-opted electoralists by opening greater space for them in the civil society upon the separation of the party's religious and political functions.

In the case of the Brotherhood, the Morsi administration saved critical bureaucratic appointments in different levels of the state as well as local governorates and state-owned press for loyal supporters of the old guard.

Access to media turned out to be another key instrument in the internal power struggle between liberals and electoralists. Media control tilted the playing field among factions as it provided greater visibility to the dominant faction while shrinking the space for its rivals. As a result, dominant factions could easily command the terms of public debate and the party's discourse, whereas marginalized factions had difficulty reaching out to the party base or other political actors. Erdoğan's faction, for instance, controlled both the public and private media and severely restricted its rivals' access to the media landscape. As a result, the party's liberals became largely invisible. The same was true for the Brotherhood. Although the movement had never managed to build a media empire as expansive as the AKP's, they still had their networks with favorable broadcasting policy and *Ikhwanweb*. These stations mostly propagated and justified the views of the dominant faction in both parties. Ennahda resembled the Brotherhood in this regard, more than it did the AKP with its limited media channels.

In short, organizational resources and access to public and private resources, including the media, formed the basis of factional power in each party. In the case of the AKP, electoralists first controlled private resources and party leadership and then the party organs and finally the media to impose their absolute control over the party organization. Liberals were almost completely sidelined or bought off with expanding incentive structures. Electoralists in the Brotherhood had followed a similar course even before coming to power. They expanded their control over organizational resources starting in the late 1980s, redesigning the executive organs and controlling the recruitment process. Command over private resources as well as the media entrenched the old guard. That is how they thwarted internal challenges posed by liberal reformists in the 1990s by purging, buying off, or marginalizing them. In the end, liberals within the Brotherhood were reduced to insignificance. The electoralist old guard was already at the helm of the organization in the wake of the revolution, and liberals posed no threat.

A similar process unfolded in the case of Ennahda, yet this time it was the liberals who had the upper hand. Indeed, they had lost the power struggle within the party to radicals in the 1980s. Only after going into exile in the early 1990s and during the party's second founding in 2012 did they prevail over their rivals inside the party by controlling recruitment, internal communication, as well as public and private resources. Liberal leadership, thanks to its growing control over the party organization in the 1990s, first purged radical Islamists and eventually sidelined electoralists by separating the religious and political functions of the party in 2016.

In the end, intraparty dynamics pushed the AKP away from liberal democracy and toward righteous majoritarianism, while it kept the Brotherhood on righteous majoritarianism throughout. And Ennahda remained committed to liberal democracy despite internal pressures in favor of majoritarianism.

Islamism and Democracy

The factional analysis offered in this book fills in the gap left by existing approaches. Modernization, in the long run, and institutional incentives and constraints provided by inclusion and exclusion, in the shorter run, may be driving factors behind Islamists' commitment to electoral politics. Structural transformation as well as sustained inclusion in (or exclusion from) politics may also transform certain Islamists' perceptions of democracy through personal experiences. However, these accounts remain incomplete without accounting for how individual-level changes aggregate to the group level (first at the factional and then the party level). Without an in-depth analysis of intraparty dynamics, I contend, we cannot ascertain the impact of modernization, inclusion, or exclusion on Islamist party behavior.

The experiences of the three parties in power have several implications with respect to our understanding of Islamism and democracy. The Turkish experience under the AKP reveals the limits of the inclusion-moderation thesis, which assumes a linear democratic habituation that starts with the inclusion of Islamists in formal politics. The case of Ennahda, in contrast, as Cavatorta and Merone argue, shows that inclusion is neither necessary nor sufficient for moderation. Yet exclusion is not a guarantee of wholesale democratization, either. In contrast to those who suggest exclusion as the basis of Ennahda's democratization, exclusion and repression have induced both radicalization and democratization at different points in the movement's history. In fact, both inclusion and exclusion worked through the internal dynamics within the party, and depending on the balance of power among different factions, the party followed different trajectories.

Second, since Islamist parties are not monoliths, the future of these parties and of democracy, at least in part, rests on the balance of power between liberals and electoralists in societies where Islamists are the most organized political force. When the balance of power among factions shifts, the trajectory of the party shifts as well. Often such shifts happen at foundational moments such as the establishment of the party or the reformation of its organization after a major setback. Organizational transitions coincided with the party's election to government, as in the case of the AKP and Ennahda, while this transition was over before the Brotherhood came to power after the revolution.

Once a faction establishes its dominance in the party, they set a course that is hard to reverse. This makes it increasingly hard to change the party from within. That is why often party change occurs through splits. A faction that fails to defeat the leadership through internal mechanisms establishes a new party with a different political agenda. This is what happened in Turkey and Egypt. When the reformists in the Milli Görüş movement failed to defeat the old guard in the party congress in 2000, they left to establish the AKP. More recently, several liberals whom Erdoğan sidelined in the past decade have formed two new parties to challenge the AKP's hegemonic Islamism. Similarly, the reformist Brothers tried hard to change the Brotherhood from within, and when they failed, they seceded to establish the Wasat Party in 1996. Several years later, the remaining reformists decided to establish their separate political organizations when they realized that they would not be able to steer the Brotherhood in a more democratic direction following the revolution. Most recently, liberals in Ennahda also parted ways when they realized they could not unseat Ghannouchi. They have yet to form a political party at the time of writing. Only in the case of the AKP has the splinter group succeeded in challenging the mother movement. A major reason is that the mother movement commands strong organizational and mobilizational resources, which new parties rarely muster. As I explain elsewhere, it was the AKP that mustered greater resources over its mother movement.[2]

Beyond Turkey, Egypt, and Tunisia

What does the experience of three Islamist parties in government tell us about other Islamist governments? The framework offered here is parsimonious enough to travel to other cases. Take, for instance, Iran. An Islamist regime established in the aftermath of a revolution by clerics has more differences than commonalities with the three countries we discussed in this book. However, factional politics in the Iranian regime closely resembles the intraparty politics studied herein. Reformists, pragmatists,

---

[2] Gumuscu, "Class, Status, and Party."

conservatives, and radicals with diverging conceptions of Islamic state and democracy contest the shape of Iranian politics and society. The coalitions they build across factions, along with the public and private resources at their disposal, determine their overall weight in the system. In turn, whoever is more powerful gets to define the terms of the Islamic regime as well as its domestic and foreign policy.[3] So far, it has been the conservatives, with occasional coalition with radicals, who have prevailed over reformists and pragmatists. Their dominance emanates from their control over key institutions such as the supreme guardianship, guardian council, assembly of experts – who selects the supreme guard – and Islamic foundations (*bonyad*) that direct most of the public and private funds.[4] Thanks to their command over such crucial resources, the conservatives have built an expansive incentive structure that sustains the loyalty of a diverse set of actors, including the Revolutionary Guards and the Basij militia. Reformists and pragmatists often ally to capture the presidency and the parliament (*majlis*), yet with significant hindrance from conservatives who control promotion and recruitment processes through their control over the guardian council. Without greater control over the incentive structure (and the myriad resources that form its basis), reformists remain weak.

We could infer similar implications for Islamist parties elsewhere, such as Hamas in Palestine, Hezbollah in Lebanon, the FIS in Algeria, the IAF in Jordan, the Islah Party in Yemen, and the Justice and Development Party in Morocco. Needless to say, these participate in mainstream politics and form a subset of the broader family of Islamist movements. Some of the findings of this book may be applicable to these cases as well.

Explaining the trajectory of radical Islamist movements is beyond the scope of this study and requires analysis of other factors, including the impact of violence on organizational behavior. Yet accounting for factional politics, as many scholars do, within such movements may still shed light on their trajectories.[5]

Beyond Islamism: Political Parties and Democracy

This book also affirms the insights of elite-based theories in the study of democratization and democratic decline and underlines the significance

---

[3] For factional differences in Iranian politics, see, for instance, Arjomand, *After Khomeini*; Moslem, *Factional Politics in Post-Khomeini Iran;* Tabaar, *Religious Statecraft*.
[4] Maloney, *Iran's Political Economy since the Revolution*.
[5] Indeed, scholars have studied internal struggles in radical organizations to explain their militarization and demilitarization. See Matesan, "Organizational Dynamics, Public Condemnation, and the Impetus to Disengage from Violence"; Ashour, *De-radicalization of Jihadis*.

of political parties in democratic transitions. The role of the political elite in the establishment and survival of democracy is as important as structural factors. In fact, real political actors play a central role in democratic transitions, backsliding, and redemocratization.

First, as Stepan reminds us, political society matters particularly at times of political transitions. They design constitutional processes,[6] negotiate the terms of the transition, and form political norms essential for a well-functioning democracy. What political actors do at the time of democratic transition matters. These are the moments of institutional influx, as Schwedler maintains, where nothing is certain. In such moments, actors' political attitudes carry greater weight than disintegrating institutions as they take new paths at these critical junctures which largely shape the new political system.

Parties also have the power to undermine already established democratic institutions and norms through constitutional hardball, court-packing, abuse of executive authority, social polarization, and amending constitutions.[7]

Thus, in each phase of regime change, political parties are at the center stage. As parties push to maximize their partisan gains – as the AKP and the Brotherhood did – or prioritize the democratic process – as Ennahda did in Tunisia – they weaken or strengthen the prospects of democracy. In cases where they choose to act upon old animosities to polarize the society by evoking (often misplaced) fears and seek revanchism against their political rivals, they compromise the future of democracy. In cases where they deliberate and engage with their rivals, they may help democracy survive.

In Tunisia, the political society, primarily Ennahda, was cognizant of this fact; the leaders of the party shunned revanchism despite (or perhaps because of) having had the most gruesome experience at the hands of the former regime. They refrained from monopolizing power, polarizing society, and evoking populist sentiments. Rather, Ennahda willingly formed coalition governments with secular parties and shared power with them. As a result, Tunisia succeeded in establishing the only democracy in the Arab world until its recent crisis. Egypt, in contrast, thanks partly to the Brotherhood's polarizing and exclusionary politics, failed because its political society failed.[8] The Muslim Brotherhood's desire to rule alone, coupled with its majoritarianism and polarizing attitude in power, alienated millions of Egyptians, whose mobilization

---

[6] Brown, "The Roots of Egypt's Constitutional Catastrophe," 81.
[7] Levitsky and Ziblatt, *How Democracies Die*.
[8] Stepan, "Mutual Accommodation," 57; Feldman, *The Arab Winter*.

delivered the Egyptian armed forces a return ticket to power. The country has descended into an autocratic regime more violent and brutal than Mubarak's.

This does not mean that Tunisian democracy is perfect in comparison though.[9] After 2014, observers cautioned of democratic backsliding due to the return of old regime figures and the delay in conducting local elections, which finally took place in 2019. Yet the former regime figures continued to creep in through newly established parties. Interestingly, Ennahda has been criticized for being lenient on the former regime elements. "Compromises," as Schwedler reminds us, "preserve many elements of existing power configurations."[10] Parties' failure to meet the economic demands of the revolution also exacerbated the crisis and exposed the regime to populist threats. President Kais Saied, a political outsider campaigning on a populist platform, came to power in 2019 and grabbed power in the summer of 2021, thereby putting the democratic achievements of the country at risk. The Tunisian people have pushed back but with no success at the time of writing.

Further, the impact of political parties is not limited to democratic transitions. Even in cases where democracy has largely been established, parties can still undermine it. The AKP, for instance, initially advanced democracy, thanks to the weight of the liberals in the cabinet and parliament, only to undermine democratic institutions later and push the country into a competitive authoritarian direction once electoralists secured power inside the party. Since then, the AKP has adopted a hegemonic Islamist outlook and, like the Brotherhood, treats democracy as majority rule.

The impact of political parties is heightened when societies are deeply polarized and vertical accountability is threatened by people's partisan attachments.[11] In such contexts, democracies are particularly vulnerable to shifts in political parties.

Party Capture, Right-Wing Populism, and Demise of Democracy

The recent experience of Islamist parties also offers insights into the rise of right-wing populism[12] today. From the Americas to Asia, right-wing populism poses a threat to democracy with its exclusionary and

---

[9] For an excellent critical analysis of democratic prospects in the country from party politics view, see Yardımcı-Geyikçi and Tür, "Rethinking the Tunisian Miracle."
[10] Schwedler, "Rethinking the Inclusion–Moderation Hypothesis," 372.
[11] See Svolik, "Polarization vs Democracy."
[12] Mudde and Kaltwaser, *Populism*; Norris and Inglehart, *Cultural Backlash*; Mounk, *The People vs Democracy*; Rogenhofer and Panievsky, "Anti-Democratic Populism in Power"; McDonnell and Cabrera, "The Right-Wing Populism of India's BJP."

majoritarian bent, antipluralist attitudes, and polarizing tendencies. Often married to ideologies as diverse as Islamism, Hindu nationalism, and nativism, resurgent populist factions within well-established conservative parties and emergent populist parties with electoral strides pose a grave challenge to democracy in old and new democracies alike.

The future of democracy is closely intertwined with the future of such parties. In cases where populist factions with autocratic leaders capture established parties, they are likely to follow a majoritarian trajectory that undermines liberal democratic institutions and triggers democratic backsliding. Party capture by autocratic populist factions in established democracies indeed closely resembles the AKP's experience in Turkey. The rightward pivot of Fidesz under Victor Orbán, PiS under Jarosław Kaczyński in Poland, and the autocratization of the Republican Party with the rise of Donald Trump in the United States are important cases in point.[13]

Political parties in the United States obviously have a more decentralized nature than the parties studied here. Yet party capture by different factions is equally significant in changing party orientation and its relationship to democratic politics. Indeed, the Republican Party had been undergoing a significant transformation wherein right-wing ideological factions have sought to capture the party for years. It has pivoted to an anti-elitist, polarizing, autocratic populist line, whereby the Democrats are treated as traitors, un-American, or the enemies of "real Americans." The party's new line thus pushes the Republicans to violate the norms of mutual toleration and institutional forbearance, essential for liberal democracy, and treat compromise and engagement with the Democrats as a cardinal sin. They have also endorsed constitutional hardball, nuclear options, and violation of established democratic norms.[14] The January 6 insurrection in fact proved how threatening party capture by autocratic factions can be to established democracies.

As facilitators of responsiveness, effectiveness, accountability, and representation, political parties are pillars of democratic regimes. They may also form the gravest threat to democracy by spreading, organizing, and mobilizing extreme ideas. Indeed, the most recent autocratic wave is driven by political parties that enable aspiring autocrats who can subvert institutional guardrails of democracy with relative ease. To make sense of these recent developments, we need to study intraparty dynamics,

---

[13] For more, see Haggard and Kaufman, *Backsliding*, 21–22, 45.
[14] Levitsky and Ziblatt, *How Democracies Die*, Chapter 8; also see Blum, *How the Tea Party Captured the GOP*.

specifically, how different factions with authoritarian (or liberal democratic) tendencies capture political parties at the expense of their liberal–democratic (or autocratic) rivals. Factions not only dictate party behavior, but they also affect a country's political trajectory. Without a better understanding of intraparty dynamics, the study of democracy remains incomplete.

Interviews

Abdellatif, Ibtihel. July 26, 2017 (Tunis)
Abdel Moula, Mohamed Nejbi. June 29, 2012 (Sfax)
Abdessalem, Rafik. July 26, 2017 (Tunis)
Aboul Fotouh, Abdel Moneim. July 18, 2007 and January 30, 2013 (Cairo)
Al Saghir, Osama. July 20, 2017 (Tunis)
Awad, Ibrahim. January 31, 2013 (Cairo)
Ayari, Mikiel Bashir. June 26, 2012 (Tunis)
Ayyash, Abdelrahman. January 11, 2016 (Istanbul), October 27, 2016 (via Skype), and August 2, 2017 (Istanbul)
Arbaoui, Noureddine. July 27, 2017 (Tunis)
Baltagy, Ammar. January 29, 2016 (Istanbul)
Bolat, Ömer. April 15, 2007 (Istanbul)
Bourguiba, Meriam. July 5, 2012 (Tunis)
Bekaroğlu, Mehmet. June 12, 2014 (Istanbul)
Ben Abbes, Aroua. July 17, 2017 (Tunis)
Çakır, Ruşen. January 5, 2017 (Istanbul)
Cherif, Youessif. June 25, 2017 (Tunis)
Chobaki, Amr. July 8, 2007 and January 29, 2013 (Cairo)
Chomiak, Laryssa. June 25, 2012 and July 18, 2017 (Tunis)
Dalenda, Largueche. June 26, 2017 (Tunis)
Darrag, Amr. August 28, 2017 (Istanbul) and October 26, 2017 (via Skype)
El-Erian, Essam. July 17, 2007 (Cairo)
El Jammali, Naoufel. July 18, 2017 (Tunis)
Elmi, Adel. June 27, 2012 (Tunis)
El-Nemr, Mustafa. October 26, 2017 (via Skype) and April 8, 2020 (via Zoom)
Fahmi, Georges. January 12, 2016 (via Skype)
Fathy, Yasser. August 9, 2017 (Istanbul)
Fouad, Khaled. August 8, 2017 (Istanbul)
Ghannouchi, Rached. July 5, 2012 and July 27, 2012 (Tunis)
Guellali, Amna. June 26, 2012 (Tunis)
Gültekin, Levent. January 17, 2017 (Istanbul)
Hajji, Adnan. July 1, 2012 (Redeyef)
Harouni, Abdulkarim. July 19, 2017 (Tunis)
Henry, Clement. January 29, 2013 (Cairo)
Hmida, Bochra Belhajj. June 27, 2012 and July 27, 2017 (Tunis)

Jeribi, Lobna. July 4, 2012 (Tunis)
Kahlaoui, Tarek. June 28, 2012 and July 19, 2017 (Tunis)
Kazzaz, Hussein. January 6, 2017 (Istanbul)
Khalafallah, Zubair. February 3, 2016 (Istanbul)
Khelifa, Oumezzine. June 28, 2012 (Tunis)
Khemiri, Imed. July 17, 2017 (Tunis)
Laarayedh, Ali. July 24, 2017 (Tunis)
Labidi, Meherzia. July 5, 2012 (Tunis), November 9, 2017 and April 15, 2020 (via Skype)
Ladhari, Zied. July 28, 2017 (Tunis)
Lourimi, Ajmi. July 18, 2017 (Tunis)
Makhlouf, Wafa. July 20, 2017 (Tunis)
Manssouri, Mohamed Nejib. June 30, 2012 (Sidi Bouzid)
Masmoudi, Radwan. July 21, 2017 (Tunis)
Milad, Zied. July 4, 2012 (Tunis)
Morou, Abdelfattah. July 24, 2017 (Tunis)
Naguib, Ahmed. February 1, 2013 (Cairo)
Nebati, Nureddin. November 15, 2006 (Istanbul)
Nouria, Asma. June 25, 2012 (Tunis)
Shahin, Emad. January 31, 2013 (Cairo)
Soliman, Osama. June 5, 2017 (Istanbul)
Şener, Abdüllatif. June 24, 2014 (Ankara)
Ünsal, Ahmet Faruk. June 24, 2014 (Ankara)
Ünsal, Fatma Bostan. January 20, 2017 (Ankara)
Yakış, Yaşar. January 28, 2016 (Ankara)
Yalçınbayır, Ertuğrul. January 13, 2017 (Bursa)
Yarar, Erol. March 15, 2007 (Istanbul)
Yarbay, Ersönmez. June 24, 2014 (Ankara)
Yenigün, Halil İbrahim. June 4, 2014 (Istanbul)
Youssef, Ahmed. January 26, 2016 (Istanbul)
Zitoun, Lotfi. July 27, 2017 (Tunis)

Anonymous Interviewees

A Turkish businessman. November 14, 2007 (Konya)
A youth member of the Muslim Sisterhood. May 24, 2017 (Istanbul)
A youth member of the Muslim Brotherhood. May 26, 2017 (Istanbul)
Group discussions with young Tunisians, various participants. July 18 and July 26, 2017 (Tunis)
Group discussion with twelve youth members of the Muslim Brotherhood. January 8, 2017 (Istanbul)
Group discussion with five local activists. June 30, 2012 (Sidi Bouzid)
Interview with three local members of the UGTT Sfax branch. July 1, 2012 (Sfax)

Bibliography

Aboul Fotouh, Abdel Moneim. 2004. "Islamic Path to Reform." *Al-Ahram Weekly*, February.
2011. "Democracy Supporters Should Not Fear the Muslim Brotherhood." *The Washington Post*, February 10. Opinions. www.washingtonpost.com/opinions/dont-be-afraid-of-the-islamists/2011/02/09/ABmMqmF_story.html
Aboulenein, Ahmed. 2012. "Morsy Appoints Islamist-Dominated Presidential Team." August 27. https://dailynewsegypt.com/2012/08/27/morsy-appoints-islamist-dominated-presidential-team/
Adalet ve Kalkınma Partisi. 2001. "AK Parti Programı," Kalkınma ve Demokratikleşme Programı, 18–20. https://acikerisim.tbmm.gov.tr/xmlui/handle/11543/926
Adams, James, Michael Clark, Lawrence Ezrow, and Garrett Glasgow. 2006. "Are Niche Parties Fundamentally Different from Mainstream Parties? The Causes and the Electoral Consequences of Western European Parties' Policy Shifts, 1976–1998." *American Journal of Political Science*. 50(3): 513–29.
AHaber. 2018. "Başkan Recep Tayyip Erdoğan Köln'de Kur'an-ı Kerim okudu (Prime Minister Recep Tayyip Erdoğan Read the Quran in Cologne)," October 2. www.ahaber.com.tr/video/gundem-videolari/baskan-recep-tayyip-erdogan-kolnde-kuran-i-kerim-okudu
Ahram Online. 2012a. "Thousands Rally Demanding Sharia Law in Tunisia," March 16. http://english.ahram.org.eg/NewsAFCON/2019/36920.aspx
2012b. "President Morsi's New Egypt Constitutional Declaration – First 100 Days – Egypt," August 12. http://english.ahram.org.eg/News/50248.aspx
2012c. "Morsi's Constitutional Declaration," November 22. http://english.ahram.org.eg/News/58947.aspx
2012d. "Brotherhood Increases MP Ratio for Constituent Assembly Ahead of Saturday Vote," March 17. https://english.ahram.org.eg/News/36977.aspx
2013a. "More 'Insulting President' Lawsuits under Morsi than Mubarak," January 20. http://english.ahram.org.eg/NewsContent/1/64/62872/Egypt/Politics-/More-insulting-president-lawsuits-under-Morsi-than.aspx
2013b. "Who's Who: Egypt's New Ministers," May 7. http://english.ahram.org.eg/News/70884.aspx
Ahram Online. 2012. "Islamists Reserve 65 Seats on 100-Member Constituent Assembly." March 26. https://english.ahram.org.eg/NewsContent/1/64/37692/Egypt/Politics-/Islamists-reserve--seats-on-member-Constituent-Ass.aspx

AIHM. 2006. "Necmettin Erbakan – Turkiye Davasi." App. No. 59405/00. Strazburg: Avrupa Konseyi.
Al Ahram. 2012. "al-wasaṭ yu'ayyid Aboul Fotouh bi-intikhābāt al-ri'āsa ba'ada tafawwuqihi 'alā al-hawā' fi al-taṣwīt al-dākhiliyy," April 30. https://gate.ahram.org.eg/News/202242.aspx
Al-Ahram Weekly. n.d. "Mohammad Badie Appoints Conservative Voices after Being Elected the Guide." http://weekly.ahram.org.eg/Archive/2010/984/eg7.htm
Al-Anani, Khalil. 2016. *Inside the Muslim Brotherhood: Religion, Identity, and Politics. Inside the Muslim Brotherhood*. New York: Oxford University Press.
Al-Awadi, Hesham. 2013. "Islamists in Power: The Case of the Muslim Brotherhood in Egypt." *Contemporary Arab Affairs*. 6(4): 539–51.
Al-Banna, Ḥasan. 1978. *Five Tracts of Hasan Al-Banna (1906–1949): A Selection from the Majmu'at at Rasail Al-Iman Al-Shahid Hasan Al-Banna*. Berkeley: University of California Press.
Albertazzi, Daniele and Duncan McDonnell. 2015. *Populists in Power*. New York: Routledge.
Al-Fathali, Hassan. 2014. "Ennahda's Ghannouchi Plays Mediator in Tunisia." Al-Monitor, December 2. www.al-monitor.com/pulse/politics/2014/12/ennahda-mediator-tunisia-president-elections-nidaa-tunis.html
Al Jazeera. 2011. "Ennahda Wins Tunisia's Elections," October 28. www.aljazeera.com/news/2011/10/28/ennahda-wins-tunisias-elections
  2017. "Erdoğan Slams CHP as Opposition March Nears Istanbul," July 1. www.aljazeera.com/news/2017/07/erdogan-slams-chp-opposition-march-nears-istanbul-170701112203655.html
Al-Masry Al-Youm. 2011. "Arba'at alf min shabāb al-Ikhwan yanḍammūn li-ḥamlat da'm «Abu al-Futuh» wa-l-jama'a tujemmid 'uḍwiyyathim," June 23. https://today.almasryalyoum.com/article2.aspx?ArticleID=301407
Al-Monitor. 2014. "Ennahda Leader Says Compromises Serve Tunisia's Interests," January 15. www.al-monitor.com/pulse/politics/2014/01/tunisia-ennahda-vp-interview-constitution-compromise.html#ixzz5uD3qW3Lc
Anayasa Mahkemesi. 1998. "Yargıtay Cumhuriyet Başsavcılığı – Refah Partisi Davasi: Karar Sayısı: 1998/1." http://kararlaryeni.anayasa.gov.tr/Karar/Content/0acac7b9-4875-4c09-a89d-16336ed73728?excludeGerekce=False&wordsOnly=False
Anderson, Lisa. 1991. "Political Pacts, Liberalism, and Democracy: The Tunisian National Pact of 1988." *Government and Opposition*. 26(2): 244–60.
Arıkan Akdağ, Gül. 2017. "Candidate Selection Process as a Tool to Shape a Party's Dominant Coalition: The Case of the AKP in Turkey." *Alternatif Politika*. 9(2): 142–63.
Arjomand, Said. 2009. *After Khomeini: Iran under His Successors*. New York: Oxford University Press.
Ashour, Omar. 2009. *The De-radicalization of Jihadists: Transforming Armed Islamist Movements*. New York: Routledge.
Atacan, Fulya. 2005. "Explaining Religious Politics at the Crossroad: AKP-SP." *Turkish Studies*. 6(2): 187–99.
Auffray, Elodie. 2013. "Zitouna TV, Islam de Fond." Liberation, February 4. www.liberation.fr/ecrans/2013/02/04/zitouna-tv-islam-de-fond_950287

Ayan Musil, Pelin and Hasret Dikici Bilgin. 2014. "Types of Outcomes in Factional Rivalries: Lessons from Non-democratic Parties in Turkey." *International Political Science Review*. 37(2): 166–83.
Ayan, Pelin. 2010. "Authoritarian Party Structures in Turkey: A Comparison of the Republican People's Party and the Justice and Development Party." *Turkish Studies*. 11(2): 197–215.
Aybak, Tunç. 2017. "The Sultan Is Dead, Long Live 'Başyüce' Erdoğan Sultan!" OpenDemocracy, May. www.opendemocracy.net/en/sultan-is-dead-long-live-ba-y-ce-erdogan-sultan/
Aydın, Ayşegül and Cem Emrence. 2016. "Two Routes to an Impasse: Understanding Turkey's Kurdish Policy." The Center on the United States and Europe at Brookings – Turkey Project 10 (December).
  2016. "Politics of Confinement: Curfews and Civilian Control in Turkish Counterinsurgency." *Contemporary Turkish Politics*, POMEPS. October 14. https://pomeps.org/politics-of-confinement-curfews-and-civilian-control-in-turkish-counterinsurgency
Ayoob, Mohammed and Danielle Lussier. 2020. *The Many Faces of Political Islam: Religion and Politics in the Muslim World*. Second edition. Ann Arbor: University of Michigan Press.
Baran, Zeyno. 2008. "Turkey Divided." *Journal of Democracy*. 19(1): 55–69.
Baron, Beth. 2014. *The Orphan Scandal: Christian Missionaries and the Rise of the Muslim Brotherhood*. Stanford: Stanford University Press.
Barrie, Christopher. 2012. "Ninth Conference: Ghannouchi Remains Leader as Ennahda Denies Any Conflict within the Movement." Nawaat. https://nawaat.org/2012/07/18/ninth-conference-ghannouchi-remains-leader-as-ennahda-denies-any-conflict-within-the-movement/
Başkan, Filiz. 2010. "The Rising Islamic Business Elite and Democratization in Turkey." *Journal of Balkan and Near Eastern Studies*. 12(4): 399–416.
Bayat, Asef. 2007. *Making Islam Democratic: Social Movements and the Post-Islamist Turn*. Stanford: Stanford University Press.
Baykan, Toygar Sinan. 2018. *The Justice and Development Party in Turkey: Populism, Personalism, Organization*. Cambridge: Cambridge University Press.
BBC News. 2011a. "Islamists Win Tunisia's Elections," October 27. www.bbc.com/news/world-africa-15487647
  2011b. "Tunisia's Islamist Ennahda Party Wins Historic Poll," October 27. www.bbc.com/news/world-africa-15487647
  2012. "Tunisians Edge Away from Sharia," March 26. www.bbc.com/news/world-africa-17517113
  2013. "Word Cloud: Morsi's Defiant Speech Stresses 'Legitimacy,'" July 3. www.bbc.co.uk/news/world-middle-east-23161987
Bellin, Eva. 2000. "Contingent Democrats: Industrialists, Labor, and Democratization in Late-Developing Countries." *World Politics*. 52(2): 175–205.
Berman, Sheri. 1997. Review of *The Life of the Party*, by Paul R Abramson, Ronald Inglehart, Herbert Kitschelt, and Kay Lawson. *Comparative Politics*. 30(1): 23.
  2008. "Taming Extremist Parties: Lessons from Europe." *Journal of Democracy*. 19(1): 5–18.

Berman, Sheri, Ronald Inglehart, Peter Katzenstein, David Laitin, and Kathleen McNamara. 2001. "Ideas, Norms, and Culture in Political Analysis." *Comparative Politics.* 33(2): 231.

Bianet. 2016. "Erdoğan'dan STK'lara: Sen Neyin Raporunu Yayınlıyorsun?" April 7. www.bianet.org/bianet/siyaset/173711-erdogan-dan-stk-lara-sen-neyin-raporunu-yayinliyorsun

2018. "AKP 2004'te Suç Haline Getiremediği Zinayı Yeniden Gündemine Aldı," February 22. www.bianet.org/bianet/insan-haklari/194571-akp-2004-te-suc-haline-getiremedigi-zinayi-yeniden-gundemine-aldi

Bille, Lars. 1997. "Leadership Change and Party Change: The Case of the Danish Social Democratic Party, 1960–95." *Party Politics.* 3(3): 379–90.

Blaydes, Lisa. 2010. *Elections and Distributive Politics in Mubarak's Egypt.* Cambridge: Cambridge University Press.

Blum, Rachel. 2020. *How the Tea Party Captured the GOP.* Chicago: University of Chicago Press.

Blumenthal, Max. 2013. "The Muslim Brotherhood's War on Egyptian Media." The Nation, March 13. www.thenation.com/article/archive/muslim-brotherhoods-war-egyptian-media/

Blyth, Mark. 2003. "Structures Do Not Come with an Instruction Sheet: Interests, Ideas, and Progress in Political Science." *Perspectives on Politics.* 1(4): 695–706.

Boix, Carles and Susan C. Stokes. 2003. "Endogenous Democratization." *World Politics.* 5(4): 517–49.

Bora, Tanıl. 2016. *Cereyanlar: Türkiye'de Siyasî İdeolojiler.* Istanbul: İletişim Yayınları.

Boubekeur, Amel. 2016. "Islamists, Secularists and Old Regime Elites in Tunisia: Bargained Competition." *Mediterranean Politics.* 21(1): 107–27.

Boucek, Francoise. 2002. "The Structure and Dynamics of Intra-party Politics in Europe." *Perspectives on European Politics and Society.* 3(3): 453–93.

Boulby, Marion. 1988. "The Islamic Challenge: Tunisia since Independence." *Third World Quarterly.* 10(2): 590–614.

Browers, Michaelle L. 2009. *Political Ideology in the Arab World: Accommodation and Transformation.* Cambridge Middle East Studies. Cambridge: Cambridge University Press.

Brown, Nathan J. 2011. "The Muslim Brotherhood as Helicopter Parent." *Foreign Policy,* May 27. https://foreignpolicy.com/2011/05/27/the-muslim-brotherhood-as-helicopter-parent/

2012. *When Victory Is Not an Option: Islamist Movements in Arab Politics.* First edition. Ithaca: Cornell University Press.

2018. "The Roots of Egypt's Constitutional Catastrophe." In *Democratic Transition in the Muslim World,* edited by Alfred Stepan, 73–90. New York: Columbia University Press.

Brown, Nathan J. and Amr Hamzawy. 2008. "The Draft Party Platform of the Egyptian Muslim Brotherhood: Foray into Political Integration or Retreat into Old Positions?" *Carnegie Endowment for International Peace Middle East Series.* 89(January).

Brownlee, Jason. 2007. *Authoritarianism in an Age of Democratization.* Cambridge: Cambridge University Press.

2016. "Why Turkey's Authoritarian Descent Shakes Up Democratic Theory." *The Washington Post.* www.washingtonpost.com/news/monkey-cage/wp/2016/03/23/why-turkeys-authoritarian-descent-shakes-up-democratic-theory/

Budge, Ian, Lawrence Ezrow, and Michael D. McDonald. 2010. "Ideology, Party Factionalism and Policy Change: An Integrated Dynamic Theory." *British Journal of Political Science.* 40(4): 781–804.

Bulut, Ömer. 2020. "AK Parti'de Büyük Değişim." Al Jazeera Turk, July 26. www.aljazeera.com.tr/al-jazeera-ozel/ak-partide-buyuk-degisim

Business News. 2014. "Habib Ellouze et Sadok Chourou préparent l'explosion de la cocotte d'Ennahdha," December 13.

Butler, Daren. 2018. "With More Islamic Schooling, Erdoğan Aims to Reshape Turkey." Reuters, January 25. www.reuters.com/investigates/special-report/turkey-erdogan-education/

Butterworth, Charles. 1982. "Prudence versus Legitimacy: The Persistent Theme in Islamic Political Thought." In *Islamic Resurgence in the Arab World,* edited by Ali E. Hillal Dessouki, 84–114. New York: Praeger.

Çakır, Ruşen. 2005. "Milli Görüş Hareketi." In İslamcılık. Second edition. *Modern Türkiye'de Siyasi Düşünce.* 6: 544–50. Istanbul: İletişim Yayınları.

Çakır, Ruşen and Fehmi Çalmuk. 2001. *Recep Tayyip Erdoğan: Bir dönüşüm öyküsü.* Beyoğlu, İstanbul: Metis Yayınları.

Çalmuk, Fehmi. 2005. "Necmettin Erbakan." In İslamcılık, Second edition. *Modern Türkiye'de Siyasi Düşünce.* 6: 550–76. Istanbul: İletişim Yayınları.

Capoccia, Giovanni and Daniel Ziblatt. 2010. "The Historical Turn in Democratization Studies: A New Research Agenda for Europe and Beyond." *Comparative Political Studies.* 43(June): 931–68.

Çarkoğlu, Ali and Binnaz Toprak. 2007. *Religion, Society, and Politics in a Changing Turkey.* Istanbul: TESEV.

Carnegie Endowment for International Peace. 2015. "2012 Egyptian Parliamentary Elections." https://carnegieendowment.org/2015/01/22/2012-egyptian-parliamentary-elections-pub-58800

Carter Center. 2012. "Presidential Election in Egypt: Final Report." www.cartercenter.org/resources/pdfs/news/peace_publications/election_reports/egypt-final-presidential-elections-2012.pdf

Cavatorta, Francesco and Fabio Merone. 2013. "Moderation through Exclusion? The Journey of the Tunisian Ennahda from Fundamentalist to Conservative Party." *Democratization.* 20(5): 857–75.

Çavdar, Gamze. 2006. "Islamist 'New Thinking' in Turkey: A Model for Political Learning?" *Political Science Quarterly.* 121(3): 477–97.

Çaylak, Adem. 2016. "İslamcı Siyasette İktidar ve İtikat." *Birikim.* 30(September): 27–36.

Çepni, Ozan. 2018. "Her yer imam, her yer hatip! MEB imam hatipleri kılavuzda 'nitelikli' yaptı." *Cumhuriyet,* April 11. www.cumhuriyet.com.tr/haber/her-yer-imam-her-yer-hatip-meb-imam-hatipleri-kilavuzda-nitelikli-yapti-956785

Çiçek, Cuma. 2011. "Elimination or Integration of Pro-Kurdish Politics: Limits of the AKP's Democratic Initiative." *Turkish Studies.* 12(1): 15–26.

Ciddi, Sinan and Berk Esen. 2014. "Turkey's Republican People's Party: Politics of Opposition under a Dominant Party System." *Turkish Studies.* 15(3): 419–41.
Çınar, Menderes. 2006. "Turkey's Transformation under the AKP Rule." *The Muslim World.* 96(3): 469–86.
  2009. "AKP ve İslami Hareketler: Defansif ve Dağıtıcı İktidar Kardeşliği." In *AKP Kitabı: Bir Dönüşümün Bilançosu,* edited by Bülent Duru and İlhan Uzgel, 307–15. Ankara: Phoenix Yayinevi.
Çınar, Menderes. 2015. *Vesayetçi Demokrasiden "Milli" Demokrasiye.* Istanbul: İletişim.
Çınar, Menderes and Ipek Gencel Sezgin. 2013. "Islamist Political Engagement in the Early Years of Multi-Party Politics in Turkey: 1945–60." *Turkish Studies.* 14(2): 329–45.
Cizre, Ümit, ed. 2007. *Secular and Islamic Politics in Turkey: The Making of the Justice and Development Party.* New York: Routledge.
Cizre, Ümit and Menderes Çınar. 2003. "Turkey 2002: Kemalism, Islamism, and Politics in the Light of the February 28 Process." *The South Atlantic Quarterly.* 102(2–3): 309–22.
Clark, Janine A. 2004. *Islam, Charity, and Activism: Middle-Class Networks and Social Welfare in Egypt, Jordan, and Yemen.* Bloomington: Indiana University Press.
  2006. "The Conditions of Islamist Moderation: Unpacking Cross-Ideological Cooperation in Jordan." *International Journal of Middle East Studies.* 38(4): 539–60.
Collectif 18 Octobre. 2006. "Textes du Collectif 18 octobre Pour les Droits & les Libertés en Tunisie à Paris." http://nachaz.org/doc-1-brocure-du-collectif-du-18-octobre-pour-les-droits-et-les-libertes/
Committee to Protect Journalists. 2012. "Proposed Egyptian Constitution Would Limit Media Freedom," December 4. https://cpj.org/2012/12/proposed-egyptian-constitution-would-limit-media-f/
  2013. "CPJ Condemns Siege at Cairo's Media Production City," March 25. https://cpj.org/2013/03/cpj-condemns-siege-at-cairos-media-production-city/
  2014. "CPJ Risk List," February 12. https://cpj.org/2014/02/attacks-on-the-press-cpj-risk-list-1/
Constitute Project. 2012. *Egypt's Constitution of 2012.* www.constituteproject.org/constitution/Egypt_2012.pdf?lang=en
  2014. *Tunisia's Constitution of 2014.* www.constituteproject.org/constitution/Tunisia_2014.pdf
Coppedge, Michael, John Gerring, Carl Henrik Knutsen, Staffan I. Lindberg, Jan Teorell, David Altman, Michael Bernhard, Agnes Cornell, M. Steven Fish, Lisa Gastaldi, Haakon Gjerløw, Adam Glynn, Sandra Grahn, Allen Hicken, Katrin Kinzelbach, Kyle L. Marquardt, Kelly McMann, Valeriya Mechkova, Pamela Paxton, Daniel Pemstein, Johannes von Römer, Brigitte Seim, Rachel Sigman, Svend-Erik Skaaning, Jeffrey Staton, Eitan Tzelgov, Luca Uberti, Yi-ting Wang, Tore Wig, and Daniel Ziblatt. 2022. "V-Dem Codebook v12." *Varieties of Democracy (V-Dem) Project.*
Cowell, Alan. 1990. "Mideast Tensions; Turnout Appears Low in Egyptian Election Boycotted by Opposition." *The New York Times,* November 30.

www.nytimes.com/1990/11/30/world/mideast-tensions-turnout-appears-low-egyptian-election-boycotted-opposition.html
Cumhuriyet. 2014. "İşte Gül'ün Köşk Karnesi." www.cumhuriyet.com.tr/haber/iste-gulun-kosk-karnesi-geleni-onaylamis-103255
2016a. "Bunlar Ateist, Bunlar Zerdüşt," May 28. www.cumhuriyet.com.tr/video/erdogan-bunlar-ateist-bunlar-zerdust-541651
2016b. "Erdoğan, Abdullah Gül'ün Gezi Parkı açıklamasını sildirdi," June 26. www.cumhuriyet.com.tr/haber/erdogan-abdullah-gulun-gezi-parki-aciklamasini-sildirdi-554183
2018. "Her yer imam, her yer hatip! MEB imam hatipleri kılavuzda 'nitelikli' yaptı," April 11. www.cumhuriyet.com.tr/haber/her-yer-imam-her-yer-hatip-meb-imam-hatipleri-kilavuzda-nitelikli-yapti-956785
Daily News Egypt. 2012. "Morsy Appoints Islamist-Dominated Presidential Team," August 27. www.dailynewssegypt.com/2012/08/27/morsy-appoints-islamist-dominated-presidential-team/
Daragahi, Borzou. 2012. "In Power, Egypt's Muslim Brotherhood Remains Secretive." *The Washington Post*, December 10. www.washingtonpost.com/world/middle_east/in-power-egypts-muslim-brotherhood-remains-secretive-defensive-critics-say/2012/12/10/31234f22-42fa-11e2-8061-253bccfc7532_story.html
Demiralp, Seda. 2009. "The Rise of Islamic Capital and the Decline of Islamic Radicalism in Turkey." *Comparative Politics*. 41(3): 315–35.
DiSalvo, Daniel. 2012. *Engines of Change: Party Factions in American Politics, 1868–2010*. New York: Oxford University Press.
Downs, Anthony. 1957. "An Economic Theory of Political Action in a Democracy." *Journal of Political Economy*. 65(2): 135–50.
Duncan, Fraser. 2007. "'Lately, Things Just Don't Seem the Same': External Shocks, Party Change and the Adaptation of the Dutch Christian Democrats during 'Purple Hague' 1994–8." *Party Politics*. 13(1): 69–87.
Dunn, Michael Collins. 1992. *Renaissance or Radicalism? Political Islam: The Case of Tunisia's Al-Nahda*. Washington, DC: International Estimate.
Duverger, Maurice. 1954. *Political Parties: Their Organization and Activity in the Modern State*. New York: Methuen & Co.; John Wiley & Sons.
DW. 2021. "Furkan Vakfı neden gündemde?" www.dw.com/tr/furkan-vakfi-neden-gundemde/a-57434769
Ehteshami, Anoushiravan. 2002. *After Khomeini: The Iranian Second Republic*. New York: Routledge.
Elad-Altman, Israel. 2005. "Current Trends in the Ideology of the Egyptian Muslim Brotherhood." *Hudson Institute*, 12.
El-Erian, Essam. 2005. "Towards the Renaissance." *Al-Ahram Weekly Online*. http://weekly.ahram.org.eg/2005/771/op71.htm
El-Ghobashy, Mona. 2005. "The Metamorphosis of the Egyptian Muslim Brothers." *International Journal of Middle East Studies*. 37(3): 373–95.
El-Gundy, Zeinab. 2012a. "Freedom and Justice Party Heads Most of Egypt's Parliamentary Committees." *Ahram Online*, January 31. http://english.ahram.org.eg/NewsContent/1/64/33333/Egypt/Politics-/Freedom-and-Justice-Party-heads-most-of-Egypts-par.aspx

2012b. "Egypt Shura Council Announces New Heads for 3 State Papers." *Ahram Online*, August 9. http://english.ahram.org.eg/NewsContent/1/64/49968/Egypt/Politics-/Egypt-Shura-Council-announces-new-heads-for%E2%80%94state.aspx

El-Hennawy, Noha. 2011a. "Defying Leadership, Brotherhood Youth Form New Party." *Egypt Independent*, June 21. www.egyptindependent.com/defying-leadership-brotherhood-youth-form-new-party/

2011b. "Brotherhood Contests over 50 Percent of Parliamentary Seats," October 25. www.egyptindependent.com/brotherhood-contests-over-50-percent-parliamentary-seats/

Eligür, Banu. 2010. *The Mobilization of Political Islam in Turkey*. New York: Cambridge University Press.

Elsässer, Sebastian. 2019. "Sufism and the Muslim Brotherhood: Ḥasan al-Bannā's wird and the Transformation of Sufi traditions in Modern Islamic Activism." *Oriente Moderno*. 99(3): 280–305.

El-Sharnoubi, Osman. 2013. "Egypt's Morsi Defies Calls to Step down, Offers Opposition Partial Concessions." *Ahram Online*, July 3.

Egypt Independent. 2009. "Brotherhood Youth Criticize Group's Structure," November 8. www.egyptindependent.com/brotherhood-youth-criticize-groups-structure/

2012. "SCAF Expands Its Power with Constitutional Amendments." www.egyptindependent.com/scaf-expands-its-power-constitutional-amendments/

Egypt Window. 2011. "Ḥizb al-Hurriyya Wa-l-ʿadāla Faqaṭ Yuʿabbir ʿan Jamaʿat al-Ikhwan al-Muslimin Wa-Lā Yujawwiz Li-Afrādhā al-Iltihāq Bi-Ghayrihi," March 15. https://old.egyptwindow.net/news_Details.aspx?News_ID=11581

Eligür, Banu. *The Mobilization of Political Islam in Turkey*. New York: Cambridge University Press.

Ennahda. 1996. The Lessons of the Past and the Problems of the Present and Future Aspirations.

2016. By-Laws. www.ennahdha.tn/النظام-الأساسي-بعد-تنقيحه-من-المؤتمر-العاشر

Entelis, John. 1997. *Islam, Democracy, and the State in North Africa*. Bloomington: Indiana University Press.

Erbakan, Necmettin. 1991. *Türkiye'nin Meseleleri ve Çözümleri*. Ankara: Semih Ofset.

Erbakan, Necmettin. 1994. "Speech in Welfare Party Parliamentary Group Meeting."

Ergin, Sedat. 2011. "Erdoğan and CHP Leader's Alevi Origin." *Hurriyet Daily News*, May 18.

Ergün, Nihat. 2015. *Adım Adım Siyaset*. Istanbul: ALFA Yayınları.

Erişen, Cengiz and Paul Kubicek. 2016. *Democratic Consolidation in Turkey: Micro and Macro Challenges*. London: Routledge.

Esen, Berk and Sebnem Gumuscu. 2016. "Rising Competitive Authoritarianism in Turkey." *Third World Quarterly*. 37(9): 1581–606.

2017a. "Turkey: How the Coup Failed." *Journal of Democracy*. 28(1): 59–73.

2017b. "A Small Yes for Presidentialism: The Turkish Constitutional Referendum of April 2017." *South European Society and Politics*. 22(3): 303–26.

2018. "Building a Competitive Authoritarian Regime: State–Business Relations in the AKP's Turkey." *Journal of Balkan and Near Eastern Studies*. 20(4): 349–72.

2021. "Why Did Turkish Democracy Collapse? A Political Economy Account of AKP's Authoritarianism." *Party Politics.* 27(6): 1075–91.
Esmer, Yılmaz. 2002. "At the Ballot Box: The Determinants of Voting Behavior." In *Politics, Parties, and Elections in Turkey,* edited by Sabri Sayarı and Yılmaz Esmer. Boulder: Lynne Rienner Publishers.
Esposito, John L. 1991. *Islam and Politics.* Third edition. Syracuse: Syracuse University Press.
  1999. *The Islamic Threat: Myth or Reality?* New York: Oxford University Press.
Esposito, John and John O. Voll. 1996. *Islam and Democracy.* Oxford: Oxford University Press.
Essam El-Din, Gamal. 2012a. "Islamists Attack 'Dictatorship of the Minority.'" *Ahram Online,* March 28. http://english.ahram.org.eg/NewsContentP/1/37945/Egypt/Islamists-attack-dictatorship-of-the-minority.aspx
  2012b. "Islamists Reserve 65 Seats on 100-Member Constituent Assembly," March 26. https://english.ahram.org.eg/News/37692.aspx
Fahmy, Ninette S. 1998. "The Performance of the Muslim Brotherhood in the Egyptian Syndicates: An Alternative Formula for Reform?" *Middle East Journal.* 52(4): 551–62.
Feldman, Noah. 2020. *The Arab Winter: A Tragedy.* Princeton: Princeton University Press.
France 24. 2013. "Egypt's Luxor Governor Resigns after Controversy," June 23. www.france24.com/en/20130623-egypt-luxor-islamist-governor-adel-al-Khayat-resigns-Mohammed-Morsi
Freedom and Justice Party. 2011. Election Program – Parliamentary Elections 2011. https://kurzman.unc.edu/files/2011/06/FJP_2011_English.pdf
Freedom House. 2013. "Freedom of the Press 2013 – Egypt." www.refworld.org/docid/5208a21a12.html
  2020. "Freedom on the Net 2019 Turkey." Freedom House. https://freedomhouse.org/country/turkey/freedom-net/2019
Gelvin, James L. 2015. *The Modern Middle East: A History.* Fourth edition. New York: Oxford University Press.
Ghannouchi, Rached. 1993. "The Participation of Islamists in Non-Islamic Government." In *Power-Sharing Islam?* edited by Azzam Tamimi. London: Liberty for Muslim World.
  2017. "Ennahda's Democratic Commitments and Capabilities: Major Evolutionary Moments and Choices." In *Tunisia's Democratic Transition in Comparative Perspective,* edited by Alfred Stepan, 15–28. New York: Columbia University Press.
Göle, Nilüfer. 2017. "Snapshots of Islamic Modernities." In *Multiple Modernities,* edited by Shmuel N. Eisenstadt, 91–118. New York: Routledge.
Gonzalez Ocantos, E. A. and J. Laporte. 2021. "Process Tracing and the Problem of Missing Data." *Sociological Methods and Research.* 50(3): 1407–35.
Grewal, Sharan. 2018. "Where Are Ennahdha's Competitors?" Rice University's Baker Institute for Public Policy Issue Brief April 26. www.bakerinstitute.org/media/files/files/e0677eb9/bi-brief-042618-cme-carnegie-tunisia2.pdf
  2020. "From Islamists to Muslim Democrats: The Case of Tunisia's Ennahda." *American Political Science Review.* 114(2): 519–35.

Grzymala-Busse, Anna. 2002. *Redeeming the Communist Past: The Regeneration of Communist Parties in East Central Europe.* Cambridge: Cambridge University Press.

Gülalp, Haldun. 2001. "Globalization and Political Islam: The Social Bases of Turkey's Welfare Party." *International Journal of Middle East Studies.* 33(3): 433–48.

Gültekin, Levent. 2005. *Şatafatlı Mağlubiyet.* 5. baskı. Istanbul: Doğan Kitap.

Gumuscu, Sebnem. 2010. "Class, Status, and Party: The Changing Face of Political Islam in Turkey and Egypt." *Comparative Political Studies.* 43(June): 835–61.

2012. "Reactions to the Arab Spring." *Yale Journal of International Affairs*, May 16. http://yalejournal.org/op-ed_post/turkeys-reactions-to-the-arab-spring/

2013. "The Emerging Predominant Party System in Turkey." *Government and Opposition.* 48(2): 223–44.

2016. "The Clash of Islamists: The Crisis of the Turkish State and Democracy." *Contemporary Turkish Politics* POMEPS 6.

2020. "Dominance and Democratic Backsliding under AKP Rule in Turkey." In *Routledge Handbook on Political Parties in the Middle East and North Africa*, edited by Franscesco Cavatorta, Lise Storm, and Valeria Resta. New York: Routledge.

Gumuscu, Sebnem and Deniz Sert. 2009. "The Power of the Devout Bourgeoisie: The Case of the Justice and Development Party in Turkey." *Middle Eastern Studies.* 45(6): 953–68.

Gunther, Richard and Larry Diamond. 2003. "Species of Political Parties: A New Typology." *Party Politics.* 9(2): 167–99.

Gürses, Mehmet. 2014. "Islamists, Democracy and Turkey: A Test of the Inclusion–Moderation Hypothesis." *Party Politics.* 20(4): 646–53.

Haber7. 2010. "Yazarını Erdoğan'a şikayet eden medya patronu," 3 March. www.haber7.com/siyaset/haber/487344-yazarini-erdogana-sikayet-eden-medya-patronu

2011. "Erbakan'ın hafızalara kazınan sözleri," February 28. www.haber7.com/siyaset/haber/717194-erbakanin-hafizalara-kazinan-sozleri

HaberTurk. 2013a. "İyi niyetli mesajlar alındı, gereği yapılacak," June 3. www.haberturk.com/tv/burasi-turkiye/video/iyi-niyetli-mesajlar-alindi-geregi-yapilacak/90588

2013b. "Cumhurbaşkanı Gül'den flaş Gezi Parkı açıklaması," June 12. www.haberturk.com/gundem/haber/851840-cumhurbaskani-gulden-flas-gezi-parki-aciklamasi

2015. "Bülent Arınç: Gül parti kurmaz ama bizi imtihan etmeye kalkmasınlar," September 11. www.haberturk.com/gundem/haber/1127415-bulent-arinc-haberturkte

Haggard, Stephan and Robert Kaufman. 2021. *Backsliding: Democratic Regress in the Contemporary World.* Cambridge: Cambridge University Press.

Hamid, Shadi. 2014. *Temptations of Power: Islamists and Illiberal Democracy in a New Middle East.* New York: Oxford University Press.

Hamzawy, Amr. 2007. "Regression in the Muslim Brotherhood's Platform?" Carnegie Endowment for International Peace, November 1. https://carnegieendowment.org/2007/11/01/regression-in-muslim-brotherhood-s-platform-pub-19686

Hamzawy, Amr, Marina Ottoway, and Nathan J. Brown. 2007. "What Islamists Need to Be Clear About: The Case of the Egyptian Muslim Brotherhood." Carnegie Endowment for International Peace. https://carnegieendowment.org/files/ottaway_brown_hamzawy_islamists_final.pdf

Hamzawy, Amr and Nathan J. Brown. 2008. "Islamist Parties and Democracy: A Boon or a Bane for Democracy?" *Journal of Democracy*. 19(3): 49–54.

Harmel, Robert and Alexander C. Tan. 2003. "Party Actors and Party Change: Does Factional Dominance Matter?" *European Journal of Political Research*. 42(3): 409–24.

Harmel, Robert and Kenneth Janda. 2016. "An Integrated Theory of Party Goals and Party Change." *Journal of Theoretical Politics*. 6(3): 259–87.

Harmel, Robert, Uk Heo, Alexander Tan, and Kenneth Janda. 1995. "Performance, Leadership, Factions and Party Change: An Empirical Analysis." *West European Politics*. 18(1): 1–33.

Hasan, Salah al-Din. 2011. "Abu al-Futuh: Arfaḍ Ta'sīs Hizb Li-l-Ikhwan al-Muslimin Fi Masr." http://salaheldinhassan.blogspot.com/2011/03/blog-post.html

Hatipoglu, Nihat. 2017. "Ulu'l emre itaat nedir?" *Sabah*, February 24. www.sabah.com.tr/yazarlar/hatipoglu/2017/02/24/ulul-emre-itaat-nedir

Heinisch, Reinhard. 2003. "Success in Opposition – Failure in Government: Explaining the Performance of Right-Wing Populist Parties in Public Office." *West European Politics*. 26(3): 91–130.

Hegghammer, Thomas. 2013. "Should I Stay or Should I Go? Explaining Variation in Western Jihadists' Choice between Domestic and Foreign Fighting." *American Political Science Review*. 107(1): 1–15.

Heper, Metin. 2002. "Conclusion – The Consolidation of Democracy versus Democratization in Turkey." *Turkish Studies*. 3(1): 138–46.

Heper, Metin and Jacob M. Landau. 2016. *Political Parties and Democracy in Turkey*. New York: Routledge.

Heper, Metin and Sabri Sayarı. 2002. *Political Leaders and Democracy in Turkey*. Lanham: Lexington Books.

Hermassi, Abdelbaki. 1995. "The Rise and Fall of the Islamist Movement in Tunisia." In *The Islamist Dilemma: The Political Role of Islamist Movements in the Contemporary Arab World*, edited by Laura Guazzone. Reading: Ithaca University Press.

Huffington Post Maghreb. 2014a. "Tunisie Polemique Mongi Rahouni," January 5. www.huffpostmaghreb.com/2014/01/05/tunisie-polemique-mongi-rahoui_n_4544792.html

2014b. "Polemique Mongi Rahoui." www.huffpostmaghreb.com/2014/01/05/tunisie-polemique-mongi-rahoui_n_4544792.html?ncid=edlinkusaolp00000003

Human Rights Watch. 2012. "Tunisie: De la prison et des amendes pour les «offenses au sacré»," August 3. www.hrw.org/fr/news/2012/08/03/tunisie-de-la-prison-et-des-amendes-pour-les-offenses-au-sacre

Huntington, Samuel. 1997. *The Clash of Civilizations and the Remaking of World Order*. New York: Simon and Schuster.

Huntington, Samuel P. 1991. "Democracy's Third Wave." *Journal of Democracy*. 2(2): 12–34.

Huntington, Samuel. 1984. "Will More Countries Become Democratic?" *Political Science Quarterly*. 99(2): 193–218.
Hürriyet. 2002. "Hazine'nin aslan payı DSP'ye," August 8. www.hurriyet.com.tr/gundem/hazinenin-aslan-payi-dspye-90112
 2012. "Siyasetin yargıyı kuşatmasına izin vermeyeceğiz," April 2. www.hurriyet.com.tr/gundem/kilic-siyasetin-yargiyi-kusatmasina-izin-vermeyecegiz-20257803
 2013a. "Cumhurbaşkanı Gül'den Gezi Parkı açıklaması," June 3. www.hurriyet.com.tr/gundem/cumhurbaskani-gulden-gezi-parki-aciklamasi-23424869
 2013b. "Bülent Arınç ilk gün için özür diledi," June 4. www.hurriyet.com.tr/gundem/bulent-arinc-ilk-gun-icin-ozur-diledi-23431837
Hurriyet Daily News. 2011. "Turkish PM Rebuffs Criticism over Press Freedom," April 13.
Hwang, Julie Chernov. 2010. "When Parties Swing: Islamist Parties and Institutional Moderation in Malaysia and Indonesia." *Southeast Asia Research*. 18(4): 635–74.
Ignazi, Piero. 1992. "The Silent Counter-Revolution." *European Journal of Political Research*. 22(1): 3–34.
Inglehart, Ronald and Christian Welzel. 2005. *Modernization, Cultural Change and Democracy*. Cambridge: Cambridge University Press.
Insel, Ahmet. 2003. "The AKP and Normalizing Democracy in Turkey." *South Atlantic Quarterly*. 102(2–3): 293–308.
International Bar Association. 2021. "Egypt Increases Use of Capital Punishment to Crush Dissent," July 28. www.ibanet.org/egypt-capital-punishment-dissent
International Crisis Group. 2012. "Lost in Transition: The World According to Egypt's SCAF." *Middle East Report No 121*. www.justice.gov/sites/default/files/eoir/legacy/2014/09/29/Lost%20in%20Transition4-24-12.pdf
IRI. 2011. "Survey of Tunisian Public Opinion, March 2011."
 2012. "Survey of Tunisian Public Opinion April 2012."
 2014. "Survey of Tunisian Public Opinion June–July 2014."
Iversen, Torben. 1994. "The Logics of Electoral Politics: Spatial, Directional, and Mobilizational Effects." *Comparative Political Studies*. 27.(2): 155–89.
Jawad, Nazek. 2013. "Democracy in Modern Islamic Thought." *British Journal of Middle Eastern Studies*. 40(3): 324–39.
Jenkins, Gareth. 2008. "AKP Strengthens Its Hold on the Turkish Media." *Eurasia Daily Monitor*, May 15. https://jamestown.org/program/akp-strengthens-its-hold-on-the-turkish-media/
Kabasakal, Mehmet. 2012. "Factors Influencing Intra-party Democracy and Membership Rights: The Case of Turkey." *Party Politics*. 20(5): 700–11.
Kalyvas, Stathis N. 1996. *The Rise of Christian Democracy in Europe*. Ithaca, NY: Cornell University Press.
 1998. "Democracy and Religious Politics: Evidence from Belgium." *Comparative Political Studies*. 31(3): 292–320.
 2000. "Commitment Problems in Emerging Democracies: The Case of Religious Parties." *Comparative Politics*. 32(4): 379–98.
Kalyvas, Stathis N. and Kees van Kersbergen. 2010. "Christian Democracy." *Annual Review of Political Science*. 13(1): 183–209.
Kandil, Hazem. 2014. *Inside the Brotherhood*. Oxford: Polity Press.

Kara, İsmail. 2014. *Türkiye'de İslamcılık Düşüncesi*. Dergah Yayınları.
Karakoç, Ekrem and Ege Özen. 2020. "Kurdish Public Opinion in Turkey." In *The Kurds in the Middle East: Enduring Problems and New Dynamics*, edited by M. Gürses, D. Romano, and M. Gunter. Lanham: Lexington Books.
Karaman, Hayrettin. 2017. "İtâat." *Yeni Şafak*, March 3. www.yenisafak.com/yazarlar/hayrettinkaraman/itat-2037056
Katz, Richard S. and Peter Mair. 1992. *Party Organizations: A Data Handbook on Party Organizations in Western Democracies, 1960–90*. London: SAGE Publications.
Kaya, Ayhan. 2015. "Islamisation of Turkey under the AKP Rule: Empowering Family, Faith and Charity." *South European Society and Politics*. 20(1): 47–69.
Keddie, Nikki. 1966. "Pan-Islamic Appeal: Afghani and Abdulhamid II." *Middle Eastern Studies*. 3(1): 46–67.
  1986. "The Islamist Movement in Tunisia." *The Maghreb Review*. 11(1): 26–39.
Kedourie, Elie. 1994. *Democracy and Arab Political Culture*. New York: Routledge.
Kepel, Gilles. 2003. *Muslim Extremism in Egypt: The Prophet and Pharaoh*. Berkeley, CA: University of California Press.
Keyman, Fuat E. and Meltem Müftüler-Baç. 2015. "Turkey's Unconsolidated Democracy: The Nexus between Democratisation and Majoritarianism in Turkey." In *Democracy, Trade, and the Kurdish Question in Turkey-EU Relations, III*, 121–29. Rome: Italian Institute of International Affairs.
Keyman, Fuat and Sebnem Gumuscu. 2014. *Democracy, Identity and Foreign Policy in Turkey: Hegemony through Transformation*. London: Palgrave Macmillan.
Khalid Amayreh. 2013. "Egypt's Unreasonable Opposition," February 18. www.ikhwanweb.com/print.php?id=30662
Khalil, Jahd. 2014. "Ennahda Distances Itself from Salafists." *Al-Monitor*, October 24. www.al-monitor.com/pulse/originals/2014/10/tunisia-islamist-ennahda-distance-salafists.html#ixzz5uOhFeevA
Kirdiş, Esen. 2016. "Immoderation: Comparing the Christian Right in the US and Pro-Islamic Movement-Parties in Turkey." *Democratization*. 23(3): 417–36.
  2018. "Wolves in Sheep Clothing or Victims of Times? Discussing the Immoderation of Incumbent Islamic Parties in Turkey, Egypt, Morocco, and Tunisia." *Democratization*. 25(5): 901–18.
Kirkpatrick, David D. 2012a. "Keeper of Islamic Flame Rises as Egypt's New Decisive Voice." *The New York Times*, March 12. www.nytimes.com/2012/03/12/world/middleeast/muslim-brotherhood-leader-rises-as-egypts-decisive-voice.html
  2012b. "Morsi Turns to His Islamist Backers as Egypt's Crisis Grows." *The New York Times*, December 7. www.nytimes.com/2012/12/08/world/middleeast/egypt-islamists-dialogue-secular-opponents-clashes.html
Kısakürek, Necip Fazıl. 2014. *İdeolocya Örgüsü*. Büyük Doğu Yayınları.
Kitschelt, Herbert. 2006. "Movement Parties." In *Handbook of Party Politics*, edited by Richard Katz and Wiliam Crotty, 278–90. London: SAGE Publications.

Kitschelt, Herbert and Philipp Rehm. 2014. "Occupations as a Site of Political Preference Formation." *Comparative Political Studies*. 47(12): 1670–706.

Kubicek, Paul. 2016. "Majoritarian Democracy in Turkey: Causes and Consequences." In *Democratic Consolidation in Turkey: Micro and Macro Challenges*, edited by Cengiz Erisen and Paul Kubicek, 123–43. New York: Routledge.

Kumbaracıbaşı, Arda Can. 2009. *Turkish Politics and the Rise of the AKP: Dilemmas of Institutionalization and Leadership Strategy*. London: Routledge.

Künkler, Mirjam and Manfred Brocker. 2013. "Religious Parties: Revisiting the Inclusion–Moderation Hypothesis – Introduction." *Party Politics*. 19(March): 171–86.

L'Express. 2014. "Constitution tunisienne: l'accusation d'apostasie interdite," January 5. www.lexpress.fr/actualites/1/monde/tunisie-une-menace-de-mort-fait-derailler-les-debats-a-la-constituante_1311699.html

Levitsky, Steven and Daniel Ziblatt. 2018. *How Democracies Die*. New York: Crown.

Lewis, Bernard. 2004. *The Crisis of Islam: The Holy War and Unholy Terrror*. New York: Random House.

Lewis, Bernard. 1994. *The Shaping of the Modern Middle East*. Oxford: Oxford University Press.

Lia, Brynjar. 2006. *The Society of the Muslim Brothers in Egypt: The Rise of an Islamic Mass Movement, 1928–1942*. Reading: Ithaca Press.

Lipset, Seymour Martin. 1959. "Some Social Requisites of Democracy: Economic Development and Political Legitimacy." *The American Political Science Review*. 53(1): 69–105.

Lipset, Seymour Martin and Stein Rokkan. 1967. *Party Systems and Voter Alignments: Cross-National Perspectives*. New York: Free Press.

Lorch, Jasmin and Hatem Chakroun. 2020. "Salafism Meet Populism." Middle East Institute. www.mei.edu/publications/salafism-meets-populism-al-karama-coalition-and-malleability-political-salafism

Lord, Ceren. 2018. *Religious Politics in Turkey: From the Birth of the Republic to the AKP*. Cambridge: Cambridge University Press.

Lüküslü, Demet. 2016. "Creating a Pious Generation: Youth and Education Policies of the AKP in Turkey." *Southeast European and Black Sea Studies*. 16(October): 1–13.

Lynch, Marc. 2009. "Conservative Gains in Muslim Brotherhood Elections." *Foreign Policy*, December 21.

Madi, Abu al-Ela. 2004. "Decades On." *Al-Ahram Weekly Online*, August 5.

Maloney, Suzanne. 2015. *Iran's Political Economy since the Revolution*. Cambridge: Cambridge University Press.

Mandaville, Peter. 2014. *Islam and Politics*. Second edition. New York: Routledge.

Mansour, Sherif. 2013. "On the Divide: Press Freedom at Risk in Egypt." Committee to Protect Journalists, August 14. https://cpj.org/reports/2013/08/on-divide-egypt-press-freedom-morsi/

Marks, Monica. 2015. "How Egypt's Coup Really Affected Tunisia's Islamists." *The Washington Post*, March 16. www.washingtonpost.com/news/monkey-cage/wp/2015/03/16/how-egypts-coup-really-affected-tunisias-islamists/?utm_term=.eca7548ae909

2017. "Purists vs Pluralists: Cross-Ideological Coalition Building in Tunisia." In *Tunisia's Democratic Transition in Comparative Perspective*, edited by Alfred Stepan, 91–120. New York: Columbia University Press.

Marks, Monica. 2013. "Youth Politics and Tunisian Salafism: Understanding the Jihadi Currnet." *Mediterranean Politics*. 18(1): 104–11.

Marsad. 2014a. "Vote sur un amendement de l'article 6: Supprimer la liberté de 'conscience,'" January 4. https://majles.marsad.tn/fr/vote/52caefeb12bdaa7f9b90f45d

2014b. "Vote sur un amendement n°42 de l'article premier," January 4. https://majles.marsad.tn/fr/vote/52c92fa112bdaa7f9b90f423

Masoud, Tarek. 2014. *Counting Islam: Religion, Class, and Elections in Egypt. Problems of International Politics*. Cambridge: Cambridge University Press.

2018. "Not Ready for Democracy: Modernisation, Pluralism and the Arab Spring." In *Revisiting the Arab Uprisings*, edited by Stephane Lacroix and Jean-Pierre Filiu, 111–40. New York: Oxford University Press.

Masress. 2013. "Akhbār Mohamed Morsi: Fahmi Huwaydi Yadʿū Mohamed Morsi Li-Intikhābāt Ri'āsiyya Mubekkira," January 29. www.masress.com/akhbartoday/69697

Massicard, Elise. 2012. "The Uses of Team Rivalry: Reconsidering Party Factionalism in Turkey." In *Negotiating Political Power in Turkey*, edited by Elise Massicard and Nicole Watts, 55–76. London: Routledge.

Massicard, Elise and Nicole Watts, eds. 2012. *Negotiating Political Power in Turkey: Breaking Up the Party*. New York: Routledge.

Matesan, Ioana Emy. 2020. "Organizational Dynamics, Public Condemnation and the Impetus to Disengage from Violence." *Terrorism and Political Violence*. 32(5): 949–69.

Maududi, Sayyid Abul Aʿla. 2002. "The Political Theory of Islam." In *Modernist and Fundamentalist Debates in Islam*, edited by Mansoor Muaddel and Kamran Talattof, 263–71. New York: Palgrave Macmillan.

McCarthy, Rory. 2018a. *Inside Tunisia's al-Nahda: Between Politics and Preaching*. Cambridge Middle East Studies. Cambridge: Cambridge University Press.

2018b. "When Islamists Lose: The Politicization of Tunisia's Ennahda Movement." *The Middle East Journal*. 72(3): 365–84.

McDonnell, Duncan and Luis Cabrera. 2019. "The Right-Wing Populism of India's Bharatiya Janata Party (and Why Comparativists Should Care)." *Democratization*. 26(3): 484–501.

Mecham, R. Quinn. 2004. "From the Ashes of Virtue, a Promise of Light: The Transformation of Political Islam in Turkey." *Third World Quarterly*. 25(2): 339–58.

Meddeb, Hamza. 2019. "Ennahda's Uneasy Exit from Political Islam." *Carnegie In Brief*, September 5. https://carnegie-mec.org/2019/09/05/ennahda-s-uneasy-exit-from-political-islam-pub-79789

Media Ownership Monitor Tunisia. 2020. "Zitouna TV," June 4. https://tunisia.mom-rsf.org/en/media/detail/outlet/zitouna-tv/

Mert, Nuray. 2009. "Sivil istibdat." Radikal, November 17. www.radikal.com.tr/yazarlar/nuray-mert/sivil-istibdat-964696/

2010. "Iki kere hayır!" Hürriyet. www.hurriyet.com.tr/iki-kere-hayir-15717056

Michels, Robert. 1915. *Political Parties: A Sociological Study of the Oligarchical Tendencies of Modern Democracy*. New York: Hearst's International Library Company.

Middle East Monitor. 2014. "Islamists Besiege TV Channel HQ for Disseminating False Information," February 15. www.middleeastmonitor.com/20140215-islamists-besiege-tv-channel-hq-for-disseminating-false-information/

Middle East Institute. 2013. "A Conversation with the FJP's Amr Darrag," May 28. http://education.mei.edu/content/conversation-fjps-amr-darrag

Milli Nizam Partisi. 1970. "Program ve Tüzük." http://hdl.handle.net/11543/801

Milliyet. 2001. "Abdullah Gül ile Söyleşi," August 27.

2010. "Bitaraf olan bertaraf olur." www.milliyet.com.tr/siyaset/erdogan-bitaraf-olan-bertaraf-olur-1277904

2013. "Bülent Arınç'tan 'Gezi Parkı' açıklaması," June 1. www.milliyet.com.tr/siyaset/bulent-arinctan-gezi-parki-aciklamasi-1717157

Mitchell, Richard Paul. 1969. *The Society of the Muslim Brothers*. Oxford: Oxford University Press.

Moslem, Mehdi. 2002. *Factional Politics in Post-Khomeini Iran*. Syracuse: Syracuse University Press.

Mounk, Yascha. 2018. *The People vs Democracy*. Cambridge: Harvard University Press.

Mozaffari, M. 2007. "What Is Islamism? History and Definition of a Concept." *Totalitarian Movements and Political Religions*. 8(1): 17–33.

MTI. 1981. The Founding Statement of the Islamic Trend Movement. https://ar-ar.facebook.com/nahdha.beb.bhar/photos/البيان-التأسيسي-لحركة-الاتجاه-الإسلامي- حركة /907690879244424/ بتاريخ- 1981-6-6 وطنةيشه لاحقا- النهضة-

Mudde, Cas and Cristobal R. Kaltwasser. 2017. *Populism: A Very Short Introduction*. New York: Oxford University Press.

Muslim Brotherhood. 1995. "The Statement of Muslim Brothers on Democracy." http://kurzman.unc.edu/files/2011/06/MB_1995_Statement_on_Democracy.pdf

2006. "Our Testimony." www.ikhwanweb.com/article.php?id=4185

2007a. "Muslim Brotherhood Initiatives for Reform in Egypt." www.ikhwanweb.com/article.php?id=797

2007b. "The Muslim Brotherhood's Program for the Parliamentary Elections of 2005." www.ikhwanweb.com/article.php?id=811

2010. "Bylaws of the International Muslim Brotherhood." www.ikhwanweb.com/article.php?id=22687&ref=search.php

Nasr, Seyyed Vali Reza. 2005. "The Rise of 'Muslim Democracy.'" *Journal of Democracy*. 16(2): 13–27.

Netterstrøm, Kasper Ly. 2015. "The Islamists' Compromise in Tunisia." *Journal of Democracy*. 26(4): 110–24.

Norris, Pippa and Inglehart, Ronald. 2019. *Cultural Backlash: Trump, Brexit, and Authoritarian Populism*. Cambridge: Cambridge University Press.

NTV. 2011. "Erdoğan: Bazı Kitaplar Bombadan Daha Tesirli (Some Books Have Greater Impact than Bombs)," June 10. www.ntv.com.tr/turkiye/erdogan-bazi-kitaplar-bombadan-daha-tesirli,V6-67sjVaUuyUC-AnarjHlg

2013. "Erdoğan: Başörtülülere Saldırdılar," June 9. www.ntv.com.tr/turkiye/erdogan-basortululere-saldirdilar,MY8fETQDTESWrDoEc5_tbQ
2020. "Cumhurbaşkanı Erdoğan: Artık bu yanlış tabuların yıkılması lazım," July 30. www.ntv.com.tr/turkiye/artik-bu-yanlis-tabularin-yikilmasi-lazim, sc2oLQfnSE2MQ3Oh2moQsQ
Nugent, Elizabeth R. 2018. "The Psychology of Repression and Polarization in Authoritarian Regimes." *Middle East Initiative.* June: 44.
2020. "The Psychology of Repression and Polarization." *World Politics* 72(2): 291–334.
2020. *After Repression: How Polarization Derails Democratic Transition.* Princeton: Princeton University Press.
Öktem, Kerem and Karabekir Akkoyunlu. 2016. "Exit from Democracy: Illiberal Governance in Turkey and Beyond." *Southeast European and Black Sea Studies.* 16(4): 469–80.
Ongun, Selin. 2015. "Fıratla Söyleşi: Erdoğan'a karşı çıkan dayağı yer." Cumhuriyet, August 17. www.cumhuriyet.com.tr/koseyazisi/346935/_Erdogan_a_karsi_cikan_dayagi_yer_.html
Öngür, Hakan Övünç. 2020. "Performing through Friday Khutbas: Re-instrumentalization of Religion in the New Turkey." *Third World Quarterly.* 41(3): 434–52.
Öniş, Ziya. 2015a. "Monopolising the Centre: The AKP and the Uncertain Path of Turkish Democracy." *The International Spectator.*
2015b. "Democracy in Uncertain Times: Inequality and Democratic Development in the Global North and Global South." SSRN Scholarly Paper ID 2641477. Rochester: Social Science Research Network.
Özbudun, Ergun. 2000. *Contemporary Turkish Politics: Challenges to Democratic Consolidation.* Boulder: Lynne Rienner Publishers.
2006. "From Political Islam to Conservative Democracy: The Case of the Justice and Development Party in Turkey." *South European Society and Politics.* 11(3–4): 543–57.
2014. "AKP at the Crossroads: Erdoğan's Majoritarian Drift." *South European Society and Politics.* 19(2): 155–67.
Özbey, Ipek. 2020. "Davutoğlu: 'Mesela Hakan Şükür siyasi ayaktı, görevli olarak gelmişlerdi!'" Cumhuriyet, July 30. www.cumhuriyet.com.tr/haber/gelecek-partisi-genel-baskani-ahmet-davutoglu-mesela-hakan-sukur-siyasi-ayakti-gorevli-olarak-gelmislerdi-1752647
Özel, Soli. 2009. "Seçimli Otoriterlik." HaberTurk, September 16. www.haberturk.com/yazarlar/soli-ozel/221616-secimli-otoriterlik
Özkul, Ismet. 2011. "KHK depreminin hasarı büyük olacak." HaberTurk, November 14. www.haberturk.com/yazarlar/ismet-ozkul/687750-khk-depreminin-hasari-buyuk-olacak
Öztürk, Ahmet Erdi. 2016. "Turkey's Diyanet under AKP Rule: From Protector to Imposer of State Ideology?" *Southeast European and Black Sea Studies.* 16(4): 619–35.
Pahwa, Sumita. 2017. "Pathways of Islamist Adaptation: The Egyptian Muslim Brothers' Lessons for Inclusion Moderation Theory." *Democratization.* 24(6): 1066–84.

Panebianco, Angelo. 1988. *Political Parties: Organization and Power*. Cambridge: Cambridge University Press.
Pargeter, Alison. 2013. *The Muslim Brotherhood: From Opposition to Power*. London: Saqi.
  2016. *Return to Shadows: The Muslim Brotherhood and An-Nahda since the Arab Spring*, Saqi.
Parsons, Talcott. 1985. *Talcott Parsons on Institutions and Social Evolution: Selected Writings*. Chicago: University of Chicago Press.
Pehlivan, Barış and Barış Terkoğlu. 2019. *Metastaz*. Istanbul: Kırmızıkedi Yayınevi.
Pempel, T. J. 1990. *Uncommon Democracies: The One-Party Dominant Regimes*. Ithaca: Cornell University Press.
Perkins, Kenneth J. 2004. *A History of Modern Tunisia*. Cambridge: Cambridge University Press.
Pew Research Center. 2013. The World's Muslims. www.pewforum.org/2013/04/30/the-worlds-muslims-religion-politics-society-overview/
Pridham, Geoffrey. 2003. "Party Systems, Factionalism, and Patterns of Democratization." In *Factional Politics and Democratization*, edited by Richard Gillespie, Lourdes Lopez Nieto, and Michael Waller, 8–30. New York: Routledge.
Przeworski, Adam and Fernando Limongi. 1997. "Modernization: Theories and Facts." *World Politics*. 49(2): 155–83.
Przeworski, Adam and John D. Sprague. 1986. *Paper Stones: A History of Electoral Socialism*. Chicago: University of Chicago Press.
Puddington, Arch. 2013. "Freedom in the World 2013: Democratic Breakthroughs in Balance, Selected Data from Freedom House's Annual Survey of Political Rights and Civil Liberties." Freedom House. https://freedomhouse.org/sites/default/files/2020-02/FIW_2013_Booklet.pdf
Quṭb, Sayyid. 2003. *Milestones*. Chicago: International Islamic Federation of Student Organizations; distributed by KAZI Publications.
Refah Partisi. 1995. "Seçim Beyannamesi." https://acikerisim.tbmm.gov.tr/xmlui/handle/11543/763
Reporters Without Borders. 2020. "2020 World Press Freedom Index Ranking," July 26. https://rsf.org/en/ranking
Reuters. 2012a. "Tunisia's Ennahda to Oppose Sharia in Constitution," March 26. www.reuters.com/article/us-tunisia-constitution-idUSBRE82P0E820120326
  2012b, April 24. *Reuters'* interview with Aboul Fotouh, April 24, 2012.
Revkin, Mara. 2012. "Parliament Names Constituent Assembly Members, but Many Refuse Their Seats." *The Atlantic Council*, June 13. www.atlanticcouncil.org/blogs/menasource/parliament-names-constituent-assembly-members-but-many-refuse-their-seats/
Rogenhofer, Julius M. and Ayala Panievsky. 2020. "Antidemocratic Populism in Power: Comparing Erdoğan's Turkey with Modi's India and Netanyahu's Israel." *Democratization*. 27(8): 1394–412.
Ross, Michael L. 2001. "Does Oil Hinder Democracy?" *World Politics*. 53(3): 325–61.

Rostow, Walt. 1971. *Politics and the Stages of Growth*. Cambridge: Cambridge Books.
Roy, Olivier. 1994. *The Failure of Political Islam*. Cambridge: Harvard University Press.
Rubin, Barry M. and Metin Heper. 2002. *Political Parties in Turkey*. Hove: Psychology Press.
Rueschemeyer Dietrich, Evelyne Stevens, and John Stevens. 1992. *Capitalist Development and Democracy*. Chicago: Chicago University Press.
Saatçioğlu, Beken 2011. "Revisiting the Role of Credible EU Membership Conditionality for EU Compliance: The Turkish Case." *Uluslararası İlişkiler/ International Relations*. 8(31): 23–44.
    2014. "AKP's 'Europeanization' in Civilianization, Rule of Law and Fundamental Freedoms: The Primacy of Domestic Politics." *Journal of Balkan and Near Eastern Studies*. 16(1): 86–101.
    2016. "De-Europeanisation in Turkey: The Case of the Rule of Law." *South European Society and Politics*. 21(1): 133–46.
Sabah. 2013a. "Başbakan'dan Gezi Parkı açıklaması," June 1. www.sabah.com.tr/gundem/2013/06/01/basbakan-erdogan-konusuyor
    2013b. "Basbakan Erdoğan konusuyor." www.sabah.com.tr/gundem/2013/06/01/basbakan-erdogan-konusuyor
Sadiki, Larbi. 2016. "Tunisia: Ennahda's 'Second Founding'." Al Jazeera Center for Studies, June 29.
    2020. "Intra-Party Democracy in Tunisia's Ennahda." Middle East Institute. www.mei.edu/publications/intra-party-democracy-tunisias-ennahda-ghannouchi-and-pitfalls-charismatic-leadership
Sanchez-Cuenca, Ignacio. 2004. "Party Moderation and Politicians' Ideological Rigidity." *Party Politics*. 10(May): 325–42.
Sarfati, Yusuf. 2017. "How Turkey's Slide to Authoritarianism Defies Modernization Theory." *Turkish Studies*. 18(3): 395–415.
Sarıbay, Ali Yaşar. 1985. *Türkiye'de Modernleşme, Din, ve Parti Politikası: Milli Selâmet Partisi Örnek Olayı*. Istanbul: Alan Yayıncılık.
    2005. "Milli Nizam Hareketi'nin Kuruluşu ve Programının İçeriği." In İslamcılık. Second edition. *Modern Türkiye'de Siyasi Düşünce*. 6: 576–91. Istanbul: İletişim Yayınları.
Sartori, Giovanni. 1976. *Parties and Party Systems: Volume 1 – A Framework for Analysis*. Cambridge: Cambridge University Press.
Sayarı, Sabri. 2002. "The Changing Party System." In *Politics, Parties, and Elections in Turkey*, edited by Sabri Sayarı and Yılmaz Esmer. Boulder: Lynne Rienner Publishers.
Sazak, Derya. 2001. "Interview with Tayyip Erdoğan." *Milliyet*, August 27.
Schedler, Andreas. 2006. "The Logic of Electoral Authoritarianism." In *Electoral Authoritarianism: Dynamics of Unfree Compettition*, edited by Andreas Schedler. Boulder: Lynne Rienner Publishers.
Scheppele, Kim Lane. 2018. "Autocratic Legalism." *The University of Chicago Law Review*. 85(2): 545–84.
Schneider, Julie. 2012. "Tunisie : d'où vient l'argent d'Ennahda?" *Le Point International*, February 10. www.lepoint.fr/monde/tunisie-d-ou-vient-l-argent-d-ennahda-10-02-2012-1430241_24.php

Schumpeter, Joseph A. 2003. *Capitalism, Socialism and Democracy*. New York: Routledge.
Schwedler, Jillian. 2006. *Faith in Moderation: Islamist Parties in Jordan and Yemen*. Cambridge: Cambridge University Press.
  2011a. "Can Islamists Become Moderates? Rethinking the Inclusion–Moderation Hypothesis." *World Politics*. 63(2): 347–76.
  2011b. "Studying Political Islam." *International Journal of Middle East Studies*. 43(1): 135–37.
  2013. "Islamists in Power? Inclusion, Moderation, and the Arab Uprisings." *Middle East Development Journal*. 5(1): 1–18.
Sever, Ahmet. 2015. *Abdullah Gül ile 12 Yıl Yaşadım, Gördüm, Yazdım*. Istanbul: Doğan Kitap.
  2018. *İçimde Kalmasın Tanıklığımdır*. Istanbul: Destek Yayınları.
Shea, Catherine. 2013. "Egypt's Morsi Continues Pursuit of New Civil Society Restrictions." Freedom House, June 18. https://freedomhouse.org/blog/egypt's-morsi-continues-pursuit-new-civil-society-restrictions
Shehata, Samer and Joshua Stacher. 2006. "The Brotherhood Goes to Parliament." *Middle East Report*. 240(October): 32.
Singerman, Diane, Amr Hamzawy, Nathan Brown, and Marc Lynch. 2007. "The Muslim Brotherhood's Party Platform." Carnegie Endowment for International Peace. https://carnegieendowment.org/files/07-11-16-muslim-brotherhood.pdf
Smith, Lydia. 2018. "Turkey Wants to Make Adultery Illegal." *The Independent*, February 27. www.independent.co.uk/news/world/middle-east/turkey-adultery-cheating-crime-president-recep-erdogan-eu-infidelity-law-a8230281.html
Sokhey, Sarah Wilson and A. Kadir Yildirim. 2013. "Economic Liberalization and Political Moderation: The Case of Anti-System Parties." *Party Politics*. 19(2): 230–55.
Soltan, Gamal Abdel Gawad, Ahmed Nagui Qamha, and Subhi 'Asilah. 2011. "Arab Barometer Survey, June 2011." *Al Ahram Center for Political and Strategic Studies*. www.arabbarometer.org/wp-content/uploads/Egypt_Public_Opinion_Survey_2011.pdf
Somer, Murat. 2007. "Moderate Islam and Secularist Opposition in Turkey: Implications for the World, Muslims and Secular Democracy." *Third World Quarterly*. 28(7): 1271–89.
  2017. "Conquering versus Democratizing the State: Political Islamists and Fourth Wave Democratization in Turkey and Tunisia." *Democratization*. 24(6): 1025–43.
Souli, Sarah. 2016. "Why Tunisia's Top Islamist Party Rebranded Itself." Al-Monitor, May 23. www.al-monitor.com/pulse/originals/2016/05/tunisia-ennahda-islamist-party-rebranding-congress.html
Stacher, Joshua A. 2002. "Post-Islamist Rumblings in Egypt: The Emergence of the Wasat Party." *Middle East Journal*. 56(3): 415–32.
Stepan, Alfred. 2012. "Tunisia's Transition and the Twin Tolerations." *Journal of Democracy*. 23(2): 89–103.
  2017. "Mutual Accommodation: Islamic and Secular Parties and Tunisia's Democratic Transition." In *Democratic Transition in the Muslim World: A*

Global Perspective, edited by Alfred Stepan, 43–72. New York: Columbia University Press.
Stokes, Susan C., Thad Dunning, Marcelo Nazareno, and Valeria Brusco. 2013. *Brokers, Voters, and Clientelism: The Puzzle of Distributive Politics*. Cambridge: Cambridge University Press.
Sullivan, Denis Joseph and Sana Abed-Kotob. 1995. *Islam in Contemporary Egypt: Civil Society vs the State*. Boulder: Lynne Rienner Publishers.
Svolik, M. W. 2019. "Polarization versus democracy." *Journal of Democracy*. 30(3): 20–32.
T24. 2013. "Babuşcu: Gelecek 10 yıl, liberaller gibi eski paydaşlarımızın arzuladığı gibi olmayacak," April 1. https://t24.com.tr/haber/babuscu-onumuzdeki-10-yil-liberaller-gibi-eski-paydaslarimizin-kabullenecegi-gibi-olmayacak,226892
Tabaar, Mohammad Ayotollahi. 2018. *Religious Statecraft: The Politics of Islam in Iran*. New York: Columbia Unviersity Press.
Tamimi, Azzam. 2001. *Rachid Ghannouchi: A Democrat within Islamism*. New York: Oxford University Press.
Tammam, Hussam. 2010. *Abdel-Monem Abu El-Fotouh: Shahid 'ala Tarikh al-Haraka al-Islamiya Fi Misr, 1970–1984*. Cairo: Dar El-Shorouk.
  2012. "The Ruralization of the Muslim Brotherhood: How Urbanism Retreated in Favor of Urbanism." Marased, Bibliotheca Alexandrina.
Tanıyıcı, Şaban. 2003. "Transformation of Political Islam in Turkey: Islamist Welfare Party's Pro-EU Turn." *Party Politics*. 9(4): 463–83.
Tekin, Üzeyir. 2004. *AK Parti'nin Muhafazakâr Demokrat Kimliği*. Ankara: Orient.
Tepe, Sultan. 2012. "Moderation of Religious Parties: Electoral Constraints, Ideological Commitments, and the Democratic Capacities of Religious Parties in Israel and Turkey." *Political Research Quarterly*. 65(3): 467–85.
  2019. "The Inclusion–Moderation Thesis: An Overview." In *Oxford Research Encyclopedia of Politics*. New York: Oxford University Press.
Tessler, Mark A. 1993. *The Origins of Popular Support for Islamist Movements: A Political Economy Analysis*. Milwaukee: Center for International Studies.
Tezcür, Güneş Murat. 2010a. *Muslim Reformers in Iran and Turkey: The Paradox of Moderation*. Austin: University of Texas Press.
  2010b. "The Moderation Theory Revisited: The Case of Islamic Political Actors." *Party Politics*. 16(1): 69–88.
The Economist Intelligence Unit. 2013. "Former Prime Minister Resigns from Hizb Al-Nahda," December 29. http://country.eiu.com/article.aspx?articleid=342624618&Country=Tunisia&topic=Politics&subtopic=F_5
Tibi, Bassam. 2008. "Islamist Parties and Democracy: Why They Can't Be Democratic." *Journal of Democracy*. 19(3): 43–48.
  2012. *Islamism and Islam*. New Haven: Yale University Press.
  2013. "A Critique of the Dominating Narrative in Western Islamic Studies." *Soundings: An Interdisciplinary Journal*. 96(4): 431–49.
Toprak, Binnaz. 1990. "Religion as State Ideology in a Secular Setting: The Turkish–Islamic Synthesis." In *Aspects of Religion in Secular Turkey*, edited by Malcolm Wagstaff, 10–15. Occasional Paper Series 40. Durham: Center for Middle Easter and Islamic Studies.

Trager, Eric. 2011. "The Unbreakable Muslim Brotherhood." *Foreign Affairs.* www.foreignaffairs.com/articles/north-africa/2011-09-01/unbreakable-muslim-brotherhood
  2016. *Arab Fall: How the Muslim Brotherhood Won and Lost Egypt in 891 Days.* Washington, DC: Georgetown University Press.
TRT Haber. 2013. "Milli İradeye Saygı mitingleri devam ediyor," June 17. www.trthaber.com/haber/gundem/milli-iradeye-saygi-mitingleri-devam-ediyor-89784.html/
Tuğal, Cihan. 2009. *Passive Revolution: Absorbing the Islamic Challenge to Capitalism.* Stanford: Stanford University Press
Tuğal, Cihan. 2002. "Islamism in Turkey: Beyond Instrument and Meaning." *Economy and Society.* 31(1): 85–111.
Tunisie Numerique. 2020. "Tunisie: La liste des 100 dirigeants d'Ennahdha," September 16. www.tunisienumerique.com/tunisie-la-liste-des-100-dirigeants-dennahdha-ayant-appele-ghannouchi-a-ne-pas-se-presenter-pour-un-nouveau-mandat/
USA TODAY. 2012. "Egypt's Opposition Leaders under Investigation," December 27. www.usatoday.com/story/news/world/2012/12/27/egypts-prosecutor-opposition-probe/1793691/
Waldner, David and Ellen Lust. 2018. "Unwelcome Change: Coming to Terms with Democratic Backsliding." *Annual Review of Political Science.* 21(May): 93–113
Waltz, Susan. 1986. "Islamist Appeal in Tunisia." *Middle East Journal.* 40(4): 651–70.
Wasat Party. 2009. "Party Program." https://kurzman.unc.edu/wp-content/uploads/sites/1410/2011/06/EGY-2011-Hizb-al-Wasat.pdf
  2013. "bayān ḥizb al-wasaṭ ʿan al-azma al-ḥāliyya," July 1.
Weslaty, Lilia. 2013. "Nominations Dans Le Secteur Public: 87% Pour La Troïka Dont 93% En Faveur Des Partisans d'Ennahdha." Nawaat, March 22. http://nawaat.org/portail/2013/03/22/93-des-nominations-dans-le-secteur-public-ont-beneficie-a-des-partisans-dennahdha/
Wickham, Carrie Rosefsky. 2002. *Mobilizing Islam: Religion, Activism, and Political Change in Egypt.* New York: Columbia University Press.
  2004. "The Path to Moderation: Strategy and Learning in the Formation of Egypt's Wasat Party." *Comparative Politics.* 36(2): 205–28.
  2013. *The Muslim Brotherhood: Evolution of an Islamist Movement.* New Jersey: Princeton University Press.
Wiktorowicz, Quintan. 2004. *Islamic Activism: A Social Movement Theory Approach.* Bloomington: Indiana University Press.
Willi, Victor. 2021. *The Fourth Ordeal: A History of the Muslim Brotherhood in Egypt, 1968–2018.* Cambridge: Cambridge University Press.
Wilson, Frank L. 1994. "The Sources of Party Change: The Social Democratic Parties of Britain, France, Germany, and Spain." In *How Political Parties Work: Perspectives from Within*, edited by Lawson Kay, 263–83. Westports: Praeger.
Wolf, Anne. 2017. *Political Islam in Tunisia: The History of Ennahda.* New York: Oxford University Press.
  2021. "Is Rached Ghannouchi Ennahda's President for Life?" POMED, July.

World Bank. 2018. "Urban Population in Turkey, Egypt, Tunisia" The World Bank https://data.worldbank.org/indicator/SP.URB.TOTL?locations=TR-EG-TN

2021. "GNI per capita, Atlas Method (Current US$)." *National Accounts Data*. https://data.worldbank.org/indicator/NY.GNP.PCAP.CD?locations=TR-EG-TN

Wuthrich, F. Michael and Sabri Çiftçi. 2020. "Islamist Parties, Intraparty Organizational Dynamics, and Moderation as Strategic Behaviour." *Mediterranean Politics*: 1–23.

Yadav, Stacey Philbrick. 2010. "Understanding 'What Islamists Want:' Public Debate and Contestation in Lebanon and Yemen." *Middle East Journal*. 64(2): 199–213.

Yardımcı-Geyikçi, Şebnem and Özlem Tür. 2018. "Rethinking the Tunisian Miracle: A Party Politics View." *Democratization*. 25(5): 787–803.

Yavuz, M. Hakan. 2003. *Islamic Political Identity in Turkey: Religion and Global Politics*. New York: Oxford University Press.

2009. *Secularism and Muslim Democracy in Turkey*. Cambridge Middle East Studies. Cambridge: Cambridge University Press.

2013. *Toward an Islamic Enlightenment: The Gulen Movement*. Oxford: Oxford University Press.

2016. "Cemaatçiler savaşı kaybetmiş Naziler gibi! Hoca'ya karşı isyan var." www.hurriyet.com.tr/gundem/prof-dr-hakan-yavuz-cemaatciler-savasi-kaybetmis-naziler-gibi-hocaya-karsi-isyan-var-40203038

2018. "A Framework for Understanding the Intra-Islamist Conflict between the AK Party and the Gülen Movement." *Politics, Religion & Ideology*. 19(1): 11–32.

Yeni Akit. 2018. "Erdoğan Özbekistan'da Kur'an okudu," May 1. www.yeniakit.com.tr/haber/erdogan-ozbekistanda-kuran-okudu-457548.html

Yenigün, Halil Ibrahim. 2014. "Turkish Islamism in the Post-Gezi Park Era." *American Journal of Islamic Social Sciences*. 31(1): 15.

Yeni Safak. 2011. "Dün nerede iseler bugün de oradalar." www.yenisafak.com/gundem/dun-neredeler-ise-bugun-de-oradalar-323681

2018. "Artık Bu Yanlış Tabuları Yıkalım," October 5. www.yenisafak.com/gundem/artik-bu-yanlistabulari-yikalim-3400059

Yeşilada, Birol. 1999. "The Refah Party Phenomenon in Turkey." In *Comparative Political Parties and Party Elites: Essays in Honor of Samuel J. Eldersveld*, edited by Birol Yeşilada, 123–50. Ann Harbor: University of Michigan Press.

Yeşilada, Birol and Barry Rubin, eds. 2010. *Islamization of Turkey under the AKP Rule*. London: Routledge.

Yetkin, Murat. 2014. "Hayrünnisa Gül: Asıl intifadayı ben başlatacağım!" *Radikal*, August 20. www.radikal.com.tr/yazarlar/murat-yetkin/hayrunnisa-gul-asil-intifadayi-ben-baslatacagim--1207895/

Yılmaz, Serpil. 2008. "Çalık'ın kullandığı kredinin koşulları." *Milliyet*, July 24. www.milliyet.com.tr/yazarlar/serpil-yilmaz/calik-in-kullandigi-kredinin-kosullari-970454

Zariski, Raphael. 1960. "Party Factions and Comparative Politics: Some Preliminary Observations." *Midwest Journal of Political Science*. 4(1): 27–51.

Zineb, Myriam Ben. 2016. "Ennahda Brings Fresh Blood to Party's New Executive Bureau." Al-Monitor, July 29. www.al-monitor.com/pulse/politics/2016/07/tunisia-executive-bureau-composition-young-senior-members.html

Zollner, Barbara. 2009. *The Muslim Brotherhood: Hasan al-Hudaybi and Ideology.* New York: Routledge.

   2021. "The Metamorphosis of Social Movements into Political Parties. The Egyptian Muslim Brotherhood and the Tunisian al-Nahda as Cases for a Reflection on Party Institutionalisation Theory." *British Journal of Middle Eastern Studies.* 48(3): 370–87.

Index

Abdessalem, Rafik, 244, 245, 250, 252, 253, 267
Abduh, Muhammad, 154
Abdülhamid II, 85
Abdullah, Talaat, 191, 192, 196
Abou Khalil, Haythem, 180
Aboul Fotouh, Abdel Moneim, 54, 158, 165, 168, 180, 201
   criticisms of Mohammed Morsi, 191–92, 194, 199
   democracy, views on, 161, 163
   imprisonment, 152, 200
   and Masr Kawiya, 181
   middle generation of Muslim Brotherhood, 154
   presidential campaign, 188
   Sharia, views on, 159, 162
   sidelining from Muslim Brotherhood, 168, 174
   women's rights, views on, 164
Abu al-Nasr, Muhammad Hamid, 168
Adalet ve Kalkınma Partisi. *See* Justice and Development Party (AKP)
Afghani, Jamal al-Din al-, 154
Ahmad Bey, 27–28
Ain Shams University, 180
Al-Ahram, 191
Al-Akhbar, 191
Al-Azhar, 180
   compared to Tunisia's Zaituna, 30
   Muslim Brotherhood's desire to control, 146, 189
   Nasser's subordination of, 29
Alexandria, 177
   concentration of educated youth, 154, 170, 180
   and "ruralization" of Muslim Brotherhood, 172
Al-Fajr, 252
Algeria, 216
   Islamic Salvation Front (FIS), 8, 13, 74, 262

Al-Gomhuria, 191
Al-Maarifa, 205–206
Amayreh, Khaled, 198
Amin, Gomaa, 169
Ankara group. *See* AKP, liberal faction within
Arab Spring, 8, 13, 17, 176
   Egypt, 143, 166, 176
   Tunisia, 224
Arafa, Sabri, 171
Arbaoui, Noureddine, 245
Arınç, Bülent, 96, 100
   defense of press freedom, 138
   engagement with protestors, 141
   liberal democrat wing in AKP, 98, 117, 118, 125, 141
   marginalization within AKP, 106, 108, 110, 115, 116
   party democracy, views on, 100, 104–105
Asyut, 171
Atalay, Beşir, 118, 141
   liberal democrat wing in AKP, 102
   marginalization within AKP, 110
Atatürk, Mustafa Kemal
   comparison with Nasser, 29–30, 188
   leader of Turkish war of independence, 28
   mausoleum, 138
Awa, Mohammed Salim Al-, 222
Ayadi, Fathi Al-, 244
Aydın, Mehmet, 103

Bab Souika, 214
Babacan, Ali, 141
   liberal democrat wing in AKP, 102
Badie, Mohammed, 155
   as General Guide of Muslim Brotherhood, 168–69, 179
   imprisonment, 200
Baha'is. *See* Egypt, minority rights
Baltagy, Mohammed al-, 174, 186, 200

Index

Banna, Hasan al-
  assassination of, 150
  formation of Muslim Brotherhood, 146, 154
  influence on old guard, 160, 162, 173
  understanding of Islam and politics, 9, 146–50, 154, 206
Bardakoğlu, Ali, 129
Bayoumi, Rashad al-, 165, 169
Belaid, Chokri
  assassination of, 231, 232
Belgium
  Catholic Party, 64
Ben Abbes, Aroua, 247
Ben Ali, Zine El Abidin
  ouster, 202, 224–26, 241
  regime of, 57, 212, 214, 222, 223
  repression of Islamists, 34, 50, 52, 203, 214–16, 221, 226, 239, 240, 253
  secularism, 32, 232
Ben Jaafar, Mustafa, 228, 233
Ben Mohammed, Imen, 248
Bhiri, Noureddine, 247
Bin Salem, Osama, 252
Bishry, Tareq al-, 178, 222
Bouazizi, Mohammed
  self-immolation and Arab Spring, 1, 202, 224
Bourguiba, Habib, 28, 208, 232
  MTI's criticisms of, 207
  relaxation of secularism, 32, 205
  removal from power, 209, 212
  secular reforms, 30, 205, 240
Brahmi, Mohamed, 233

Cairo, 1, 17, 143, 146, 189
  concentration of educated youth, 154, 170, 180
  and "ruralization" of Muslim Brotherhood, 172
Çelik, Ömer, 109
Chammam, Mohammed, 209, 211
Chammen, Bechir, 245
Chebbi, Ahmed Najib, 233
Chorou, Sadeq
  electoralism in Ennahda, 203, 209, 213, 214, 225, 232, 237, 244
  exile, 215
  regime repression, 239
  Salafi ties, 226
  sidelining within Ennahda, 226, 245, 249
Çiçek, Cemil, 103, 108
cold war, 63, 86, 96
Coptic Christians. *See* Egypt, minority rights

Dakahlia, 171
Davutoğlu, Ahmet, 103, 126
  attempt to capture AKP, 116–18
  resignation from AKP, 110, 142
da'wa religious activism, 15, 93, 95, 101, 147, 148, 155, 161, 170, 171, 187, 205–207, 225, 246, 248
Demirtaş, Selahattin, 134
democracy
  definition of, 10
  democratic backsliding, 11, 21, 263–66
Democratic Constitutional Rally (RCD), 214, 226
democratization, 10
din wa dawla (religion and state), 98, 147, 157, 158, 207, 251
Doğan Media Company, 115, 138
Doğan, Aydın, 115
Doulatli, Zied, 223

Egypt
  colonial rule, 27, 146
  democratic transition, 144
  economic development of, 31, 36–38, 45
  Egyptian Bloc, 184
  Egyptian Current Party, 181
  Free Officers' Coup, 29, 150
  Freedom and Justice Party (FJP), 3, 54, 172, 179, 182, 197
  independence, 28
  Islamic middle class, 34
  Islamic Society (Jamaat al-Islamiyya), 146, 151, 195, 205
  Labor Party, 152
  Masr Kawiya, 181, 191, 194
  military intervention, 41, 57, 144, 200–201, 264
  minority rights, 163–65, 171, 183, 193–94
  Napoleon Bonaparte's invasion of, 27
  National Council for Women and the National Council for Childhood and Motherhood, 183
  National Democratic Party (NDP), 153
  National Salvation Front (NSF), 192
  Ottoman rule, 27
  political transition, 189–90
  reform and modernization, 27, 146
  religious conservatism in, 38–39, 238
  Renaissance Party (Nahda), 180
  secularism, 28, 32
  Tamarrod (Rebellion) movement, 198–99, 233
  terror attacks, 146, 152
  2010 revolution. *See* Arab spring
  war with Israel, 151

Eker, Mehdi, 109
Ellouze, Habib
  electoralism in Ennahda, 203, 225, 232, 235, 237, 238
  regime repression, 239
  Salafi ties, 230, 252
  sidelining within Ennahda, 245, 249
Emre, Süleyman Arif, 87
Ennahda
  AKP, comparison with, 253, 261
  coalition-building. *See* Tunisia, Troika government
  constitutional process, 235–36
  democratic commitments, 3, 14, 37, 50, 55, 202, 204, 219–20, 224, 228, 255, 260
  democrats within. *See* liberal faction
  economic policies, 36, 254
  electoral losses, 81, 237
  electoralist faction, 203, 213–15, 225
  exile, 34, 215–16
  internal communication, 249–52
  Islam and democracy, understanding of, 220, 222, 230–31, 235–36
  liberal and electoralist factions, struggle between, 216, 225–26, 232
  liberal faction, 5, 21, 80–81, 204, 241–42, 254
  media presence, 252
  moderation, explanations for, 52–54, 238–41, 260
  Muslim Brotherhood, comparison with, 15, 258, 259
  organizational structure, 242–43
  party finance, 246–47, 258
  party platform, 212, 223
  political compromise, commitment to, 41, 59, 223, 233–34, 236–38, 263
  protests against, 57
  radicals within. *See* electoralist faction
  recruitment and promotion, 244–46
  repression of, 215, 221
  Salafism, competition with, 221–22, 231–32, 258
  second founding, 19, 21, 77, 80, 241
  selective incentives, liberal control over, 247–49
  Shura Council, 242–43
  Tunisia's political transition, role in, 17, 18, 39, 224, 226–28
  women in, 247–48
Ennaifer, Hamid, 205, 207
Erbakan, Fatih, 86, 136
Erbakan, Necmettin, 97
  centralized style of rule, 100, 103, 106
  electoralism, 89, 94
  founding of Milli Görüş, 86
  legacy in AKP, 132, 136
  majoritarianism, 91, 94
  resignation as prime minister, 88, 95–96
  understanding of religious mission, 87, 90, 93–94
Erdoğan, Recep Tayyip
  adultery, attempts to penalize, 103
  conflict with Gülen movement, 117
  Davutoğlu, power struggle with, 116–18
  delegitimization of opposition, 124, 133–35, 195
  educational reform, 129, 130
  executive presidency, 125–26
  freedom of assembly, approach to, 138–39
  Gezi Park protests, response to, 139–41
  Gül, power struggle with, 110–12
  Islamization project, 41, 95, 100–101
  judicial reform, 120, 123, 125
  Kurdish movement, approach to, 134–35
  leader of electoralist faction, 84
  leader of Istanbul group, 96, 98
  liberal challengers, 261
  majoritarianism, 131, 142
  media, control over, 114–16, 259
  Milli Görüş, influence by, 86, 118–19, 132
  monopolization of power in AKP, 17, 19–20, 77–78, 105, 142
  Morsi, comparison with, 144, 190, 196, 233
  outreach strategies, 95, 97
  party chairmanship, 104–105
  party finance, control over, 112–14, 258
  personality cult, 127–28, 130
  political ban, 95, 102
  press freedom, restrictions on, 101, 136–38
  recruitment, control over, 108–10, 112, 258
Erian, Essam el-, 158, 163, 168, 174, 179, 186, 199
  co-optation by Muslim Brotherhood old guard, 168, 179
  imprisonment, 152, 200
  middle generation of Muslim Brotherhood, 154
  views on gender and religious minorities, 165
Eroğlu, Veysel, 109

296   Index

Essebsi, Beji Caid, 232, 233, 236, 243
Essid, Sami, 252
European Council, 82, 102
European Court of Human Rights, 102
Ezzat, Heba Raouf, 188
Ezzat, Mahmoud
  control of Muslim Brotherhood's finances, 175, 258
  influence over Mohammed Morsi, 189
  old guard of Muslim Brotherhood, 155, 165, 168, 169, 174, 175, 179, 187

Fırat, Dengir Mir Mehmet, 112

Germany, 64
Ghalioun, Burhan, 222
Ghannouchi, Rached, 205, 213, 230, 236, 237, 261
  conciliation, belief in, 225, 227, 231, 233, 237
  criticisms by radicals, 254
  democratic principles, adherence to, 202, 215, 218–20, 224, 227, 235, 238
  elections, approach toward, 213
  exile, 211, 214, 215, 240
  imprisonment, 208, 209
  Islamic democracy, doctrine of, 57, 209, 211, 219, 248, 251–52
  leadership of liberal faction, 21, 80, 203, 225
  media, influence over, 252
  MTI, participation in, 207, 208, 210
  non-violence, 216
  party finance, control over, 246, 258
  party leadership, influence over, 204, 216, 226, 241
  party rules, approach to, 247, 253
  philosophical writings, 13, 204, 206
  recruitment, control over, 243–46
  return to Tunisia, 212, 225
  Sharia, view of, 159
Gharbiya, 172
Ghazali, Mohammad al-, 206
Ghozlan, Mahmoud, 179
Gökalp, Ziya, 95
Görmez, Mehmet, 129
Gül, Abdullah, 109, 142
  clash with Erdoğan over intra-party democracy, 103–104
  freedom of expression, support for, 137–38
  Islamist background, 100–101
  legal reform, 123, 125, 126
  liberal democrat wing in AKP, 96–98, 102, 103, 106, 117, 141
  marginalization within AKP, 108–12
  pro-government smear campaign, 115–16
  protestors' rights, defense of, 138–41
  rule as president, 78, 110–12, 120
Gülen movement, 57, 116–17, 121–22, 126, 135
Gülen, Fethullah, 116, 121, 130
Güler, Hilmi, 109
Gulf War, 103

Habib, Mohammad, 159, 168
Harakat al-Ittijah al-Islami (Islamic Tendency Movement)
  goals of, 207–209
  inspiration by Muslim Brotherhood, 207
  repression of, 211–12
  rifts within, 209–11
Harakat al-Nahda. *See* Ennahda
Heshmat, Gamal, 165, 172, 186
Hizmet. *See* Gülen movement
Hmida, Bochra Belhajj, 248
Howeidy, Fahmi, 188, 194, 222
Hudaybi, Hasan al-, 151
Hudaybi, Ma'mun al-, 155, 168
  old guard of Muslim Brotherhood, 155, 156, 159, 161
hudud punishments, 159, 182, 214
Hungary, 23
  Fidesz, 44
Hussein, Mahmoud, 179

Ikhwan al-Muslimeen. *See* Muslim Brotherhood
Ikhwanweb, 174, 198, 259
India, 23, 164
  Bharatiya Janata Party (BJP), 44
Indonesia
  Prosperous Justice Party, 74
intraparty politics
  coalitions, 65–6
  dominant alliances, 63, 71–73, 257–58
  external factors, 6, 62–65, 256
  importance of, 61–62
  party change, 63
  power games, horizontal, 68–71
  power games, vertical, 66–68
Iran, 74, 160, 207, 261–62
  Basij militia, 262
  Iranian revolution, 94, 206
  Revolutionary Guards, 262
Iraq, 13, 103, 134, 250
Islam
  and democracy, relationship between, 2–4
  essentialist approaches to, 2–4, 9, 23, 255
Islamis parties
  incentive structure, 70–71

Islamist parties
  aggregation, 6, 7, 24, 49, 61
  coalition-building, 7, 77
  democracy, commitment to, 4, 7–12, 73–74
  democratic procedures, internalization of, 4
  effect of intra-party dynamics on, 4, 6–7, 74–75, 256–57
  electoral and governance pressures, 53–55
  electoral politics, commitment to, 8–9, 255–56
  factions within, 6–7, 41, 49, 58, 59
  as ideological parties, 7–8
  incentive structure, 5, 7, 19, 61, 66–67
  inclusion-moderation thesis, 25, 42–50, 62, 260
  individual preferences, 7
  middle class, importance of, 26, 34, 35
  modernization, effect of, 25–38
  as movement parties, 14–15
  organizational resources, 5
  political participation, effect of, 5, 46–50
  power distribution, 5, 12
  variation among, 2–3, 6, 260
Islamists
  electoralist, 4–5, 11–14, 75–77
  liberal, 4–5, 11, 75–7
Istanbul group. *See* AKP, electoralist faction within
Italy, 66

Japan, 66
Jebali, Hamadi, 221, 222, 225, 232, 233, 244
jihad, meaning of, 93, 151
jihadi groups, 22, 255–56
  in Egypt, 152–53, 155
  in Europe, 240
  in Tunisia, 231
Jlassi, Abdelhamid, 221, 225
Jordan, 1, 13
  Islamic Action Front (IAF), 8, 48, 49, 74, 262
Justice and Development Party (AKP)
  anti-pluralism, 132–36
  authoritarian turn, 3, 13, 14, 17–18, 36, 37, 56, 82, 86
  battle with Gülenists. *See* Gülen movement
  closure case, 120
  coalition talks, 117–118
  delegitimization campaigns, 133, 135
  electoralist faction within, 77–78, 103–104
  Ennahda, comparison with, 204, 228, 234, 236, 242, 245, 250, 252, 253

  formation of, 19, 77, 82
  freedom of assembly, 138–41
  freedom of the press, 136–38
  hegemonic Islamization, 41, 128–31
  internal and external communication, 114–116
  Islamist presidentialism, 126
  Kurdish question, approach to, 117, 133–35
  liberal faction within, 19–20, 101–103
  liberalism to electoralism, swing from, 83–84, 105, 133, 141–42, 259
  Milli Görüş, departure from, 98–101
  Milli Görüş, pivot to, 118–20, 135–36
  moderate early period, 2–4, 35, 55, 78
  Muslim Brotherhood, comparison with, 144, 145, 199, 202
  organizational rules, changes in, 105–108
  party finance, 112–14, 258
  recruitment and promotion, 108–110, 258
  righteous majoritarianism, 78–79
  sidelining of military, 57, 121
  splinter groups, 142, 261
  2010 referendum, 123–25

Kaczyński, Jarosław, 265
Karamollaoğlu, Temel, 135–36
Karker, Salah
  exile, 215
  marginalization in Ennahda, 216
  radical wing in MTI, 209–11, 240
  sidelining within Ennahda, 226
  time in exile, 211
Katatni, Sa'ad al-, 155, 172, 179
  as chairman of People's Assembly, 185–6
Kavala, Osman, 140
Kazzaz, Hussein, 171, 179
Khayat, Adel al-, 195
Kılıç, Haşim, 124, 125
King Farouk, 148, 150
Kısakürek, Necip Fazıl, 126–27
Kurtulmuş, Numan, 110
Kutan, Recai, 97
Kuwait, 13, 48
  Hadas (Islamic Constitutional Movement), 8
Kuytul, Alpaslan, 135

Laabidi, Farida, 247
Laarayedh, Ali, 221–33, 244, 247
Laarayedh, Amer, 245
Labidi, Meherzia, 247, 248
Ladhari, Zied, 245, 247
Lakhoua, Sheikh Mohammed, 214
Lebanon
  Hezbollah, 8, 13, 46, 74, 262

Libya, 1, 13, 231, 250
London, 215, 252
Lourimi, Ajmi, 221
Luxor, 195

Madi, Abu al-Ela
  criticisms of the old guard, 167, 171–73
  middle generation of Muslim Brotherhood, 154, 156
  Mohammed Morsi, disagreements with, 199–200
  resignation from Muslim Brotherhood, 170
  Wasat Party participation, 157
Malaysia
  Malaysian Islamic Party, 74
Malek, Hasan, 175
Mansoura University, 180
Maqsoud, Saleh Abdal, 190
Marzouki, Moncef, 228, 236, 237
Mashhour, Mustafa, 155, 168
Maududi, Sayyid Abul A'la, 9, 206
Mekki, Abdellatif, 245, 254
Menzah, 211
Milli Görüş Hareketi (National Outlook Movement), 15, 34, 86, 98–100, 104, 119, 127, 128, 130, 132, 135, 142, 161, 214, 216
  alliance with Turkish nationalists, 134
  antipluralism, 92–94
  comparison with Ennahda, 219–20
  comparison with MTI, 207, 208, 212
  comparison with Muslim Brotherhood, 197
  critique of secular-republicanism, 86–88
  departure of reformists from, 97, 106, 261
  influence on AKP. *See* AKP, turn to Milli Görüş line
  instrumentalist approach to democracy, 88–90, 121
  liberal wing, 94–96
  majoritarianism, 84, 90–92, 95
  origins of, 85–86
  parties associated with, 86
  role of party leaders, 105–106
  state repression of, 86
Milliyet, 115
Minya, 171, 172
Misr25, 198
modernization theory, 25–26
Mohammed Ali Pasha, 27
Morocco, 1
  Justice and Development Party, 13, 262
Morou, Abdelfattah, 205, 212, 214, 232, 244, 247, 254

imprisonment, 208, 209
Islamic Tendency Movement, participation in, 207
liberal democratic tendencies, 203, 209, 211, 234–35
MTI, participation in, 207
Morsi, Mohammed, 17, 172, 185, 191, 236
  attacks on civil liberties, 195–97, 233
  election as president, 20, 36, 40, 53, 54, 144, 145, 165, 187–88
  Ikhwanization, 189–92, 194–95, 259
  involvement in Muslim Brotherhood, 155, 176, 179, 187
  majoritarianism, 56–57, 192–93
  ouster, 200
  popular mobilization against, 192, 198–200, 204
  referendum campaign, 80, 193–94
Mrad, Nejib, 245
MTI. *See* Harakat al-Ittijah al-Islami (Islamic Tendency Movement)
Mubarak, Hosni, 40, 188
  approach to Islamist movements, 50–52, 143, 152–54, 158, 174, 175
  electoral authoritarian rule, 53, 79, 143, 153, 176, 183, 223
  legacy of authoritarian institutions, 189–92, 195–98, 264
  ouster, 143–44, 176–77, 198
Muslim Brotherhood
  Constituent Assembly elections, 184–86
  constitutional amendments, 178–79
  coup against. *See* Egypt, military intervention
  delegitimization of protests, 56–57, 59, 144, 197–200
  democracy, weak commitment to, 38, 50, 144, 149, 201
  democratic norms, rejection of, 14
  domination of political transition by, 3, 144, 176–77, 181–82
  electoral politics, commitment to, 4
  electoral program, 182–84
  electoral support, 54
  electoralist faction, 20, 38, 145, 259
  Ennahda's departure from, 220, 223, 228, 236, 248
  equal citizenship, debates over, 163–64, 193–94
  exile, 18
  founding ideology of, 9, 146–48
  global influence of, 13
  gradualism, 151–52
  Guidance Bureau, 167–68
  Ikhwanization of the state, 189–90
  instrumentalism, 161–62

internal communication, 172–75
internal coup, 168–69
internal disagreements, 74, 156–57
Islamization, 160–61
liberal faction, 4, 40, 49, 79, 145, 155–56, 261
majoritarianism, 53, 79–80, 255, 263
media, control of, 190–91
middle generation, 154
old guard, 79, 154–55, 177–78
party finance, 175–76
political and religious activism, 162–63, 180–81
political participation, 52, 143, 152–53, 179–81
presidential elections, 186–88
press freedom, infringements on, 196
professional associations, impact of, 47, 157
recruitment and promotion, 169–72
referendum, 193–94
reformists, purging of, 165–66, 181
role of university youth in, 154
ruralization, 170–71
second founding, 19, 77, 153
Sharia, debates over, 159–60
Shura Council, 166–67
state repression of, 29, 34, 50–51, 150–51
Tunisian Islamism, influence on, 206, 217
women's rights, approach to, 30, 144, 164–65, 182–83, 248
Mzali, Fethia Mokhtar, 208, 210

Nahdawis. *See* Ennahda
Nasser, Gamal Abdel
comparison with Bourguiba, 30
Islamist movements after death of, 32, 151, 153
repression of Muslim Brotherhood, 34, 50, 150, 154
secularism, 28–30, 188
Nokrashy, Mahmoud Fahmy El
assassination of, 150
Nouri, Mohammed, 223

Orbán, Victor, 265
Ottoman Empire
fall of, 28
Islamic legacy, 88, 128, 129
İttihat ve Terakki Cemiyeti (Committee of Union and Progress), 85
reform and modernization, 26–28, 85, 125
Ounissi, Sayida, 247
Özal, Turgut, 103

Paris, 215, 222, 233, 243
personal status code
Tunisia, 30, 213, 214, 223, 230, 248
Turkey, 28–29
Poland
PiS (Law and Justice), 265

Qaradawi, Yusuf al-, 206
Qur'an, 9, 30, 90, 127–30, 147, 154, 205, 206, 217, 221, 231, 235
Qutb, Sayyid, 240
followers in Muslim Brotherhood, 150–51, 154–55, 168, 206, 243
influence on Tunisian Islamists, 216, 219

Rakibi, Mohamed el-, 185
Rida, Rashid, 154
right-wing populism
Brazil, 23

Sabahi, Hamdeen, 188
Sadat, Anwar
approach to Islamist movements, 32, 50, 151
assassination of, 152
Saied, Kais
presidential power grab, 202, 204, 254
Salafiyya, 154
Salama, Abdel Nasser, 191
Saleh, Sobhi, 185
Şener, Abdüllatif, 106, 141
liberal democrat wing in AKP, 98–100
marginalization within AKP, 110
Şener, Nedim, 137
Shafik, Ahmed, 40, 188
Shahin, Emad, 189, 198
Shams, Mohammed, 181
Sharqiyya, 171, 172
Shater, Khairat al-
control of Muslim Brotherhood's finances, 258
exile, 175
founding of Ikhwanweb, 174
imprisonment, 200
influence over Mohammed Morsi, 189
old guard of Muslim Brotherhood, 155, 168–69, 172, 179, 184
presidential nomination, 187
Shi'a. *See* Egypt, minority rights
Sidi Bouzid, 17, 202
Şık, Ahmet, 137
Sisi, Abdel Fattah al-, 3, 200
Smiai, Ahmed, 245

300 Index

socialist parties
  authoritarian tendencies, 23, 43, 61
  comparison with Islamist parties, 7, 24
Sousse, 206, 221
Soylu, Süleyman, 110
Suez Canal, 27
Sultan, Essam, 154, 156, 157, 185, 200
Sunna, 9, 147, 217, 231, 235
Syria, 13, 134, 231, 250

takfir (excommunication), 222, 235
takhassus (specialization), 248, 251
Tantawi, Mohamed el-, 185
Tilmisani, Omar al- (General Guide of Muslim Brotherhood)
  death of, 20, 79, 155, 168–69
  participation in formal politics, 151–52
  and reformist wing, 153–54
Trump, Donald, 265
Tunisia
  Ben Achour Commission, 226
  Congress for the Republic (CPR), 228–29
  democratization in, 4, 13, 202–203, 226, 238, 250–51, 264
  doctors' coup, 212
  economic development of, 31, 36–38, 224, 254
  Ettakatol (the Democratic Forum for Labor and Liberties), 228–29
  independence, 28
  Islamist movements in, 52–54, 205–207
  modernization, 27–28
  National Dialogue Quartet, 234–35, 243
  Nidaa Tounes Party (NT), 232, 233, 237, 250, 258
  October 18 movement, 222–23, 226–27
  Ottoman rule, 27
  post-revolutionary developments, 17
  religious conservatism in, 38–39, 230–31
  revolution of 2010. *See* Arab Spring
  Salafis in, 231–32, 237
  secularism, 28, 30, 32, 224
  strength of civil society, 57
  student activism in, 32, 211, 221
  Troika government, 228–29, 231–34, 236–37, 246, 252
  Tunisian General Trade Union (UGTT), 234
  2021 power-grab. *See* Saied, Kais
  women's rights, 30
  Zaituna mosque-university, 30, 205, 208
Turkey
  authoritarian turn, 3, 82, 142
  constitutional reforms, 123–25
  democratic backsliding, 122, 131
  Diyanet (Directorate of Religious Affairs), 29, 87, 89–90, 128–30
  economic development of, 31, 35–36
  EU candidacy, 19, 82, 102–103, 141
  February 28 process, 95–96, 116
  Felicity Party (SP), 97, 135
  Furkan Foundation, 135
  Gezi Park protests, 82, 137, 139–41
  independence, 28, 85
  Islamic middle class, 34
  Islamist political culture in, 105–106, 111
  MAZLUMDER, 135
  as model for Arab world, 3, 13
  1980 coup and Turkish-Islamic synthesis, 32
  Peoples' Democratic Party (HDP), 134
  political participation of Islamist movements, 50–53, 86
  press freedom, 138
  Republican People's Party (CHP), 85, 117, 120, 133
  secularism, 28, 87, 88, 99
  state repression of Islamist movements, 85–86
  support for US war in Iraq, 103
  True Path Party (DYP), 95
  2016 coup attempt, 18, 126, 127, 129
  Virtue Party (FP), 96–98, 106
  Welfare Party (RP), 8, 75, 93–95, 97
  westernizing reforms, 28, 87

United Kingdom, 64
United States of America, 23, 240
  Republican Party, 47, 265
Ünsal, Ahmet Faruk, 107, 109, 135

Vatan, 115

Wafd Party, 150, 152, 184
Wasat Party, 20, 145, 157–58, 166, 170, 174, 185, 199, 200, 261
World War I, 28, 85
World War II, 150

Yalçınbayır, Ertuğrul
  liberal democrat wing in AKP, 98, 100–102
  marginalization within AKP, 100–101, 110, 112
Yarbay, Ersönmez
  liberal democrat wing in AKP, 98, 100

marginalization within AKP, 108
  views on party finance, 113
Yazıcı, Hayati, 109
Yemen, 1, 13, 250
  Islah Party, 8, 48, 74, 262
Yıldırım, Binali, 109, 118, 126
Youssef, Bassem, 196

Zaafarani, Ibrahim, 180
Zengin, Bahri, 94
Zindani, Abdul Majeed al-, 49
Zitoun, Lotfi, 229–30, 240, 254
Zitouna TV, 252
Zoghlami, Wassila, 247
Zoghlami, Yamina, 247

CPSIA information can be obtained
at www.ICGtesting.com
Printed in the USA
LVHW020857080323
741174LV00004B/205